BARACK OBAMA AND
TWENTY-FIRST-CENTURY POLITICS

Barack Obama and Twenty-First-Century Politics

A Revolutionary Moment in the USA

Horace G. Campbell

PlutoPress
www.plutobooks.com

First published 2010 by Pluto Press
345 Archway Road, London N6 5AA and
175 Fifth Avenue, New York, NY 10010

Distributed in the United States of America exclusively by
Palgrave Macmillan, a division of St. Martin's Press LLC,
175 Fifth Avenue, New York, NY 10010

www.plutobooks.com

British Library Cataloguing in Publication Data
A catalogue record for this book is available from the British Library

ISBN   978 0 7453 3007 5   Hardback
ISBN   978 0 7453 3006 8   Paperback

Library of Congress Cataloging in Publication Data applied for

This book is printed on paper suitable for recycling and made from fully
managed and sustained forest sources. Logging, pulping and manufacturing processes are expected to conform to the environmental standards of
the country of origin.

10 9 8 7 6 5 4 3 2 1

Designed and produced for Pluto Press by
Curran Publishing Services, Norwich

Simultaneously printed digitally by
CPI Antony Rowe in England, UK
and Edwards Bros in the United States of America.

*This book is dedicated to my wife
Zaline Makini Roy-Campbell
and all of the offsprings of Hannah Wimbish
who have struggled for a better world
in the USA since 1828.*

CONTENTS

PREFACE AND ACKNOWLEDGMENTS

This is a book about *Ubuntu* and our shared humanity. It came out of a deep desire to communicate the optimism and hope of a new generation who want to break with the old ideas of racial hierarchy and militarism. In the process, I have sought to draw on my training and experience as an intellectual and activist to this project of healing and peace. The book seeks to harness traditions of truth and social justice in order to inspire a generation who want to embark on a straightforward project of peace, life, health, and saving Planet Earth. Every day, while this book was being written, the urgency of these four tasks became clearer and more imperative.

By the time this book was completed, the rupture in the US society had deepened to the point where there was open talk about impending violence from disgruntled sections of the population. The economic depression and the distress felt by large sections of the population were being exploited by fringe right-wing forces in the United States. Rising unemployment, hunger, homelessness, and despair crept in as the mortgage crisis and home foreclosures cascaded throughout society. Of the more than 310 million US citizens, more than 150 million were a paycheck away from homelessness. Mainstream policy analysts who had supported the imperial overreach were silenced by the challenges before society. Within the discipline of political science, rational choice ideas were shattered. Conservatives jumped into the midst of this conundrum to spread confusion as to the nature of the economic depression. In the absence of a strong and vibrant progressive movement to clearly articulate the capitalist roots of the economic crisis, along with possible alternatives, conservative action groups with links to the business community reproduced myths of "rebounds." The populism of the conservative action groups gained credence as the federal government rolled out numerous schemes to save the big banks and automobile companies while the poor were losing their homes.

After a vibrant election campaign, the Obama grassroots campaign folded and those who had been mobilized and inspired by the promise of hope and change were left without clarity on the ways forward. The popular movements of workers, anti-racist elements, peace activists, environmentalists, and women's groups are now searching for a way to regain the momentum that was the highlight of the "Yes we can" movement in 2007 and 2008.

From all corners of the globe there are demands for a fundamental restructuring of society in order to repair the human spirit and save Planet Earth. It is the escape from spiritual death and the repair of the human spirit that is driving the youth of today. This repair and healing of human beings will inspire the reordering of the spaces they inhabit so that bridges are built to connect humans. Another form of reparation will involve an all-out drive to clean up the toxic dumps and reverse global warming. The failure of the Copenhagen summit on climate change in December 2009 stands out as an example of the inability of those who resist change to fully grasp the need for conversion from the thinking in politics and economics that brought us the mode of economic organization that is destroying the planet. Everywhere there are signs of the "tipping point," but those in business of polluting the planet, especially the coal, oil, and gas industries, have been so powerful that they have placed short-term profits before the future of Planet Earth.

Many people from the networks for environmental justice supported Obama's campaign. This was only one of the many networks of networks that had acted autonomously to support the candidacy while building a movement to educate society that there had to be a break. The concept of the break is central to recursion in fractals, just as the geometry of nature provides an analytical framework for understanding some of the ways forward. Old concepts of rationality and domination over nature and over other humans have influenced Western thinking, and this thinking held back human capabilities.

In all societies, citizens are seeking creative ways to rethink the priorities for humanity. Obama's election took place in the middle of the push forward to the era when new forms of energy could engender new thinking. Just before the completion of this book, experiments relating to the collision of protons at the Large Hadron Collider (LHC) in Switzerland fired up people's imaginations, especially in the scientific community.

"Plans for the supercollider include experiments that could go a long way in proving and disproving theories regarding dark matter, other dimensions, supersymmetry, whether smaller particles exist, and other theories in particle physics."[1] As the scientists observed, this was a new era of physics. This era is now opening up possibilities for profound transformations of the relations between humans, and the relations between humans and nature. Intentional actions by humans to live in harmony with nature and with each other open revolutionary possibilities for wealth creation and for the global eradication of exploitation, racism and gender discrimination. Yet, trapped by the ideas and conventions of liberalism and militarism, the US government remains torn between the past forms of economic organization and the multiple challenges of breaking from old forms of destruction, war, and greed. While the US government was spending trillions of dollars on war, the European Union took the head in the research associated with particle physics and the collison of protons.

OUTLINE OF THE BOOK

In the nine chapters of this book, I seek to elaborate on the convergence of forces to sharpen the revolutionary moment, and concentrate on the ideas and organizational forms that will distinguish this moment from previous moments.

Chapter 1 lays out the conceptual framework of the book, and argues that Obama is not a revolutionary, but is caught up in a revolutionary moment in world history. The revolutionary moment in US politics is underscored by the convergence of forces that brought the country's politics to an inflection point at the wake of the election season of 2007–08. At the revolutionary moment, Obama, as a student of the black liberation school, tapped into the humanist philosophy of Ubuntu and the optimism embedded in the message of hope. This was the same hope and optimism that had buoyed blacks when they were regarded as less than human (by the three-fifths clause) in the United States, to assert their humanity and win their civil rights. This first chapter interrogates the traditional sense of revolution, which is often the violent overthrow of existing order by self-proclaimed revolutionaries. The analysis relocates revolution within the context of fundamental transformation in society, sustained by a consciousness of the challenges of the moment and bound to a new form of thinking among the rank and file of the society. *Barack Obama and Twenty-First-Century Politics* is an attempt to clarify the revolutionary ideas and the harnessing of the energies of youth for a fundamental break with old politics, economics, militarism, and racism. The Obama election campaign's quantitative task of mobilizing over 3 million small donors, close to 8 million volunteers, 13 million e-mail addresses and more than 2 million Facebook partners induced a qualitative change in the politics of the United States. This superlative quantitative organizational capacity, which engineered the election victory in November 2008, is the essence of a leap in politics. The ideas relating to a quantum leap and quantum politics alert us to political and economic philosophies that are more appropriate to the realities of the twenty-first century, where separation and compartmentalization have no meaning.

It is the combination of the new energy and light that emerged from the inflection point that sparks questions on the need for a new framework for analyzing politics. In South Africa, the term Ubuntu emerged to point to the ways in which we share a common humanity. This chapter links praxis with principles, and lays the ideational carpet for the chapters that follow.

Chapter 2 analyzes Obama's upbringing against the backdrop of the history of Hawaii and the genocidal traditions that were unspoken in that island. His mother, Stanley Ann Dunham, imbued in the young Barack Obama a respect for diversity and the importance of hard work. This chapter draws attention to the five women who influenced Obama's training. The early training from his mother was buttressed by the example of his grandmother. Obama's experiences as a community organizer on the South Side of Chicago in the state of Illinois are analyzed in the context of how the non-profit sector had been used to blunt the enthusiasm of young people who were eager to change the world. Throughout the chapter, the history of the neo-liberal model of "grassroots organizing" is brought out to highlight the ways in which the system manipulates youths.

Obama's journey to Kenya in 1988 brought to the fore his search for a sense of purpose in his life. Our text surveys the contradictions of a settler society and how Obama attempted to navigate these contradictions. The final section of the chapter brings out the linkages between the personal and the political, and elevates the importance of Michelle Obama in the search for a new politics in the United States. The conclusion to this chapter links the old racist ideas to the new eugenics which is cloaked in the biotech experiments of the twenty-first century.

Chapter 3 examines the history of racism and sexism in the politics of the United States. Militarism and masculinity have been celebrated as the twin virtues of Hollywood and the United States. It was a sexist conception of the world that is based on manliness and patriarchal values. Ben "Pitchfork" Tillman (governor and later senator representing South Carolina) epitomized the leader who mobilized the white working poor on the basis of the persecution and murder of African Americans. The ways in which the ideas of Anglo-Saxonism reproduced whiteness in the United States are brought out in this chapter. One of the core arguments of this book is that the mainstream intelligentsia have been stymied by the investment in whiteness. In the Latino community the ideals of whiteness have created massive confusion about the future of society. The book argues that this confusion is being mitigated by the new revolutionary openings in Latin America and the resolute stand of African descendants and indigenous peoples. From Bolivia to Ecuador and Paraguay to Venezuela, new forces are calling for profound changes in the entire American region. This new epoch of revolution is a major corrective to the counter-revolutionary era that was inspired in the era of Ronald Reagan, when an alliance with anti-communist and racist elements from California to El Salvador wreaked death and destruction.

The Obama campaign built on the revolutionary gains of the civil rights movement and the continued quest for real equality in American society. This chapter introduces the reader to the revolutionary traditions of Harriet Tubman and her principles of self-organization.

Chapter 4 highlights the ways in which the ideas of self-organization were brought to bear to confront the machinery of the Democratic Party. Since the time of Franklin Delano Roosevelt in 1932, the Democratic Party has been organized around ethnic politics, ethnic blocks, and party bosses. These party bosses are then linked to real estate developers and bankers in the urban centers. The history of major party bosses is replete with characters such as Carmine DeSapio of New York and Richard Daley of Chicago. Averell Harriman became governor of New York out of this form of ethnic patronage politics.

From 1992 through 2008, the Democratic Party machine was dominated by the Clintons. It was their absolute control of the machine that gave the Clintons the sense that a Hillary victory was inevitable in the Primary elections. Non-US readers will be introduced to the multi-million-dollar business of political consultancy in the United States in this chapter.

Chapter 5 uses the case of South Carolina to highlight the shift in the Democratic Party, and show how the forms of self-organizing and self-mobilization that were set in motion by the Obama campaign defeated the old entrenched machinery of party bosses. This chapter comprises the heart of the thesis of this book. It spells out how the confluence of 'fractals' and Ubuntu will inspire new modes of political organizing.

Using fractal insights of scaling and self-similarity, the chapter examines the forms of organizing by young people in Iowa and South Carolina to highlight the nuts and bolts for future political campaigns – electoral and non-electoral – across the world, in which each person becomes empowered to believe that they can make a difference, and which, in classical fractal formation, can be replicated over and over.

It was in the midst of the primary season when the investment house Bear Stearns collapsed in March 2008. This chapter explores the linkages between economics and politics, and brings out the intellectual impoverishment of a society where the statements of a preacher were deemed more newsworthy than an interrogation of the corrosive powers of bankers.

There are a number of books on Obama. There are books by journalists, by Democratic Party operatives, by political consultants and by academics. The dominant narrative from these books has been provided by journalists who have been preoccupied by immediatism and the strategic markers laid out by foundations and think tanks. Many of these texts are geared towards the current power struggles within the ruling elements, and they reproduce the conscious and unconscious biases that hinder our sense of a shared humanity. The limitations of the mainstream press were so pronounced during the election season that many journalists were not paying attention when they were in the midst of the transition from the old to the new. The slow death of a newspaper, the *Rocky Mountain News*, was one reminder that the heyday of old conception of the celebration of the conquest of the West was coming to an end. This reality struck me during the Democratic National Convention in Denver. I had traveled to the mile-high city of Denver to be a witness to the historical moment, where we could grasp the relationship between the burdens of the past and the tasks of the future. It was in Denver that we saw the full force of youth. From all over the country, and indeed from all over the world, young people converged on Denver, Colorado, to witness history. These young people were very involved in discussions about a green future. Chapter 6 delves into the mindsets and zeal of the young people who provided the energy for the Obama movement. Hitherto, it was the belief of the party and political class that young people would not vote. But Obama, in his campaign, generated a level of enthusiasm that became a new index of the political temperature in the country by political pundits.

Because Obama's thinking of including all became the guiding philosophy, the management of diversity within the campaign was one of the hallmarks of the convention. The full impact of these efforts to include all was on display at the caucuses of those who hitherto had been termed "minorities." It was in the Hispanic/ Latino caucus that I observed the effectiveness of Michelle Obama as a campaigner. The chapter seeks to bring out the synergy between Michelle Obama and Hilda Solis as one sign of the future of US politics.

Chapter 7 brings out how the elections were confronted with the planning and machinations of big capital. The election campaign was overshadowed by the events of September 2008, and especially September 15, when it was announced to the world that Lehman Brothers, one of the top five investment banks in the United States, had collapsed. Weaving the challenges of the management of the collapse in the midst of an election campaign is the thrust of this chapter. Our task here is to draw out how the economic terrorism of capitalism was being leveraged to slow down Obama's campaign.

This chapter brings to the reader the ground operation which placed millions of workers/volunteers into play and unfolded in a manner that made victory inevitable. It lays out the vivid imagery of the wall of youth that was to be found in the campaign offices all over the country. Respect, Empower, Include, were the words repeated by campaign workers as they navigated the spaces of a new politics. It is out of the experience of the new politics that organizing itself was revolutionized through the nested loop of a network of networks. The strength of these networks withstood the rabid and racist provocations of the right during the campaign.

Chapter 8 emphasizes the need for people at the grassroots to use the bottom-up, self-mobilization model of the Obama campaign to support and hold him accountable, since "the task of restructuring US society is huge." As the lessons from past counter-revolution have shown, the problems cannot be solved overnight. This chapter draws on the message of fractal optimism, which is the idea that the networks of networks created by the bottom-up, self-mobilization of the grassroots form the kernel of a new move towards a revolutionary form of organizing. This optimism is further hinged on the knowledge that "the election of Obama opened the space for new grassroots leadership ... that is emerging at new sites of politics in relation to differing issues such as homelessness, need for health care, employment, pension, environmental repair, anti-racism and the peace movement ... [which has] the potential to shake the complacency of the consensus that maintained the capitalist system" (from Chapter 8).

How could a progressive movement intervene in this situation, where the contradictions were being heightened at a pace which meant the spark for a massive confrontation could break out at any time? What would be the outcome of a new rupture in society? This was the question that I posed from the beginning when I started to follow the implications of the Obama presidency in 2006. From the outset, I saw many parallels with the challenges for the abolitionist movement at the time of the Civil War in 1860.

Barack Obama inherited two wars and a rising conflagration in Pakistan. On top of this commitment to continuing wars founded on disinformation and lies, the moment of September 2008 brought to the fore a perilous situation in which banks were more dangerous than standing armies. Without clear leadership and explanation about the direction of the society, the demobilized peace forces were left to follow the heightened conservative representation of the nature of the economic crisis.

Free-market myths had been so ingrained in our society that real social questions of health, education and cleaning up the environment could not be properly addressed because of the hostility by sections of the Republican political leadership to social programs for the benefit of society at large. For two centuries these elements have used the resources of the state at will, privatizing gains and socializing losses to the point where these barons of finance and industry were trapped by their old instincts and ideas.

This debate on intrusive government took on added significance during the long deliberations on health care reform during 2009 and early 2010. After a very sharp debate in society at large, the US Congress passed an Act providing for partial reform of the health care system in March 2010, the Patient Protection and Affordable Care Act, HR 3590. This historic Act for the first time extended mandatory medical care to 94 percent of US citizens, adding another 32 million people to the health care system. Under this law, insurance companies can no longer deny people health care on the basis of pre-existing conditions. Young people are allowed to stay on their parents' insurance until age 26. It extends coverage for senior citizens and strengthens Medicare. However, the Act does not include a single payer system in which the government is able to provide health insurance for all. In reality, what was called health care reform in the United States was a victory for the health insurance industry, biotech corporations, big pharma, and health maintenance organizations. Despite the weakness of the reforms, the conservative forces branded the health care reform a "government takeover." From the summer of 2009, a relatively new political formation named the "Tea Party Nation" took the forefront in the opposition to the Obama administration. The mainstream media provided this fringe group with enough media spotlight for many to believe that these were speaking for the majority of the population, especially white citizens. Emboldened by the permissive climate of racism and open hostility to black leaders, they heaped invectives at elected black leaders and spewed out the most brutal homophobic statements.

It is precisely in this political climate, where intense insecurity is being generated, that this chapter stresses the importance of revolutionary non-violence to inspire new networks of peace and justice to intervene in politics.

In the last chapter, we return to the concept of healing and Ubuntu. It introduces a unified emancipatory approach: liberating humanity from the mechanical, competitive, and individualistic constraints of Enlightenment philosophy, and reunifying humans with each other, the Earth, and spirituality. In tandem with much of the current discourse on fractal wisdom, this intervention calls for a revolutionary paradigmatic transformation – but one that is intrinsic to human knowledge and human capacity to intervene to stop the destruction of the planet.

Obama drew on the ideas of Ubuntu, and in turn inspired a new force of youthful energy to join the campaign. This soul and energy force was manifest in the tremendous outpouring of the collectivities of people of different races, classes, genders, sexual orientations, and ages coming forward to give meaning to the campaign message, "Yes we can."

American feminist Alice Walker called on the president to govern with happiness. Reflecting on the positive mood inspired by Obama on the night of the election, and the mood of happiness of the multiracial and multinational gathering, Walker wrote, "A primary responsibility that you do have is to cultivate happiness in your own life."

This book seeks to build on the call for happiness in order to inspire an understanding of Ubuntu as the core theory of the politics of inclusion for the twenty-first century.

ACKNOWLEDGEMENTS

I concluded early in February 2007 that the election cycle of 2008 was pregnant with change and ought to be engaged with thoroughly. I had traveled to Kenya in December 2007, and shared with Tajudeen Abdul Raheem (a peace activist and worker for social justice) my sense of the moment that was unfolding. After an initial hesitation about the unfolding process, Tajudeen encouraged me to document this as part of present history. My elder brother Eusi Kwayana shared the perception of the dangers of the rupture, and was continuously pointing to the danger signs where progressives should be vigilant.

From India, Sreeram Chaulia perceived the candidacy of Obama as a symbol that could galvanize other oppressed people to challenge entrenched forces. Sreeram was a firm partner in this project, and the completion of this book owes much to his energy and to his insights into the limitations of mainstream political science. My wife and partner, Zaline Makini Roy-Campbell, Sreeram and Usha Damerla were enthusiastic supporters of this project to document the election as history was unfolding.

Wazir Mohamed was very forthright that progressives could not be on the sidelines. Within the progressive community, there were intense discussions on the merits of an Obama campaign as opposed to support for the Green Party and the candidacy for president of Cynthia McKinney. This alternative from outside the two mainstream parties was compounded by the fact that Ralph Nader also declared and later ran a presidential campaign in 2008. I was engaged with my local peace activist colleague Howie Hawkins, and I benefited from his insights into the conditions of the larger working-class movement and trade union dynamics.

I am grateful to the owners of the platform *Black Commentator* for their enthusiastic support for my first foray into the proposition that Ubuntu could be a useful framework for understanding the Obama phenomenon. In February 2008 they published "Barack Obama, Fractals and Momentum in Politics." Later during the campaign, *Black Commentator* published two other essays and the response reinforced to me the need to develop the arguments for a thorough analysis of the moment.

I want to acknowledge the importance of the work of James

Boggs, *The American Revolution: Pages From a Negro Worker's Notebook*, in the understanding of the phases of the revolutionary processes in the United States.

Throughout the world of fractals, there were communications from those who were encouraging me to develop the argument in a full-length manuscript. The book *Biology of Belief* by Bruce Lipton reinforced the arguments that had been laid out in a book on *African Fractals: Modern Computing and Indigenous Design* by Ron Eglash. I acknowledge the importance of the Eglash's *African Fractals* in informing the theoretical framework of this book. Fanon Wilkins was another colleague who was grappling with the implications of an analysis of fractal thinking and fractal wisdom. Fanon Wilkins was among those who kept a close watch on the cultural explosion that was bubbling in the hip hop movement. Dr Rickey Hill of Mississippi Valley State University was also enthusiastic about the importance of fractals, and wanted us to analyze them even further in relation to an understanding of jazz and politics.

My sisters Ifi Amadiume and Barbara Ransby were influential in setting out the implications of a radical feminist analysis for the new ways of knowing. In our discussions, Barbara Ransby (one of the original six leaders of the Black Radical Congress) not only drew from her grasp of the influence of Ella Baker but sought to inspire a new generation that would build on that legacy in new conditions. At the end of the primary process, I traveled to Denver for the Democratic National Convention. I enjoyed the hospitality of Tanya Beer, a former student who felt passionately about justice. Her husband, Matt Myers, was working on a film on the dislocation of the First Nation peoples from Arkansas to a patch of land in northeast Oklahoma. Before the start of the convention, Tanya, Matt, and I hiked in the hills above Denver. It was during these walks that Matt spelt out the theme of his *Tar Creek* documentary, depicting one of the worst environmental disasters in the United States. Matt Myers was participating in a process of establishing a way to expand reparative justice by bringing forth the truth about what happened to the First Nation peoples from Arkansas.

I am grateful to Matt and Tanya for opening up their home to me during the period I spent in Denver at the Convention. I was not an official delegate but went to enough sessions to get a good sense of the old giving way to the new. I am also grateful to Annette Walker for her insights into Colorado politics, and for her knowledge of the Five Points area of Denver, Colorado.

As with any major political undertaking of this sort, numerous persons contributed to the inspiration behind this book. I gained inspiration from women like Barbara Roy and Rosemary Mealy who did not flinch in their understanding that the dynamic of the moment was bigger than Barack Obama. At the moment of the elections in November 2008, I was buoyed by the stories of women far away in Iran and in Brazil who sent up supplications and prayers for change. Throughout the writing of this book I had in mind the young people from all continents who wanted change in the twenty-first century. Emily Erickson was one of the millions of young people who made tremendous sacrifices to engage with the campaign, and were embarking on their own journey of Ubuntu. I want to acknowledge her energy and initiative in the search for healing.

Over the period of writing, I have benefited from discussions and sessions with many in the peace, reparations, and justice movements. My sisters from the Grannies for Peace movement from New York were exemplary in their solidarity with this project. I am extremely grateful to all those who contributed their time while I was in the field during the election period. Marc Obas and Jill Littlejohn were among those who agreed that I could identify them as people who spent time with me. There were many others who prefer to remain anonymous.

Since that time, I have benefited from my discussions with close colleagues, especially those who were thinking through the political implications of the big bailout of the banking sector and the fact that the economic decline and fall of the dollar will be prolonged and painful. I have become indebted to many people who read drafts of chapters, so many that I could not begin to name them all. Sreeram Chaulia and Wilson Aiwuyor stand in a special category in their pedantic work with me to ensure the completion of the project. Both Sreeram and Wilson wanted us to bring out the importance of fractal optimism and the new possibilities from an informed self-organized population. They have throughout provided detailed feedback and encouragement.

My immediate family and my political family were enthusiastic supporters in many ways. Wazir Mohamed from our political family (called Rodneyites) was among the first to organize a session in Binghamton in March 2007 for a serious reflection on the meaning of the Obama candidacy in the context of war and economic depression. Sections from the rump of the International Caucus of the Black Radical Congress (BRC) were also very supportive. My brother Canute Distin and his wife Julie, Joy Jeffrey, and Patricia Daley pushed and encouraged me in ways that ensured that I focused on getting the manuscript out while teaching and balancing a hectic schedule. My daughter Kurwa Nyigu not only contributed materially to my field research and travel in North and South Carolina but also brought her own insights into the unfolding changes in that region when we worked there in October 2008. Philip Owusu, Dara Walker, Amber Murrey-Ndewa, Rosalina Edwards, David Johnson, and many others read drafts of chapters and made valuable suggestions. Adam Hochschild, Patricia Rodney, and Patricia Daley were among those who enthusiastically endorsed the project at the outset. I would like to thank Roger Van Zwanenberg of Pluto Books for his encouragement and patience during the process of writing this book.

Finally, this book emanated from the optimism of those who want to live in peace. There was no financial contribution to this project from any political party, foundation, or non-governmental organization. I want to specifically thank Makini and Samora for their patience while I labored to complete this task. I drew spiritual energies and encouragement from all of those who stood up so that we can now make a difference.

1

REVOLUTIONARY MOMENTS AND RUPTURES

Barack Obama has been called the first Internet president. He has been called the first black president. He has been called a healer for the twenty-first century. For many from the grassroots, he has been hailed as the first community organizer who brought the skills of bottom-up political organizing to the national stage in order to win power in electoral politics. It was this bottom-up organization nested into a tightly controlled core serving as the basis for welcoming and inspiring self-organizing cells of volunteers, donors, contributors, and other participants that ushered in a new mode of politics.

Obama's winning strategy has completely changed the face of electoral politics, so much so that technology experts noted that the way political campaigns are organized in the United States will never be the same again. Obama and his team utilized the tools of social networking, the Internet, cell phones, and YouTube unlike any previous political campaigns.

More importantly, the political campaign took place in a period when there were profound changes in the international political system and in the nature of the US political economy. After the Second World War, the United States emerged as a hegemonic power with the US dollar as the currency of world trade. In the midst of the campaign, the financial crisis and destabilization of the financial oligarchy produced temporary panic in the ranks of the rulers. For a short moment, there was even talk of martial law and the suspension of bourgeois democratic rights.

At the moment of the collapse of the US financial system in September 2008, the tremendous powers placed in the hands of the government had a sobering effect on society, as previous economic behemoths such as AIG, General Motors, and the banks rushed to seek state subsidies. Interestingly, it was in the same period of the financial crisis that one former chief economist of the International Monetary Fund (IMF), Simon Johnson, stated that the bankers had carried out a coup d'état.[1] Johnson was referring to the coercion of the US Congress to bail out the financial services sector during the greater depression that started in 2007. Congress voted over US $700 billion to prop up a banking sector that had been involved in the unregulated $600 trillion market for over-the-counter derivatives.

The cascading effects of the financial crisis have not fully reached the consciousness of US citizens. Millions are unemployed, official poverty rates have skyrocketed, and millions are losing their homes because of foreclosures. For a short time, banks and bankers continued to dominate the discussion by claiming that the "big banks were too big to fail."[2] Yet, others who had been following their activities wrote about *The Sellout: How Three Decades of Wall Street Greed and Government Mismanagement Destroyed the Global Financial System*.[3]

To pre-empt calls for a new mode of economic organization, the financial oligarchs considered new schemes to thwart democratic participation. Not to be outdone, the crude racists in the United States are calling for a military coup. They have shouted that Obama was not born in America. They have appeared in public with guns and labeled each one of his proposed programs as Marxist/socialist. They have sought to roll back the new thrust of citizenship that promised a multicultural and multiracial democracy.

This book is based on the proposition that a new concept of shared humanity must be the basis of social collectivism if humans are to survive the challenges of the twenty-first century. Laying out some of the elements of the revolutionary moment, I seek to question some of the received ideas about revolution, especially the idea that a revolution requires armed struggle and a vanguard party. My analysis seeks to outline the strengths of networks that arise out of the principles of self-emancipation and self-organization.

A cultural revolution that had used the codes of "dancing in the streets" and "fight the power" prepared American society for a rich cultural intervention. The powers of the film, media, and music industries in the United States are waiting for the moment when human creativity can be turned from the making of profits from mindless violence to opening up society for profound changes. Bottled-up scientific possibilities are awaiting this upsurge of human energy and creativity so that big corporations do not turn humans into cyborgs. Barack Obama was elected in a period when some scientists were promising a future of technological singularity and the deepening of genetic perdition.[4]

There is a very small coterie of creative filmmakers and cultural workers who seek to use the artistic medium to educate and warn of the dangers of the technological fix that is trying to orchestrate the genetic and behavioral control of society. These artists and producers have exposed the possibility of film and television playing a role in reversing the dumbing-down of youth. My effort in this book is to answer a question that James Boggs asked over 30 years ago, "Why in the age of mass media, do we remain ignorant of how the social and political decisions which affect our daily lives are made?"

How can working people intervene to ensure that the chaos produced by the crisis does not devour us as humans? I will argue in this book that in order to be human we need to belong to and have a sense of community. The process towards realizing that we live in a human community will begin to break down the hierarchies that sustained capitalism over the past 300 years.

The question posed by the book is whether convergence of political, economic, environmental, military, and social challenges for American society at the time of the election of Barack Obama constitutes a revolutionary moment.

This book holds that it does.

REVOLUTIONARY MOMENTS: LESSONS FROM THE FRENCH AND CUBAN REVOLUTIONS

Generally a revolution is defined as a sudden overthrow of the existing social, economic, and political order. But revolutions such as the Cuban Revolution of 1959, the Chinese Revolution of 1949, the Russian Revolution of 1917, the French Revolution of 1789, the American Revolution of 1776, and the Haitian Revolution of 1804 arose out of moments when the ideas supporting or propping up the old order had become unsustainable. Usually, there are events that mark the maturation of a revolutionary process, but this process begins in the womb of the old society. The maturation to the point of a critical break from the old takes place when the ideas, organization, and leadership of the new rising forces can decisively remove the old order from political and social power.

In this sense, the revolutionary moment is not tied to one event such as the march into Havana of the Castro revolutionaries on January 1, 1959, or the storming of the Bastille on July 14, 1789. Events such as the storming of the Bastille in July 1789 were episodic, but the revolutionary process had to work itself out through contending ideas, forms of organization, and the subsequent emergence of Napoleon Bonaparte.

In France, the bourgeoisie and the working class temporarily unified to overthrow the feudal lords, the monarchy, and the retinue of military forces that propped up pomp and privilege. Because of the social weakness of the working classes and their theoreticians, the revolution was hijacked by the more organized section of the rising maritime and commercial bourgeoisie. The revolutionary theoreticians for this historic intervention had prepared society with new ideas of liberty, equality, and fraternity. During the course of this revolution, the outmoded ideas of feudal absolute monarchy based on the total centralization of power in the hands of the Bourbon kings were overtaken by the accumulation of capital and the egalitarian demands from below.

Napoleon Bonaparte emerged out of the militarism and "reign of terror" inside the revolution. Violence begat violence as the revolutionary fervor of the French marched throughout Europe. Feudal lords opposed liberty, and the clash of ideas produced war. War weakened the revolutionary forces, and Napoleon corrupted the ideals of liberty. Napoleon did not challenge the chauvinism and imperial traditions of the monarchy. Ultimately, as the struggles in France unfolded, the ideas of liberty in Europe proved compatible with enslaving others.

The most outrageous aspect of the French imperial pursuit in the name of revolution was the failed attempt to re-establish slavery in Haiti. Scholars in Europe who celebrated the revolution in France failed to link this weakness of the French Revolution when it came to Africans and crimes against the peoples of Haiti.

A second example of the revolutionary moment is Cuba. The old ideas of semi-feudal land ownership (latifundia), white supremacy, and cultural repression through the church, in alliance with imperialism, had been overtaken by the demand for independence in Cuba since 1933. Though the outmoded ideas of the plantation owners had worn thin, a brutal dictatorship was kept in power by the military with the support of the government of the United States. Beginning in 1955, with the assault on the Moncada barracks, Fidel Castro sought to clarify the ideas of independence and reconstruction in Cuba. His speech, "History will absolve me," served as the intellectual and ideological marker for consolidating independence and defeating the landed property owners in Cuba. Che Guevara deepened the theory of revolution and independence by linking the fortunes of revolution in Cuba to a worldwide revolution.

Despite Cuba's extension into the orbit of the Soviet Union in the period of the Cold War, the ideological commitment to revolutionary change had such deep roots in Cuba that the leadership and the Cuban experiment survived to serve as the forerunner for the modern revolutionary moment in the Americas. Che Guevara had advanced and supported one of the central principles of *Ubuntu* when he declared, "the true revolutionary is guided by strong feelings of love."

Fifty years after the triumph of the Cuban revolution, the peoples of the Americas are at the cusp of a different revolutionary moment, one where there are new political movements in the Caribbean and Latin America raising questions of justice and societal transformation. In these deliberations in Bolivia, Ecuador, Paraguay, Venezuela, and other parts of Latin America, there is an entirely new feature that has been brought into the discussion. That is the role of the ideas of indigenous peoples in shaping the new political cultures that can emerge out of the challenges to the old ideas of domination over nature and dominion over other human beings. Indigenous forces have registered the fact that it is no longer possible to write and deliberate on revolution as if the indigenous and former enslaved are non-persons. These debates on revolution involve a fundamental transformation in people's consciousness about the worth of all humans, while radical feminist consciousness has deepened the understanding that revolutionary ideas must challenge patriarchal ideas about the family, sexuality, relationships, state, and politics.

Citizens in the United States are proud of the revolutionary traditions that overthrew British colonialism. The inherent weakness of that tradition was revealed in the second revolutionary moment: the period of the Civil War and Reconstruction. There were two other revolutionary moments – the period of the suffragettes and the US workers, and the civil rights revolution of the 1960s. In writing on the American Revolution over 40 years ago, James Boggs outlined the challenge to US citizens posed by the revolutionary struggles in Latin America.

It would be unrealistic to expect the people of the United States to come directly to the aid of the Latin American revolutions on any large scale. The grievances and issues which underlie these revolutions and which propel them to success are in Latin America itself. But there are going to be many, many shameful episodes similar to that of the attempted invasion of Cuba in 1961 which will shake up the people of the United States, make them squirm, and force them to question themselves and their government. The spread of the Latin American revolutions means that before the people of the United States there lies a painful period of decline in prestige and in confidence, both in themselves and in their governments, similar to that which the British have been experiencing with the decline of their empire. All this will help to deepen the general revolutionary crisis in this country.[5]

Boggs was writing from the vantage point of the Detroit cultural and political struggles during the civil rights revolution. This revolution had sought to make a break with the crude racism of the Jim Crow era. However, just as the revolutionary fervor of the period of the Civil War was overturned by Jim Crow and counter-revolution, the civil rights gains were reversed by Reaganism and the conservative counter-attack.[6] In its crudest forms, the Reagan regime forced citizens of the United States to choose good over evil. George W. Bush deepened this ideological coercion with the slogan of "you are either with us or against us."

Within the context of this book, I will represent the period 1980–2008 as a period of counter-revolution.

The contemporary revolutionary moment is emerging after years of counter-revolutionary ideas and leadership, which were clearly expressed in the governing alliance in the United States from the period of Ronald Reagan in1981 to George W. Bush in 2008. The current decline of US imperialism and the rise of new forces are challenging the anti-imperialist and peace forces to place the question of a new internationalism of working people at the forefront of international politics.

This revolutionary moment can be grasped in relation to the current balance of forces internationally and domestically within the United States.

NEW CONCEPT OF SHARED HUMANITY

I propose that we are not speaking of revolution in the traditional sense (seizure of state power by self-proclaimed revolutionaries). We are talking about a fundamental transformation. It is well known that we are in the midst of a technological revolution. What is less appreciated is how our modes of thinking lag behind the profound changes that offer new capabilities for humans to live in peace in the twenty-first century and to dispense with centuries-old back-breaking work. There are transformations at the levels of conscious-ness, at the level of material organization, at the level of gender relations, and at the level of our relationship to the planet Earth and the Universe. These transformations in consciousness are taking place at the same time as the old ideas that legitimated individual accumulation at the expense of social needs are in disarray.

There are fundamental transitions taking place before our very eyes. Global warming, hurricanes, health pandemics, and global social dislocation demand urgent action. Neo-liberalism and the rule of the World Trade Organization have threatened the physi-cal elimination of billions of citizens. The pauperization of billions continues every day as the giant monopolies seek to extend their powers to the remotest parts of the planet. Yet, despite the trium-phant posturing of those who proclaimed that there were no alternatives, it is now clear that we are in a period of systemic crisis that goes beyond the financial system. There is now an end to the long period of US hegemony, and one of the many challenges will be to manage this depression so that the crisis of capitalism and the competition between the competing capitalist centers does not break out into war. The labels for the varying manifestations of crisis and decline − energy crisis, food crisis, environmental crisis, climate change, financial crisis, and so on − conceal a fundamental crisis in the ideation system of unlimited accumulation of wealth.

It can be stated that, globally, the collapse of capitalist ideological hegemony is taking place in slow and imperceptible forms. Inside the United States, the conjuncture is still dominated by confidence about the ability of US capitalists to re-engineer the system so that American corporations can dominate international finance. The US government has partially nationalized large sectors of the economy (banks, insurance, automobiles, and so on), but the almost religious aversion to a discussion about the democratic content of state control of the commanding heights of the economy ensures that the capitalists socialize the losses and privatize the profits. The task of this book is to contribute to the radical critique of capitalism, and strengthen the social forces that are committed to reversing the depoliticization of citizens.

Throughout the culture wars in the United States, the cultural outpourings of the most oppressed sections of the population have acted as an antidote to complete dehumanization. Cultural expressions from rhythm and blues artists as well as jazz musicians ushered in a veritable cultural revolution where citizens were braced to resist the ideological onslaught of rugged individualism, greed, and the celebration of war. When cultural artists came together to sing "We are the world" in the midst of a famine in Ethiopia, they were signaling another possibility for the role of Hollywood and the media. Instead of violence as entertainment, there was a window being opened to the possibilities of film and television (along with new media) for education, inspiration, and creative responses to political realities.

Progressive film-makers were marginalized as the Pentagon suborned screenwriters and producers to cultivate the glorification of war and imperial adventures in the society. Michael Moore is only one of the many film-makers who have used the medium of film to sharpen the critique of capitalism and to narrate this tale of greed and corruption, to query whether the whole incentive structure, moral values, and political economy of American capitalism are fit for human beings.

Cultural and intellectual leaders in the United States have been groping for ways to move society from fear, recrimination, violence, and racial intolerance to principles of love, mutual respect, and proactive engagement. In this search, leaders such as Nelson Mandela have been an inspiration. Mandela embraced the values of peace over revenge or spite and hate. Despite the imperfections of that process, the principles of peace and the life-affirming ethos of Ubuntu echoed from Southern Africa to all parts of the globe.

UBUNTU

Within the liberation traditions of Africa, there is the idea of healing and reconciliation associated with the concept of Ubuntu. Translated, Ubuntu means cooperation, forgiveness, healing, and willingness to share. This concept, though emanating from Southern Africa, is not limited to that region. It reflects a philosophical system that is found in all indigenous societies. One feminist scholar summed up Ubuntu in this way:

> *Ubuntu* is an ancient philosophy founded on the notion of communalism, (I am because we are), driven by attributes such as truth, justice and compassion. This philosophy does not discriminate on

the grounds of race, economic affluence, social status or gender. It is a flow of life that is the same for every member of the human race. *Ubuntu* is not only tied to human life. It also concerns itself with respect for animals and the environment. The adoption of such a philosophy therefore seeks to create a balance between the self and others, as well as between the internal and external.[7]

In the process of searching for ideas about community, it is necessary to interrogate the linear conceptions of "progress" and "unlimited growth." Out of this interrogation, I have found the ideas about Ubuntu most useful as a guide to the new proposals needed for the twenty-first century. Ubuntu combines the optimism of the civil rights revolution (and the cultural outpourings associated with that revolution) with the technological revolution, and articulates an ideal of working towards a common humanity. The idea of Ubuntu starts from a philosophical position that regards humanity as an integral part of ecosystems that lead to a communal responsibility to sustain life. Human value is based on social, cultural, and spiritual criteria. Natural resources are shared on principles of equity among and between generations. It is the antithesis of the idea of "competitive advantage."

This idea of sharing and cooperation comes up against the history of individual self-interest, rational choice, states of conquest, and the politics of might as right. Though this idea of Ubuntu is underdeveloped in the pantheon of contemporary revolutionary ideas, I believe that it can strengthen the new directions for the twenty-first century. Desmond Tutu, the South African activist, had outlined the principles of Ubuntu as:

> the principle of caring for each other's well being and a spirit of mutual support. Each individual's humanity is ideally expressed through his or her relationship with others and theirs in turn through recognition of the individual's humanity. Ubuntu means that people are people through other people. It also acknowledges both the rights and responsibilities of every citizen in promoting individual and societal well being.[8]

In this moment, it is crucial that we grasp the sense that we are people through our relationships with other people. This is fundamental to breaking the hierarchies that created the bifurcated citizenship between whites and non-whites. (By bifurcated citizenship, I mean the 200-year history that produced a hierarchy of citizenship, starting from the US Constitution which denied blacks, First Nation peoples, and women the rights to full citizenship.) One of the essential aspects of this moment is to deepen the challenge to the ideas of white supremacy so that progressive individuals who oppose institutional racism come to the fore to denounce the concept of whiteness. It is worth acknowledging the dictum of James Baldwin when he proclaimed, "As long as you think you're white, there's no hope for you."

Encoded in this challenge is the task to interrogate the linearity that placed Europeans at the higher level of human transformations. In the past, some Marxists had argued that the forms of societal organizations that developed in Europe (communalism, slavery, feudalism, capitalism, and socialism) were necessary for human societies before they could think of alternative forms of organizing. It was this stage-by-stage concept that rendered some "revolutionaries" unable to grasp the crimes of the transatlantic slave trade and the crimes of the American Holocaust against the First Nation peoples.[9]

Although some of these "radicals" understood the crimes that were committed, it was the view that these were "unfortunate" byproducts of "progress" and the "development of the productive forces." Analyses of "accumulation by dispossession" contributed to our understanding of past and present imperial expansions, but the gendered and racial manifestations of imperial plunder were not developed. We need to grasp the interdependence of peoples in all parts of the world regardless of race, nationality, gender, and sexuality, so that the unity of peoples transcends borders.

The World Social Forum provided a space for the anti-globalization campaign. This campaign contributed to the critique of market fundamentalism. A new concept of shared humanity must be acted upon so that this revolutionary moment accelerates the dismantling of the military industrial complex and unleashes a process of conversion of factories so that goods for humans are produced instead of gadgets for war and mass murder. The technological advances offer new possibilities for us to rethink the meaning of economics, but old conceptions of work still linger with thoughts of a regenerated manufacturing sector. Revolutionaries will have to refine the new meanings of work as humans focus on the fulfillment of individual potential as the fundamental aim of the organization of society.

ELEMENTS OF THE REVOLUTIONARY MOMENT

The current revolutionary process has opened up completely new questions for society. There are numerous areas in American political and economic life where we can discern the exhaustion of the old ideas. The exhaustion of "liberalism" has pointed to the need for active citizens who participate in all spheres of life so that democracy rises above the procedural motion of elections. There are many areas where the need for active citizenship appears, but I want to highlight five.

The first element of this moment is represented in the end of the financial and economic hegemony of the United States. When Alan Greenspan testified before the US Congress in 2008 that the old monetarist ideas were wrong, it was a public admission of the failure of the neo-liberal economic mode of organization. Both liberal and neo-liberal economic thinking and organization are now going through a profound crisis. We have come to the end of the period of the "consumer-led economy." In all areas of life, the question is being raised whether the public good will be placed over private interests. Will US citizens continue to be complicit in the plunder of the resources of the planet?

The stimulus packages of the Obama administration provide a profound acknowledgement that only massive state intervention can save the present economic system. Gone is the concept that priority should be given to freedom for capitalists to indulge in unlimited accumulation without regulation. (This was called Reageanomics, and practiced to the hilt by Wall Street.) This has collapsed like a house of cards, and the financial bubble is having a ripple effect on all aspects of social and economic life. There is now a desperate attempt to save capitalism through nationalization without accountability and control by workers, communities, and the mass of producers.

One year after the moment of the collapse of Lehman Brothers, the same Alan Greenspan predicted that the financial crisis would happen again because of "speculative excesses." Greenspan said, "The crisis will happen again but it will be different." Hiding behind old formulations about human nature, Greenspan and the ideologues of private accumulation could not grasp the fundamental contradiction between private accumulation and the social production of wealth. When the crash comes again, will the capitalist classes be able to carry out another coup d'état? Thomas Jefferson wrote in early 1802 that "banking institutions are more dangerous to our liberties than standing armies."[10]

When these words were written, the US banking system was not yet international. Two hundred years later, the banking system and the financial services sector of the economy are not only more dangerous, but these institutions have interlocked themselves with the barons of the military industrial complex. The Carlyle Group and Blackrock Inc. (a government adviser, giant federal contractor, and private money manager) epitomize the political and economic power of the financial and military oligarchy. Breaking the entrenched powers of the bankers, insurance, and militarists will require a clear and concerted mobilization and education of citizens.

Neo-liberal capitalism has exhausted its capacity for coherence, and there is a disintegration of the ideological hegemony of the Anglo-American capitalist classes. The current crisis of capitalism has delivered a major blow to the post-1945 system. In the words of Samir Amin, "The principle of infinite accumulation, which defines capitalism as synonymous with exponential growth, and the latter, like cancer, results in death ... the restoration of the system, which is not impossible, will solve no problems, but rather aggravate them."[11]

This does not mean that we are witnessing the collapse of capitalism. The ability for the system to reconstitute itself will rest on the forms of organization and the ideas that will emerge to challenge the capitalist classes internationally. Already, within the international system, there is recognition that the period of US dominance where the US dollar acts as the reserve currency is coming to an end. Temporarily, much of the debate going on about economic restructuring is taking place in a context where political leaders have little knowledge about the way the economy works. We now know that George W. Bush was rendered *Speech-less* by the extent of the economic collapse.[12] Speculation and bubbles left policymakers unable to grasp the devastating consequences of their casino-type behavior for the lives of billions of humans. Arrogance and conceit prevent those in power from grasping the irony that in the short run, it is the Chinese political leaders who are among the forces holding up the dollar as the reserve currency of international trade.

Nouriel Roubini commented that this period of the fall of the dollar will last more than a decade.[13] I agree that the process of managing the combined pressures of huge budget and trade deficits will compound the decline of the dollar. Excessive debt cannot be cured with future debt. It is a matter of time before many countries diversify their reserve holdings away from the dollar. When this moment arrives, the United States will no longer be able to finance its deficits based on the resources of other societies. The decline of the dollar has accelerated, and the diminution of the status of the dollar will be long and tortuous, with many twists and turns. Jingoism, militarism, and chauvinism have always been the tools of a ruling class in decline. To defeat this jingoism, it will be crucial for peace and justice forces to intervene to end the reliance on hard military power for the sustenance of the economic system. It is here where the questions of ideological clarity meet up with the forms of organization that will emerge out of this conjuncture of the global capitalist crisis.

Second, and tied to the first area in which active citizenship is needed, is the idea that American society can consume the wealth and resources of the planet by the militarization of the Earth (with a promise of domination from space) and the unlimited expansion of wars and military bases. This expansion had (in the past, during the Cold War) been justified in the name of rolling back communism. During the Bush era, militarization was justified in the name of "the war on terrorism." For a short while, the discourse on "globalization" was also employed to conceal the pillage of the natural resources of the planet. The fabrication of a major terrorist threat, and the spread of lies about weapons of mass destruction in Iraq, were used to mobilize the citizens of the United States to support militarism and wars at a moment when society needed to retreat from its long history of foreign military interventions. Militarism and the permanent war economy in the United States were the corollary of unilateralism and the celebration of warfare to reproduce the culture of domination.

The third element is the restriction on scientific research and creativity by Newtonian concepts of hierarchy and conservative religious values. The convergence of information technology, nanotechnology, biotechnology, and cognitive technologies, along with new breakthroughs relating to solar energy, holds the promise of a break in the reliance on fossil fuels. It is acknowledged in the scientific community that nanotechnology is revolutionary. One leader for Federal research had noted that:

> Nanotechnology involves moving individual atoms and molecules, building machines using molecular building blocks, and creating new kinds of materials and structures from the bottom up. Science and technology on the scale of a nanometer is revolutionary. It could change the way almost everything works – from medicines to computers, from clothing to skyscrapers – and lead to new products not yet imagined.[14]

Referring to this as bottom-up science, scientists have acknowledged the revolutionary potential of these converging technologies, and the reality that nanotechnology allows engineers to develop machines and structures that are much smaller than anything humans have been able to produce until now. Ray Kurzweil went further, arguing that with the future research in nanotechnology, "The crossover of the tipping point where solar energy will be less expensive than fossil fuels in almost every situation is within five years."[15]

The challenges, principles, and potential from this new scientific revolution that is ongoing in our lifetime cannot be fully appreciated because of the eugenic thinking of the educational system. An in-depth study of the moral and ethical issues for this technology is constrained by an educational system geared towards dumbing down and incarcerating youths of color. The ethical choices offered by new technologies can only be fully explored in a new context where the democratization of knowledge and information lays the basis for new citizenship.[16] Human society is not waiting for the United States to change its educational system as these scientific breakthroughs accelerate. American society lags behind because of the failure of its leadership to unleash an appreciation of the complexity and nuances of quantum mechanics. The emphasis on finance, insurance, and real estate reinforced the belief that science and scientific appreciation were secondary to greed and speculation.

The fourth element of this moment is the end of the Fordist consumer-led economy that is destroying the planet Earth. Millions of citizens are aware that there must be a revolutionary break with the US "culture of contentment" that is exacerbating global warming. This realization that the existing way of life is unsustainable is at the pivot of the failure of the old order. If present production and consumption patterns are not changed, the impact on our biosphere will be astounding: the air and water we depend on will become increasingly polluted; the soils will erode; and more and more forests, habitats, and biodiversity will continue to be lost. If the entire population of the Earth were to produce and consume at present US levels, we would need three planet Earths. The need to implement more environmentally friendly and socially responsible economic activity has never been greater, and for these reasons this moment is one that strengthens the call for Earth Democracy.[17]

Environmental justice and green consciousness are challenging the old ideas of those who trumpet the development of the productive forces. The linearity of certain socialists has also been challenged by this moment. From the ecological crisis, there is an emergent radical critique of capitalism itself.

The fifth element of the old idea was the effort to entrench the most racist and eugenic ideas to support racism and racist government policies at all levels. The old forms of urbanization, unequal access to health care, cancer alleys (such as the heavily polluted 85-mile stretch of the Mississippi River from Baton Rouge to New Orleans, Louisiana), and the forms of policing to oppress in order to reinforce and reproduce conservative public policy are now being challenged more forcefully. The primordial ordering principle of US society precedes the above four areas, and there are pressures from everywhere to shatter the racist assumptions embedded in US philosophy of democracy and freedom. The election of Barack Obama has not changed the racist structure of US society, but it demonstrated that the permanent division between working people cannot be supported to maintain the hegemony of the capitalist class.

These are just some of the contradictions, and we cannot chart the full contradictions of capitalism in this short commentary. The elements of the revolutionary moment have not reached the climactic stage in society. But these challenges are apparent to working people, and the contradictions are breaking out at a pace where the old media and instruments of psychological warfare and mind control cannot control the information conveyed to citizens. What is missing so far is the clarity of revolutionary ideas, the new forms of organization, and the resolute leadership that can mobilize the energies of the youth for a fundamental break with the old politics, economics, militarism, and racism.

BEYOND VANGUARDISM IN THE TWENTY-FIRST CENTURY

There are real possibilities for new directions in political organizing offered by the model of self-organization and self-mobilization of social networking. The self-organization and self-mobilization of the different social forces that were drawn into the political process in the United States in 2008 during the election campaign raised new directions for the understanding of revolutionary organization. A society cannot realize the potential for revolutionary change without revolutionary organizations.

During the twentieth century, the idea of a vanguard form of organization with the most advanced cadres in the leadership was the accepted idea of revolutionary organization.[18] The proposal of a vanguard party leading the revolution had been developed in the Bolshevik Revolution, and ideas on the role of the elite revolutionary forces were inscribed in revolutionary theories during the twentieth century. Then, it was the view that there had to be violent armed struggles in a revolution.

According to an interpretation of the ideas of Vladimir Lenin, workers, revolutionaries or those who want change need to organize together in a party, based on the principles of "democratic centralism," which aims to gain a decisive influence in the class struggle. The most advanced sections of the industrial working class were to be the vanguard of the revolution. One of the ultimate aims of the class struggle and the creation of the party was revolution and its seizure of power. Under this principle, the party would be strictly centralized, with all members expected to submit to party decisions, speak in one voice and act in one way. Without this "vanguard" injecting its politics into the working class (who, it is asserted, can only reach trade union consciousness by their own efforts), a revolution would be impossible.

Rosa Luxemburg, the German revolutionary, critiqued the ideas of "democratic centralism and vanguardism," and pointed out that there had to be room for the spontaneous activities of workers and peasants. She argued that ideas that were necessary for the conditions of a society such as nineteenth-century Russia could not be generalized for other societies. Despite the specificity of her critique, and the fact that the debate took place in the heat of actual struggles, intellectuals and political experts drew a false dichotomy between the need for organization and spontaneity. What was clear from the history of revolutionary praxis in the twentieth century was that there could be no revolution without organization. The challenge was to be able to build an organization that could be inclusive and welcome the ideas and actions of the most oppressed of the society.

Inside the revolutionary traditions of the United States, the ideas of vanguardism have been critiqued by various forces. The autonomy and independence of many radical formations led them to reject the underlying assumptions of vanguardism. Eugene Debs, one of the founders of the American Socialist Party in the early years of the twentieth century, believed that radical organizations had to have a "broad tent in which all trends within the socialist movement were represented in the same organization, because it would organize more people."[19]

Similarly, in the black liberation movements, the revolutionary forces, especially women such as Ella Baker, rejected the underlying assumptions of elitism and great male leaders. The experiences of blacks in the anti-slavery struggles, in the Garvey movement, and later in the freedom movement were that black people had to be self-reliant at the level of theory. This radical democratic vision was evident in the civil rights revolution. It was in this period that the principles of non-violent revolution were articulated by Martin Luther King Jr. In breaking his silence over the war in Vietnam, King opposed militarism and violence and called for a "radical revolution of values."[20]

As Martin Luther King Jr. moved in the direction of organizing workers, in particular sanitation workers in Tennessee, he was assassinated. The assassination of many of the leaders of the civil rights revolution was an effort to destroy radical ideas and organizations. Yet the lessons of this period nurtured new ideas on revolutionary organization.

Walter Rodney, a Caribbean revolutionary, escaped the pitfalls of scholars and thinkers who believed that they could chart the struggle for the working classes. In an interview in 1980, he noted:

> There is both from a theoretical point of view as well as from the point of view of anyone engaged in politics, a clear distinction between spontaneity in protest and the organization of that spontaneity and the self-organization of the people so that they can carry themselves from one stage to a higher stage.[21]

Here, Rodney was reasserting the communication of Marx to the First International that "The emancipation of the working class must be carried out by the working class themselves."[22] Marx's concept of self-emancipation had been smothered by crude Leninism, which demanded that revolutions be led by vanguard organizations.

Vanguardism was not restricted to the revolutionary parties. "One-party democracies" from Algeria to Zaire had sprung up in Africa. From Indonesia to Iraq, authoritarian leaders sought the refuge and discourse of democratic centralism. In most of these societies, there was a lot of centralism but very little democracy. Societies such as North Korea and Zimbabwe, under Kim Il-sung and Robert Mugabe respectively, produced strong leaders out of supposedly revolutionary parties, so that the central committee replaced the party and ultimately, the supreme leader replaced the party. Josef Stalin had refined this form of vanguardism and the cult of the personality as one component of the degeneration of the Bolshevik Revolution in the Soviet Union.

Vanguardism was to be found in political parties all over the world, and mainstream parties adopted elements of vanguardism. Within the United States, the political leadership of the Democratic Party acted as a vanguard, making decisions for the rank and file. Throughout the twentieth century, a boss system had developed that took decisions out of the hands of voters. Within the black liberation movement in the United States, there were elements of vanguardism, and this was to be found in the elitism of the leaders of the civil rights movement. Would the civil rights movement be based on grassroots organizing or the elite who, a generation earlier, had been called "the talented tenth"? Ella Baker had elaborated on a radical democratic vision that proclaimed the necessity for bottom-up organization and for the political education of the masses so that the masses would be able to be agents of their own liberation.

Baker had been an activist throughout most of the twentieth century, and observed the pitfalls of vanguardism in the Communist Party and in the top-down civil rights organizations such as the Southern Christian Leadership Convention (SCLC) and the National Association for the Advancement of Colored People (NAACP). It was the aversion to vanguardism that inspired her to work with the freedom fighters of the fourth revolutionary moment in the United States, the moment of the civil rights revolution.

Baker had insisted on bottom-up forms of organizing, on participatory democracy, and for all forms of organization to be based on democratic decision making. Building from the traditions of the church, she asked, "would leadership flow from the pulpit to the pew or from the pew to the pulpit?"[22] In the two-way flow, she had stressed the importance of the pew. Her revulsion to vanguardism had emerged from the celebrity civil rights leaders who were venerated by the media. These celebrities appeared in communities to organize when there was a lot of national media, but would leave after all of the media attention dissipated. Communities were then left to the mercy of police and Ku Klux Klan retaliation.

The Mississippi Freedom Democratic Party (MFPD) had been built on the model of a non-hierarchical organization where the consciousness of the people could take them from one level of awareness to the next. Fannie Lou Hamer, who was born into a sharecropping family, had matured as one of the grassroots mobilizers who rocked the national consciousness in 1964 at the Democratic National Convention. Her emergence had made more credible the idea of Baker that "give the people the light and they will find their way." Robert Moses and the leaders of the Student Non Violent Coordinating Committee (SNCC) had taken the principles of Ella Baker and joined a massive movement that attempted to move US society from its racist and militarist moorings to an inclusive and more democratic society.

The elementary gains of the civil rights revolution were hijacked after Ronald Reagan came to power in the United States in 1980. Conservatives studied the organizational techniques of the civil rights struggles, and set about the task of building a conservative grassroots revolution in the United States. This conservative revolution, which was based on ideas of Christian fundamentalism, became a formidable force in US politics and gave militarism a social base among sections of the white working class.

A non-profit sector at home coupled with humanitarianism abroad completed the picture of disaster capitalism. Hurricane Katrina in New Orleans exposed the calumny of neo-liberalism and individualism. First, every aspect of the Bush administration and its ideas of individual self-interest was exposed by Hurricane Katrina. Second, this natural disaster also sent another warning about global warming. This hurricane was like a metaphor on the entire system of capitalism and the human condition at the start of the twenty-first century.

It was therefore not by accident that the cultural revolution from below shaped the radicalism of US society. During the 1960s, James Boggs, who was a worker in Detroit, noted in his pamphlet on the American Revolution that the crude materialism that shaped vanguardism had to be transcended.

> The American Revolution does not necessarily have to start from economic grievances. Nor does it have to start with the American working class in the lead. The development of capitalism in the United States has generated more than enough contradictions to pose the question of the total social reorganization of the country. Some of these contradictions relate to sheer poverty and the workers' life in production. Others are just as important and have even wider bearing on the quality of social existence. Man is imaginative and creative. His needs go far beyond the realm of the material.

Boggs was way ahead of his time when he called for revolutionary imagination:

What is man's greatest human need in the United States today? It is to stop shirking responsibility and start assuming responsibility. When Americans stop doing the one and start doing the other, they will begin to travel the revolutionary road. But to do this they must use as much creative imagination in politics as up to now they have used in production. The fact is that the more imaginative Americans have been in creating new techniques of production, the less imaginative they have been in creating new relations between people. Americans today are like a bunch of ants who have been struggling all summer long to accumulate a harvest and then can't decide how to distribute it and therefore fight among themselves and destroy each other to get at the accumulation.

The greatest obstacle in the way of the American people beginning to behave like human beings rather than like animals is the great American illusion of freedom.[23]

CLASSICAL MUSIC MEETS JAZZ

While the Bush administration dithered in the face of hundreds of thousands of persons stranded in New Orleans, genuine grassroots organizations leapt into motion to expose the reality that elements of Ubuntu still resided within the population of the United States. Church groups organized food and clothing, assisted whole neighborhoods to relocate, and contributed generously to those who had been rendered homeless by the hurricane and the breached levies.

The Obama campaign for the presidency tapped into this spirit, with the added advantage of the new information technologies to redefine the election process and set in motion millions of volunteers. This campaign brought together a tight organization that could tap into the enthusiasm and spontaneity of millions of volunteers. Every political party had access to the new technologies. What was significant was the way in which the Obama organization tapped into the new technologies so that the ideas and capabilities of grassroots forces could make a decisive statement in relation to a bottom-up approach to participation. It was this bottom-up principle, along with the lessons of a democratic vision of transparent leadership, that Jeremy Bird likened to classical music meeting jazz.

In classical music, it is the conductor who wields the baton and holds the power over the orchestra. Gene Koo captured the command position of the orchestra conductor when he argued that:

The superstructure of the campaign is traditional, top-down command-and-control (with information flowing upwards, of course). At the roots the campaign – as is typical for most volunteer efforts – comprises ad hoc mesh networks. It's in inserting strong, tightly-knit teams that the campaign has made the greatest innovation.[24]

From the historical record, we get a window on the tight-knit organizational structure from the book by David Plouffe, *The Audacity to Win: The Inside Story and Lessons of Barack Obama's Historic Victory*. David Axelrod (chief strategist for Obama's 2008 election campaign and now senior advisor to Obama) and David Plouffe effectively retained the hierarchy of the enterprise, but in the process also ceded a tremendous amount of autonomy to its middle managers in an effort to build a more dynamic and scalable operation.[25]

One commentator noted that the strong control by the Obama campaign organization "mixed timeless traditions and discipline of good organizing with new technologies of decentralization and self-organization."[26]

Once this meeting and mixture took place, the energy, the force, and the power of jazz could not be contained. It had broken out in the campaign and was set to be a key component of the revolutionary moment. A genuine form of "network power" was emerging from a generation that spent a considerable amount of time on the Internet and using social networking tools. The ability to reach, influence, and mobilize millions of youth had been honed by progressive cultural leaders during the cultural revolution.

Musician Lauryn Hill had been a forerunner in the struggle against sexism and racism, calling for "freedom." Inside the hip hop movement, artists for peace struggled against misogyny and masculinity. Obama embraced the peace wing of hip hop, and young people in South Carolina dubbed him the hip hop presidential candidate.

Throughout the two years of campaigning, the style and substance of Barack Obama offered a new sensibility to political leadership. Writers of differing intellectual and ideological persuasion have remarked that "Obama's social networking was the real revolution." New visionaries emerged in the election cycle, and these far-sighted elements worked early in the primary campaign to harness the tools of social networking with its tremendous communication capabilities and aggressive database development. This social networking tipped the balance between hope and change on one side, and four more years of Republican conservatism on the other. It was here where ordinary people did extraordinary things and where small interventions added up to register big changes.

Commercial entrepreneurs had for years been reading the book on social networking by Malcolm Gladwell, *The Tipping Point: How Little Things Can Make a Big Difference*. In this book, the concept of momentum for change is explored, but confined to the goal of selling products and the cycle of profits. Gladwell defined a tipping point as a sociological term, "the moment of critical mass, the threshold, the boiling point." He further elaborated on "how ideas and products and messages and behaviors spread like viruses do." These ideas have many lessons for radical politics in our time.

In my opinion, not only was the Obama campaign's self-organization unique in terms of unleashing the potential of the youth, it also achieved a qualitative leap in the forms of political organizing through quantitative means.

In this respect, the forms of politics broke the old vanguardism of the left, and the leaderism and bossism of the Democratic Party. This is why the lesson of the defeat of the Clinton machine is so significant. The election of Obama was followed with great interest by millions around the world who wanted their own grassroots organization to challenge entrenched interests. People around the world have for long been rendered hopeless, because they do not believe they are able to mobilize against the establishment and succeed. They will be most interested in studying the Obama campaign to learn and to take heart that the "system" is not unbeatable.

I shall use the words of Boggs to wrap up this section:

> The American people must find a way to insist upon their own right and responsibility to make political decisions and to determine policy in all spheres of social existence – whether it is foreign policy, the work process, education, race relations, community life. The coming struggle is a political struggle to take political power out of the hands of the few and put it into the hands of the many. But in order to get this power into the hands of the many, it will be necessary for the many not only to fight the powerful few but to fight and clash among themselves as well.[27]

After Obama's election, racist ideas came to the fore, with the extremism of the conservative forces threatening the kind of violence that promises to make the prediction of Boggs come through. The working classes had been divided on racial lines, and the old white

working classes have been awakened to the erosion of the investment in whiteness. Similarly, the old Left leadership treated the
white working class as an abstraction so that there were no strong
bases to make a break with the capitalist classes. New leaders are
emerging as communities are fighting a defensive battle against the
old divisive ideas of white supremacy.

The election of Obama opened the space for new grassroots leadership. Essentially, this opening can progressively weaken the few
who have always held on to power. Zack Exley commented long
before November 4, 2008 that, "Win or lose, 'The New Organizers'
have already transformed thousands of communities – and revolutionized the way organizing itself will be understood and practiced
for at least the next generation."[28]

There is a new grassroots leadership that is emerging at new
sites of politics in relation to differing issues such as homelessness,
need for health care, employment, pensions, environmental repair,
anti-racism, and the peace movement. The *network of networks* has
created a new layer of political leadership in society, which has the
potential to shake the complacency of the consensus that maintained
the capitalist system. For example, a network such as that of breast
cancer survivors appeared as a force in politics to change the health
care system. This network remains independent of political parties,
but is organized to defend the interests of women. It was within
these new layered sources of network power that citizens discovered
their capacity for distributed collective action.

Obama tapped into the deep yearning for change from the
counter-revolutionary period. A glimpse of the revolutionary energy
was seen on the Mall in Washington on January 20, 2009. Obama
himself dug deep into the revolutionary memories and ideas of Tom
Paine in order to inspire the millions who wanted to make change
real. Obama was being pushed by the momentum of the demands
for peace and justice. Can he be pushed further?

REPARATIONS AND REVOLUTION

The role of the anti-capitalist forces in this period is to be able to
build new politics, new ideas, and new networks using the self-
organization, self-confidence, and self-mobilization that had grown
out of the challenge to the financial wizards and their military
backers. Emancipatory politics as a component of the democratization process draws from the richness of the lessons of the previous
struggles for democracy. There was the clarification of the reality

that the old politics of exclusion based on tribal enclaves were not instructive regarding a number of democratic questions. The politics of inclusion is a bedrock principle of emancipatory politics.

The Obama campaign adopted an approach to society that was broadly inclusive and open to all groups. The recognition of the democratic changes in the society heralded a new chapter in US society, beyond the politics of divide and rule that had persisted from the period of the conquest of the First Nation peoples and the annexation of the territories of Mexico. This conception of inclusive politics was an effort not just to defeat the Republicans but also to foster structural transformations in the dynamics of society, where blacks, Latinos and other groups had full citizenship. It is in the realm of the politics of inclusion that the alliances between peace movements, the workers' movement, the environmental justice movement, the transgender movement, the anti-racist movement, the women's movement, and the reparations movement have room for building new militants and new sites of politics beyond elections. Such an alliance will be necessary to hold the Obama administration accountable, building a new force inside the United States while aligning with the peace movement globally.

This movement must continue to champion the call for the reduction of the US military budget and the dismantling of the offensive military planning of the "war on terror." The US working class has no stomach for the kind of patriotism that supported the PATRIOT Act and the illegal invasion of Iraq. There must be intensified work in the peace movement for the United States to withdraw from Afghanistan. In the short run, the extreme racists will seek to dominate the political space, and this extremism will itself force liberals to take a more decisive stand on institutional racism.

One of the weakest aspects of the Old Left is its failure to embrace the new abolitionism and the centrality of the anti-racist struggle. This Left has also been deaf to the reparative claims of the oppressed. In the United States, the historic Left has consciously distanced itself from the reparations movement. It is within the ranks of the indigenous peoples, sections of the Latino communities, and in the African American community that there is a clear understanding of the links between reparations, healing, and revolutionary change.

Reparations should involve atonement, healing, justice, reconciliation, and the repairing of what has been broken. In essence, the reparations movement requires a break with the past crimes of capitalism and racism. This movement demands that society step back from the celebration of progress and atone for the genocide of millions of Africans and indigenous persons. Like the civil rights movement of the 1960s, this reparations movement is broad, with a progressive wing working for the overthrow of capitalism and one wing that consider reparations as monetary compensation.

In reality, monetary compensation is only one form of repair. The others are restitution, rehabilitation, and guarantees of non-repetition. It is on the question of the guarantee of non-repetition that the Left and revolutionary forces of the African descendants have joined with indigenous peoples and other oppressed peoples to redress the crimes of colonialism, slavery, imperialism, and occupation. This reparations movement draws from the historic lessons of the struggles against Nazism, and informs the peace and justice forces in Palestine and other sites of occupation and humiliation.

The ruling class in the United States has cut off the people from the international discussions of the World Conference against Racism. The lobbies for colonialism and warfare are for the moment stronger than the forces opposed to militarism and occupation. It is significant that no section of the traditional Left or trade union sector in the United States supported the call for the United States government to re-engage with the World Conference against Racism. Thus far, the Israeli lobby has registered itself as a force stronger than the peace and reparations movement. However, the slow build-up of the struggles and alliances between Latin America and Africa in the changed world situation has placed the ideas of majority and minority in a quandary.[29]

NEW MILITANTS AND SITES OF POLITICS

Obama is not a revolutionary, but he has been caught up in a revolutionary moment in world history. The electoral campaign of Obama rode on a wave of peace and change desired by ordinary Americans and peace-loving citizens globally. There are limitations to the electoral project insofar as the task of restructuring US society is a gigantic one that cannot be done overnight. Obama may not be the solution, but is a small step in the direction of making the break with the old binary conceptions that dominated enlightenment thinking.

The laws of unintended consequences that will emanate from this break can lead to a new direction with the new positive bottom-up organizing for transformation to a democratic society where all can live in peace. Additionally, the demographic shifts and the self-confidence of formerly oppressed communities have been leading to an awakening among blacks and Latinos. Although they are minorities in the United States, they are a majority in the world. What in the United States is portrayed as a race question is, on a world scale, the question of the rights of the majority of the human race.

The delegitimization of neo-liberal experts has already opened room for creative and humorous broadsides against the bankers and their protectors. Humor, creative uses of social networking, youth energy, and new images can galvanize the society to a point where these bankers no longer have a chokehold over the society. However, beyond humor, there is need for new organizations. The embryo of the new forms of organizing is already there in the networks organizing for life, decent education, and for peace.

In practical terms, the *networks of networks* form the kernel of the new move towards a revolutionary form of organizing. These networks create spaces for creativity and transcend the racialized spaces of society. Quantitatively, the more networks that are available, the more there is the possibility of a leap. This leap is central to Quantum politics.

C. L. R. James noted that revolutions are not carried out in parliaments, they are only registered there. It is also appropriate to remind the reader of another claim by James, "The leaders of a Revolution are usually those who have been able to profit by the cultural advantages of the system they are attacking."[30]

In the Haitian Revolution, Toussaint L'Ouverture emerged from the ranks of the enslaved to champion the ideas of freedom and liberty. Toussaint had profited from the cultural advantages of a revolutionary era. Barack Obama profited from the revolution in social networking and the rich heritage of the civil rights movement.

The victory of Obama is the first step to weaken the Right. Where we go from here will depend on the ideas, organization, and leadership that will develop in this period. This book is intended to support ideas about twenty-first century revolution.

CONCLUSION

The election of Barack Obama as the president of the United States was an extraordinary event in world history. What his election meant was that a sizeable section of the US population felt that something new was required. Sufficient numbers from the white working class voted for him to ensure victory. Yet the long history of racism and sexism guarantees that it is only a prolonged popular struggle that can seriously challenge institutional racism in the United States.

There is now the potential for new organizations building on the former revolutionary moments in the history of the republic.

Historians have identified four previous revolutionary periods in the United States: 1776–83, 1860–77, 1919–29, and 1954–73. Revolutionaries understand the limitation of bringing fundamental changes from within the White House in the United States. Barack Obama, as a person, cannot fundamentally alter the conditions in the society. However, like Abraham Lincoln at the time of the US Civil War, his election arose at a moment of many transitions. Abraham Lincoln was pushed by the radical abolitionists who understood that saving the Union could not be separated from the abolition of slavery. At that revolutionary moment, the growth of Lincoln pushed him to the point where he understood that the promise of the founding fathers and the American Revolution of 1776 could not be fulfilled if society persisted on the basis of enslaving others.

Long agitation, a forceful abolitionist movement, and war shifted the force in the United States. Lincoln was cut down so that the democratic vision could not then prevail. Obama was elected at another moment when American society was being forced to choose. The spectacle of wars, militarism, and the collapse of the financial system forced hard choices on society. Trained in the ideas of liberalism, Barack Obama had read Lincoln, and had accepted the proposition that there could be a "more perfect union."

What Obama could not address was whether this union and democratic society could exist within the present mode of economic organization. The collapse of the financial services sector, the nationalization of banks, and the fall of the dollar presented challenges that few leaders had faced in US society.

Informed and mobilized youth brought new energies to the political table. Social networking tools that were being used for entertainment were harnessed by the young to intervene. Web 2.0 technologies served to revolutionize the nature of political organizing. At the same moment, new innovations were being rolled out that challenged the old forms of economic organization. Scientific cooperation across borders led to sharing of information to challenge the intellectual property rights orientation of transnational corporations. The Ubuntu of shared humanity met with the Ubuntu of the open source movement. When these two conceptions of Ubuntu converged in the election campaign, there were innovative interventions that fundamentally changed politics.

During the campaign, it was imperative to find a way to reach youth that was effective and able to bridge social and racial differences. In many ways, the ground had been prepared by the new abolitionists who were inside the hip hop revolution opposing the prison industrial complex (that is, those businesses and organizations involved in the repressive apparatus that warehouses primarily black and brown people in the United States). This hip hop movement combined the positive and the negative, and the campaign was able to draw out the most positive forces. These positive forces set the words of optimism to music. *Yes we can.*

A clear understanding of the nature of US politics and the limitations of the structures of conservatism means that Barack Obama would only be trapped by this social system if those who are being drawn into the *Audacity of Hope* do not build their own political movement and political organization.

In the efforts to build a new political formation, whether it is called a party or not, the task for the producers and working people in the society will be to deepen the traditions of self-liberation in order to bring light to those who have been blinded by the devastating culture of ignorance. We should not underestimate the tasks of regeneration of real humans in the twenty-first century.

It is only a bottom-up movement built on the principles of self-emancipation and self-mobilization within many organized movements that can prevent Barack Obama from becoming a tool for the Wall Street forces and the exhausted militarists. Failure of the movement would mean that the Obama administration would perpetuate the counter-revolutionary moment from Reagan to Bush.

Self-mobilization, self-organization, and the politics of inclusion will create new spaces so that the political space will be expanded beyond the media, the lobbyists, and the ritual spaces of the White House, Congress, and the Senate Chambers. Safe and clean neighborhoods, children who are reared to respect all human beings, and a society that supports the repair of planet Earth await these new self-organizing forces.

The campaign of Barack Obama is the story of hundreds of thousands of ordinary people. These are the people who are participating because they believe that politics can mean something again. It is apt to conclude with the words of Martin Luther King Jr., "Our only hope today lies in our ability to recapture the revolutionary spirit and go out into a sometimes hostile world declaring eternal hostility to poverty, racism and militarism."

Chapter 2 details the political education of Barack Obama.

2

THE POLITICAL TRAINING
OF BARACK OBAMA

From the time of his birth, Barack Obama was confronted with the questions of healing, Ubuntu, the building of a non-racial democracy, and the need for new modes of politics and political organizing. These tasks emerged slowly as he grasped the strength and weaknesses of his formal education in Indonesia and Hawaii, and then more profoundly as he grasped the limits of the concept of "charity" while he was a community organizer in Chicago. Yet it was the very same experience as a community organizer that promoted his understanding of the important linkages between humans, and the need to take themselves from one level of organizing to the next, which is at the heart of self- emancipation.

By any criterion, Obama was an educated person. He had graduated from the Ivy League Columbia College in New York City and had gone on to graduate magnum cum laude from another Ivy League Law School at Harvard University. At this citadel of learning, Obama became the president of the *Harvard Law Review*. From this position as its first African American president, Obama could have had any number of plum jobs, as a partner in a prestigious law firm, a clerk for the top judges, or a faculty member at a leading university. Yet he chose to return to Chicago, to the site of politics that he had embraced as a community organizer after he graduated from university. He had become painfully aware that formal education about equality and democracy had severe limitations. From the moment of his full understanding of the struggles of his father and the nature of racism and colonialism in Kenya, Obama seemed to have made a decision about a political career. It was a career that required a break with the old vanguardist politics, old methods of top-down organizing, and outmoded forms of uniformity and hierarchy that placed tremendous powers in the hands of corporations.

This chapter will briefly explore Obama's self-education as an organizer, and especially the lack of principle among politicians after the death of Harold Washington. His stewardship in Chicago taught Obama many of the lessons that had been learnt from the civil rights movement and those members of Student Non Violent Coordinating Committee (SNCC) who internalized the ideas of Ella Baker. Obama had discovered the potency of community organizing, and found the link between the new technological advances and grassroots organizing. This provided the context for his break with old conceptions of vanguardism, the monocultural mind, and the top-down politics of conventional political parties.

We will begin by locating Obama in the multiracial context of Hawaii, paying attention to the role of his mother in his political education. From this, we examine the influence of his grandparents during the crucial years while he was learning from their experiences in the capitalist depression. Our exploration into his years in the field as a community organizer in Chicago is meant to set up an understanding of how the positive and negative lessons from this immersion into community enabled Obama to seize opportunities as they unfolded with new techniques for organizing and social networking.

Obama matured in the United States when giant corporations had exploded and supported a new form of conservative management that dictated total control over life and human relations, to the point where these corporate entities had acquired patents on over 100,000 genes. Blinded by the "monoculture of the mind," they had placed patents on animals, plants, and microorganisms. The convergence of information technology, biotechnology, nanotechnology, and cognitive technologies had ushered in a revolution of ideas about life, but ideas about social relations had remained at the level of the nineteenth-century conception of life. The nineteenth-century construction of the world was in "mutually exclusive categories thus banishing multiplicity and pluralism as well as pluralism and connectedness."[1]

Bruce Lipton has taken this conception of connectedness to deepen our understanding of how human beings can only be fulfilled when we evolve as a community. This community will be the basis for enhancing our humanity. Lipton termed this understanding of community as knowledge based on fractal wisdom. While the convergence of new technologies opened vast opportunities for new forms of human relations, this potential remained buried, waiting like a seed for the right conditions for germination.

In 1980, when Obama was 19 years old, the US Supreme Court ruled that as long as living organisms had been genetically engineered and could be deemed "human-made inventions," it was possible to patent life forms. This radical change in the understanding of life was taking place when the patenting of life and cloning shifted the terrain of politics, and ushered in a new politics for the twenty-first century that was associated with the genetic revolution.

The genetic revolution – like slavery, civil rights, and the Cold War before it – is such an event. In time, it may overshadow them all.[2]

In the United States, the politics of the genetic revolution had become entangled with the politics of stem cell research and ideas about when life began, but lurking not far behind were the ideas of eugenics. Obama was designated a black person by virtue of the fact that his father was a black person, an African from Kenya. But from the time of his youth, Obama had to wrestle with outmoded ideas of racial determinism while seeking to reconcile his humanity with that of others who had been abused and violated.

Born in Hawaii, the 50th state of the United States, Barack Obama was the child of people from two continents. It was his lifelong aspiration to reconcile the reality of his heritage (what he called his inheritance) and to rise above the ideas of superiority and inferiority of human beings. In this enterprise of understanding the core principles of love, reconciliation, peace, and forgiveness, his mother, Stanley Ann Dunham, was a key teacher and motivating force. While Obama was a youth, she continuously posed ontological issues to him about what it is to be a human being. Her optimism imbued in the young Obama one core element of his political training – the idea that all humans should have the right to live on the planet Earth as free human beings. It derived from the egalitarianism that she had pursued in her own life while in Hawaii and in Indonesia, as she sought to escape the stifling confines of a settler society. For this search, the mainstream media called her a "romantic" and "a free-spirited wanderer."[3]

Her understanding of equality had challenged the old determinism and Lockean concepts of property that justified the ideas of individual self-interest. The equality that was promised in the US Constitution had been premised on an acceptance of the ideas of private property as the basis for citizenship, the superiority of the

European forms of political and economic organizing, the centrality of men as breadwinners of the family, and rigid heterosexism. The function of these ideas was to impart values of patriarchy, masculinity, and individualism, with a brand of militarism that was baptized patriotism.

Schooling in the United States provided a basic civic education for the maintenance of the social structure and smooth functioning of the system. Formal education for all in the United States emerged out of decades of political struggles. At the dawn of this republic, Obama could not have been a citizen of the United States. In 1787, non-whites were counted as three-fifths of a person for the purposes of electoral balancing in the former slave states. The "one drop" theory designated that a person with one drop of non-white blood was non-white. Such was the perverseness of academe that decades of writings by official journals in the profession of political science did not seriously challenge this bifurcated citizenship.

Stanley Ann Dunham was born into a community where, although her parents were members of the working class, her European heritage positioned her to enjoy the privileges of white supremacy. At the age of seven in Texas, she was cursed as a "nigger lover" because she dared to play with a young black girl, breaking the segregation barriers even before the legal dismantling of *Brown v. Board of Education*. Throughout her life, she objected to the reproduction of white privilege and revolted against the class, gendered, and racial underpinnings of the educational system.

When Samir Amin wrote about education in societies where the division of labor and the class divisions are obfuscated by the seemingly smooth integration of classes and a high degree of social mobility,[4] the dysfunctional nature of the educational system had not yet created widespread alienation and growth of the prison industrial complex. There was still an industrialized sector of the economy that provided wage labor for the vast majority of US citizens. By the end of the twentieth century, deindustrialization, unemployment, and sharp inequalities combined to ensure that education in general, and political education in particular, had led some writers to reflect on the logic of "savage inequalities."[5] In order to cover up this savagery, there is an elaborate apparatus to "manufacture consent" using "make believe media: the politics of entertainment."[6]

Obama's political training took place in a context where the ideas and values of his mother elevated him above the savagery and mediocrity that awaited him in the celebration of genocide as progress.

He reinforced the importance of human communities and sought to inspire the difference between individuality and individualism. The idea of community is central to his training as a politician.

Initially, he had been recruited to work on the basis of the principles of community organizing that had come from Saul Alinsky.[7] Obama inserted himself in the community on the South Side of Chicago in 1985, two years after the election of Harold Washington as Mayor of Chicago electrified the city to new possibilities. Three years into community organizing, Obama began to understand the limitations of the old Alinsky model of organizing. It was ultimately a safety valve for the system. Community organizing and foundation support could not make up for the lack of state intervention to supply decent education, health for all, and a clean environment. Obama's tenure as a community organizer coincided with a time when the professionalization of community organizing diverted energies away from the full empowerment of people at the grassroots. Conservative think-tanks and foundations flourished in the period after Reagan, when community organizing was overtaken by new "faith-based initiatives." It was ironic that Obama himself had been recruited as a community organizer by one such faith-based initiative, of the Roman Catholic Church in Chicago.

His autobiographical work, *Dreams from my Father: A Story of Race and Inheritance,* provides enough insights into the thinking and practices that shaped Obama and his attempt to shape the politics of the twenty-first century. As a descendant of two settler societies (Hawaii in the United States and Kenya in East Africa), his journey towards reconciliation with his father led to his self-discovery and propelled him to excellence and to shattering the bondage of inferiorization.[8]

In exploring the use of the powerful imagery and language of redemption in his autobiography, we will seek to understand how he unearthed the transformative possibilities of redemption. Was he moving to the same plane as the philosophers who used the ideas of redemption to call for emancipation from mental slavery? During the anti-slavery period, images of escape from Babylon and redemption were powerful sources of inspiration, education, and mobilization. At the start of the twentieth century, secular elements internalized more materialistic and deterministic approaches to revolutionary politics, and eschewed the use of images such as redemption. Instead of arguing for the full liberation and emancipation of the working peoples, there was the stages theory of history, pointing to the need for the liberation of white workers as a prerequisite for the tutelage of other workers. Moreover, the racist nature of some of the working-class organizations ensured that African Americans had to be self-reliant at the level of intellectual and ideological creativity.

Obama dug deep into this reservoir of creative energy in searching for a brand of politics that was non-conflictual, while not succumbing to "moral cowardice." The emancipatory ideas of liberation fighters for non-racial democracies and peace, and the redemptive messages of Mahatma Gandhi and Martin Luther King Jr., inspired Obama, but there were also five women whose influence imbued a brand of feminist sensibility that is now so evident in his style, manner, and speech. The five women were Harriet Tubman, Obama's mother, his grandmother, Ella Baker, and Michelle Obama. In this chapter, we look at the influence of the last four of these women. In the next chapter on "Confronting Racism and Sexism in US Politics," we shall examine the influence of Harriet Tubman's self-organizational principles on Obama.

UBUNTU AND NON-RACIAL DEMOCRACY

When Obama's mother moved to Hawaii, she had followed the migratory path of the children of many working people after the Second World War. By the time of the annexation of the Islands by the United States in 1898, the indigenous Hawaiian citizens had become a minority in their own society. When the peoples were incorporated into the Union in 1959, "the legend was made of Hawaii as the one true melting pot, an experiment in racial harmony."[9] Despite this melting pot theory, a physical and cultural decimation of the indigenous peoples had followed the path of the mass genocide of native peoples in the United States in the wake of European exploration and settlement.[10] David Stannard's study on Hawaii brought out the specific dimensions of the genocide in the experience of the islands' indigenous peoples. His book, *Before the Horror: The Population of Hawaii on the Eve of Western Contact*, documented the devastating consequences for a society in which, in less than 50 years after Western contact, 90 per cent of the population had perished.

There was no question that genocidal violence and biological warfare had taken place in Hawaii. The experience of cultural and physical genocide reinforced the phenomenon of what Claudia Card termed "social death." This was the phenomenon where actual genocide and cultural oppression are reinforced by the recursive processes of loss of social vitality, loss of identity, and thereby loss of meaning for one's existence.[11] In *Dreams from my Father*, Obama himself used his own style to reflect on this form of social death.[12]

According to the memory of his grandfather, Stanley Dunham, the family immersed itself in this society, living alongside different peoples while seeking mutual understanding. The anti-racism of the Dunham family was imprinted in their social relations, so that Obama's grandparents made a wide circle of friends, including Japanese Americans, Native Hawaiians, blacks, Chinese, and others. From these relations with the inheritors of indentureship and segregation, the Dunham family learnt the history of physical and cultural death that had been reinforced by the exploitation of the migrant laborers. After the decimation of the indigenous peoples, the European plantation owners had imported hundreds of thousands of Chinese, Filipino, and Japanese workers to work on the sugar and pineapple plantations. Ronald Takaki, one of the descendants of the migrant workers on the plantations, documented the ways in which racism was the driving force behind the plantation management policies before and after Hawaii's annexation by the United States.[13]

As a keen student of human society even before her formal training as an anthropologist, Obama's mother was able to penetrate the hype about Hawaii being the paradise of the Pacific. She grasped the real content of the history, and the realities behind the advertisements that were being crafted to sell Hawaii as a major tourist destination. Hawaii in 1960 was fast becoming a truly multiracial society where Asian Americans were in the majority and 20 per cent of the population came from mixed heritages. Like her parents, and in the face of the sexism and patriarchy that supplemented racism, Ann shunned the privileges of the settler community and gravitated towards those who were seeking to ascertain their humanity in the face of the history of exploitation and racism.

It was not surprising then that Ann gravitated towards the first African student to enroll at the University of Hawaii, in 1959: Barack Obama, Sr. She married him at a time when such marriages were illegal in 15 states of the United States. Obama Jr. himself revolted against the ugliness of the concept of miscegenation in his autobiography.[14]

A spirit of love sustained Ann and Barack Obama Sr. as young persons facing relatives who were skeptical that they could overcome the lurid and ugly past of the United States. Ann had listened very carefully to the stories of the Land and Freedom Army in Kenya and the criminal violence committed by the British. She immediately became a supporter of Kenyan independence, and understood the tyranny of Britain that propelled the freedom fighters to struggle for their rights. So while the Anglo-American media disparaged the Kenyans (talking about the "evil" Mau Mau), the mother of Barack Obama was imbibing another reality. Obama Jr. was a beautiful offspring of the love between two persons.

On his part, Barack Obama, Sr. conveyed messages of hope for freedom while identifying with the promise of a multiracial democracy in the United States, starting in Hawaii. When he graduated from the University of Hawaii in 1963, Kenya was gradually moving towards independence, but the society could not shed the legacies of ethnic manipulation and brutal exploitation. This was the theme of struggle that Obama Sr. reiterated when he spoke at Barack Jr.'s high school on his second convalescing trip to Hawaii in 1971.[15]

Barack Obama was receiving one lesson from his father that would influence his thinking on Kenya and the world. The other lessons were being imparted by his mother. She communicated the values of self-development, hard work, and sacrifice.

LESSONS IN UBUNTU

To reiterate, human sympathy, willingness to share, love, and forgiveness are the key aspects of Ubuntu. When Barack Obama Sr. departed from Hawaii to go to Harvard in 1963, the two-year-old Barack Jr. was left to be reared by his mother and grandparents. However, Ann did not denigrate or berate Obama Sr. for leaving. She had understood the struggles for independence in Kenya, and kept up correspondence with him while he was there. She forgave him and moved on to continue her own path of self-realization while nurturing the young Barack with the spirit of love and forgiveness.

In 1963, Ann divorced Barack Obama, Sr. and married Lolo Soetoro, an Indonesian student. Her second marriage required Ann to move to Indonesia. Thus, at the age of six, the young Obama was now being given another lesson by the multicultural, multi-ethnic and multireligious society that was Indonesia, and he was always conscious of this.

Obama was receiving another practical geography lesson and becoming immersed into another diverse society. Even as a child, he was not blind to the atrocities that had befallen Indonesia after the US-assisted 1965 military coup against Sukarno. When Obama was writing his autobiography in the 1990s, it was already known that over half a million Indonesians had been slaughtered.[16] This lesson of repression could not be avoided in the Soetoro household in Indonesia, because it inserted itself in all spheres of life, to the point where it affected the life chances of Lolo – his new father – and shattered the possibility of a proper relationship between a US citizen and an Indonesian who did not support repression.

This was the overriding atmosphere as Barack Obama attended primary school in Indonesia, while his mother awakened in him an interest in knowledge. She taught him about the ongoing civil rights struggles in the United States, and the importance of knowledge and power.[17]

Here then were the crucial years for the formation of the ideas, values, and political education of Barack Obama. As a politician, Obama referred to his mother as "the dominant figure in my formative years. ... The values she taught me continue to be my touchstone when it comes to how I go about the world of politics."[18] In his autobiography, he elaborated on the values she taught him: honesty, fairness, straight talk, and independent judgment. These ideas and values were reinforced in numerous ways.

Ann was therefore a pivotal catalyst in assisting Barack Obama to grow up with new ideas grounded in forgiveness and love. According to the *New York Times*, "She always felt that marriage as an institution was not particularly essential or important," said Nina Nayar, who later became a close friend of Ms. Soetoro. "What mattered to her," Ms. Nayar said, "was to have loved deeply."[19]

Her influence challenged Obama to bring this principle of caring to the center of his life. His determination to follow a life of service and become a community organizer stemmed from the ideas that he learnt about nurturing, cherishing, and caring. These ideas are at the core of the Lela principle, the belief that the qualities of nurturing and caring should be shared collectively and promote life. Ron Eglash, in his book on the understanding of fractals, especially African fractals (*African Fractals: Modern Computing and Indigenous Design*), has elaborated on the iteration of the Lela principle from the family unit to the societal level. In all spheres of life, public and private, the qualities of nurturing and sharing are shared collectively and aim at promoting life.[20] Ann gave Obama a reference point for his new education. This reference was reinforced by his grandparents, especially his grandmother, Madelyn Payne Dunham, whom he affectionately called "Toots."

TOOTS AND THE DIGNITY OF WORK

If his mother was the anchor of the Lela principle in Barack Obama, the role models for his sense of purpose were his grandparents, especially his grandmother. Obama described her in one of his speeches as "a woman who helped raise me, a woman who sacrificed again and again for me, a woman who loves me as much as she loves anything in this world."[21] His sister, Maya Kassandra Soetoro-Ng, noted in an interview that "he has our mother's romantic tendencies but our grandmother's pragmatic tendencies."

What were these pragmatic tendencies? They included being realistic about the tasks ahead and being focused on these tasks. Obama himself called this trait "Midwest prudence." It was also respect for work, working people, and the quiet determination of women to contest patriarchy.

"Toots" is the anglicized version of *tutu*, the Hawaiian word for grandparent. Madelyn Payne was born in 1922 in Augusta, Kansas, and matured in the midst of Jim Crow and the Great Depression. She frequently told Obama stories about the real conditions of the working people throughout the Depression.

Madelyn married Stanley Dunham in 1940. When he went off to war, she had to struggle to support her only child, Ann. During the war, she toiled as one of the millions of women who had been mobilized for wartime production, on a bomber assembly line. Her work in the factory was to steel her in patience and understanding of the dignity of work, and she never shunned forms of employment that others frowned upon. Writing in his autobiography, Obama related the intolerance of his grandparents to the Jim Crow conditions of the South. When his parents challenged the school principal over segregation in the school grounds and the fact that their daughter was harassed for playing with a black girl, his grandfather was told by the principal, "You best talk to your daughter, Mr. Dunham, white girls don't play with coloreds in this town."[22]

The family could not tolerate this crude prejudice, and left the South for the West: California and Washington State, and eventually Hawaii. When the family arrived in Hawaii, Madelyn worked for a bank from 1970 onwards, and retired as a vice president in 1986. Even though she achieved this position, her chances for promotion had been circumscribed by the male-dominated workspace.

These details became relevant insofar as his grandparents were the caregivers to Obama after his mother dispatched him back to the United States in 1970 so that he could cope with the American system of education. It was his grandparents who supported and encouraged him while he fumbled in the idyllic world of the privileged high school – in his own words, "an incubator for island elites."

It was while living with his grandparents that Obama became a voracious reader. In his own words, he would lock himself in his room and read. As a "black" child in this "white" household, Obama immersed himself in books, going to the library to read books on East Africa and becoming absorbed in "the writings of James Baldwin, Ralph Ellison, Langston Hughes, and Malcolm X, only to find "the same anguish, the same self-doubt, a self-contempt that neither irony nor intellect seemed able to deflect."[23]

The anguish and self-doubt were not assisted by the reality of the world in which they lived. The following story is often repeated and was reflective of the world of Obama. His grandparents had an argument over Madelyn's request that her husband drive her to work, because she had been "hassled" at a bus stop by a beggar. Stanley was angry because, as Obama retold the story, '"She told me the fella was black.' He whispered the word. 'That's the real reason why she's bothered. And I just don't think that right.'" Obama added, "The words were like a fist in my stomach, and I wobbled to regain my composure."[24]

Later, during the presidential election campaign and the controversy over Jeremiah Wright, Obama would repeat the narrative of this episode and draw considerable criticism. But the episode exposed the putrid and all-pervasive reach of racism in the United States. Madelyn saw Obama as her grandson, but had been ensnared by her own reference points. The loneliness that Obama felt at that moment in his life was compensated for by his work and his admiration for the work ethic of his grandmother. Although very much alone in his thoughts, he was undergoing a process of transformation. The respect for the dignity of work that he learnt from his grandmother was one of its components.

Obama recalled the work ethic of his grandmother, and how everyday she awoke at 5 am to go to work even though in the workplace she had been passed over for promotion because of sexism. His mother would tell Toots "that the bank should not get away with blatant sexism." But Toots did not complain. She took pride in her work.

Toots believed in the importance of caring and hard work. In this, she shared with Gandhi and others the enduring belief that all working persons should live in dignity. It was the belief of Gandhi that sanitation workers were worthy of respect, and that a society's

approach to the most downtrodden workers revealed its commitment to true freedom and dignity. This approach to freedom was
also inspired by the struggles of working-class leaders inside the
United States. But Martin Luther King Jr. combined this commitment to freedom and dignity with the support for working people.
It was thus not by accident that the last campaign of Martin Luther
King Jr. was his engagement with the struggles for the poor and
sanitation workers in Memphis, Tennessee. These traditions would
inspire Obama towards community service, and led him to Chicago
for the next stage of his political training and education.

TRAINING AS A COMMUNITY ORGANIZER IN CHICAGO

From the time he left high school in Hawaii, Obama was aware of
the difference between education and training. When he told his
friend Frank that he had been accepted by Occidental College in
California, Frank retorted,

> You're not going to College to get educated; you're going there
> to get trained. They will train you to want what you don't
> need. They'll train you to manipulate words so that they don't
> mean anything any more. They'll train you to forget what it is
> that you already know. They'll train you so good, you'll start
> believing what they tell you about equal opportunity and the
> American way and all that shit. They'll give you a corner office
> and invite you to fancy dinners, and tell you you're a credit to
> your race.[25]

Frank was not advising Obama not to go to college, he was advising
him to stay "awake" so that he did not succumb to the ideology of
individualism, the survival of the fittest, and material self-interest.
At Occidental College, Barack Obama began to find his voice, and
underwent a process of self-discovery. In his first public speech
at an anti-apartheid rally to support the divestment campaign, he
related how he surprised himself in the way he held the attention
of the students. His colleague Regina congratulated him, because he
spoke from the "heart." But Obama was still full of self-doubt. He
was searching for a sense of community. This search influenced his
transfer to Columbia University in New York City, but the dog-eat-
dog atmosphere of Manhattan troubled him. After his graduation,
he worked for one year as a research assistant for the publishing

and consulting firm Business International Corporation in New York. This job, with all of its possibilities, did not endear him to corporate America.

It was while he was in college that Barack Obama understood that:

> What I needed was a community. I realized, a community that cut deeper than the common despair that black friends and I shared when reading the latest crime statistics, or the high fives I might exchange on the basketball court. A place where I could put down stakes and test my commitments.[26]

In pursuit of this test, Obama decided that he wanted to be a community organizer.[27] He applied to community groups all over the country, until he was hired by a faith-based community group working on the South Side of Chicago.

As a community organizer in the Altgeld Gardens public housing project in the mid-1980s, Obama, then 23, quickly emerged as a tireless and pragmatic advocate for the community – traits that characterize the kind of president he says he wants to be. This is how the media presented Barack Obama when he had announced his candidacy for the presidency of the United States. In the same story, Michelle Obama said,

> His work as a community organizer was really a defining moment in his life, not just his career. It helped him decide how he would impact the world – assisting people in defining their mutual interests and working together to improve their lives.[28]

In his autobiography, Obama himself pointed out the importance of working in the community. During the 1980s, as one component of the conservative thrust to break down the role of government, there was a major emphasis on community organizations. It is significant that when academics and the popular press theorize about community and community organizing, they erase the history of community building and solid communities among the First Nation peoples. Hence, when mainstream political scientists credit Alexis de Tocqueville as the first major theoretician to study community and community organizing in the United States, they usually overlook the fact that de Tocqueville never analyzed black or First Nation communities.[29] De Tocqueville used unrepresentative communities as the basis for his study of American society, and for the next

150 years, scholars drew on his analysis without challenging the undemocratic and genocidal background that provided the context for these studies.[30]

In the political training of Obama, the writings and insights of de Tocqueville are important insofar as Saul Alinsky, the guru of community organizing in the United States, had been influenced by the Frenchman. Writers since Alinsky have drawn attention to the unrepresentative model of the New England communities that de Tocqueville studied, and the elaborate institutional design that grounded the principle of "popular sovereignty." De Tocqueville did write against slavery,[31] but his praise for American communities where power was decentralized to facilitate popular control was written at a time when elsewhere in the United States, human beings were enslaved. The levels of participation through popular elections might have been higher in the United States than in Europe in 1831, but women and blacks did not have the same rights as white men to participate in community activities.

This qualification is central to moving towards a new sense of community as, in the twenty-first century, many communities in the United States are facing real challenges from the crisis of unemployment, state-induced spread of addictive substances,[32] and the dysfunctional educational system. The other major reason for the qualification is that the theoretical basis of de Tocqueville's innovations about the democratic benefits of associational life did not challenge the property relations that formed the basis of the political relations. Some of these qualifications are now clearer in a period when biotech companies want to repeal the 13th Amendment so that corporations can "own" humans again. Obama was still to learn these qualifications from his own experience of serving in Chicago for more than three years.

It was as if Obama himself was to serve as a reference point for future studies of political organizing and associational politics, insofar as Chicago had been the proving ground for most of the social work studies on community organizing. Saul Alinsky (1909–1972) is considered the founder of modern community organizing in the United States. He was born in Chicago in the period after brutal attacks on the working class associated with the suppression of trade union activity in the Chicago stockyards. It was in Chicago that workers had fought the major battles for the eight-hour-day, and the Haymarket memorial stands in the history of working peoples all over the world who celebrate May Day.[33]

At the start of the twentieth century, the spatial organization of working-class communities was explicitly arranged on ethnic lines in order to divide the workers and break the potential for militant trade union action. This division of workers was based on "Anglo-Saxonism," that is, the belief that white Anglo-Saxon Protestants (WASPs) evolved from a superior breed of humans and that all other ethnic groups (such as the Irish, Italians, Jews, Polish, Greeks, Armenians) were inferior and could only move up the hierarchy on the basis of their ability to attain the levels of intelligence, efficiency and prudence of WASPs.[34] Anglo-Saxonism in the United States was reinforced by institutional racism, so that blacks bore the brunt of the divisions and manipulation of communities.[35] Through creative measures, working peoples sought to thrive in their communities, but the entrenched repressive power of the state was deployed in the "survival of the fittest" ideology embodied by the demobilizing ideas of "manifest destiny."

Worker organization had been undertaken by trade unions, but by the time of the Depression and Prohibition, Chicago had become one of the central sites for gangsters and political fraudsters. No section of the "associational" life of Chicago could escape this gangsterism. So powerful were these gangsters and so prevalent were gangland killings that their names (such as Al Capone) became part of American folklore. Politics in the state of Illinois became inextricably interwoven with the world of gambling, racketeering, kickbacks, prostitution, police violence against workers, and shady contracts.

It was in this climate of super-exploitation and violence that Saul Alinsky had become a community organizer. After serving as a juvenile officer, he planned to do participant observation research on the Mafia in Chicago, and ingratiated himself with the Mafia boss Frank Nitti – heir to Al Capone's empire.[36] After his internship as a "honorary member of the mob," Alinsky worked closely with the Left in organizing the CIO (the Congress of Industrial Organizations). He became famous in the late Depression period when he consciously sought to move beyond trade union organizing to community organizing in the disparate ethnic groups that were divided and exploited in the Back-of-the-Yards neighborhood that had been characterized as a "jungle."

Alinsky believed that community organizing was the best way to empower the dispossessed, and worked to develop "organization of organizations," comprised of all sectors of the community – youth committees, small businesses, labor unions, and most influential of all, the Catholic Church.[37] This initiative was innovative for its time in the white community, and Alinsky initiated the Back-of-the-Yards Council, staging a series of successful pickets, strikes, and boycotts which won small concessions from the city and the entrepreneurs. His book, *Reveille for Radicals* (1946), was like a manifesto which called upon America's poor to "reclaim American democracy." The success of Alinsky's model of organizing, spelt out in books and magazines, spread throughout the United States, and he was invited by community groups all over the country to assist urban communities in their struggles for rights.

However, unlike the Left and the more radical sections of the US political spectrum, Alinsky's *Rules for Radicals* (1971) advocated that community organizers must work within the existing social system.

This position of radicals seeking room to maneuver within the system assured the more far-sighted elements of the Chicago establishment that the tactics and strategies of Alinsky, while appearing radical, were not a real threat to the social system. One of the major capitalists in Chicago, Marshall Field, started to finance Saul Alinsky, and thus began the period in American politics of the paid community organizer who was hired by an umbrella community organization.

Obama had studied Alinsky, and made a conscious decision to work within the system for social change. He agreed with many of the organizational principles of Alinsky, especially the need to:

- fight majority tyranny
- teach people the actual exercise of their formal rights
- give people courage to form individual judgments
- enable social action between individuals across social boundaries.

Obama was a disciple of Alinsky in other ways, as he was a paid organizer, funded by the church to go in and organize a community with which he had no real links. Obama had envisioned this job as part of his process of "redemption." He had moved to Chicago in the wake of the euphoria over the mayoral victory of Harold Washington. Before the election of Obama in 2008, Washington's period as mayor of Chicago (1983–87) was remembered as one of the high points of coalition building across communities. An African American had been able to organize a multiracial coalition to defeat the machinery that controlled the city hall. It must be stressed that Washington himself was not victorious because of charisma, but because of a long tradition of grassroots organizing that had been challenging the Daley machine. When Obama signed up as a community organizer in 1985, he had been optimistic that, with a progressive mayor, he could do grassroots organizing to change the conditions of deindustrialization and wretchedness.[38] He devoted the bulk of his autobiography to the lessons learnt during the three years that he worked on networking, coalition building, and listening as a community organizer.

The one major lesson that he learnt from all of his efforts was that the people had to take the lead in change, and that community organizing alone could not change the fundamental and embedded forms of exploitation and alienation. Those in the media and blogosphere who have written about Obama's years as a community organizer have concentrated on the glowing statements that the members of the community made about him,[39] but Obama himself was more modest about his accomplishments in Chicago. Gradually, he was exposed to the real imbalances of power and the lack of principle among politicians, especially black politicians, after the death of Harold Washington in November 1987. He watched the spectacle as the machine politicians bought off one section of the black leadership and manipulated others, in a context where "there was a loss of independence and initiative among community based organizations." In this situation, the Alinsky student who had recruited Obama noted that "The more Obama worked as an organizer, the more he became convinced that the most serious problems he confronted couldn't be solved on the local level. People were still poor, kids were out on the corner selling drugs, schools weren't working."[40]

Obama understood very clearly that talk about race could not make effective politics. After immersing himself in a church in order to find community, he took note of the strident nationalism dressed in religious clothing, and learnt over the next ten years how nationalism could thrive as "an emotion but flounder as a program for transformation."[41] This was the challenge – how could society transform the conditions that Obama encountered in the Chicago communities? It was very clear that the small victories that could be won, such as removing asbestos from buildings, had to be the stepping stones in a larger struggle, so that people could be taken from one level of consciousness and organization to the next.

These lessons of grassroots organizing were not only being learnt by those who wanted to transform conditions of environmental degradation and alienation. The conservative forces were also studying the impact of community-based organizations, and foundations began to develop a new sector of the economy called the non-governmental (NGO) sector. At home and abroad, this *conservative alternative* mushroomed and became one arm of the neo-liberal project to downsize government.[42]

Obama left Chicago in 1988, but he did not leave behind the community and his contacts there. However, there was another dynamic at work in policy circles. Ronald Reagan and Margaret Thatcher had given political force to an intellectual movement that supported a very conservative agenda for the United States. Foundations and institutions of higher learning aided and abetted what Nelson Blackstock called *The FBI's War on Political Freedom*.[43] Universities joined this assault on progressive ideas in order to ingratiate themselves with a conservative federal bureaucracy.

The idea of using grassroots organizations as a social cushion for large-scale discontent inspired a new brand of politics, intellectual engagement, and masculinist thinking. The deployment of homophobia as a social and political weapon reinforced old-fashioned sexism in society. In this environment, closeted activists became a rich prey for the conservatives.

Many activists of the 1980s believed in the possibility of reforming the system without tearing it apart. However, the idealism of activists such as Obama would be overtaken by a strident campaign that enveloped the United States after the election of Ronald Reagan. Conservative foundations and think-tanks blossomed, and vigorously promoted the idea that if effort was focused on making conditions good for corporate owners (investors), they would provide for all Americans.[44]

Schools of public administration in the Ivy League universities started programs on the non-profit sector, while books were written on how *Philanthro-Capitalism* could save the system.[45]

The project embedded in books such as *Philanthro-Capitalism* had been preceded by the influential study by Robert D. Putnam, *Bowling Alone: The Collapse and Revival of American Community*. Putnam developed the concept of social capital, and decried the falling participation of citizens in community organizations. What the social scientists of the non-profit sector could not explain was why there was "declining membership in specific formal organizations" at the time when billions of dollars were being spent on the non-profit[46] sector of the economy. With immense funding from the same foundations and the prestige of Harvard University, Putnam did not connect the declining membership in community organizations to the conservative overdrive and the professionalization of community organizing, which was leading to the depoliticaization of traditional community-based organizations.

More importantly, Putnam made references to the legacies of the civil rights movement and the deep traditions of community within African American spaces without a proper analysis of the extensive program of the government to "infiltrate, disrupt and otherwise neutralize" the social movement that provided the base for community organizations.[47] This disruption was followed by the devastation wreaked by the crack cocaine epidemic, and the forms of city planning that destroyed poor communities in creating highways for the suburbanization of the United States.

Putnam did not connect "civic engagement and social capital" with the original community of humans in the United States, the Native American community. This community, along with the tight-knit African American communities, held the line against the crack epidemic and the wholesale liquidation of progressive ideas in society. Afro-centrism and concepts of reparative justice filled the political void to combat ideas of individual self-interest. Under Ronald Reagan, William Jefferson Clinton, and George W. Bush, there were drastic cuts in spending in all areas of life – housing, schools, public hospitals, public transportation, infrastructure, job programs, welfare, and so on – while the rich accumulated vast sums and established numerous community foundations to ensure that the Allard Lowenstein model of political organization prevailed. (The Allard Lowenstein model of organizing refers to organizers who appear radical but are working closely with security agencies.)

The remobilization and re-engagement of youth was awaiting another vision, that of communities that transcend racial divisions and sexual orientation. Malidoma Some presented another concept of community in his book *The Healing Wisdom of Africa*, and did not have to seek refuge in the discourse on "social capital" or "civic capital." His definition was simple and straightforward:

> Community is important because there is an understanding that human beings are collectively oriented. The general health and well being of the individual are connected to a community, and are not something that can be maintained alone or in a vacuum. Healing, ritual and community – these three elements are vitally linked.[48]

Obama had joined a church in Chicago in 1987, but he felt restless and wanted to be more connected to his family in order to find peace in the community that he adopted. After his acceptance by Harvard University in 1988, he set out to Kenya to make peace with his inheritance.

SEARCHING FOR LIFE PURPOSE AND HEALING IN KENYA

From the time Obama was a child, he had spent his time in the library reading books on Kenya. As he matured, he began grasping the contradictions of the Kenyan form of colonial apartheid, and was disabused of romantic conceptions of Africa. While he was at Columbia University, his father died, and he remained troubled by his lack of connection to his Kenyan family. One sister visited him while he was a community organizer in Chicago, and her stories of the politics of Kenya and the tribulations of his father intrigued him even more. Slowly, he was learning about the economic, racial, ethnic, and regional divisions in Kenya, and how these had a direct impact on his family. Obama's memory of his father was influenced by the optimism of his mother and by his father's short visit to his high school in Hawaii. He understood that his father believed in transcending divisions between humans.

When Obama arrived in Kenya in 1988, society was reeling from a new round of the politicization of ethnicity by post-colonial elites.

As Obama Jr. visited relatives, he learnt of the role of his father in the struggles for intellectual decolonization after he returned to Kenya from Harvard in 1963. Kenya had become an independent republic after a violent struggle for self-determination. Obama Sr. had been caught up in this anti-colonial battle, and was arrested as a youth because he was attending the anti-colonial rallies of the Kenya African National Union. When he received a scholarship as part of the Kenyan airlift of East African students to the United States, his sojourn in the United States saved him from the polarization and divisions that were pursued by the British.[49] Anthropologists and other social scientists worked over time to reproduce "the ideology of tribalism" in Kenya, and Cambridge University in the United Kingdom was particularly active in this enterprise. Obama Jr. would not have known in 1971 that when his father was praising the possibility of a non-racial democracy in Hawaii, he was also reflecting his own dreams for Kenya.

As an educated African, Obama Sr. had been employed by the government and served as an economic adviser. But in 1965, he responded to the economic planning of the government that had been presented in a government document entitled "Sessional Paper No. 10." In 1965, at the height of the Cold War, Kenya was caught in the middle of continuing anti-colonial struggles. President Jomo Kenyatta sided with the United States in the unfolding wars for self-determination in the Congo. Tanzania had carved out a path of non-alignment and the Zanzibar revolution of 1964 had radicalized all of East Africa. Obama Sr. maintained a sober independence of thought in the midst of this turbulence, and was offended by the manipulation of regionalism, racialism, and ethnicity by the Kenyatta regime. In his attempt to contribute to the debate, he wrote an article in the then influential *East African Journal* expressing his opinions on "Sessional Paper No. 10." Obama Sr. was specific and to the point. He wrote that the document was "neither African nor socialism," and opposed the ideas of private property and private enterprise that preserved the status quo in Kenya. He supported the consolidation of land for Africans within the context of the growth of cooperatives.[50]

Obama Sr. elaborated his critique of the government plans by arguing that the over-emphasis on economic growth was unacceptable in so far as growth in the economy could not be separated from educational transformation, the cultural upliftment of the people, and changes in the social conditions. He advocated a model of economic change that was based on building up the economic chances of the people from below instead of the trickle-down economics that was inherent in the plan to attract foreign investment.

Because he wrote about a real egalitarianism and the possibility of transforming the apartheid conditions of Kenya, Obama Sr. lost his job with the government. He was cast out of the class of educated and upwardly mobile Africans who benefited from the Africanization of exploitation after "Sessional Paper No. 10."[51]

However, the disquiet among the peoples of Kenya about the polarization in society led to fissures in the government, and brought about a break between Vice President Oginga Odinga and President Kenyatta. Progressive trade unionists were killed, and parliamentarians who did not go along with the crude manner of accumulating wealth were publicly denounced and castigated by Kenyatta. Car accidents became a regular form of death for those who opposed the government. Masculinity and patriarchal attitudes reinforced the politicization of ethnicity, and Obama Sr. was caught in the midst of this retrogression.

He suffered because he was a Luo, not because he was an insider in the Kenya Peoples Union. It was in this climate of extrajudicial killings, persecution, and harassment that Obama Sr.'s life became interwoven with alcohol and unemployment. A car accident in 1971 was a close call, and it was in the aftermath of this accident that

Ann invited him to Hawaii to convalesce. During this convalescence in 1971, the ten-year-old Obama spent time with his father. His father told him, "You are an Obama. You should be the best."

Obama Sr. escaped death in 1971 only to join the ancestors in November 1982 during a period of extreme turbulence. After the intensification of the Cold War in 1980, the internal politics of Kenya could not escape the reality that the country had become an outpost for British and US military activities in the Indian Ocean. Opposition to the activities of the government affected all sections of the society, leading to the harassment and incarceration of intellectuals. A failed military coup against the government of Daniel Arap Moi precipitated another round of repression, and scores of political leaders escaped into exile. This was the year that Barack Obama Sr. died in a car accident at the age of 46.

REDEMPTION

Obama learnt the intricate details of Kenyan and East Africa politics while he was on his healing journey. Using the skills of a writer and the narrative form of conversation, he used encounters on his safari to draw out the contradictions of British policies in East Africa. He was brought face-to-face with village life and the conditions of existence for millions of people who survived without clean running water and electricity. Through the voice of his grandmother, he reconstructed the history of the Luo people as he heard it, and the full history of his grandfather. Traveling between the villages and homesteads of relatives, Obama was exposed to the complexities of the gendered roles in the rural areas, and the crisis of masculinity as it was compounded by colonial relations.

It was in a village that he began to sort out the complexities of masculinity and the insecurities that had been generated in the village community. Through the stories of his grandmother, he learnt of the nuances of the life of his grandfather, Hussein I. Onyango, who had worked as a cook and was called "houseboy," and the struggles of his father. After listening for days to these stories he finally asked to read the letters of his grandparents and his father. From a close reading of his grandfather's passbook and his father's letters soliciting a scholarship in the United States, he reflected on the depth of the cultural and physical oppression that has deformed all those who came in contact with colonial oppression. I want to quote at length to bring the reader the words of Barack Obama after he read the old crumpled letters of his father and grandfather.

This was it, I thought to myself. My inheritance. I rearranged the letters in a neat stack and set them under the registry book. Then I went into the backyard. Standing before the two graves, I felt everything around me – the cornfields, the mango tree, the sky – closing in, and I was left with only a series of mental images. Granny's stories come to life.

After reflecting on the "force of will" of his grandfather and his father, he retraced their journey as he understood the desperation of their time and the necessity to reinvent themselves. He continued,

> I dropped to the ground and swept my hand across the smooth yellow tile. O Father, I cried. There was no shame in your confusion. Just as there had been no shame in your father's before you. No shame in the silence fear had produced. It was the silence that betrayed us. If it weren't for that silence your grandfather might have told your father that he could never escape himself or re-create himself alone. Your father might have taught those same lessons to you. And you, the son, might have taught your father that this new world that was beckoning all of you involved more than just railroads and indoor toilets and irrigation ditches and gramophones, lifeless instruments that could be absorbed into the old ways. You might have told him that these instruments carried with them a dangerous power, that they demanded a different way of seeing the world. That this power would be absorbed only alongside a faith born out of hardship, a faith that wasn't new, that wasn't black or white or Christian or Muslim but that pulsed in the heart of the first African village and the first Kansas homestead – a faith in people.

It was here that Barack Obama reinforced his identity as a human being while reconciling himself to the political realities of the societies that defined him as black, as a Luo, or as an African.

> For a long time I sat between the two graves and wept. When my tears were finally spent, I felt a calmness wash over me. I felt the circle finally close. I realized that who I was, what I cared about, was no longer just a matter of intellect or obligation, no longer a construct of words. I saw that my life in America – the black life, the white life, the sense of abandonment I'd felt as a boy, the frustration and hope I'd witnessed in Chicago – all of this was connected with this small plot of earth an ocean away, connected by more than the accident of a name or the color of my skin.[52]

We can imagine that in his vision of redemption, Obama was taking the words of emancipation from mental slavery one step further. He was reinforcing the connectedness of all human beings. In the estimation of this writer, this was when Obama made the decision that he was going to soar and be a beacon of light for the new relations between humans, transcending race, ethnicity, and religion. But before Obama made the plunge into the world of electoral politics, there was one more lesson for his training. This was the importance of networks of networks among the grassroots, and sharing his life with other human beings.

MICHELLE ROBINSON: THE PERSONAL IS POLITICAL

Our exploration of the political education of Obama has so far dwelt on his parents, grandparents, and his foray as a community organizer in Chicago. With his new confidence as a human being who was labeled black in the United States, Obama set about distinguishing himself. At Harvard, he went into the Ivy League and its rituals with clear ideas of what he wanted to accomplish. From the first year when he joined the *Harvard Law Review*, Obama made it known that he was involved in establishing a new style of intellectual and political leadership in the United States. He ran in the election to become the president of the *Harvard Law Review,* and made history by winning it and becoming the first "designated" African American to hold that post. According to the *New York Times*, "The eight law-review issues Obama presided over included articles on the Rev. Dr. Martin Luther King Jr., and gender and racial discrimination in retail-car negotiations."[53]

Obama found a position as an intern in a Law Firm, Sidley & Austin in the summer of 1989. It was during this internship that he met Michelle Robinson, who was then a first-year associate at the Chicago law firm (now Sidley Austin Brown & Wood). It was through Michelle that Obama's understanding of the African American experience moved from one understood through books and the years as a community organizer to that of a person functioning within a family inside the black community.

Michelle Robinson had been born on the South Side of Chicago. Her parents were working people whose forebears had left South Carolina at the height of the Ku Klux Klan violence and the Great Depression. Michelle grew up as a conscientious young African American, traveling to Georgetown, South Carolina, connecting with the history and memory of the brutal repression after

Reconstruction. After high school, Michelle was accepted at Princeton and later went to Harvard, graduating in 1988. Because of her social background, she was excluded from the professional black women who constituted the Chicago black elite. This elite was part of a national club of blacks whose political orientation was similar to the upper classes of the United States, and it was through the mouthpieces of this elite that anti-immigrant sentiments were fanned inside the black community. In order to escape identification with the poor, their clubs and debutante balls provided the cultural orientation to disguise their political alliance with the new conservatism. They vacationed at Martha's Vineyard in Massachusetts and flipped between the higher echelons of the two political parties. Skin color and status were very important to this elite in so far as they accepted the biological definition of "race," and there was a "brown paper bag test" to decide if someone was eligible to be part of this black elite.[54] This elite was offended in 1988 when Jesse Jackson referred to his forebears who were domestic servants.

Obama escaped the frivolities and insecurities of this elite in so far as he was brought up in a "white" family, but he expressed his disquiet at the shallowness of the upper classes and the "smallness of their politics." Michele was also an outsider to this class by virtue of the occupations of her father and mother, who were ordinary working-class people. Future integration into the black professional classes awaited her. As two outsiders, both graduated from Ivy League schools, these two people found that they had a lot in common. They were disciplined, focused, and aspired to change society.

Obama courted Michelle, and they were married in Chicago in 1992 after he graduated from law school. Through Michelle, her parents, her brother, and the wider extended family, Obama began to understand the layered social and racial nature of the black community of Chicago. As a graduate of Harvard and a member of the black professional class, Michelle grew impatient with corporate law and sought employment with the City of Chicago, "to pursue a public life." It was during her interview that she met Valerie Jarrett, one of the top insiders in Chicago black politics. Jarrett had been a holdover from the Harold Washington administration into the Daley administration. Her links with the black ruling circles stretched from Chicago across the country, and included many important power brokers.

Michelle soon introduced Obama to Valerie Jarrett, and the three formed a political alliance that gave Obama links to the black middle classes without formally joining any of their fronts and clubs. By the time Obama decided to enter electoral politics, he had built links with a coterie of "successful black business persons such as Martin Nesbitt who would form the kernel of his kitchen cabinet."[55] Would these "pragmatic" alliances degenerate into "equivocation" and "moral cowardice" on the part of Obama? This was the outstanding challenge of the liberalism that Obama had internalized in his understanding of democracy in the United States. It is possible to see Barack Obama wrestling with the contradictions of the political establishment of the United States when he became a US Senator. But this is to anticipate.

From this base, Obama moved his key alliances from the study circles examining the ideas of Ella Baker to the Lakefront elements of the North Shore of Lake Michigan. In his book, *The Audacity of Hope,* Obama reflected on the pragmatism of navigating these different social waters in Illinois politics. He queried whether pragmatism would lead to moral cowardice. Obama and Michelle navigated the treacherous waters of Illinois social and political life without being infected by the greed that had made Chicago notorious. There was a prominent example of this greed and corruption after Barack Obama won the presidency, when the governor of Illinois, Rod Blagojevich, attempted to sell his Senate seat to the highest bidder.[56]

Obama began to learn how to share his life with a confident, brilliant, and disciplined black woman. His political education was now being reinforced by the personal. His own sensibility as one seeking to transcend the pits of racial division was reinforced by a woman whose life reflected the interconnection of the struggles between race, gender, and class in the United States. Both Obama and Michelle were for a short while members of a loose study group that reflected on the ideas of Ella Baker. Barbara Ransby had been writing and speaking on the importance of Ella Baker for the black freedom movement and for the feminist movement in the United States. The principles of grassroots organization put forward by Ella Baker had influenced the activists of the SNCC and professional community workers.

Ella Baker represented a figure in the movement for social justice who spanned the generations of those fighting against Jim Crow, against exploitation during the Depression, and against the conservatism of Reagan. She had honed her skills in working with the youth during the civil rights era, and advised them that they must develop autonomous networks independent of the professional civil rights leaders. The key principles she imparted were:

- Challenge the centralization of authority.
- Disseminate political knowledge.
- Develop the technical skills and local organizational capacity of the poor, students, and working people.
- Devolve expertise.
- Generalize intellectual activity.
- Widen genuine democratic participation.

Obama and Michelle studied and internalized these principles as they made decisions about where they would fit in the political future of the United States.

CONCLUSION

Obama studied political science in 1981 at Columbia University, and had been inundated with the ideas of liberalism and enlightened self-interest that were associated with the Chicago School of Milton Friedman. He grasped the limitations of the theories and ideas about rational actors in society, and sought to gain a better understanding of the driving forces behind social change. In his quest for a new education and new ideas, he benefited from his early exposure to the multi-ethnic and multiracial context of Hawaii, his multi-ethnic experience of Indonesia, and his own inheritance in relation to the background of his father. These exposures sharpened the realization that the concepts of individualism and private property must be understood in the cultural context of the form of democracy that had evolved in the United States.

Ron Takaki, another citizen who had been raised in Hawaii, had taken the limitations of liberal democracy and implored the youth of America to build on this foundation in order to extend the true meaning of democracy. Takaki called the equality of the US Constitution a "proposition," and argued that the political struggle in the United States was to make this equality a reality. Using Abraham Lincoln's Gettysburg Address to highlight how key struggles can afford the opportunity to deepen democracy, Takaki argued that the principle of equality outlined by Lincoln remained the "unfinished work of Americans."[57] Takaki did not discuss whether this equality was possible within the context of capitalism and the forms of economic organization that exploited humans.

In many ways, Obama shared the same view that the principle of democracy was work in progress. In *The Audacity of Hope*, he

wrote that the constitution "is not a static but rather a living document, and must be read in the context of an ever-changing world."
He remarked how his grandmother read to him "the opening lines
of the Declaration of Independence and told me about the men and
women who marched for equality because they believed those words
put to paper two centuries ago should mean something." Barack
Obama repeated these words in a letter to his daughters days before
his inauguration.

Obama shared the dream of Abraham Lincoln for a more perfect
union, and used this formulation in his speech during the election
campaign in his call for American society to transcend the defor-
mities of racism and racial determinism. He shared the dream of
his mother for a more inclusive society, and the dream of Martin
Luther King Jr. for all of God's children to see themselves as humans.
Obama and Michelle's dream of inclusiveness was a departure from
the old politics of exclusion and division. The test was to build a
movement to take these principles to government.

In this chapter on the political training of Obama, we used periods of his life to illuminate aspects of the new education that he
received. The experiences in Chicago gave him practical experience
on the positive and negative lessons of community work. By the time
he left this internship, the conservative onslaught had despoiled the
innocence of thousands of well-meaning youths who wanted to do
community service. Obama wanted to be in a position to make a
break with the divisions and insecurities that had been extended by
the neo-conservatives.

Obama understood that the politics of transformation had to be
nested in a wider sense of humanity than the past Anglo-Saxonism
of the founding fathers. It was this transformation that took Obama
above the need to parrot homage to "capital" in all of his formulations. As a human being in the United States, Obama was preoccupied with how to make a break with the iterations of destruction
and institutional racism. From his formal and informal education,
we will suggest that Obama was troubled by this reality.

We quote from an ongoing discussion on racism in the United
States:

How people have been accepted and treated within the context
of a given society has a direct impact on how they perform in
that society. The racial worldview was invented to assign some
groups to perpetual low status, while others were permitted
access to privilege, power and wealth. The tragedy in the US has

been that the policies and practices stemming from this world view succeeded all too well in constructing unequal populations among Europeans, Native Americans and peoples of African descent. Given what we know of the capacity of normal humans to achieve and function within any culture, we conclude that present day inequalities between so called racial groups are not consequences of their biological inheritance but products of historical and contemporary social, economic, educational and political circumstances.[58]

We now turn to how the Obama campaign intersected with the long struggle to confront racism and sexism in US politics.

3

CONFRONTING RACISM AND SEXISM IN US POLITICS

Racism is not the whole but the most visible, the most day-to-day the crudest element of a given structure. ... We must look for the consequences of this racism on the cultural level. Racism, as we have seen, is only one element of a vaster whole: that of the systematized oppression of a people.

Frantz Fanon

At the core of the heart of the race problem is the sex problem.

James Weldon Johnson

From the dawn of the republic, there has been a divergence between the creed of democracy, democratic participation, and elections on one side, and the reality of inequality, especially slavery and sexism, on the other. Racism and sexism were two forms of exploitation and discrimination that perpetuated the division and weakness of the majority of the population. For the purposes of this chapter, racism emanates from a set of ideas, practices, attitudes, actions, and institutional structures that systematically subordinate a person or group because of their color. Sexism refers similarly to attitudes, actions, or institutional structures that systematically subordinate a person or group because of their sex. Sexism is usually buttressed by the belief in heterosexism: that is, the belief that normal sexual relations should be between humans of different sexes. Genetic engineering, nanotechnology, and robotics raise new challenges for the twenty-first century as the repression and conservatism of the neo-liberal era placed US society in a league of its own on questions of racism and sexism.

When Barack Obama took the podium to speak in Philadelphia on March 18, 2008 on the question of race and racism, he sought to project the promise of repairing the flawed democratic traditions of the United States. His speech entitled, "A more perfect union," strengthened a line of thought that sought desperately to break the crippling ideas of white supremacy, black inferiority, and machismo in American society. Decades of political struggles to enrich the content of democratic participation had been met by violence, countervailing forces of greater inequality, and crude eugenics dressed in liberal clothes.

Obama's task of setting forth on a better future was not a minor challenge. Abraham Lincoln had tried to confront it by telling the nation in 1863 that African Americans had to be included in the democratic vision of the United States.

Lincoln used the formulation of the need for a "more perfect union" in the midst of the war against enslavement, veritably the second revolutionary war for democracy. At the site of one of the bloodiest battles of the war against slavery in 1863 at Gettysburg, Lincoln invoked the promise of freedom and equality of the Constitution of the United States to remind citizens of the unfinished work of creating a government for the people, by the people.[1]

For this democratic creed to be credible, African Americans and women had to be recognized as persons. Two hundred years after the birth of Lincoln, the history of the United States did not reconcile itself to the democratic demands of large sections of the population. Lincoln, who himself harbored racist ideas, had been educated and pushed forward by the militant abolitionists, notably John Brown, Frederick Douglass, and Harriet Tubman. These freedom fighters had struggled to give meaning to democracy.

But attempts to repair the rigid inequalities of the society were short lived. The violence and lynching of the period of Jim Crow rolled back the limited legal advances for citizenship that had been achieved between 1865 and 1877. Ideas of equality could not then prevail in a society based on property rights, military expansion, and imperial annexation. Altering the stark division of the world between persons and property required a major intellectual leap that American society was not yet prepared for. After the Civil War and Reconstruction, the old religious and biological argument about black inferiority was renewed and adapted by changing its appearance. In the words of Frantz Fanon, "It has had to undergo the fate of the cultural whole that informed it."[2]

The ideological and political victory of the Southern planter elite nourished and supported the masculinist theories that were popularized in the society. Leaders of the Southern "plantocracy" initiated the campaigns of sexualized racism, lynching, whipping, and intimidation. Personalities like Benjamin Tillman epitomized this brand of politics, and inspired forms of persecution that would be later cultivated with greater success by Adolf Hitler in Germany.[3] Academics and journalists gave legitimacy to the violent actions of the Ku Klux Klan by reproducing and popularizing the ideas of eugenics, that intelligence and other personality traits are genetically determined and therefore hereditary.[4] Today, in the face of the new "liberal eugenics," the role of the US financial and academic community in refining theories about the master race clarifies the implications of the current investment in whiteness in the genetic engineering industry.

Sexual exploitation took a new form after the development of the cinema, where racial and sexual stereotypes were reproduced to fulfill the emotional needs of a society that had earlier enjoyed the Saturday night outings of the lynch mob. Hollywood became the vector for the celebration of genocide against the First Nation peoples and for the reproduction of racial stereotypes.[5]

Violence on the streets, disenfranchisement, segregation, division of ethnic neighborhoods, and rape were enshrined as components of the politics of exclusion and oppression. Up to this day, the institutions of higher learning of the United States continue to venerate leaders such as Benjamin Tillman, Theodore Roosevelt, and Thomas Jefferson. After Ben Tillman and numerous Klan heroes, Strom Thurmond and his heirs such as Joe Wilson ensured that the ideas and practices of "scientific racism" found a special place of honor in society up to the first decade of the twenty-first century. Would this deformity be compounded by present-day genetic engineers who want to breed a new group of superhumans?

The question of who could decide who or what should be human took democracy to an entirely new level, beyond the simple question of voting and participating in elections. Yet the challenge of who could make decisions about the future of the scientific community was tied up with the democratization of information, the democratization of knowledge, and full participation of all citizens. Racism in the American educational system in the twenty-first century ensures that society is approaching levels of segregation more sophisticated but no less nefarious than in the period of Jim Crow.[6]

A process of re-segregation at the moment of the election of Barack Obama in 2008 is perpetuating educational apartheid and holding back the full potential of American society.[7] Segregated schools, communities wracked by environmental racism, high unemployment, a medical apartheid complex, along with the prison industrial complex reinforce a new social conservatism that does not disguise its appeal to white chauvinism and reaction.[8]

From the history of the struggles for civil rights and the rights of women, the general level of political mobilization of American society had reached the point where Obama's message in Philadelphia struck a responsive chord. Obama addressed his own opposition to the extreme racism of the Ku Klux Klan and the opposition to interracial relationships that had spurred on the Klan. During the election campaign, the newly developed Birther movement questioned Obama's place of birth, but the real subtext was the reality that his father was black and his mother white. The Birther movement was a continuation of the wedge issues of the conservatives: abortion, homophobia, and same-sex marriage.[9] After eight years of the politics of social conservatism and division, a leader had emerged in the society that preached connectedness between humans. Obama established himself as a person, a human being – not a "black" candidate. Moreover, he personified the leadership values that he preached, and reflected society's need to move beyond racial categorization.

By the start of the twenty-first century the Human Genome Project settled the question of racial differences between humans.

DNA studies do not indicate that separate classifiable subspecies (races) exist within modern humans. While different genes for physical traits such as skin and hair color can be identified between individuals, no consistent patterns of genes across the human genome exist to distinguish one race from another.[10]

It is now acknowledged that racism is quite independent of race. Many social scientists would agree that racism evolved out of the convergence of white supremacy and "white" capitalism – out of the oppression and exploitation of peoples of African descent and other people of color.[11]

If race is not biological but a social construction, then would it not require a massive social movement to advance the struggle against racism? This is the new political terrain, as the cumulative effects of the historic campaign against racism and sexism dictated that far more than legal questions were at stake. There was an intractable contradiction between the forms of property and capital accumulation and the well- being of the majority of the citizens. Patriotism, militarism, masculinity, and patriarchy reproduced structural, physical, racist, and gendered violence. The struggle against racism could not be completed in an election cycle, but had to be built on the previous efforts to roll back racism and sexism.

The quest for democracy in the United States has passed through five phases of struggles which became markers for the enrichment of political culture. They were:

1. The revolutionary war of 1776–1783 and the far-reaching claims for representative democracy against the "three-fifths of a person" label for African Americans.
2. The Civil War and the struggles for citizenship by African Americans climaxing between 1859 to 1877.
3. The struggles of women and workers in the era of eugenics.
4. The civil rights struggles of the mid-twentieth century.
5. The twenty-first century struggles for the full democratization of society.

Space will not allow for a detailed exposition of these five phases. Our analysis in this chapter will focus more on the first, second, and third periods. The details of the civil rights revolution are too well known to bear repetition here, and the fifth phase will be addressed in the last chapters of this book. Our entire project of seeking a transformation of the politics for the twenty-first century builds on the view that has often been expressed of the civil rights revolution, that it was a "moment when ordinary people did extraordinary things." Obama himself has said repeatedly that he "stood on the shoulders of the giants" of the anti-racist struggle.[12]

What has emerged from the historical record is the fact that racism and sexism held back the creativity and solidarity of the population. Recent scholarship on the vigorous promotion of whiteness pointed out that sections of the labor movement embraced these ideas, "adopted them and at times murderously acted on them."[13] If racism was pervasive, sexism was even more nefarious in so far as the ideas of male supremacy were embraced and promoted by sections of the oppressed. Lynching became the clear sign of sexualized racism in the political culture, as women such as Ida B. Wells and Anna Julia Cooper created the traditions of independent thought and action. Ella Baker carried forward this tradition imparted to the civil rights workers, and inspired the networks that eventually elected Obama.

Sexual oppression was reinforced by a virulent heterosexism in the fifth period, to the point where in 2007 Chris Hedges wrote *American Fascists: The Christian Right and the War on America.*

In 2008, Sheldon Wolin made the argument in *Democracy Incorporated: Managed Democracy and Inverted Totalitarianism* that if the United States does not radically alter course, it will become a totalitarian state. Because of the nature of US society, Wolin saw this as a rush towards what he called "inverted totalitarianism." This designation of fascism had been linked to the neo-conservative forces to the point where the very notion of democracy in the United States was being discredited by large sections of the international community. This author has desisted from labeling the conservativism in the United States "fascism" in so far as the autonomous politics from the reconstruction and civil rights period had lodged a reservoir of democratic political culture outside of the mainstream political parties. Wolin had understood the importance of the democratic political culture outside political parties, and had placed the question of the repression of African Americans at the center of the rush towards totalitarianism. Wolin argued that:

> The significance of the African American prison population is political. What is notable about the African American population generally is that it is highly sophisticated politically and by far the one group that throughout the twentieth century kept alive a spirit of resistance and rebelliousness. In that context, criminal justice is as much a strategy of political neutralization as it is a channel of instinctive racism.[14]

From the birth of the republic, society had to confront racism. The Obama campaign was one other step to rise above the instinctive racism of society. Our effort will lay out the broad outlines of the emancipatory ideas that evolved out of these periods, and how they strengthened the appeal of the Obama campaign for the presidency. The conclusion of this chapter reflects on the conjuncture of the economic depression and the challenge of strengthening democratic relations.

PHASE I: THE ELECTORAL COLLEGE AND "THREE-FIFTHS OF A HUMAN"

Two weeks after the election of Barack Obama in November 2008, an editorial in the *New York Times* called for the abolition of the Electoral College. The Electoral College is the system where the election of the president of the United States is conducted in each of the 50 states as a separate contest. In the editorial the newspaper noted:

> The Electoral College is more than just an antiquated institution: it actively disenfranchises voters and occasionally (think 2000) makes the candidate with fewer popular votes president. American democracy would be far stronger without it.
> There is no reason to feel sentimental about the Electoral College. One of the main reasons the founders created it was slavery. The southern states liked the fact that their slaves, who would be excluded from a direct vote, would be counted — as three-fifths of a white person — when Electoral College votes were apportioned.[15]

There it was in 2008: the principal newspaper of the United States reminding society that the system of electing the president had been shaped by enslavement of Africans. There is a national popular vote movement calling for the abolition of this system without thorough discussion of the undemocratic foundations of the Electoral College. Three times since the Civil War in 1865, the Electoral College has awarded the presidency to the loser of the popular vote.

The most recent example of the 2000 election brought international attention to this undemocratic legacy of slavery. This was the case where Al Gore won the popular vote by more than half a million votes but still lost the election to George W. Bush.[16] Gore lost the election because there was widespread disenfranchisement of hundreds of thousands of citizens, especially blacks, on the grounds that they were felons. The evidence of criminal manipulation of elections was linked to a strategy by Karl Rove to maintain a permanent Republican majority and a permanent Republican in the White House.[17]

From the beginning of the United States as a republic up to 2000, manipulation, disenfranchisement, and criminal intimidation with clear racial considerations prevented the development of democratic expression. Polling data from both presidential elections of 2000 and 2004 had overwhelming evidence that, in particular states, officials made it harder for black and brown citizens to vote. In 2000 and 2004, the states of Florida and Ohio carried forward a long tradition of disenfranchising black voters. Jeb Bush, then governor of Florida, went back to the practices of Jim Crow and slavery to disenfranchise blacks. The Office of the Governor was implicated in the notorious fraud associated with the 2000 election. When the

Supreme Court intervened to legitimize the theft of the elections, citizens were reminded that it was the same court that had (100 years earlier) legalized segregation and Jim Crow in the *Plessy v. Ferguson* decision.

Mainstream political scientists wrote articles about "institutional legitimacy" when it was acknowledged throughout the United States that this was a stolen election.[18] It fell to those involved in the fight for democracy to expose the fact that it was the same Supreme Court that had been supporting the neo-conservatives in undermining the Voting Rights Act.[19] The more there were investigations into the "flaws" of the system of voting, and the calculated and determined efforts at intimidation and suppression of black voters, the more it became clear that these were not technical questions that could be fixed by better laws, but social issues that had to be linked to a thorough reconceptualization of the concepts of who is human, who has the right to vote,[20] and who should be able to participate in the democratic process.

The republic had been founded on the Aristotelian principle that there were two categories of humans: citizens and slaves.

After the Haitian Revolution, the idea of an independent black state frightened the founding fathers of the United States. Following the first three elections, leaders wanted to develop a system that guaranteed power in the hands of slave-owners. Thus, the founders of the republic adopted a constitutional amendment (the 12th) that pointedly preserved the centrality of slave labor for the political economy. In order to maintain this system of bonded labor, the owners of the slaves claimed, by right, the political power that would increase their wealth and economic power.[21] In order to strengthen the voting power of the slave-owning states, the Constitution designated African Americans as three-fifths of a person.[22] The same political class that disenfranchised blacks also disenfranchised women.

Objectively, although both women and blacks had an interest in fighting for democratic change in the United States, in the first 70 years of the republic, the ideas of white supremacy were deployed. White woman were denied the right to vote, but poor whites (men and women) were mobilized by the ideas of Manifest Destiny to support expansion and enslavement. Racism, as an ideology, rendered all non-Europeans throughout the world as sub-humans. According to this white supremacist view, the closer you are to white skin and straight hair, the "closer" you are to being completely human.

The defense of inequality and property rights thus found a coherent space in the intellectual base of the new society. The ideas of John Locke on private property, individualism, the state of nature, and rationality shaped the thinking of the US intelligentsia, and inspired the view that there was a "science of human nature." In 1993, the *Harvard Law Review* published a detailed article on "Whiteness as Property."[23] In this article, Cheryl Harris detailed the liberal basis of property rights, and linked white supremacy to the concept of property. Harris concluded that whiteness was tied to two fundamental concepts, that of the social identity of supremacy and that of subordinating others. What Harris was also arguing was that bourgeois democracy had naturalized whiteness in the United States. This critique of the property basis for liberal bourgeois democracy had been made for decades by Africans who opposed the idea that they were considered property.

David Roediger has argued that denial of this problem among whites has crippled the intellectual culture of the United States, with important consequences for liberal and conservative ideas.[24] This weakness in the intellectual culture has been compounded by the Hobbesian concepts of enlightened self-interest and the war of all against all.[25] The philosophies of Hobbes and Locke continue to provide the moral and political legitimacy for the liberal democratic state, when humanity is now in a new period and needs the ideas of Albert Einstein, Mahatma Gandhi, Martin Luther King Jr., and Harriet Tubman.

Once the escalator myth was accepted – that there was a hierarchy of beings with higher and lower forms of humans – the enslavement of Africans was justified on religious and pseudo-scientific grounds.[26] Sexual racism developed as one aspect of the dehumanization of Africans.

This sexual and racial ideology justified untold brutality in the United States. The enslavement of blacks was accompanied by the mental enslavement of whites. Whites could only be freed from mental slavery if the blacks freed themselves from actual enslavement. Exploitation, enslavement, sexual repression, racism, and genocide disfigured the society. Political scientists have gone to the Frenchman Alexis de Tocqueville to find justification for defining the United States as a democratic state in this period, but the statement on the undemocratic nature of the system was written in blood by the sacrifices of those who resisted the barbarism of a deformed society.[27]

It was the organized and spontaneous opposition to this

barbarism that formed the political dynamic before the Civil War in 1861. It was the African American and First Nation peoples who nurtured the humanity of all, and fought with all means possible against barbarism. Freedom takers such as Denmark Vessey, Gabriel Prosser, Nat Turner, and millions of unsung heroes fought against slavery and provided the foundation on which Obama built.

On February 10, 2007, Obama declared his candidacy for the presidency of the United States at the Old State Capitol building in Springfield Illinois, where Abraham Lincoln delivered his "House divided" speech in 1858. In his address, Obama made similar comments, but did not deal with the racism and sexism in politics head on. He used the formulation, "the smallness of our politics" to bring home the point on the history of "the big problem." Obama presented himself as a post-partisan politician who could unify people and bridge divisions. In this endeavor, Obama carried forward the traditions of Harriet Tubman, who fought slavery and racism, and distinguished between racists and those decent citizens who wanted to be in the ranks of the anti-racist and anti-sexist forces.

PHASE II: THE CIVIL WAR AND THE STRUGGLE FOR DEMOCRACY

While Obama drew inspiration from Lincoln, his announcement concealed a more important role played by the progressive movement in Lincoln's campaign. A focus on individualism has sought to suggest that the abolition of slavery came from Lincoln's genius. Social studies texts in secondary schools portray Lincoln as the man who "freed" the slaves. However, the reality was that it was the enslaved that freed themselves, and unleashed a political process that was unstoppable to the point of engulfing the society in a great Civil War.

In *Black Reconstruction in America*,[28] W. E. B. Dubois explained how legal and military skirmishes preceded the actual outbreak of war. The small war in Kansas, the activities of the underground railroad, and the militancy of the abolitionists had made the question of ending slavery the number one question in society. A Republican victory in the 1860 election resulted in seven Southern states declaring their secession from the Union even before Lincoln took office. Both the outgoing and incoming US administrations rejected secession, considering it rebellion. Dubois outlined the split in the military, and the extent to which the anti-racist and anti-slavery work of the abolitionists had inspired generals and officers with "abolitionist sentiments." This split in the military continues to be instructive in the fight against the more conservative factions of the military, who celebrated the conquest of the lands of the people of Mexico and genocide against the First Nation peoples.

Objectively, the material conditions of the North supported free labor over slave labor, but subjectively, the ideas and ideology of white supremacy held back the Northern industrialists. It devolved to the organized and spontaneous actions of the oppressed to force the political question that could only have been resolved at that time by warfare.

Cedric Robinson's book *Black Movements in America* (1977) spells out the fundamental role of the militant and revolutionary abolitionists who were opposed to slavery.

Lincoln was not himself opposed to slavery, and only wanted to maintain the Union. Writing to Horace Greely on August 22, 1862 he admitted that:

> My paramount object in this struggle is to save the Union, and is not either to save or to destroy slavery. If I could save the Union without freeing any slave I would do it, and if I could save it by freeing all the slaves I would do it; and if I could save it by freeing some and leaving others alone I would also do that.[29]

Lincoln was not to know then that the anti-racist momentum at that moment had gone far beyond a preoccupation with the future of the Union. Enslaved Africans were determined to force the historical question about the future of the society. Lincoln himself had said on more than one occasion that he believed in the inferiority of blacks, but he underestimated the extent to which black Americans would go to press their claims for their humanity. In this regard, Lincoln could be considered a gradualist. The South had declared war, and Lincoln had no choice but to face the questions of racism and slavery.

Cedric Robinson identified three groups of abolitionists: the gradualists, the militant abolitionists, and the revolutionary insurrectionists.[30] In this narrative of the foremost progressive movement of the nineteenth century, Robinson made distinctions between abolitionists such as William Lloyd Garrison, and revolutionaries such as John Brown, Martin Delaney, Frederick Douglass, and Harriet Tubman.

Black people wanted freedom and nothing short of freedom. The

Supreme Court decision of 1857 in *Dred Scott v. Sandford* heightened the challenges for citizenship and freedom. Chief Justice Roger B. Taney's decision said that slaves were "so far inferior that they had no rights which the white man was bound to respect." Blacks were forcing the question of the law. Would politicians and citizens in the North break an unjust law by assisting escaped slaves, thus violating the Fugitive Slave Law? There was a network of citizens all over the North who opposed this law.

A full elaboration of this major military struggle in the United States and the decisive role of black troops in the victory of the North would take us too far into the history of the United States. This area of scholarship has been well documented by W. E. B. Dubois and Cedric Robinson.[31] Small vignettes of the crucial role of blacks in the war have emerged in films such as *Glory*, the story of the 54th Massachusetts regiment, but the full story has not been revealed: that by the end of the war, there were more blacks serving in the Northern army than the entire Confederate army. Black troops were decisive for the victory of the North in the Civil War.

PHASE III: AUTONOMOUS ORGANIZING AND THE HARRIET TUBMAN PRINCIPLES

Although the literature on the fight against slavery and war had focused in the past on military activities, the day-to-day rebellion of the enslaved was just as important as open wars. In this rebellion, the role of African women was vital to the anti-slavery ideology. This was in part because of the social relations and social reproduction under slavery. In the United States, First Nation peoples were excluded, killed, and placed on reservations. Capitalists seized their lands to generate agricultural and mineral wealth. At the top of society was the capitalist class, the industrialists who were the driving force behind the economy. Below the capitalists and the wealthy landowners were the independent yeoman farmers and sections of the white working classes. Though exploited, these elements identified with the privileges of whiteness. White women were oppressed on the basis of their place in the society, but the ruling-class white women acted as ideological props for the system as a whole. They were presented as repositories of white civilization, sexless and pure, while the white slave masters and overseers carried out untold sexual assaults and sexual violence on black women.[32] Opinion makers worked hard on the investment in whiteness to bind all whites, irrespective of class, to the ideology of white supremacy.

Among people of African origin, there was a small layer of free blacks who were independent artisans and craftspersons, with a few wealthy ones in Louisiana. In the main however, the blacks were seen as a commodity, as property to be owned, bought, and sold. At the bottom of this hierarchy of humans was the black female. It was from here that the most militant anti-slavery and anti-racist ideas flowed. The black woman became the principal agent for the anti-slavery struggle because she felt the brunt of rape, violation, and day-to-day outrages on top of the hard work of plantation life. On the auction block, black women were stripped naked and handled like cattle. Forced sex and forced procreation were both degrading components of the devaluation of the personhood of the black woman. Slave narratives and the oral histories of millions of black women testified to the widespread rape and violation which was meted out.[33] It is this testament by the violated women that has sharpened the understanding of the kind of relationship that Thomas Jefferson maintained with Sally Hemings.[34]

Through her body, the system of slavery and capitalism was reproduced. It was not by accident that the anti-sexist and anti-racist forces came from the ranks of black women. Novelists such as Octavia Butler (*Kindred*) and Toni Morrison (*Beloved* and *Sula*) have used fictional characters to bring to life some of the inner struggles of black women under enslavement. Beyond fiction, there is the memory of millions of outstanding women, with the truly exceptional ones such as Harriet Tubman and Sojourner Truth celebrated by history. These women influenced and gave courage to other women in the women's movement.

The bravery and fortitude of millions of enslaved women were passed down to nurture the anti-racist movement. Harriet Tubman holds a special place among them. Born in enslavement, she developed and strengthened one of the crucial networks of freedom known as the underground railroad. After the Civil War, she was one of the leaders and organizers of the women's movement in the United States. Tubman bequeathed many principles, but we want to articulate the most important that were inherited by the Obama organization:

- We must fight against all odds.
- Achieve a high level of organization and preparation that come from the study of the terrain, the differing political forces, and the

history of the United States. Tubman had an indefatigable thirst for knowledge, and she studied law, history, geography, politics, religion, and astronomy. She believed in the necessity of close-knit networks that enabled the underground railroad to function, while at the same time supporting spontaneity, self-organization, and self-mobilization. The anti-slavery movement depended on mobilization at all levels: personal, community, regional, and national.

• Be a deeply spiritual person and aspire to love instead of hate.
• Believe in freedom from oppression – mental and physical slavery.
• Believe in the rights of women. Tubman was unafraid of big military forces, slave masters or other oppressors. She was ready to defend herself and her supporters, and her belief in victory inspired others to fight for freedom.

The relevant point for the comparison between Barack Obama and Lincoln is that there was an autonomous political force independent of Lincoln. This independent force outside of the mainstream parties was able to push society in an anti-racist direction. Without a clear anti-racist and anti-sexist force in society, those in the state could not be expected to carry forward the full anti-racist program to ensure that blacks could live in the United States as citizens.

RECONSTRUCTION AND THE THIRD PHASE

For our analysis, it was the militant abolitionists who seized the initiative and pushed Lincoln. Lincoln was able to grow and rise to the requirements of advancing the process of democratization. The articulators of freedom made bold attempts in the period of Reconstruction to shift the politics of the society, but the social forces which assassinated Lincoln worked overtime to assassinate the anti-racist movement and the democratization project. Would Reconstruction lead to the reconstruction of capital and free labor throughout the country, or be the basis of a form of capitalism girded by various forms of unfree labor such as sharecropping? The answer came out of political struggle. The violence of the former slaveholders settled the question on behalf of sharecropping, lynching, and the forms of Jim Crow that lasted until the middle of the twentieth century.

The heart of the Reconstruction plan was laid out in two measures: the 14th Amendment to the Constitution and the

Reconstruction Act. The 14th Amendment was passed in June 1866 and ratified in 1868. It was designed to protect the rights of Southern blacks and restrict the political power of former Confederates.

The 15th Amendment gave the right to vote to African Americans. With the right to vote, the politics of the United States was temporarily changed with a burst of participation by black males. Armed with the right to vote, to register, and to participate in the official political process, 1,465 black elected officials held political office in the South over the next decade.

On a per capita and absolute basis, more blacks were elected to political office during the period from 1865 to 1880 than at any other time in US history. In legislatures, they put forward radical and far-reaching proposals that for the first time brought social services such as public education, public health, and public sanitary services.

Despite the far-reaching implications of the Amendments to the Constitution, the force of law was not enough to beat back the entrenched ideas of racism.

COUNTER-REVOLUTION

Lincoln's assassination robbed the abolitionists of an ally in the White House. President Andrew Johnson, Lincoln's successor, did not support the radical Reconstruction that had been unleashed, and signaled to white Southerners that they had an ally in the White House when he vetoed the Freedmen's Bureau Bill. President Johnson called it unconstitutional and too expensive. This was the beginning of a major struggle between the contending forces to roll back the rights of blacks and to entrench racism in a new form, albeit with more violence and repression.

Dubois placed the question of labor and property at the center of this struggle between the black laborers (former slaves) on one side and the Southern planters who wanted a new relationship with the Northern industrialists on the other. In *Black Reconstruction* (1998), Dubois reminded the reader that the Civil War was an attempt to reduce black labor to unlimited exploitation.

According to Dubois, there were three phases of terrorist violence against blacks in the South. First was the phase of disregard for law which follows all wars. Then it became a labor war, an attempt to force workers to agree to the terms of the capitalist. Next it changed to a war between laborers, blacks, and whites.[35]

Sexualized violence was also at the center of this racism.

BENJAMIN TILLMAN, SEXUALIZED VIOLENCE, AND THE CONSOLIDATION OF RACISM

Throughout the United States, the temporary alliance between the abolitionists and the Republicans gave way to the increased tensions over economic relations in society.

As early as 1843, the process of enveloping Irish immigrants with the virus of white racism had led one observer to comment:

> It is a curious fact, that the Democratic party, and particularly the poorer class of Irish immigrants in America, are greater enemies to the negro population, and greater advocates for the continuance of negro slavery, than any portion of the population in the free States.[36]

Right up to the twentieth century, the official position of immigration officials and other bureaucrats was to drill home the importance of whiteness to immigrants. Chinese and Mexican immigrants were spared this chauvinism, but sections of the immigrant population from India sought to internalize the ideas of white supremacy. This position continued into the twenty-first century.

The other oppressed group that was ensnared by the ideas of racism was white women fighting for the right to vote.

Coming out of enslavement, the abolitionists had pushed for the right to vote for blacks, and the burst of energy relating to reconstruction in health, education, sanitation, and agriculture was testament to the vigorous attempts to change society. But the leaders of the women's movement were not at one with the black leadership, and in 1870, Susan B. Anthony along with Elizabeth Cady Stanton moved to ingratiate themselves with the Democratic Party, the party of the Ku Klux Klan, after the passing of the 15th Amendment of the Constitution gave the right to vote to black men.[37]

Thus was an alliance strengthened between racists and oppressed women in the period after reconstruction. The short-lived effort to bring Sarah Palin into the 2008 presidential election as a factor was one desperate attempt to go back to the tradition of using white women as a foil for the spread of racist violence. Violence in the name of defending white women became the justification for one of the longest waves of racist violence and murders in the United States.

There is now a new burst of scholarship that is centralizing the fact that the question of white supremacy was tied to conceptions of manhood, and that the appeal of Ku Klux Klan and other terrorist groups was not just to racism but also to masculinity.[38] These scholars have broken the old stereotypes of black men, and have brought to the fore the full extent and depth of sexual terrorism in the United States. "Splitting a nigger woman" had become the euphemism all over the South of the United States to describe the rape of black women, since it was considered not only "a white man's prerogative but also a way to express his anger and contempt."[39] Sexual terrorism reinforced political disenfranchisement and economic exploitation in the form of sharecropping. Dorothy Roberts has explored the relationship between eugenics and sexual terrorism, and defined sexual terrorism as "willful denial of female reproductive and bodily rights and wholesale suppression of one half of humanity on grounds of socially constructed gender norms."[40]

The Ku Klux Klan was one of the pre-eminent organizations to enforce sexual terrorism after 1866, insofar as it is now understood by feminist scholars that the Klan was based on the deployment of calculated sexual violence. Saturday night parties of lynching, castration, and burning the bodies of black men, concealed an even more profound and widespread rape and violation of black women. Rape was one of the most forceful expressions of sexual terrorism and white supremacy. This terrorism was pervasive, intense over nearly a century, and served as the basis for the ideological coherence within a system of "racial dominance long marked by forced sex and procreation."[41]

The Klan combined all aspects of terrorism in the history of the United States: political, economic, racial, and sexual.

Political terrorism was the violent disenfranchisement of blacks up to the passing of the Voting Rights Act in 1965. It was rigidly enforced by the Black Codes and other local statutes. Blacks were denied the right to vote by grandfather clauses (laws that restricted the right to vote to people whose ancestors had voted before the Civil War), poll taxes (fees charged to poor blacks), white primaries (only Democrats could vote, only whites could be Democrats), and literacy tests.

Economic terrorism was the systematic exploitation and robbery of blacks, rigidly enforced through the system of semi-slavery called sharecropping. This was a system where blacks worked on white farms and were continuously in debt to the point where in the 1950s Martin Luther King Jr. met Southerners who had never seen the US currency.

Lynching and racial terrorism were used as methods of social control to keep blacks exploited as sharecroppers. After the withdrawal of the Federal army in 1877, blacks had no legal recourse against assaults and brutal exploitation because the Jim Crow justice system was all-white: police, prosecutors, judges, juries, and prison officials. Sexual terrorism involved routine rape (especially gang rape) and sexual torture and mutilation of women, especially black women. On the other side of this terrorism was the sexual torture and emasculation of black men by mobs of Klansmen, validating the claim that masculinity ("real manhood") was the exclusive prerogative of white men.[42]

The career of Benjamin Tillman and the terrorism that was meted out in South Carolina are emblematic of this multi-faceted terrorism. Born to a slave-holding family in South Carolina in 1847, Tillman signed up to fight for the Confederate army in 1864. During Reconstruction, in the face of black elected officials, he organized Red-shirted paramilitary forces to kill, maim and terrorize blacks. He was one of the thousands of landowners who organized disgruntled former rebels to wreak violence and lynching.

Like the Klan and other vigilante organizations, Tillman strove to redeem white men in the face of challenges for rights by black workers, and to reconstruct white patriarchal authority. Tillman and his ilk set about the mobilization of poor white men with no skills, and believed that "racial conscience was a matter of domination and terror not cooperation."[43] The rise of Tillman to be the governor of South Carolina, serving from December 1890 to December 1894, highlighted the career of many politicians who manipulated the ideas of white racism.

Moving from the State House to the Senate in 1895, Tillman took his message across the United States. He was re-elected in 1900, 1906, and 1912, and served from 1895 to his death in 1918. It was from this national stage that Tillman argued that blacks should be exterminated if they attempted to exercise the franchise, asserting that "The negro must remain subordinate or be exterminated."[44]

This violent self-assertion by masculinists and militarists marked the political culture of the South throughout the twentieth century. Tillman cultivated the "pitchfork" as his image to represent himself as a farmer, but he depended on militaristic terror against black people and political opponents.

Yet today the cover-up of these crimes is manifest in the ways in which Tillman is hailed as a great educator for having initiated building of two universities – Clemson University and Winthrop

College – and the Charleston Naval Shipyard. Two US Navy ships were named after him.

I walked through Winthrop College during the election campaign of 2008, and marveled that students in the twenty-first century would be learning in an institution where openly fascist ideas were not challenged. After President Theodore Roosevelt entertained Booker T. Washington in the White House, Senator Tillman commented that "The action of President Roosevelt in entertaining that nigger will necessitate our killing a thousand niggers in the south before they will learn their place again."[45]

LONG-TERM LEGACIES OF THE THIRD PHASE

The role of Tillman as a propagandist for the ideas of white supremacy and sexualized racism was established during his period in the Senate, when he undertook extensive lecture tours of the United States in order to ensure that his version of the history of the South become central to the national consciousness. From his position as a member of the United States Senate Committee on Armed Services, Military Affairs and Chairperson of the Committee on Naval Affairs, 1913–18, Tillman used his influence to extend the role of the armaments industry and championed the extension of the southern version of reconstruction.

In this enterprise, he was able to inspire the celebrated study of the Ku Klux Klan called *The Clansman*.[46] It later influenced the celebrated movie, *The Birth of a Nation*. This film started the long tradition of involving Hollywood in the transmission of sexualized racism. It depicted the South as the bastion of American values and a space that had been violated by the Civil War. The film depicted Reconstruction as a disaster because black people could never be integrated into US society as equals. Representing the "three-fifths" strategy as the answer, the film and the propaganda of leaders such as Tillman presented the violent actions of the Klan as the basis for returning the United States to true democracy.

David Blight's book *Race and Reunion: the Civil War in American Memory*[47] traced the way in which the entire society internalized this racist interpretation of the Civil War and Reconstruction. David Brion Davis argued in an essay on "The Enduring Legacy of the South's Civil War Victory" that:

The United States is only now beginning to recover from the Confederacy's ideological victory following the Civil War. Though the South lost the battles, for more than a century, it attained its goal: that the role of slavery in America's history be thoroughly diminished, even somehow removed as a cause of the war. The reconciliation of North and South required a national repudiation of Reconstruction as "a disastrous mistake"; a wide-ranging white acceptance of "Negro inferiority" and of white supremacy in the South; and a distorted view of slavery as an unfortunate but benign institution that was damaging for whites morally but helped civilize and Christianize "African savages."[48]

EUGENICS AND THE IDEOLOGICAL VICTORY OF THE SOUTH

If novels such as *The Clansman* and films such as *The Birth of a Nation* were popularized in the twentieth century as important phases of US politics and culture, the ideas of eugenics became permanently fixed as the way of explaining the differences between "races." Immigration officials such as Francis Amasa Walker had been opposed to immigrants "of inferior races," and from his position, helped to popularize the idea that Anglo-Saxons should stem the flow of mongrel races in order to halt racial suicide.

Sexualized racism, along with the twentieth-century fear of immigrants, predisposed the ruling classes and the institutions of higher learning to accept the theory that "social characteristics were heritable and deviant behavior was biologically determined."[49] Biological determinism took hold in society as the United States instituted punitive measures against black people, which were justified by state officials on the grounds that there were biologically determined traits that predisposed blacks to criminal activity and "deviancy." By the end of the twentieth century with the war on drugs, biological determinism buttressed sexualized racism and was reinforced with an all-out war against black women who were deemed "unfit to have children." This all out war against the poor refused to accept the institutional and cultural forces behind racism and racist thinking and actions. To cover up exploitation, major capitalists in the United States financed research and publications, so that the names of Carnegie, Harriman, Kellogg, Rockefeller, and other barons of industry were associated with the funding of researchers, universities, and organizations dedicated to "weeding out those of the bad breed."

At the apex of this research network was the Eugenics Record Office (ERO) at Cold Spring Harbor Laboratory in New York, which gained international notoriety as a center for eugenics and human heredity. The long-term consequences of the research output of the ERO are still being felt in the society today.

Respected scientists and top universities such as Stanford, Harvard, Yale, and Princeton espoused race theory and race science. Stanford president David Starr Jordan originated the notion of "race and blood" in his 1902 racial epistle "Blood of a Nation." In it, the university scholar declared that human qualities and conditions such as talent and poverty were passed through the blood. Master race theories reinforced sexism, chauvinism, and homophobia, and nurtured fascism internationally. "Deadly American race science of eugenics that idealized a blond, blue-eyed superior race" inspired scientists and policymakers who were of the view that "some 90 percent of humanity was to be eliminated using various methods."[50] Such a proposition was not practical from the point of view of the need for labor by the capitalist classes, but the idea of wholesale elimination of target populations gained root, and was circulated through popular mediums such as country fairs, magazines, and respectable academic platforms.

German efficiency and organizational skills ensured that the wholesale elimination of people was more concentrated and more successful in Germany. Up to the present, the citizens of the United States are not totally aware of the close collaboration between US foundations and researchers, and the scientists in Germany who were to take the eugenic thesis to the highest level.[51] If the atrocities of the Nazi Holocaust were concentrated on a short period of 1933–45, the eugenic ideas of the ruling elements in the United States had a longer period of gestation, and found new advocates in the field of human genetics.

Race science took root to the point where, throughout the twentieth century, notable scientists such as Arthur R. Jensen reinforced the hereditary school of thought on race and intelligence.[52] From the ERO to the scholarship of Arthur Jensen in the 1960s and Richard Herrnstein at the end of the century, the eugenic ideas of subordinating "inferior beings" became entrenched in the politics and institutions in the United States. Such was the influence of the eugenics movement that no less a person than the former president of the United States, Theodore Roosevelt, wrote on the duties of the "right kind of citizen of the right type" and the prevention of the "wrong people from breeding."[53] Like its militaristic counterpart the Ku Klux Klan between 1880 and 1940, the eugenics camp proved to be a dominant social movement.[54]

Positive eugenics has been described as selective "breeding" to improve the characteristics of an organism or species. Negative eugenics involved the systematic elimination of so-called undesirable biological traits. The sterilization laws that were orchestrated in the United States before 1945 were based on the need to ensure positive breeding. Every area of US social and economic life was negatively affected by eugenics thinking.

Harriet A. Washington explored the long history of the widespread sterilization of black women in relation to eugenic ideas, and how the experimentation on blacks in the medical profession was shielded by eugenic thinking. The 40-year experiment on blacks that was carried out in the Tuskegee syphilis study confirmed a deep suspicion that the medical profession was tainted by eugenic ideas. Institutionalized racism and sexism in the field of medicine and in the health services received better cover in the era of neo-liberalism, when "liberal eugenics" sought to separate itself from the "authoritarian eugenics of Hitler" in order to support better investment in genetic enhancement.

Michael J. Sandel has been at the forefront of exposing the dangers of genetic enhancement, and the new investment in creating children with the sex, height and genetic traits "of the perfect child."[55] The questions associated with the huge investment in whiteness connected with this field of genetic enhancement have been brought to the fore by Dorothy Roberts in *Killing the Black Body*.[56] It is in these studies that we get full exposure to the kind of thinking that spawns the Birther movement, and how race shapes the new area of genetic engineering.

Institutionalized racism (especially in the areas of education, medicine and the prison industrial complex) took root in the United States to the point that neither Supreme Court decisions such as *Brown v. Board of Education* nor legal measures such as the Civil Rights Act of 1964 and the Voting Rights Act of 1965 could dent the depth of racist thinking and its impact on the society. Indeed, immediately after the Supreme Court passed the landmark *Brown v. Board of Education* decision in 1954, William F Buckley, one of the top conservative thinkers in the United States, commented that "whites had every right to discriminate against blacks because whites belonged to 'the advanced race.'"[57]

Despite and in fact because of the advances of the civil rights movement in the fourth phase, a new form of racism emerged in the form of racial profiling. Legal segregation of the Jim Crow era was replaced by a new Jim Crow of mass incarceration. Policing urban communities and exploitation has reached the point where "There are more African Americans under correctional control today – in prison or jail, on probation or parole – than were enslaved in 1850, a decade before the Civil War began."[58]

Driving while black was dangerous in most parts of the United States because of the constant harassment by the police. This racial profiling and "the war on drugs" ensured that one in three black people in the United States under 25 will become enmeshed in the courts, prison, or post-prison experience. Of all US prisoners, about 67 percent are people of color, although people of color make up only about 30 percent of the US population. The United States imprisons more persons per capita than any other country. Black men and women are disproportionately held within the system of courts, prisons, and surveillance.

Institutionalized racism ensured that in every area of social engagement – housing, education, employment, health, and police interface – black and Latino people were worse off than in the period of the civil rights revolution. Conservative public policy under successive governments rolled back social programs as neo-liberalism gave more support to racists and sexists. In order to win elections, xenophobia and anti-black racism were deployed by successive leaders, with the media taking racist and sexist stereotypes to new heights.

Ronald Reagan had campaigned from the outset in 1980 with a clear message to Southern segregationists. George Bush, Sr. developed an explicit advertisement with Willie Horton as the portrait of the threatening criminalized black male. Not to be outdone, Bill Clinton used coded language while attacking rap artists such as Sister Souljah.

Racism, homophobia, and religious fundamentalism became dominant ideas under George W. Bush Jr. to the point where wedge issues of abortion, homophobia, followers of Islam, and patriotism defined the political culture. Sexism, the cult of masculinity, militarism, and religious fundamentalism carried all the hallmarks of fascism in the Bush/Cheney administration.[59] Neo-liberalism gave cover to liberal eugenics. Under liberal eugenics, there were new assertions of the need for private individuals to have the right to genetic enhancement. It was in this climate that we heard new claims about the future of technological singularity in the twenty-first century.

EUGENICS AND TECHNOLOGICAL SINGULARITY

When the first discussion on technological singularity appeared at the end of the twentieth century, it was predicted by Ray Kurzweil that humanity would reach it by 2045. By the start of the twenty-first century there were new projections about the possibilities for this new era, when "our intelligence will become increasingly non-biological and trillions of times more powerful than it is today—the dawning of a new civilization that will enable us to transcend our biological limitations and amplify our creativity."[60]

According to this vision of the future of the twenty-first century, we are moving to the stage of transhumans, where the convergence of four technologies promises to alter the form, substance, and direction of human nature and civilization forever. These are nanotechnology, biotechnology, information and communication technologies, and cognitive technologies. It is the era when these technologies are deployed with computer simulations of the human brain. All four technologies have the capability of creating impacts even more profound than those historically unleashed by the Industrial Revolution or the Nuclear Age. All claim to advance the quality of human existence and consider dangerous side-effects to be manageable. In 2010, futurists were predicting that by 2013 a super-computer would be built that exceeds the computational capabilities of the human brain.

As computers become more powerful, numerous, and cheap, the futurists predict they will reach the point where they can be programmed to have a mind (intelligence, self-awareness, emotional richness) indistinguishable from a human's. Ray Kurzweil predicted that the first artificial intelligence (AI) will be built around a computer simulation of a human brain, which will be made possible by previous, nanotech-guided brain scanning.[61]

Given the history of eugenics, the role of Nazi scientists during the period of fascism, and the history of racist ideas, there are profound challenges for humanity in this period. Not only will this new period of robotics and transhumans change the fundamental laws of production and production relations, the balance between humans and superhumans will have definite implications for demo-cratic participation in society. Superhuman intelligences may have goals inconsistent with human survival, and the preconceived ideas of racial hierarchy could have a new lease of life.

In 1971, Sidney Wilhelm wrote a book with the provocative title *Who Needs the Negro?*[62] In this book, Wilhelm argued that with automation and technological change, black labor in the United States would become unnecessary. Millions of industrial jobs have been lost in the past 30 years, consequent to the deindustrialization of the United States, with devastating consequences for cities, the quality of life, and public policies. Instead of conceptualizing new meanings for the reorganization of society beyond the export of jobs to zones where labor was totally at the mercy of capital, the neo-liberal agenda called for more policing in an era when political power was concentrated in fewer and fewer hands.

It is with this background that those who oppose racism follow carefully the discussions on technological singularity and the suggestion by researcher Hugo de Garis that AI might simply "eliminate the human race, and humans would be powerless to stop them." This concern had been powerfully presented by Bill Joy after a discussion with Ray Kurzweil. In a well-publicized article in *Wired Magazine*, Bill Joy raised the alarm of the future elite who will be making decisions for all other human beings. He warned:

> Technologies such as human cloning have in particular raised our awareness of the profound ethical and moral issues we face. If, for example, we were to reengineer ourselves into several separate and unequal species using the power of genetic engineering, then we would threaten the notion of equality that is the very cornerstone of our democracy. We are aggressively pursuing the promises of these new technologies within the now-unchallenged system of global capitalism and its manifold financial incentives and competitive pressures.[63]

Quoting Carl Sagan, Joy added, "This is the first moment in the history of our planet when any species, by its own voluntary actions, has become a danger to itself – as well as to vast numbers of others."

The election of Barack Obama as president of the United States took place at a time when the debates on new technologies and new forms of slavery required informed and democratic participation.

CONCLUSION: DEMOCRATIZATION AS A PROCESS

One year before Dr. Martin Luther King Jr. was assassinated in 1968, he called for a revolution of values for the United States to move from a "thing-oriented" to a "person-oriented" society.[64] He argued that democracy and the anti-racist struggle in the United States could not be successful until there was a revolution transcending spiritual death. His warning about the approach to spiritual death is even more pertinent in the era of technological singularity and transhumans in the twenty-first century.

Our analysis of the history of racism and sexism and the impending transformations of the biotech century lead us to the view that technological singularity, at its core, is a profound spiritual challenge. Therefore, materialistic conceptions of change and democratic participation will be impotent before the challenge of technological singularity. The debate on whether we are persons or semi-machines has placed the question of democracy on an entirely new terrain.

In his speech on spiritual values, Dr. King not only challenged the racism, sexism, and militarism of the United States, but he also challenged the deeply held view of Western European philosophy that separated humans between rational and non-rational beings. In her critique of reductionism and western rationalism, Mary Midgley reminds us that in Greek and Roman societies, slaves were non-persons.[65] This distinction between persons and non-persons was deepened in Western thought by enlightenment philosophers such as Immanuel Kant.

Midgley's critique of Kant and rationalist thinking has also inspired our call in this book for democratic discussion and more informed interventions on genetic engineering, nanotechnology, and robotics. Joy and Midgley were calling on society to step back from the celebration of technology for the sake of technology, so that there can be a better grasp of the dangers for the hierarchy and survival of humans. Midgley had critiqued the theoreticians of AI more than 30 years ago, arguing that "the theories will not solve the real social and moral problems the world is facing, either through genetic engineering or using machines. These schemes still seem to me to be just displacement activities proposed in order to avoid facing our real difficulties."

Global warming, environmental destruction, world hunger, militarism, and disease are urgent questions that demand focused attention by humans. Racism and sexism in the United Sates have blocked its ability to focus attention on the need of humans. In effect, what the United States has exported in the past hundred years has been its racist ideology and not democratic values. International investment in whiteness has blunted the struggles to transform the legacies of exploitation and oppression. From China to Brazil and from Japan to India, acceptance of white supremacy continues to hold back the transformation of human relations.

Our exploration of the roots of slavery in the United States was to remind the reader that things can be disposed by other humans, and that slaves were more like things. "Things can properly be used as means to human ends in a way in which people cannot. Things have no aims of their own; they are not subjects but objects. Thing-treatment given to people is exploitation and oppression."[66]

Dr. King questioned the rationalist thought that had inspired the Constitution of the United States and justified the enslavement of Africans and the mass murder of the First Nation peoples. In our introduction, we saw how framers of the US constitution treated Africans as non-persons, and how the definition of the African as three-fifths of a person deformed the political culture of the United States. The same mindset of the rational thinkers had rendered women non-persons and deepened the systematic corruption of society.

How can society celebrate the human spirit in the twenty-first century to get away from the binaries of persons and things, spirit and matter, mind and body, black and white, heterosexual and homosexual, and those divisions that held back human creativity and tremendous energy?

RACISM AND THE OLD LEFT

The confrontation with racism and sexism has also brought to the forefront the ideas and practices of those who in the past were called the Left. The materialism and linear thinking of the radical left meant that the race question was made subsidiary to the class question. A variant of social Darwinism was applied to social trans-formation, to the point where the Marxist schema of communalism, slavery, feudalism, capitalism, and socialism was accepted as the path for all humans. According to this understanding of human transformation, Europeans had advanced beyond feudalism, and other peoples were therefore "inferior." Economists from both the right and left conflated "progress" with capitalist expansion. For Marxists of the twentieth century, the question of racism had to await the struggles of capitalism.

These Marxists had forgotten the admonition of Karl Marx that "Labor cannot emancipate itself in the white skin where in the black it is branded."[67] C. L. R. James also explored the dialectical relationship between race and class when he noted that "The race question is subsidiary to the class question in politics and to think of imperialism in terms of race is disastrous. But to neglect the racial factor as merely incidental is an error only less grave than to make it fundamental."[68]

Despite this insight, those who have borne the brunt of racism and sexism in the United States have found the social movements for democracy wanting. Women in general, and black and brown women in particular, have been most insistent that the question of sexism must be central to the opposition to racism and class exploitation. In the fifth phase of confrontation with racism and sexism in the United States, radical feminists, especially black radical feminists, have been the ones to place the issues of gender and sexuality at the center of the new democratic struggles.

Cathy Cohen's book, *Boundaries of Blackness: AIDS and the Breakdown of Black Politics,* called on black political leaders to challenge homophobia and sexism in their communities.[69] This challenge had also been reinforced by Harriet Washington's study of *Medical Apartheid,* which called on society to ensure that there is democratic control over scientific research on biological and chemical warfare.[70] The case of the attempts of Wouter Basson in South Africa to develop a virus that could kill blacks and leave whites was a story of how far the sickness of racism had reached in the scientific community.

BEYOND THE LIMITATIONS OF LIBERAL THOUGHT

The civil rights movement had been one of the more profound moments in the struggles for democracy in the United States by building on the advances of previous struggles. Building on the anti-racist and anti-sexist struggles against slavery, the movement against Jim Crow, and the movement against eugenics, the civil rights movement sought to align itself with the intellectual roots of the liberal traditions of the United States. Despite the limitations of the liberal democratic reference, the social roots of the civil rights movement were established in the freedom struggles of the enslaved, and the spirit of love and emancipation.

More than once in his presidential campaign, Obama drew attention to the fact that he was standing on the shoulders of those who had sacrificed in the social struggles. He used the code of the North Star to make reference to the political education that he received from Harriet Tubman. In his book on the electoral victory of Obama, *The Audacity to Win,* his campaign manager David Plouffe wrote that,

It's a reminder of how and why we won. We never forgot why we were running. That was our North Star. And we held that North Star in our sights at all times. We made many mistakes along the way, but we always remembered that we were running because, as Barack put it, the dream so many generations had fought for was slipping away.[71]

Obama drew from the civil rights movement, which drew from the long traditions of the freedom struggles in society. The important point is that there were many forces making the civil rights revolution: preachers, students, workers, activists, and what are called unsung heroes. Obama studied the techniques and organizational strengths of each of these movements, and made special note of the contribution of Ella Baker.

This was a woman who struggled for over six decades, linking the real lived experiences of the struggles against the Ku Klux Klan to the struggles against sexism right up to the 1980s. She was one of the most important influences on the young militants of the civil rights revolution. She called on young people to think of transforming the entire social structure. She inspired the ideas of participatory democracy, collective leadership, and shunned "leaderism." She was on of the most outspoken opponents of male chauvinism in the movement. Her mantra was that those organizing must work with people where they are. These were the ideas that had carried the massive struggles that led to the Civil Rights Act and the Voting Rights Act.

In particular, the Voting Rights Act of 1965 was supposed to represent a major victory in the democratic struggles in the United States. Given the success of the Klan, Jim Crow, and the traditions of Benjamin Tillman, black people had been denied the right to vote in most of the Southern states of the United States. In 1952, in 24 counties of the "black belt" region of the South, not one black person had been registered to vote. Although voter registration increased after the Act in the seven states where disenfranchisement had been most explicit, the Justice Department of the United States had to be vigilant to ensure that blacks could exercise the franchise.

Institutionalized racism and embedded sexism in US society after the election of Ronald Reagan dictated that far more than electoral victories was needed to excise the cancers of racism and sexism from society. Rooting out racism and sexism and the ideas of white supremacy required an acknowledgement by society that it was suffering from sickness. It required the kind of reparative justice that had been mandated by the World Conference against Racism in 2001. However, in the main, white citizens in the United States were in denial about the true history of racism. Reparations provided the basis for a possible healing from the cancers of racism and sexism.

This kind of acknowledgment of the mental sickness required a leap in the consciousness of society for the majority to understand that racism is a white problem and that it was the task of whites to be engaged in the struggle against whiteness. The spirit of this chapter is to agree with James Baldwin that "as long as you think that you are white, there's no hope for you." This author is also agreeing with the observation of David Roediger that "racial identities are not only Black, Latino, Asian, Native Americans and so on, they are also white. To ignore white ethnicity is to redouble its hegemony by naturalizing it."[72]

Obama had been part of a generation that aspired to break ideas of subordination and domination. In his speech to the Democratic Party National Convention in 2004, Obama had said clearly that "There is not a liberal America and a conservative America – there is the United States of America. There is not a Black America and a White America and Latino America and Asian America – there's the United States of America." Liberals cheered the speech but failed to grasp its challenge to the naturalizing of whiteness. Obama was using his own biography to get beyond the traditions of blame and punishment. Invoking the principle of Ubuntu that "I am my brother's keeper, I am my sister's keeper that makes this country work," he sought to project the interconnectedness of all citizens of the United States, that "alongside our famous individualism, there's another ingredient in the American saga. A belief that we're all connected as one people."

Obama was attempting to balance the ideas of individualism and the collective ideas of Ubuntu. Dr. King had also subscribed to this principle of Ubuntu. He warned, "An individual has not started living until he can rise above the narrow confines of his individualistic concern to the broader concerns of all humanity."[73]

Obama was suspended between the future of Ubuntu and the past ideas of what constituted liberal democratic values. As a politician running in the United States, he could not do otherwise. Like Lincoln, Obama had accepted the promise of democracy as a proposition. Lincoln was pushed forward by the Civil War. Would a social movement emerge from the capitalist depression to push Obama away from the limitations of liberal thought?

One possibility came from the massive mobilization associated with the 2008 elections. Obama was to insert himself into a new social movement, and as he grew with this movement, new possibilities for democratic participation emerged in the election. This was explicit in the primaries of the election cycle to which we now turn.

4

GRASSROOTS ORGANIZING CONFRONTS THE MACHINE

Very few revolutions start with a conscious attempt to take power. No revolution has ever started with everyone in the country agreeing with the goal of the revolutionary movement. It is clashes, both ideological and physical, among segments of the population and usually the whip of the counter-revolution which give the revolution its momentum. Sometimes the revolution is violent, sometimes it is non-violent, but always it is the revolution. Sometimes those in the revolution are conscious of the consequences of their actions, sometimes they are not, but always there is action.

James Boggs, *The American Revolution*

This statement at the start of the civil rights struggle summed up the essence of the ways in which the anti-racist struggle in the United States was bound up with the battles for a new mode of social organization and new relations between human beings. The actions of millions of citizens who were claiming their rights as citizens have been called the civil rights revolution. It was a classic case in which some were conscious of the consequences of their actions. This revolution had to tackle the race question head on. There could be no dichotomy between race and class.[1]

Though James Boggs did not link sexual oppression and sexism to the race, class, and nation challenges, he was clear that the revolution had to be multi-faceted, with many sites, many fronts of struggle. In Chapter 3, I detailed the interconnections between racism and sexism in the United States. Racism and sexism divided blacks from whites, men from women, and gays from straights. It was this division that was exploited throughout the twentieth century to mobilize the Ku Klux Klan to unleash counter-revolutionary violence and attacks against blacks. Throughout the struggle for civil rights in the post Second World War period, those whites who opposed racism had to confront their whiteness. Whiteness and property reinforced money, and money reinforced whiteness. Despite the fact that it was the capitalist classes and the most powerful sections that benefited from the great waves of US wealth, "the pro-wealth policies of the right have enjoyed substantial low and middle income support, particularly among religious voters enlisted by cultural faces of conservatism."[2]

It was the potential unleashed by the civil rights and peace movements that propelled the period of conservatism and neo-liberalism from the time of Ronald Reagan to the present. Barack Obama went back to the grassroots organizing of the Freedom Riders and built on the traditions and tactics of this period in order to capture the leadership of the Democratic Party. (The Freedom Riders set out to challenge the status quo by riding various forms of public transport to challenge laws or customs in the Deep South that supported segregation). In the process, Obama became suspended between the traditions of revolution and counter-revolution.

The defeat of the Clinton machine of the Democratic Party brought to an end a period of US politics when blacks were officially excluded from the top echelons of the party. In order to mobilize to become the candidate of the Democratic Party, Barack Obama fell back on the organizational tactics, the self-confidence, the ideas of self-organization, and the openness of the radical grassroots organizing of the 1960s. There was a clear link between the challenges of the 1964/68 Mississippi Freedom Democratic Party (MFDP) and the Obama election campaign. Obama acknowledged this historical fact when he addressed the Democratic National Convention in Denver.

This chapter begins with the story of the MFDP and the historic struggle for black delegates to be seated at the 1964 Democratic Party Convention in Atlantic City. Although this story of Fannie Lou Hamer and the Student Non Violent Coordinating Committee (SNCC) has been retold many times by many different sources, it remains an epic story in the history of the United States in so far as the sharecroppers of the South were willing to confront entrenched interests to break out of semi-feudal exploitation.[3] These struggles of the freedom fighters also exposed a phenomenon in the United States known as "limousine liberals." These were the liberals of the North who wanted the movement for civil rights to be organized in scripted legal boundaries where white philanthropy could dictate the issues. Massive voter registration drives and getting out the vote for elections was the most commitment that would come from the liberal elements who did not understand the sicknesses and exploitation of "white nationalism." Within the Democratic Party each leader had their favorite "negro" who could pacify the voters and deliver some of them to the voting booth at election time. When Obama appeared, it was expected that he was simply leveraging for the usual spoils handed out to black politicians and preachers.

We now know that the prolonged civil rights struggle opened the legislative process that brought about the Civil Rights Act of 1964 and the Voting Rights Act of 1965. Beyond this legal struggle lay the prolonged fight against brutal exploitation, biological determinism, segregation, mass incarceration, and the criminalization of black youths. It was in this prolonged fight to confront racism and sexism that the liberals exposed their fickleness in the face of institutional racism. Faced with the legitimate linkages between peace and civil rights, the liberals capitulated before the militaristic onslaught of the Cointelpro (counter-intelligence program) which physically eliminated activists.[4] Liberals opposed racism in words but not really in deeds. Robert Kennedy started out as a liberal activist from the North. Once he tied his future to the alliance of black and Latino workers with the peace movement, he was assassinated in 1968.

Martin Luther King, Jr. had started out embracing the liberal creed of equality and the importance of individual accumulation, but once he became involved in the peace movement and linked this movement to the rights of workers, he was transformed into a passionate defender of the rights of all. Starting out inside an elitist and patriarchal movement of preachers, King grew into one of the foremost revolutionary activists in the United States, calling for a revolution of values to avoid "spiritual death." Once King started down the road of a critique of capitalism, imperialism, and militarism, he was assassinated in Memphis, Tennessee. Similarly, the assassination of Malcolm X, Medgar Evers, and countless others occurred in a context where hundreds of millions of dollars of resources were expended on infiltrating, disrupting, marginalizing, and/or subverting groups suspected of being subversive. Challenging racism in the United States is still considered subversive, with the mass media and the mainstream establishment using all means to discredit those who are considered "black power revolutionaries."[5]

It was in the areas of cultural production that the revolution of the 1960s broke racial barriers to mobilize young people. Whether it was the poetry of Langston Hughes and cultural spokespersons who termed themselves "poets of the revolution," or Jimi Hendrix's irreverent rendition of the national anthem, the cultural revolution challenged racist power structures. Gradually, young people stopped singing in codes, so that when Martha and the Vandellas sang "Dancing in the street," there was an explicit message in the song for youths to rise up and join urban uprisings against oppression. H. Rap Brown, one of the leaders of SNCC, played songs such as "Dancing in the street" while organizing. From the music of rhythm and blues to the hip hop songs of fighting the power, the music, art, and culture of this period shook the foundations of the republic. In their fight back, conservatives focused on cultural struggle.

Lynne Cheney and William Bennett (Secretary of Education under Reagan) were frontline generals of this culture war. One of the goals of this war was to purge those on the left from the academy while deepening and refining the ideation system of supremacy. Lynn Cheney as head of the National Endowment for the Arts, Dick Cheney at the Pentagon and later as vice president inspired the counter-revolutionary forces to go all out to purge society of ideas of social justice. Neo-conservatism and "patriotism" became vehicles for the mobilization of poor white workers against their own interests.

In order to appear patriotic, leaders of the Democratic Party such as Henry "Scoop" Jackson of Washington State had become advocates of robust militarism. The period of the New Deal in the 1930s had ushered in a period of an alliance between labor, blacks, and small capitalists, but after the era of McCarthyism, the Democratic Party embraced militarism with the same zeal as the Republicans. Federal spending to stimulate the economy during the New Deal gave considerable weight to precinct bosses and ward leaders of the party. The party machinery in the urban areas became bases for political patronage.

In the United States, mainstream politics, and especially the urban politics of the Democratic Party, took on the aura of an impersonal mechanical operation. A well-oiled machine that greased the palm of party operatives became central to the procedural process of electing officials which was called democratic participation. Grease, corruption, and negative images of backroom deals were associated with the most sordid figures in US politics.

The mindset of mechanic extended beyond the political organization. Mechanical thinking embraced a Newtonian world view with the attendant ideas of dominion – dominion over blacks, dominion over women, dominion over nature, and dominion over the planet. The supremacy of the males, especially white males required that politics was in the hands of rational and scientific persons. Blacks and women were supposed to be emotional and irrational.

Political leadership required cold and calculated thinking, and the party machinery delivered the right person who came through the machine. "By conceptualizing reality as a machine rather than a living organism, (science) sanctioned the domination of both nature and women."[6] Hillary Clinton and Bill Clinton worked to control the machine after 1992, and Hillary Clinton used the discourse of equality to make her claim to control the Democratic Party machine.

Mayor Richard Daley, Sr. has entered the history books as a machine politician in Chicago. The sordid nature of "pay to play" politics was revealed to a younger generation after Barack Obama was elected president in 2008, when the governor of Illinois, Milorad "Rod" Blagojevich, was charged with "conspiracy to commit mail and wire fraud and solicitation of bribery." "Pay to play" was one clear manifestation of the nexus between the machine, money, and politics in the United States, where democracy was sold to the highest bidder. The media, the institutions of higher learning, religious institutions, small business, big business, security, and intelligence personnel were all ensnared by patronage, bribery, and the selling of influence that was called "democracy" in the United States. However, by the end of the twentieth century, the business of politics had become so huge that a special class of entrepreneurs emerged. These were called "political consultants." Consultancy for politicians had become such a thriving enterprise that the "entrepreneurs" developed their own trade association, the American Association of Political Consultants (AAPC). Political careerists and entrepreneurs polluted and diminished the vestiges of democratic participation.

As a mainstream politician, Obama embraced and employed consultants. David Axelrod, who had worked in Chicago politics since the era of Mayor Harold Washington, was the "political consultant" for Obama when he campaigned to be senator in 2004. In this chapter we will use the formulation "Obama campaign" to point to the grassroots energy that catapulted Obama to the world stage. However, the grassroots forces should not always be seen as being dominated by other parts of the campaign. There were three main parts of this Obama campaign. The first consisted of Barack Obama and Michelle Obama, along with the Chicago insiders and family friends such as Valerie Jarrett, Marty Nesbit, and Eric Whitaker. The second part of the Obama team consisted of the paid political operatives such as David Axelrod, David Plouffe, Robert Gibbs, Peter Rouse, and firms such as Blue State Digital and the multimillion dollar organization called GMMB. This second part of the team was so big that there had to be a division of labor between the capitalist enterprise of Axelrod (AKP&D Message and Media, a political consulting firm) and the giant pubic relations operations of Jim Margolis (GMMB).

It is the third part of the Obama campaign that I am seeking to highlight. The third part consisted of the millions of volunteers who were mobilized in the Primary campaign to nominate Obama as the candidate for the Democratic Party. Political education and political literacy was a prerequisite for many of the volunteers, so that they could dispel myths and disinformation about the US society. It is this third part that I call the grassroots organization of the Obama forces. The Obama campaign for the nomination of the Democratic Party mobilized millions of citizens who had not previously been engaged in political campaigns.

Marshall Ganz, one of the tutors at Camp Obama, had learnt his lessons on community and grassroots organizing from the SNCC, and had gone on to write a doctoral thesis on grassroots organizing for Harvard University.[7] Ganz had participated in the recursive process of building a local grassroots organization within a local community that could have an impact at the levels of state, region, and nation.

In this chapter, our analysis will focus on that branch of capital called the Democratic Party, and its evolution to the Clinton period. Hillary and Bill Clinton had become leaders in the Democratic Party in the early 1990s, and through the moguls of finance, reinforced the ideals of neo-liberalism and militarism. Would the Obama effort to gain the presidency of the United States belong to the traditions of limousine liberals and technology geeks, or to a tradition that recognized the need for prolonged popular struggle? This was one of the challenges of bringing something new to the arena of electoral politics while building a movement that was stronger than the machinery of any mainstream political party.

Obama launched his campaign as an outsider to the party machine. He started the campaign with three principles: campaign with respect; build it from the bottom up; and finally, no drama. It was the bottom-up approach of self-organization and self-mobilization that defeated the old Democratic Party machinery. James Boggs had outlined the unintended consequences of the struggles for rights in the United States. He noted, "Reforms and revolutions are created by the illogical actions of people. Very few logical people ever make reforms and none make revolutions. Rights are what you make and what you take."[8]

Obama was taking the rights that had been snatched from millions after the 1877 compromise. Taking these rights required twenty-first century mobilization while opening up new questions for democracy and radical change.

Below, I chart the nature of the party machine and the importance of the Obama victory over this machinery, whose task was to undermine the democratic participation of voters.

REVOLUTIONS BY ORDINARY PEOPLE – THE MISSISSIPPI FREEDOM DEMOCRATIC PARTY

The story of the historic challenge of the MFDP in 1964 is now legend. Yet it is necessary to retell the story of poor working-class forces that had been organized to fight for their rights in the Deep South. Fannie Lou Hamer was one of the hundreds of black women who had been sterilized without her knowledge or consent. She had been a timekeeper on a Mississippi plantation for 18 years before becoming an activist in the struggle for freedom. Fannie Lou Hamer, Rosa Parks, and Ella Baker represented a new cadre of women who challenged gendered stereotypes. Trained by SNCC as a grassroots organizer; Hamer had been involved in the challenges to politicians such as James Eastland, and had emerged as a spokesperson for the MFDP at Atlantic City in 1964. James Eastland was the kind of Southern Democrat who had dominated the Democratic Party between 1877 and 1960. Lyndon Johnson (D) from Texas had been selected by John F. Kennedy at the Los Angeles Convention as running mate in 1960 so that Johnson could rally the Southern segregationists to the Kennedy campaign.

In 1963 John F. Kennedy was dead, cut down by bullets from assassins.[9] Kennedy had been pushed by the street force of the Freedom Riders to consider seriously the need for civil rights. Global anti-communism preached from Washington was compromised by pictures of police dogs harassing school children. This was the political and revolutionary climate that produced the boldness and self-confidence of Fannie Lou Hamer and sharecroppers who wanted full citizenship. The MFDP had been organized as a challenge to senators such as James Eastland (head of the Senate Judiciary Committee). When Ms Hamer began her testimony before the 1964 Convention, President Lyndon Johnson personally intervened to divert attention from the legitimate demands for democratic representation.

Johnson had been monitoring the Convention from his office in the White House. When Ms Hamer was about to make the case for the rights of blacks in the South, Johnson immediately called an impromptu press conference in order to silence her. As a gesture to silence the civil rights movement and to divert attention from the struggle for representation, the Democratic Party leaders shuffled, procrastinated, and intervened to offer the MFPD two seats at the Convention. This compromise would have enabled the racist delegation from Mississippi to maintain their positions in the party while appeasing two delegates from the MFPD. As a matter of principle, the MFPD rejected the two seats.

For Johnson, who had become president in 1963 after the assassination of John F. Kennedy, party unity and winning elections were far more important than the rights of the Fannie Lou Hamer and millions of poor black people in the United States. Unlike the mainstream analysis, which downgraded this challenge by the MFPD, Kwame Ture (also known as Stokely Carmichael) dealt with this struggle as a component of a larger revolutionary struggle.[10]

Carmichael recounts his experiences with the freedom protests, as well as efforts to challenge segregation in many parts of the south. A key theme running through these struggles was the autonomy of youth.

OBAMA'S LEARNING FROM THE ELLA BAKER PRINCIPLES

Many of the tactics and strategies of the MFDP struggles were to reappear in the campaign of the Obama organization in the effort to transform the politics of American society. The Mississippi Freedom Summer of 1964 (a campaign to register as many African American voters as possible) had been a grassroots campaign in one state that had reverberations all over the South and at the national level in Washington D.C. Here were two fractal processes at work: the similarity of local campaigns and a recursive process that percolated to the top of politics. The Obama campaign was benefiting from a tradition of leadership and organization that had been honed from the anti-slavery struggles and refined by grassroots leaders such as Harriet Tubman, who had laid down the principles for resistance and survival against the Ku Klux Klan, and Jim Crow. Barack Obama had been a student of the tactics of Ella Baker while in a study group in Chicago, and understood the interconnections between leadership, power, and autonomy for the local community.

Leadership, power, and autonomy within the period of the digital revolution were far more challenging concepts as the values of militarism and deformed masculinity had compromised the understanding of power. Moreover, the deployment of military power by Donald Rumsfeld and the Pentagon required a more focused understanding of people, power, and community in the twenty-first century. Conservative forces had organized new movements such as the Promise Keepers (an international conservative Christian organization for men) and the anti-tax, racist Tea Party protests. Populist racism of the Benjamin Tillman genre was seeking to make a comeback after Barack Obama emerged on the scene, but the vestiges of the hip hop movement constrained many white youths from embracing the open chauvinism and xenophobia of the Tea Party movement.

Through the hip hop revolution, the songs of fighting the power had connected civil rights activists to the songs of defiance of those resisting the prison industrial complex. A revolutionary consciousness from Toussaint L'Ouverture to Tupac Shakur transcended boundaries to link the anti-racist struggles to revolutionary struggles.[11] Just as in the song "Revolution" the lyrics of Bob Marley had proclaimed that "it takes a revolution to make a solution," the power of black American music had taken its place in the cultural revolution that broke down the exclusionary barriers of Jim Crow. Jazz musicians such as John Coltrane and Miles Davis pushed music to new heights so that capitalists could not keep down or exclude this powerful creative force. The Obama campaign recognized the power of this creative force, and throughout the 2008 campaign called the movement a fusion of classical music and jazz.

The songs and music of this period survived and inspired a new genre which was to be called hip hop. Songs of freedom and freedom dreams of the twenty-first century drew heavily from civil rights, and Tupac Shakur and Kanye West were just two examples of hip hoppers whose parents were involved in the civil rights revolution. Their memory and understanding complemented the in-depth record of the processes of self-empowerment of the most oppressed. Barbara Ransby's rendition of the centrality of Ella Baker to the tactics of self-mobilization and self-organization buttressed the alternative narrative of the civil rights struggle, which was different from those writing on social capital and public choice.[12] It was the radical democratic vision of women such as Ella Baker and Fannie Lou Hamer that reinforced revolutionary organizational techniques. Without being schematic, it is important to sum up the key points of revolutionary organization that were inherited from the previous generations of resistance. Most important was the importance of bottom-up organization. Bottom-up self-organization required political literacy among grassroots forces. Second, grassroots organizers had to be knowledgeable about the local and global conditions. Third, these grassroots forces had to be self-reliant and self-confident.

In a racist society, radical and revolutionary forces had to be anti-racist, anti-sexist, anti-homophobic, and tolerant of the rights of others. Religious tolerance was a very high principle. This meant that the militant atheism of some on the left had to be respectful of religious views. A democratic spirit which was anti-authoritarian and anti-militaristic was also essential in this new revolutionary organization. It was not by accident that Ella Baker saw grassroots women as potent forces in the new self-organized community units. SNCC had followed the policy of going to people where they were located, whether in churches, mosques, temples, or on the corner. Radical grassroots organizers had to have organic links with their communities.

The women of the Ella Baker and Fannie Lou Hamer period underlined the reality that civil rights struggle could not be separated from anti-sexist struggle, and countered the great male narrative that has built the civil rights struggle solely around the idea of a leader such as Martin Luther King, Jr. Teaching and learning were reciprocal relations where "student" and "teacher" roles are not fixed. Everyone's experience contributed to shaping the agenda.

The training of volunteers for the Obama primary campaign followed the traditions of the freedom schools, and imparted the radical democratic vision of the anti-racist and anti-sexist leadership from the grassroots. From Team Obama and from the public-motivating website, MyBo, it became clear early that in the "David and Goliath" contest between Barack Obama and Hillary Clinton, the identification of grassroots leaders would be the key to counter the vast financial lead that had been built up by the Clintons. From Obama's experience as a community organizer, the lessons of the 1960s, and the experiences of the grassroots campaigns across the country, the Obama campaign distilled a number of ideas about leaders.

The first task was to identify, recruit, and develop leadership. Second was the challenge to develop community around that leadership. Third was to build resources from within the community.

Thus, however poor the community was, it was the task of the community to empower itself.

In the Obama camp's training for activists, three principles were stressed: the importance of leadership, community, and power from the grassroots.[13] With the tools of the information communication technologies that could reach millions more in a shorter time, this new grassroots flame changed the political geography of the United States. The interdependence between technology, new media, and field organizing of the old type reaped dividends for the new movement of "hope" and "change." New media forms challenged the chokehold of the old media, which had been compromised by its financial connections to the checkbook politics of the past.

At an organizing conference at Shaw University in North Carolina in 1960, Ella Baker had called on youth to draw on their own strengths and to form their own organizations. Baker spurned the kind of "charismatic" and media-driven individuals who were not involved in the communities where people lived. This identification and deployment of grassroots "power" had inspired the formation of the SNCC, and it was the same kind of leadership building that had brought Fannie Lou Hamer to national prominence. SNCC was multiracial, and combined the energy of grassroots activists from the South with committed and optimistic youth from the North. Robert Moses spelt out the ways in which grassroots organizers such as Fannie Lou Hamer could find their voices:

> Small meetings and workshops became the space within the black community where people could stand up and speak, or in groups outline their concerns. In these sessions people were feeling themselves out, learning how to use words to articulate what they wanted and what they needed. In these meetings, they were taking the first step towards gaining control over their lives, and the decision making that affected their lives, by making demands on themselves.[14]

Learning how to use words to articulate what they wanted was the same principle of self-empowerment that was utilized with great success for the volunteers who were trained at Camp Obama. Marshall Ganz fell back on these traditions, and this could be seen at work throughout the campaign. Michelle Obama adopted this storytelling when she related the story of her father at the Democratic National Convention in Denver. Optimistic and tech-savvy youth grounded with community formations and leaders from all walks of life. The power of words and the new technology meant that the Obama campaign produced more than 1,100 YouTube videos. By the end of the Primary season, these videos had been viewed 53.4 million times.

In the YouTube training communication that was circulated widely to Obama volunteers and paid organizers across the country, the Obama team encouraged volunteers to tell their story in order to motivate other volunteers and activists. Just as Obama told his story in *Dreams from my Father*, each volunteer was encouraged to tell their story so that the power of their narrative could inspire others. A grassroots person with a questionable background and history of anti-social behavior could not lead others. Thus the very act of telling stories acted as one way to attract social forces who wanted change. It was also a basis for community intelligence. Would this story prevail once the team Obama won the election? This continues to be the challenge for radical activists who supported the Obama campaign.

During the struggles of the 1960s, meetings in Mississippi had been conducted so that sharecroppers, farmers, and ordinary working people could participate, empowering them in the process. In order for SNCC to engage in this process of unleashing self-empowerment and self-organization, there had to be an organizational framework to respond to the outpouring of social energy that came rushing forth to defeat Jim Crow. It was this fusion of an organization with the flexibility and capability to engage ordinary people that the Obama team learnt.

Just as in the civil rights movement, this mix of organization with leadership linked to self-mobilization and self-empowerment allowed "ordinary people to do extraordinary things." Thus, the Obama campaign affected ideas about radical political organizing for the twenty-first century.

The extraordinary achievement in the 2008 election cycle was the defeat of an entrenched political machine. According to Jeremy Bird of the Obama campaign, the organization was akin to classical music coming together with jazz. The improvisation of jazz came from creativity, skill, and self-organization, but a certain level of structure and organization was needed. For the music to explode, the jazz improvisation had to take center stage and to assume its own recursive path. It was this new form of organizing that will be the central analysis of twenty-first century politics.

The improvisation and spontaneity of grassroots networking was unleashed with even greater force to build a ground operation that changed the game of US politics and propelled Barack Obama to the presidency of the United States. This was the first time ever that a person who was not (initially) a direct beneficiary of the bigger capitalists was able to mobilize millions of grassroots supporters to finance a major campaign of a dominant political party. Organizing and leadership development within the Obama campaign had brought about a phenomenon where 13.5 million citizens contributed to the campaign, 4,000 activists (mostly young people) were trained full-time in organizing, and thousands of local leadership teams took responsibility for achieving objectives in their communities.

Songs of jazz and the blues from the civil rights period were being sung again with gusto as Sweet Honey and the Rock sang, "We who believe in freedom cannot rest till freedom comes." Various versions of "Wake up everybody" (especially the version by Harold Melvin and the Blue Notes) became the rallying song for this campaign, as the message of "hope" coupled with the enthusiasm of motivated citizens had created a new dynamic. When hip hop artist will.i.am produced the music video "Yes we can" featuring well-known actors and musicians singing and rapping to an Obama speech, there were over 12.7 million viewings of it on YouTube.

BEYOND VANGUARDISM

Prior to this dynamic, the possibility of a progressive grassroots form of presidential engagement had become more and more remote. A culture of corruption in American politics had dictated that candidates in major elections needed large amounts of money. Politics was driven by money. Big money, as a manifestation of oligopolistic capitalism, gave rise to money men, solicitors, money bundlers, and high-end lobbyists. Elections in the United States became "the hostage of money." As Jeffrey Birnbaum puts it, "The country's first primary is not held in New Hampshire, but on K Street in Washington [the lobbyists' main drag], on Wall Street in New York, and on Michigan Avenue in Chicago."[15]

Kevin Phillips had outlined how the elementary democratic form of society had been corrupted by this concentration and centralization of wealth.[16] Politics in the United States was therefore likened to the vanguardism of the rich, where wealth had corrupted democracy. Elections became another branch of capitalism, providing opportunities for those with huge sums to lobby and strengthen their faction of the processes of accumulation and profiteering.

Vanguardism on the left and on the right had proscribed the unleashing of grassroots power to the center of politics. William

Domhoff has asserted that the Democratic Party had in the past acted like a vanguard party.[17] In his analysis, the party elite of the Democrats made decisions on behalf of the base with a coterie of bankers, developers, and ward bosses. It was this elite around the Clintons that sought to dictate the decision-making process of the Democratic Party elections in 2008. The Clintons saw themselves as the advanced section of the democratic machine.

Vladimir Lenin wrote about a vanguard in the communist movement, where the most advanced elements of the working class along with the revolutionary intelligentsia led the revolution.[18] Throughout the twentieth century, Marxist-Leninist parties had attempted to impose this concept of vanguardism on the movements for revolutionary change. Beginning with the Bolshevik Party under Stalin, the party gradually replaced the people and the vanguard replaced the party.

In principle, the two dominant parties in the United States (the Democrats and the Republicans) operated in many ways that were similar to top-down Marxist parties. The control of the party by top capitalists had led Domhoff to conclude that "the power elite involves itself in the candidate selection process through the simple, direct, and often very unsubtle means of large campaign donations that far outweigh what other classes and groups can muster."[19] Obama's grassroots movement swept aside the old party machinery of the Democratic Party which had been built up since the time of Franklin Delano Roosevelt (FDR) in the 1930s.

The engagement of millions of grassroots contributors in Obama's primary campaign made a tremendous difference both in the competitiveness of the Primary season and in the general elections in November 2008.

THE CONSERVATIVE COUNTER-OFFENSIVE IN THE UNITED STATES BEFORE THE RISE OF THE OBAMA PHENOMENON

In the introduction, I highlighted the ways in which the US government moved decisively to infiltrate, disrupt, marginalize, subvert groups, and if necessary assassinate those who were militantly against racism. The transformation of traditional non-profit organizations in the era of neo-liberalism was taken one step further down the road of counter-revolution when the grassroots conservatism and the machinations of the "radical right" under George W. Bush worked hard to mobilize the poor against their own interests.[20]

This devaluation of the struggles of grassroots and oppressed peoples had been engineered by the intervention of the super-rich and their tax shelters called "foundations," which sought to direct an understanding of the civil rights struggle into the intellectual corridors of free market ideas and rational choice politics.

While it is generally agreed that the forces of the civil rights and peace movements shaped the politics of society at a critical turning point for society, mainstream writers have sought to develop a monopoly on the research and writings on this civil rights revolution, and in many ways have sought to marginalize the voices and words of those who were footsoldiers of the civil rights struggle. The major studies from Ivy League universities pay inordinate attention to the lessons of the civil rights period, but with the objective of silencing the power of ideas and organizing from below.

American rulers were sufficiently jolted by the far-reaching implications of grassroots mobilization to produce a steady stream of rational choice political scientists, diversity counselors, and social work specialists who now seek to be authorities on the civil rights movement.

However much the foundations and their benefactors sought to monopolize the thinking of what grassroots work should be, the radical traditions of the anti-capitalist forces persisted so that universities and the well financed non-profit sector did not have the final word on grassroots organizing. It was in the environmental justice movement that there were new grassroots initiatives, defying the traditional forms of organizing. This is a new process in so far as many of forms of grassroots organizing that were refined within the context of the civil rights revolution have now been co-opted by a new international front for capital in the multi-billion-dollar industry called the "NGO sector." In the past, the grassroots organizers had challenged hierarchies and top-down politics. However, during the era of neo-liberalism, there were new "professionals" with the right kind of training in grant-writing and public administration who were acting as "service providers for the poor."[21]

As one aspect of counter-revolution, the stamp of communism had been bestowed on civil rights workers. Ronald Reagan had distinguished himself in the state of California during the 1960s as a rabid anti-communist. Conservative foundations and billionaires had deployed intellectuals to study the grassroots organizing of SNCC and the Black Power movement to adopt these tactics on behalf of the rich. One group that emerged in this manner was the militant anti-abortion forces. A reactionary revivalism dominated the Reagan era to the point where "wealth, money-culture ethics and corruption went beyond the venality of government and politicians, to weigh parallel distortions in ideas, policy making and fashion."[22]

The nomenclature of Reagan Democrats emerged within the politics of the United States to identify those elements of the white working class who betrayed their class interests to join with the rabid conservatism of the Reagan presidency. Reagan had ingratiated himself with the most conservative sections of the military industrial complex and the Southern elements that were being encouraged to flee the Democratic Party. Reagan's trip to Mississippi was not only symbolic. It was sending a message to Southern politicians that the Federal government under Reagan would not interfere when the local officials violated the Voting Rights Act of 1965. "States' rights" in the United States remains a coded message to support segregation and overt institutional racism. With the media as a tool in the hands of the reactionary revivalism under Reagan, the distortion of grassroots politics was most evident when the very concept of revolution was turned on its head to describe the Reagan period as "the Reagan revolution." Reagan took militarism further with a promise to dominate the Earth from space through a strategic defense initiative. The transformation of the Republican Party under Reagan began with a massive attack on the trade union movement and the working class in general. One of the first actions of the Reagan administration was to shackle and chain workers of the Professional Air Traffic Controllers Organization (PATCO) who were involved in an industrial dispute with the government. Reagan's mass dismissal of PATCO members – and their blacklisting from further federal employment – was the biggest, most dramatic act of union-busting in twentieth-century America.

Yet through ideological coercion, millions of workers supported Reagan and the Republican Party, and became known as Reagan Democrats. What is less well known about this period is the psychological scars that were visited on society by the tremendous investment in the ideas of greed, individualism, and imperial machinations. While the civil rights period had sought to interrogate the traditions of sexualized violence, genocide, and plunder, the Reagan years led to a glorification of warfare. Towards the end of the Reagan years, one group of Democratic leaders formed the Democratic Leadership Council (DLC) in an explicit effort to move the Democratic Party from its social democratic moorings, which had been established under the New Deal policies of FDR and the Great Society (anti-poverty) programs of Lyndon Johnson. Reagan and the conservative polices from 1980–2007 continue to be central to an understanding of US society because the ideas and tactics of Reagan assisted the transformation of the two principal political parties in the United States.

The dominant wing of US capitalism had calculated that a militaristic superpower status of the United States was preferable to a form of collaborative imperialism that had been developing with the Trilateral Commission under President Jimmy Carter. Three branches of capital favored this approach: the financial services industry, the oil and gas industry, and armaments manufacturers. Other sectors such as Big Pharma and the agribusiness transnationals were not far behind these three.

Bill Clinton and the DLC supported the armaments sector and the big financiers, and at the same time subsidized massive investment in the technology sector. Robert Rubin, treasury secretary under Bill Clinton, was the glue for the oligopolistic capitalists and militarists. There was a loose alliance between the new tech entrepreneurs and the military industrial complex. The transformation of the Democratic Party to the neo-liberal side of society had been swift in the period after the attempts by Jesse Jackson to become the Party's presidential candidate.

THE ATTEMPTED INTERVENTION OF JESSE JACKSON

In the euphoria of Harold Washington's victory as mayor of Chicago in 1983, Rev. Jesse Jackson entered the race as a candidate for the Democratic Party in 1984. His candidacy elicited widespread support from grassroots communities and the progressive alliance among labor, environmentalists, the peace movements, the women's movement, and the civil rights forces was dubbed the "rainbow coalition."[23]

Such was the enthusiasm that the Jackson campaign won a number of primaries and registered more than 2 million new voters in the 1984 primary season. A similar contest in 1988 created fright at the top leadership of the Democratic Party after Jackson received more that 7 million votes. Earlier in 1982, the party had created the category of superdelegate to avoid the emergence of non-establishment candidates such as Jesse Jackson. The campaign of Jesse Jackson had brought back the social forces from the peace and civil rights movement that had deserted the Democratic Party after 1968.

After the challenges of the MFDP in 1964 and the confrontations of Chicago in 1968, the Democratic Party had established a commission to democratize the selection of the presidential candidate. The commission headed by Senator McGovern brought new rules to ensure that all delegate selection procedures were required to be open, and party leaders could no longer hand-pick the convention delegates in secret. The commission recommended that delegates be represented by the proportion of their population in each state. In an effort to broaden participation by women, youth, and peoples of color, the commission mandated quotas for proportional black, women, and youth delegate representation.[24]

This was a major effort to bring the party into the twentieth century and to change the backroom politics that had led to the selection of Woodrow Wilson, Franklin Delano Roosevelt, and John F. Kennedy. After the Jesse Jackson explosion in 1984 and 1988, the pent-up outpouring of progressive grassroots participation had led to the establishment of a system of superdelegates to choose the presidential candidate for the Democratic Party.

Superdelegates were the ultimate insiders of the Democratic Party machine, and their role was supposed to be a safety valve to ensure that the Democratic Party did not select another losing candidate such as George McGovern in 1972.[25]

After the reforms of 1972, George McGovern had lost the election, and the party saw its business as winning elections, not in ensuring progressive grassroots activism and mobilization. Voter registration drives at elections were good enough for democracy. For the chroniclers of the nexus of wealth, power, and politics, the Jesse Jackson campaigns had added nuisance value and color to the party but were not to be taken seriously.

Robert Rubin from the banking sector, David Geffen from the entertainment sector, and hundreds of new millionaires from the technological and telecommunications industries had become active in the Democratic Party under Bill Clinton. These powerful rich elements joined the regional capitalists who had grown rich under Lyndon Johnson and were at the top of the party, along with figures such as Chris Dodd, John Kerry, Edward Kennedy, Nancy Pelosi, and Jay Rockefeller.

In the middle of the party were the new forces that had become empowered through the knowledge economy. These were the phalanx of political active citizens who were employed in education, telecommunications, information technology, research, and in the professions from law to psychiatry. Besides these forces in the middle were the political representatives who were subordinated to the big money and big political leaders at the top. Political representatives in Congress were dependent on the linkages between the professional consultants and the big-money forces at the helm of the party.

According to the Pew Research Trust in 2008, the average cost of contesting a seat in the US Congress was US$1.1 million.[26] Money and politics reinforced neo-liberalism in the United States. It was necessary to dig into the pool of past civil rights activists to give legitimacy to this new direction.

Vernon Jordan and Ronald Brown (as prominent black leaders) have written their accounts of their role in the party. They were brought into the top echelons of the reorganized Democratic Party to ensure that it remained legitimate in the eyes of the urban poor. Jordan, a former director of the Urban League, had received tutelage from Robert Straus, who was for four decades one of the top power brokers in US politics. Brown had served as an aide to Edward Kennedy and became the chairperson of the Democratic National Committee after the Jackson challenge. Brown was a tireless fundraiser for Bill Clinton. When Clinton became president in 1992, Brown was named commerce secretary. It was during his second term that Bill Clinton used the party and the machinery to serve the interests of the top elements of the US capitalist system so that the internal balance of power within the party marginalized the McGovern and anti-militarist forces.

The DLC had completed the transformation of the party into an instrument for the new rich. The chosen face card in the 2008 election, Hillary Clinton, wanted to cash in on the resentment of the working peoples against the policies of George W. Bush with an updated populism. It was the closeness of the grassroots challenge of the Obama message of hope that led to real consternation at the higher levels of the party. In order to grasp the significance of the Obama victory, it is necessary to recount the nature of machine politics in the Democratic Party and the class warfare that has always been waged against working people.

THE DEMOCRATIC PARTY AND THE HIERARCHY OF POWER

The trend towards the marginalization of anti-racist grassroots forces was one component of a view that, to win elections, the Democratic Party had to win back the Reagan Democrats. Winning Reagan Democrats and financial deregulation had been the hallmark of the Bill Clinton period. Welfare reform completed the canvas of the Clinton administration supporting legislation against the poor and vulnerable. However, this pro-capitalist activism of the Democratic Party was not new. What was new were the unprecedented levels of inequality in American society.

During the 20-year period of the Reagan revolution and neo-liberalism, the super-rich increased their share of the national wealth of the United States. By 2005 the top 1 percent of the population had taken in over 21 percent of the gross income. In 1986, this 1 percent had only taken in 11.3 per cent of the gross income.[27] Paul Krugman has brought attention to the "great wealth transfer" in society, where the higher a citizen goes up the income scale, the greater the rate of capital accumulation.[28] Emmanuel Saez from the University of Berkeley has traced the level of income disparity, and showed that the present concentration of wealth has reached levels not seen since 1928.[29]

During the 2008 election season, the Democratic Party lambasted the Republican Party as the party of the rich and powerful. But in the United States, the operation of politics for the economic gain of a few is as old as the Republic. The form of politics to serve the rich was one component of the counter-revolution after the seizure of power from the British colonialists. The basic revolutionary principle of the American Revolution of 1776 was that "people could and should think for themselves and should and could accept responsibility for making social, economic and political decisions." At that time (before the Haitian Revolution of 1791) the American Revolution was the most thorough revolution of its time in so far as that this nation was founded by a great revolution which inaugurated an age when "it gave men and women a new concept of themselves as self-governing human beings, i.e. as citizens rather than subjects."[30]

The challenge then was to ensure that the concept of citizenship applied to all, regardless of sex or race. Racism trumped revolution, so that from the birth of the Republic the revolutionary concept of self-governing citizenship had been undermined by racism. This racism which was always a component of the capitalist relations of society raised its head fiercely after the Haitian Revolution, and the concept of the African as a sub-human (or three-fifths of a human) being became entrenched in the counter-revolution and the organization of Party politics. The new leaders after the revolution in 1776 used state power to seize the assets of the fleeing colonial overlords. These assets were shared between the victorious revolutionaries, who maintained a system of bonded labor-slavery.

Thomas Jefferson (one of the chief ideologues of the principles of freedom and the American Revolution of 1776) founded the Democratic Party in 1792 as a congressional caucus to fight for the Bill of Rights and against the elitist Federalist Party. Jefferson wanted to centralize power in the hands of the plantation class at the expense of the rising industrial classes in the North. He became the first leader of this Democratic Party to be elected president of the United States in 1800. At that time, the name of the party was Democratic Republican. With the tabulation of the enslaved Africans as three-fifths of a person for electoral purposes, the Democratic Party used the government to subsidize the planters.

Aside from Thomas Jefferson and Andrew Jackson, the first leaders of the republic were also militarists and expansionists. James Monroe, who was elected as president in 1816, is now associated with the Monroe Doctrine, which carved out the Western hemisphere as an American sphere of influence.

Jackson was associated with the infamous Indian Removal Act. This was the official destruction of the lives of the First Nation peoples in the areas east of the Mississippi River. He was also branded as a "war hero" because of his military operations against the Seminole people who were defending their sovereignty.

During the second half of the nineteenth century, the Republican Party represented the rising industrial capitalist class, which dominated the railroad, banking, and manufacturing sectors of the economy. Abraham Lincoln became the first president from this party, and although the humble origins of Lincoln are stressed by historians, the Republican section was the party of the super-rich and was unapologetic in its defense of Anglo-Saxon values. Republicans had supported the gradual abolition of slavery because bonded labor held back the spread of industrial capital in the United States.

In Chapter 3, we outlined how although objectively the Republicans should have supported emancipation, it was the subjective force of the deep will for freedom from the oppressed blacks that forced the resolution of the Civil War. The shallow commitment of the Republican Party was revealed in 1877 when it abandoned the Reconstruction project and turned a blind eye to the terrorist campaigns of the Ku Klux Klan and extreme racist elements. The Republican Party had compromised on Reconstruction, and it was a gentlemen's agreement of US politics that the Democratic Party would be the organization of the extreme segregationists. This reality influenced millions of African Americans to support the

Republican Party up to the time of the election of Franklin Delano Roosevelt in 1932.

While the Democratic Party in the South was controlled by planters, in the Northern cities, it became the political organization of new immigrants seeking to integrate, especially Irish, Italian, and Jewish immigrants, with strong support from the Catholic hierarchy. Although the United States was a secular society with the separation of church and state, religion always played a very strong role in the political struggles in society. Though the Democratic Party was described as a "coalitional, pluralistic party," this pluralism reflected the diversity of the rising social forces that sought political representation. It was very strong in urban areas, and many immigrants found a base for their community within this organization. Woodrow Wilson was elected president on the platform of the Democratic Party, but he was an unashamed racist who did not hide his admiration for white supremacist ideas.

By the start of the twentieth century, the Democratic Party consisted of small businesspeople, professionals, trade unionists, farmers (along with the former slaveholders who now maintained the sharecropping system), bankers, regional capitalists, and those who were kept out of the old Eastern establishment. Yet the same forces that were exploited by the WASP establishment internalized all of the prejudices against blacks, Latinos, Chinese, and other non-white people.

Hence, in the urban areas of the North, immigrants from Europe dominated the party and shared many of the bigoted ideas of the Southern Democrats. Organizationally, the party was based on state and local organizations with strong support from organized labor.[31] The election of Franklin Delano Roosevelt in 1932 brought about a new transformation of the party, balancing the New York commercial bankers in the party along with the agribusiness, farm machinery and southern elements. Urban working-class elements were pacified with the New Deal, and the base of the party became a vehicle to vote in elections. It was corroded with "incentives" and other forms of patronage, bribery, and a contract system linked to gangster-type persons. As early as the 1930s, US political scientists were writing on "The Political Party versus the Political Machine."[32]

In many ways, the machines of the Democratic Party operated like vanguard parties, organized around a party boss or a small autocratic group that commanded enough support to maintain political and administrative control of a city, county, or state. The party boss of a major city such as New York City would be connected to party bosses across the country. It was in New York City that Tammany Hall became the symbol of a disciplined organization that could guarantee the election of a particular candidate and also ensure the passage of legislation through the power of an organization created for political action.[33]

Despite differences between the Democratic and Republican parties, both worked to discourage the emergence of a third party that was strong enough to represent the interests of working people. Together, the leadership of both parties deployed chauvinism and eugenic ideas to divide the electorate. During the twentieth century, anti-communism and militarism were the forces that united the interests of the two parties. Throughout this period, the Democratic Party still maintained that it was the party of the common person.

In 1904, it had instituted a system of primaries to choose candidates, but it was so complex that it continued to favor the party bosses. In Northern cities where blacks could vote, such as Boston, Chicago, Philadelphia, and New York, the party bosses treated blacks with disrespect. Up to 2008, African Americans did not have the kind of freedom to vote and participate that they did in the period 1865–76.[34]

From the victory of Franklin Delano Roosevelt (FDR) in 1932, the Democrats held power continuously until 1968 (except for the eight years of Republican leadership under Dwight Eisenhower from 1952 to 1960). Senator James Eastland (D) from Mississippi served in the US Senate for 36 years and was head of the Senate Judiciary Committee for 25 years. John Stennis and Trent Lott were two other representatives from this state who did not hide their openly racist ideas. Speaking at the 100th birthday of Strom Thurmond in 2002, Lott reminisced that when Thurmond ran for president in 1948, "we voted for him. We're proud of it. And if the rest of the country had followed our lead, we wouldn't have had all these problems over the years, either."[35] Such was the brazenness and boldness of the racism of representatives from Mississippi.

Recent scholarship on the rise of "radical conservatism" in the United States has properly focused on the linkages between the state politics of Mississippi and its influence on national politics. Joseph Crespino's book on Mississippi is only one of the many sources that ask us to go beyond the immediatism of the political moment to grasp the ways in which the resistance to the civil rights movement inspired the resurgence of radical conservatism in the United States.[36]

When faced with the historic struggles for civil rights, the Northern sections of the party wanted to have it both ways. They wanted to maintain their alliance with the Southern political forces like James Eastland while encouraging blacks to wait for carefully guided reforms. Thus, in the midst of the civil rights struggles, liberal foundations from the North disbursed large sums to support voter registration drives. Voter registration was seen to be safe and non-confrontational for the system. Since 1964, large sums were expended by foundations for voter registration drives while the political parties found new and old ways to "dilute the black vote."[37]

LEADERISM, VANGUARDISM, AND THE PARTY BOSS

Party machines were controlled by bosses, who organized "the manipulation of certain incentives to partisan political participation: favoritism based on political criteria in personnel decision, contracting, and administration of laws."[38] It was not essential that the bosses were elected officials. The boss usually emerged from the ethnic group that was in control of the party machinery. Throughout the late nineteenth and early twentieth centuries, Irish immigrants and Irish political bosses mushroomed across the big cities, with the definition of certain jobs being reserved for the Irish, who had become white.

Tribalism flourished as the competition between Irish, Italian, and Jewish immigrants expanded the tapestry of ethnic politics in the United States.[39] Because the Irish immigrants had been very active in the nineteenth century, their role in the political machine has been extensively documented along with the policies of job reservations that accompanied the control of the machine.[40] Numerous books and articles have reproduced the history of the boss system, and it is now an accepted fact of history that the system dominated US politics.[41]

Throughout the late nineteenth and early twentieth centuries, US politics had been dominated by party bosses such as Huey Long (Louisiana), Ed Crump (Mississippi), Theodore Bilbo (Mississippi), Frank Hague (New Jersey), Edward Kelly (Illinois), and James Curley (Massachusetts). Of these bosses, probably the most famous was Edward Joseph Kelly (May 1, 1876–October 20, 1950), who served as the mayor of Chicago from 1933 to 1947.

Another famous party boss within this tradition, Richard J. Daley, inherited the Kelly machine and became the mayor of Chicago, serving or 21 years, from 1955 to 1976. Daley's machine was credited with controlling one of the most well-known systems of patronage in the United States, and it was his machinery that was credited in ensuring the nomination of John F. Kennedy in the democratic contest of 1960.[42]

Although Daley had been immortalized by those who have written on Chicago in 1968, the bosses in the New York political system became national legends. James Farley, who served under the Roosevelt administration, emerged from the New York system after organizing the election campaign of FDR. From this same tradition also emerged the notorious Carmine De Sapio. In 2004, when he passed away at 95, the *New York Times* described him as a "King-maker" and the last of the Tammany Hall bosses.

After the militant strikes of the CIO (Congress of Industrial Organizations), the Federal government turned to organized criminal forces to attack trade unionists in order to "root out communist influences." During the Cold War, organized criminal elements had been integrated into the political machinery of the United States in order to undermine the social aspirations of the trade union and civil rights movements. Support for the state of Israel was as important as anti-communism in determining the spoils of political patronage in the big cities. Before the clashes in the streets of Chicago at the Democratic national Convention in 1968, elements of the gangster section of the capitalist class were aligned to the Democratic Party machine in both Chicago and New York.[43]

Mainstream political scientists and academics who analyzed this penetration of the party by gangsters have minimized the importance and role of the party bosses in reproducing a certain form of conservatism while the Democratic Party represented itself as a party of reform.[44]

TECHNOCRATS, BOSSES, AND POLITICAL PATRONAGE

Hand in glove with these bosses were powerful bureaucrats who awarded government contracts. After the New Deal, the ability of bosses to dispense patronage and contracts increased. The Second World War, urbanization, and the building of expressways and parks, government buildings, military bases, and other facilities strengthened the possibilities for the direction of "incentives." The story of Robert Moses (to be distinguished from Robert P. Moses, the radical leader of SNCC), the master builder of New York, exposed the history of both the chauvinism and hierarchy within the higher political circles, along with the machinations of differing ethnic leaders. Moses was descended from the German Jewish immigrant section of New York. Trained at Yale and Oxford, he internalized the basest prejudices of the WASP and English aristocracy, and used the power of the state and became corrupted by it for 44 years.[45]

From the point of view of reconstruction for the twenty-first century, the career of Moses is instructive about the ways in which power was used to displace hundreds of thousands of poor and black people to make way for the rich to move and have leisure. The processes of suburbanization and urban renewal were to have profound implications for the political parties and for the mode of capitalism after 1945.[46]

Three points are worth noting for the link between urbanization and party politics. First, was the role of the banks and financial institutions in the housing sector, and the links between mortgages, financial instruments, and politics. Second was the deepening of the ideas of ownership and property rights that promoted a certain brand of conservatism in the suburbs. Third was the hollowing out of the inner cities, and the disregard for the lives of African Americans, Latinos, and other peoples of color. It should be added that the crack cocaine epidemic of the 1990s was supposed to complete the decimation of the inner cities in order to prepare for twenty-first-century gentrification.

FROM BOSSES TO POLITICAL CONSULTANTS

After Carmine De Sapio, because of the negative aspects of those charged with criminal offenses from the party machinery, the use of the term "boss" has no longer been in popular usage and has been replaced by the word "consultant." Political consultants became as sophisticated as business consultants in top corporations of the United States. Consultants were paid by candidates to make strategic decisions about communications, media, the allocation of campaign staff, and hundreds of details associated with US election contests. Karl Rove and Dick Morris were the two of the more well-known consultants by the end of the twentieth century. Mention has already been made of their trade association, the AAPC. According to this trade association, political consulting became a multi-billion-dollar industry which services more than 50,000 public elections held in the United States each year. This association lists over 59 tasks, including polling, setting up staff organization for candidates, message, strategy, day-to-day campaign management, message dissemination, issues and opposition research, speech writing, scheduling and advance work, canvassing and voter contact by phone, volunteer coordination, direct mail production and printing, "get out the vote," website creation, and maintenance. Before the economic meltdown of 2007, political campaigning was neck and neck with auto, Big Pharma, and retail advertisement in bringing in revenues for the advertising industry. There was no place for amateurs in this new era of building political machines.[47] It was estimated that five sectors of the economy spent approximately US$8.72 billion lobbying politicians in the ten year period 1998–2008.[48]

Mark Penn was one of the famous consultants of the Clinton machine who symbolized the interconnections to financial houses, public relations and marketing firms, and polling and political campaigns. It was under his guidance that Hillary Clinton was influenced to run a muscular campaign to show that the Democratic Party could be just as tough as the Republicans in the fight against terrorism.

THE CLINTONS INHERIT THE PARTY MACHINERY

The Vietnam War period was another watershed era, when the Democratic Party became divided between the Hubert Humphrey/ Henry "Scoop" Jackson wings of the party, and Eugene McCarthy/ George McGovern branches.[49] Henry "Scoop "Jackson was a supporter of the military industrial complex who formed the Coalition for a Democratic Majority (CDM). Two major conservative trends emerged out of the CDM. The first was the Project for a New American Century (PNAC) and the second was the DLC. After the tumultuous rise of the PNAC and its star leaders such as Donald Rumsfeld and Dick Cheney, the world knows more about the "neocons" and their robust militarism.[50] What is not generally known is that the PNAC was a bipartisan venture, and that many who were rejected as diehard conservatives had been tutored by and worked under Daniel Patrick Moynihan.[51]

The second spin-off from the CDM was the DLC, which had been formed in 1985. "Liberal hawks" in the Democratic Party were motivated by the desire to show that they supported a strong military at home and intervention overseas. Because of the importance of the state of New York and the importance of the Israeli lobby, the other feature of the DLC was its support for the state of Israel. The other work of the DLC was to diminish the influence of the radical grassroots activists who had joined the party in the context of the Rainbow Coalition. In these ways, the DLC shared some of the same worldviews as the PNAC. Jesse Jackson called the DLC the Democratic Leisure Class, because he was very aware that the "centrist" position of the DLC was meant to marginalize the grassroots forces that had been mobilized against Reagan.

Daniel Patrick Moynihan and Pamela Churchill Harriman were among those from the party establishment who mobilized the political resources to move to the right in the aftermath of the Reagan victories. The person who was named chairperson of the DLC was Al From, but he was operating in a context where party heavyweights such as Sam Nunn, Dick Gephardt, Joe Lieberman, and Pamela Harriman were seeking to move the Democratic Party away from the New Deal coalition of workers, farmers, civil rights organizers, and trade unionists.

Though he had been roundly condemned by the civil rights movement, Moynihan ran to become a senator in New York in 1976. His connection to the Democratic Party machine assured him of victory, and he remained a senator from New York until he retired in January 2001. Hillary Clinton inherited his Senate seat in 2001.

Pamela Harriman (daughter-in-law of Winston Churchill), the widow of Averell Harriman, was one of the insiders in the machinery of politics in New York. The Harrimans were part of the railroad and banking group that dominated US society in the late nineteenth century. Mrs. E. H. Harriman, the mother of Averell Harriman, had been one of the most enthusiastic supporters of the eugenics movement, and had donated land for the research station at Cold Spring Harbor.

These were the forces of the DLC that selected Bill Clinton to be the person to revive the Democratic Party after 12 years of rule by Ronald Reagan and George Bush Sr.

The Clintons have now left their own version of the relationship of the DLC and the Democratic Party in their books and memoirs. It is to this record that the reader can go to verify the political orientation of Hillary Clinton. From this history, it would not be a surprise to read Mark Penn characterizing Hillary Clinton in December 2006 as: "We are more Thatcher than anyone else."[52] It was the tough and militaristic character of Margaret Thatcher that was supposed to be sold to US society in the campaign of Hillary Clinton. This Thatcherite side of the Clintons had been obfuscated by the clever technique of Bill Clinton of speaking from the left and the right. This was called the "politics of triangulation."

During the Clinton presidency (1993–2000), the Democratic

Party served the interest of Wall Street. Robert Rubin's ascendancy as treasury secretary strengthened the new rich, and the Goldman Sachs culture of greed and power was promoted as neo-liberalism. Foreign policy initiatives all served the biggest capitalists. Whether it was the Trade Related Intellectual Property Rights agreements for the biotech companies, agricultural subsidies for the agribusiness interests, or the lowering of standards of the Environmental Protection Act, the conservative policies of Bill Clinton eased the road for the brisk neo-conservatism of George W. Bush. This tradition of speaking from the right and left at the same time was also manifest in the Clinton's record on labor and the rights of immigrants. While courting the unions, Clinton pushed through the North American Free Trade Agreement (NAFTA) to support US corporations, and it was under his presidency that casino-type operations gained a new lease of life under treasury secretary Robert Rubin.

In the absence of political bosses, Terry McAuliffe, Dick Morris, James Carville, Mark Penn, and Paul Begala were to emerge as leading consultants in the Democratic Party when Bill Clinton ran for re-election in 1996. Before he fell out with the Clintons and ravaged them in print, Morris was determined by *Time* magazine to be "the most influential private citizen in America." As a political consultant, he did not distinguish between Republicans and Democrats. His consulting firm served inside the United States and outside. Through linkages to the International Republican Institute and the National Democratic Institute, it sold American forms of democracy and consulting overseas.

Consultants in the twenty-first century were very similar to party bosses in the early twentieth century. However, because of the size and complexity of campaigns in the twenty-first century, fundraising was separate from advertising and public relations. It was this division of labor that placed Terry McAuliffe and Mark Penn as two central elements in the Clinton machine, each working to ensure that Hillary Clinton became president. After the untimely death of Ron Brown, Terry McAuliffe became the chief fundraiser for the Clintons. His tireless efforts to raise money and to dominate the machine are now recorded for history in the book *What a Party.*[53] McAuliffe related in this book how, during the 1996 contest, Bill Clinton could sit at his computer and link to most, if not all, the sites of the Democratic machine in the country.

For the peoples of the world, the most striking record of the Clinton administration was the campaign to ensure that the United Nations did not intervene to stop the genocide in Rwanda in 1994. When the fastest genocide was taking place, the Clinton administration lobbied other members of the UN Security Council ensure that the United Nations did not intervene.[54] This was the same president who represented himself as a friend of blacks, and was lovingly labeled as the "first black president." This was before the era of YouTube could deliver statements he made in the most rural communities. Hillary Clinton failed to delve into this episode in her book, *Living History*.[55] It was the same Hillary Clinton who reworked the real story of her visit to Bosnia when she was the first lady in order to present herself as a muscular leader who would be ready to lead the United States from day one as president.

Insofar as Hillary Clinton was not a native-born New Yorker, it was the Democratic Party machine that ensured her victory in the 2000 election for the Senate. When she became a senator for New York, Bill Clinton made a public spectacle of opening an office on the historic 125th Street in Harlem. It was a signal by the Clintons that the black operatives of the New York machine were now part of the Democratic Party. Charles Rangel, Basil Paterson, David Dinkins, and Percy Sutton were four big shots in the New York party who had been kept on the periphery when Di Sapio and Harriman ruled it.

The move of the domicile to New York was to set the stage to be at the center of the machinery of the party. Harold Ickles, Mark Penn, and Terry McAuliffe were the frontline generals of the Clinton machine as it built up the financial resources for the 2008 contest. Lynn Forester (Lady de Rothschild), wife of the European banker Sir Evelyn Robert de Rothschild, was also a fundraiser for the Democratic National Committee. She was a frontline supporter of the Hillary Clinton bid for the presidency. She represented the twenty-first-century version of Pamela Harriman. In his book *What a Party*, McAuliffe has recorded for posterity the linkages between finance capital, hedge fund managers, and the fundraising abilities of the Clintons. McAuliffe had maneuvered to become the chairperson of the Democratic National Committee after 2004 in preparation for Hillary to run for the presidency in 2008.

The collapse of the Clinton machine in 2008 did not take place in a vacuum. It arose out of a new form of grassroots organization for the twenty-first century. In this David versus Goliath contest, the toolkit of the Obama machinery of hope demonstrated how ideas and organization can prevail in a transformed political situation.

CONCLUSION

The transformation of the Democratic Party under the Clintons strengthened its racist roots. Our analysis of the two differing forms of grassroots organization in the United States was to highlight the fact that the activism of the peace movement and the civil rights movement was very different from the "radical conservative" grassroots engineered by the neo-conservatives. Our analysis also brought out the experience of Mississippi racists, and how the ideas of institutional racism and chauvinism found a base in the North. It was the New Deal policies of the Democratic Party that provided the resources for the re-engineering of the United States with the highway system that developed suburbanization. Master builders such as Robert Moses of New York implemented the Mississippi model of societal organization, and this model of racism took root in the form of projects of urban renewal.

Party bosses profited from the contracts to real estate entrepreneurs and a new group of Democrats called "developers." These three forces, the bankers, the developers, and the party bosses, held the machinery of the party together. By the end of the twentieth century, the sophistication of the business of elections required a new cadre for the vanguard. These were called "consultants." These elements served as a bridge between the top political representatives and the biggest capitalists. The interface was through fundraising.

In the process of refining this new area of accumulation, the discipline of political science was compromised. Because the workers for the multi-billion-dollar consultancy business came from the discipline of political science, entire new fields of social science were being developed in line with the division of labor of the consulting arrangements. Conservatism, complacency, and institutional racism marked the tenure of both the academics and the political practitioners. Academics could not escape the culture wars of the conservative onslaught.

However, the optimism and energy of the civil rights movement was still alive in society. This contest came out in the primary campaign between Hillary Clinton and Obama. We now turn to how Obama's message of hope created a dynamic that intervened to challenge the Clinton money machine. We argued that the American Revolution that James Boggs witnessed had been smothered by counter-revolution, but had not disappeared. There were lingering traditions reflecting two broad tendencies. The first was that of grassroots peace and justice organizers who did not cease after small gains were made. This was the experience of Robert P. Moses and those members of the SNCC who are still involved in radical politics and pursuing *Freedom Dreams*.[56] Moses was one positive example of the radical imagination who, up to the present, continues to be involved in the frontline struggle for decent education. A second positive example was the self-organized and self-confident community activist who could step up to empower new forces, especially the youth. These forces were supported by the creativity and inspiration of the cultural artists who predicted that change was coming.

In Chapter 5, we will articulate how the Ubuntu of shared humanity met the Ubuntu of the open source movement. Our analysis will examine how the social networking tools employed by Team Obama made a break with the machine. It is in Chapter 5 that the reader will grasp how Obama succeeded in establishing a new pattern of democratic/election campaign that might form the reference point for democratic politics in the twenty-first century.

5

FRACTAL WISDOM AND OPTIMISM IN THE PRIMARY CAMPAIGN OF 2008

By the time of the primary campaign of 2008, US society had been readied for two possible directions. It was either going to deepen the conservatism and militarism of the counter-revolutionary era or there was going to be change. A mortgage crisis and two wars in Iraq and Afghanistan increased joblessness and the massive concentration of power in the hands of neo-conservative forces. Citizens were in fear and on the defensive in the period of incessant psychological warfare called "the war on terror."

Candidates for the Democratic Party had to choose between the perpetuation of psychological warfare and the hyper-militarism of the conservatives or a new mode of politics where ordinary persons were empowered to become citizens participating in the electoral process and not mere consumers gullible to the projections of pollsters and focus groups.

In one of the longest and costliest contests within the Democratic Party, Obama and his multi-layered team confronted the old party machine. In the process of mobilizing the tools of social networking, the triple O strategy (Online Obama Operation) of Team Obama utilized Web 2.0 technologies to set in motion a twenty-first-century primary campaign. It was a campaign against the party machinery of the Clintons in which the Obama Online Operation created the biggest political upset in history.

This major intervention in the political process was made possible by the unleashing of the creative spirit of a large section of the population. This spirit was energized by the candidate himself and the optimism to confront the "smallness" of US politics.[1] This optimism was communicated in "Yes we can" and the predisposition to expect the best, or at least a favorable outcome. This optimism was grounded in an abiding faith in humans, a religion of love, and the doctrine that this world is the best of all possible worlds.

It was the same optimism that had been communicated by Harriet Tubman and lived out by Obama's mother, "Don't see things as they are right now, kind of imagine what they might be."

David Plouffe, one of the key members of the team, has been using this formulation to analyze the new politics that emerged from the fractal organizational techniques engaged by the Obama campaign in the election. Bottom-up principles of empowerment drew new networks into the political process. These networks in turn broke the vanguardism of the machine and the domination of the bosses/ consultants. One central element of the break was the "virtual mechanism for scaling and supporting community action." The repetition of the building community action across the country involved repeating self-similar patterns of community organizing by the grassroots. Together with the break from the professional consultants and the unleashing of millions of volunteers, these elements mobilized principles of fractal geometry. It is this combination of patience, wisdom, and fractal organization that we examine in this chapter.

CAMPAIGNING AS A HUMAN BEING, NOT A BLACK CANDIDATE

Obama was not the first citizen of African descent to run for the candidacy of the Democratic Party. In 1972 Shirley Chisholm, the congressperson from Brooklyn, had been a candidate for president of the United States, and the first woman of any race to seek the nomination of a political party for that office. Jesse Jackson, Al Sharpton, and Carol Mosley Braun had also competed. But it was the Obama challenge that transformed the party and American politics.

This transformation emanated from a number of factors. First, Obama ran as a human being and not as a black candidate. Second, the new ideas of Ubuntu – shared humanity – inspired a transcendence of the hierarchal idea of whiteness and blackness, firing up the young in the process; and third, the deployment of fractal principles of organizing had a transformative impact on both the volunteers and on the overall organization.

Most importantly, the Obama candidacy was "for real:" that is to say, it sought to win the nomination of the Democratic Party and the presidency of the United States. It was not part of the tradition of "leverage politics" by black candidates to bargain with the top officials of the party for positions and handouts.[2] The Obama campaign was bringing to a close the long tradition of certain blacks running in campaigns in order to gain some breadcrumbs in the Democratic Party.

Electoral politics and the methods of challenging the Right had divided the Left and those who call themselves progressives in the run-up to the 2008 primaries. Within the labor movement, the conservatism of the mainstream American Federation of Labor-Congress of Industrial Organizations (AFL-CIO) had historically lent support to the Clinton machine.

Inside the peace movement, the question of Israel and the issue of Palestine had led to the silencing of large sections over the US war against terror. The environmental justice movement was torn between the Green Party, the candidacy and platform of Cynthia McKinney, and those environmentalists who wanted to stand above politics.

For the women's movement, the candidacy of Hillary Clinton created a major contradiction. Conservative and liberal feminists in the Democratic Party supported Hillary in droves, while radical feminists warned of the dangers of *Sexual Decoys and Imperial Feminists*.[3] Radical black feminists such as Alice Walker and Grace Lee Boggs were clear from the outset that something new was afoot in the form of Obama.

If the labor, peace, environmental, and women's movements were divided, the black liberation movement was split down the center, between those who eschewed "bourgeois" politics and those who calculated that it was not possible to stand above electoral politics in an era of counter-revolution.

Objectively, there were some black spokespersons who opposed Obama on the grounds that he was unelectable. Tavis Smiley led a running opposition to Obama based on umbrage over Obama's lack of participation in his television shows. Mainstream operatives, from Andrew Young, Charles Rangel, and Maxine Waters to Vernon Jordan and Robert L. Johnson, the founder of Black Entertainment Television, pledged early and loudly for the Clintons. There were a few persons such as Maya Angelou who had maintained a long friendship with the Clintons and stuck with them. Some blacks who termed themselves radicals called for support of John Edwards or the creation of a third party. Of the historic black radicals from the civil rights period, it was Imamu Amiri Baraka who was the most forthright in calling for an assessment of the moment and the importance of Obama's connection to the moment.

There were certain sections of the black intelligentsia who were so wrapped up in racial history that they provided fodder for talking heads on the cable shows who wanted to remind younger citizens of the Bradley effect.[4] Martin Kilson of Harvard University stood out among the contributors to the online weekly *Black Commentator* in the ways in which he grasped the historic continuities from the period of the Civil War and the traditions of radical black theology. Henry Louis Gates, another well known black intellectual, had been equivocal about Obama because of his close ties to the Clinton insider Vernon Jordan.

There were black professionals, especially lawyers, who came out early in support of Obama. In the main, however, the black intelligentsia stood aloof during the primary season. There was no such equivocation from the rank and file of the most oppressed sections of the population. The black poor calculated the stakes, followed events closely, and when time came to intervene in South Carolina, they acted decisively and shifted the tone and content of the electoral struggles, sending signals to Latinos and the poor that the progressive grassroots forces could not sit on the sidelines.

Above all, the forces that made the campaign possible were the youth of America. They organized in networks, and turned tools of enjoyment and leisure into tools of education to break the traditions of the "dumbing down" of America. Obama connected with the youth by embracing their knowledge. Very early in the campaign, the team was able to garner the vision of Chris Hughes, one of the founders of the social networking Internet site Facebook. In the tapping of Hughes and an incredible youthful media group, Obama demonstrated that he not only shared young people's aspirations to be full humans in the coming era of technological singularity, but also was a forward thinker, willing to learn and understand the challenges of emerging technologies.

Obama had the capability of making the bond that people felt as he told his stories. It was this emotional relationship building that inspired young people as they surged in the political arena and confounded the consultants who continued to believe that the youth would not vote. A new multi-cultural and multi-national youth culture was emerging and was searching for levers of self-expression. Many found their voices in the Obama campaign of 2007–08.

HOPE AND CHANGE

The Obama campaign was nourished from the beginning by the engagement of a progressive grassroots force which was like a seed waiting for the right conditions for germination and growth. Slogans of "Hope," "Change," "Fired up, ready to go" and "Yes we can" sprung from different sites of the poor and the most oppressed. In recursive processes, they spread across society, inspiring a new generation that had been written off by the political machine.

Hope trumped despair and apathy as thousands of young people were inspired to tap into their potential. Each slogan had a message that came from historic campaigns of women, youth, workers, or the peace movement. "*Si Se puede*" ("Yes we can") had been the slogan of the United Farm Workers. The song by Sam Cooke "A change is gonna come" had ushered in the civil rights movement, and Tupac Shakur had given an urgent message of the need for peace in his song "Changes." Martin Luther King, Jr. had called on youth to recognize the fierce urgency of "Now," and Obama used the same urgency to call for a break with the "culture of fear."

Obama constantly referred to the "fierce urgency of now" in detailing the conjuncture of the 2008 primary and the electoral contest. The specter of another four years of Bush's policies gave the 2008 campaign extraordinary international attention. Hence, while the Hillary Clinton team presented her as the US version of Margaret Thatcher, the Obama campaign called the Iraq war a "dumb war" which should never have been started. From the house-to-house and door-to-door efforts, a stream developed into a mighty river to register the opposition to war and fear-mongering, and to wash away Hillary Clinton's machine.

In his memo to Hillary Clinton, Mark Penn had argued for her taking a masculinist and militaristic line. Right up to the election Penn did not believe that Obama could win. Other memos from inside the Clinton camp urged her to insist on showing her "strength" and "experience."

Mark Penn developed a line of argument that was later picked up by Sarah Palin and the Birthers when he wrote in his now infamous memo, "I cannot imagine America electing a president during a time of war who is not at his center fundamentally American in his thinking and in his values." Penn proposed targeting Obama's "lack of American roots."[5] For Penn and his forces, the multicultural America promised by Obama should have been saved for 2050.

Unlike the divisive top-down operation of Penn, the Obama team operated like an organization grounded in the grassroots template of the civil rights movement. It was an effort to build a bottom-up movement, training leaders who would develop capacity in their own communities and have the energy and motivation to link local action with national purpose. It was a campaign plan based on the principle of "scaling up" to change society. The replication of the training of leadership across the country was also based on another fractal principle, that of self-similarity.

SCALING, SELF-SIMILARITY, AND RECURSION IN THE CAMPAIGN

The grassroots challenge to the Clinton machine presented an effort to make a break with the old top-down party which was a "hostage to money" and professional consultants.[6] This break is central to recursion, one of the five elements of fractal geometry. The simplicity of the break with the old in the process of the Obama campaign was manifest in the fact that the Obama campaign was able to mobilize more local volunteers on the ground in key states earlier than the Clinton campaign. This was especially important for caucus states, where a massive ground operation was necessary.

On the ground, face-to-face mobilization was especially important in smaller states and caucus states. There was a feedback loop between volunteers and the fundraising capabilities so that the more volunteers there were, the more the campaign was able to raise small contributions, the total of which could now be counted in hundreds of millions of dollars. Fundraising facilitated and strengthened the campaign organization so that the ambitious 50-state strategy would have resources.

As the feedback of volunteers, resources, and strengthened organization took root, there was confidence and optimism which fertilized grassroots planning. Bruce Lipton argues that such optimism will be strengthened by fractal wisdom.[7]

Fractal wisdom, which breaks linear and mechanical thinking, is itself grounded in possibilities of spiritual renewal. This renewal is linked to the harmony between humans and humans, and between humans and nature. Fractal wisdom seeks to capture the geometry of nature. In the most basic sense, fractals are defined as small parts that represent the whole while displaying the same level of complexity at any scale. Another definition of fractals is that they are mathematical models that mimic nature.

For example, if you understood the campaign to be like a cauliflower, you would see the fractal concept of self-similarity at work. Once you took the cauliflower apart you would see that the pieces, however small, mirror the structure as a whole. This was the same with the Obama campaign. The structure of the house-to-house formations in one community, say in Iowa and South Carolina, would be replicated county by county across the two states and then replicated state by state to reflect the overall national campaign.

Instead of focusing primarily on "battleground states," the Obama campaign organization had agreed with Howard Dean (chairman of the Democratic National Committee, DNC) that there should be a 50-state strategy, and it campaigned in a state such as Idaho, a caucus state where for generations the Democratic Party had not competed. It was the optimism that enriched the networks that were being formed and inspired the victory. Networks of networks based on cooperation and participatory individuals propelled new action.

Jeremy Bird, the field organizer in South Carolina, repeatedly told the story of the impact of shooting a video of house meetings. These videos were then sent to other communities to motivate volunteers and to give them an idea of what was being done. From the communities the videos were sent to Chicago, and from Chicago to websites of MyBO and My Barack Obama. Grassroots organizing and online technology had converged to make a break with the old pattern of electoral politics. The extensive use of YouTube for a primary campaign was a new lesson for politics.

The other important point was to place the new tools in the hands of local organizers. The web as a new tool for organizing, empowerment, and connecting people was developed in the Obama campaign like no other political campaign in the United States. David Plouffe, Chris Hughes, Marshall Ganz, Jeremy Bird, and other frontline players of the Obama team have written or spoken on their methodology. This was the most fundamental network, the frontline team that fused skilled consultants and professionals with the old tactics of the Mississippi Freedom summer. David Axelrod had emphasized this break with the old when he instructed his ad team, "Forget everything you ever learned about politics. This guy is different. This race is different. And if we do the same old thing, we're going to debase the thing that makes us unique."[8]

UBUNTU MEETS UBUNTU

Obama's story of inclusion, his message of healing, informed by the strategic concept of shared values and shared humanity (Ubuntu), made the campaign unique and created the basis for transformed volunteers who participated in a transformative political process.

After the defeat of the Democratic machine, *Atlantic Monthly* magazine grasped this new politics of inclusion by noting,

> Hillary's campaign had failed to understand that America was in the midst of a national passage from the old-style confrontational politics of the boomer generation – a divisiveness perfected by both the Clinton and Bush administrations – into a new style of Netroots politics, open-sourced and inclusive, multi-racial and multicultural.[9]

The testing ground for this multi-cultural vision had been represented in the Rainbow Coalition of Jesse Jackson and the anti-racist movement. In his speech to the Democratic National Convention in Boston 2004, Obama had declared, "there's not a Black America and a white America, a Latino America and Asian America, there's the United States of America." This message of hope and shared values shaped the methodology of the campaign.

Shared values had provided the context for cooperation, relationship building and trust. It was the same kind of trust and cooperation that characterized the campaign organization of Michelle Obama, Valerie Jarrett, Steve Hildebrand, Chris Hughes, David Axelrod, David Plouffe, and Robert Gibbs. There had to be trust between a frontline team of gays and straight, black and white, women and men, young people and seasoned consultants.

When Obama had announced on YouTube that he was a candidate for the Democratic Party nomination, there were seven other candidates. Of these, the two most well known were Hillary Clinton and former senator John Edwards (North Carolina). Within a few months, the social networking tools deployed by Obama placed him in the top tier of this large field of candidates. The web platforms were used with skill to highlight different aspects of his life story.

At the start of the twenty-first century, new computing power paved the way for a fundamental shift in how content and value was socially and collaboratively co-created through the World Wide Web. Web 2.0 technologies opened the door for the democratization of information so that the Internet could become a collaborative platform where organizations, individuals, corporate entities, or political groups could use the collective power of distributed users to capitalize on data access and network effects with extraordinary consequences for the elaboration of new networks.

Vanguardism and control of information were being broken as the second generation of web development facilitated information sharing and collaboration. It must be stated that the technology had to be rooted in people. One key theme running through this mobilization of technological resources was the truism of Lawrence Lessig; "the people own ideas."[10]

The innovations generated by the Web 2.0 environment challenged the old forms of media and information sharing, as social networking opened the door for new communities. The exponential growth of this technology also led to groups who wanted to ensure that the web was more democratic and that all citizens would have access to software. This free and open source movement based on the free software concept was also called Ubuntu.

The improvement of content and innovation had been engaged by the Howard Dean campaign of 2004 for the Democratic Party presidential nomination, but it was the Ubuntu of shared values in the message of Obama along with the Ubuntu of the open source movement that made the fundamental shift for the politics of the twenty-first century. The Obama campaign was caught between the open source future and the profit-making past, and this was most manifest in the management of the My Barack Obama web platform. In 2004 there had been a group organized around the concept of "netroots" who wanted to *Crash the Gates,* the euphemism for defeating the old party machine.[11] Crashing the gates and creating people-powered politics at the grassroots had to be nested in Ubuntu at the philosophical and software levels. There had to be a coherent organizational framework with a structure that was sensitive to the limits of the old vanguard political boss system. All campaigns in the 2007–08 election cycle had access to the same technological tools that were available to the Obama campaign. Inside the Democratic Party, the PR teams were able to tap into the same media.

The Obama team established Camp Obama to develop the best conditions for using the social networking tools of building communities, to learn the positives and negatives of the Jesse Jackson Rainbow Coalition and the Howard Dean campaign, and to train new volunteers who were coming forward. There was no discrimination in the Camp Obama training environment.

The most comprehensive account of Camp Obama is in lectures on *Distributed Leadership* by Marshall Ganz, which have been replayed on YouTube since the election of Obama. The very title of *Distributed Leadership* in the Obama campaign signaled something new, insofar as this reflected an attitude to political organizing and management. Distributed leadership meant that all volunteers being trained in

Camp Obama were to see themselves as change agents in their own right – as motivators, leaders, and sources of inspiration to others.

The staff at Camp Obama motivated these volunteers to act as trainers in their own communities. Processes of empowerment that gave voice to the volunteers became the basic starting point, and like the Mississippi Freedom Democratic Party (MFDP), everyone was encouraged to speak so that there would be no possibility of trivializing volunteers. The vetting process of volunteers had to be sophisticated enough to weed out agent provocateurs, yet sensitive enough to inspire those with exuberance but lacking in experience.

In the process of tapping into national narratives, a neighbor-to-neighbor tool was developed which gave this vetting process increased legitimacy. Volunteers at Camp Obama had to be focused to understand that volunteering was not a trivial part-time matter but one that required engagement and commitment. Camp Obama required participants to be like a dedicated cadre of a movement without the strict ideological commitment of a vanguard party. What the Camp provided was a context for the building of teams which would be working together over a long time.

Camp Obama drew on the experiences of freedom summers and community organizers from all over the country. The most important point that was stressed was the difference between organizing for services (non-profit and social services work) and organizing for political power. When the call for activists exceeded expectations, the Obama campaign headquarters was able to take Camp Obama on the road to Super Tuesday states: New York, Georgia, Idaho, California, Missouri, Arizona and so on. To staff the seminars, the campaign brought in veterans of community organizations, union organizers, and religious leaders — each of whom was free to tweak the curriculum. The best, most brilliant folks from faith-based organizing, online organizing, community-based organizing, and union organizing all collectively came together to work on Camp Obama.

Marshall Ganz, who had been schooled by Ella Baker and Robert P. Moses in Mississippi 44 years before, had brought his experiences as an organizer for the United Farm Workers and the Robert Kennedy campaign of 1968. He testified that that the first thing the staff did was to organize the volunteers into teams based on Congressional districts, with around eight persons per team.

They were taught to tell their own story instead of salivating over Obama's story. "It is about looking for sources of values."[12] In his lecture in 2009, Ganz identified five elements of creating a new leadership. These were:

- motivation through mastery of the art of narrative
- relationship building, which is about commitments to common interests
- structuring
- strategizing
- producing measurable outcomes.

In this case, the measurable outcome was the defeat of the party machinery of the Clintons.

PROVING GROUND IN SOUTH CAROLINA

The experiences of Anton Gunn and Jill Littlejohn as volunteers for the campaign in South Carolina are good examples of the new approach to tolerance and transformative politics. Driven by the message of Hope, Jill M. Littlejohn emerged in upstate South Carolina as one of the dynamic young leaders of the Obama campaign. As co-chair of the young democrats for Greenville County, she threw her energy into making links all across South Carolina for the Obama primary campaign. Motivated by the Obama campaign, she threw herself into local government politics for the first time.

Anton Gunn became the political director of the Obama campaign in South Carolina, and connected with the Obama head-quarters in Chicago to link the structure of the national campaign to a grassroots movement. *Time Magazine* called Gunn the leader of Obama's "grassroots army" in South Carolina.[13]

In a previous chapter, we identified South Carolina as the site of the most brutal forms of sexism and racism. It was from the bowels of Greenwood, South Carolina that the enthusiasm of one woman brought out the slogan "Fired up, ready to go." Edith Childs (who led the chant for Obama at a rally in South Carolina in 2007) had been an NAACP (National Association for the Advancement of Colored People) organizer in the 1970s and was a local activist in Greenwood. On June 15, 2007, when Obama traveled to Green-wood on a wet day, he was dispirited because of the size of the audience and even more tired by the long journey and the inclem-ent weather. Edith Childs sought to encourage the tired Obama with her chant, "Fired up, ready to go." It was a chant from the grassroots civil rights period.

Here was a recursive process where a grassroots chant and response slogan learnt from the struggles of an earlier era nourished and enriched a national campaign. "Fired up, ready to go" was recorded as a song in Seattle and was one of the more well-known chants of the Obama campaign after that. In the words of Obama, it showed how one voice could change a community, a county, a state, and a nation.

It was in South Carolina that black professional political forces had been most compromised by the Democratic Party machinery. The leader of a black megachurch and a state senator with a consulting firm had been paid a retainer of US$15,000 by the Clinton campaign. In November 2007, more than 60 of the most prominent leaders of the church made a grand appeal for Hillary Clinton and endorsed her to be the nominee for the Democratic Party. This endorsement by the ministers was a recursion of the old pattern of political campaigning which the Obama team was breaking.

It was the job of pastors to deliver their flock, and the Clintons' ad team would bring in the information. The Obama campaign was challenged to rise above this top-down endorsement without directly challenging the pastors. For this, Michelle Obama and Oprah Winfrey joined in a massive rally which sent a message beyond South Carolina.

South Carolina had nursed both the clear signals of slogans of resistance and the subliminal communication from coded messages of more than one hundred years of fighting Jim Crow. Within the United States, members of every community develop codes to speak to each other. University graduates and fraternity and sorority brothers and sisters have codes from their rituals. There are codes for professionals, the street, sports buffs, and most importantly, the grassroots. It was important for the Team Obama campaign to understand the codes, decipher them, and communicate directly and indirectly to possible supporters. Anton Gunn used the codes of the hip hop revolution as he dubbed Barack Obama "the hip hop candidate." This designation was not without its pluses and minuses.

Social networks had been an important strategy for survival within the state of South Carolina. Poor folks had been manipulated by the rich during the nineteenth and twentieth centuries, and political powers used the memory of the confederate flag to stimulate division. The confederate flag, the banner of the slave masters, was and remains a symbol of white supremacy, fear, hate, and the lynch mob. Right up to the twenty-first century, this symbol of segregation and hate was proudly flown over the dome of the state capitol.

Political passions were always very taut because of the depth of the oppression in South Carolina. From Greenwood County in the North West to Beaufort County in the South, the racial memory on both sides meant that communities were tight-knit. Politics required a personal touch, and hence house-to-house meetings meant a lot. To be contacted by someone who was known in the community meant a lot in South Carolina. Jeremy Bird related the impact of the videos of house and community meetings where people were telling their stories. Even though this form of voicing and testifying had been taught at Camp Obama, the visual evidence of black and white communities building the Obama movement in South Carolina had an electric effect on the campaign. Videos of house meetings were sent across the state to motivate other communities, and from South Carolina to Chicago to motivate the national campaign. Both Michelle Obama and Oprah Winfrey added to the energy of South Carolina, and the subliminal message was communicated by Oprah at a massive rally in December 2007 when she asked, "Are you the one?"

Oprah Winfrey (herself a child of James Eastland's Mississippi who had risen to the pinnacle of TV talk show presentation), had noted, referring to Obama, "It's a question the entire nation is asking – is he the one? South Carolina – I do believe he's the one." "He's the one." Celebrity endorsement of political aspirants is as old as politics in the United States, but the endorsement of Oprah carried with it the following of 8 million viewers who watched her television show every day. Her appearance at a rally in a stadium of over 30,000 persons strengthened the support among women. One of the real dangers of her message of deliverance by the chosen one was that, in the past, deliverers had accrued so much power that they became the problem. Whether the negative aspects of leaderism and deliverance would plague Obama had to await the euphoria of the campaign. At that moment in December 2007, the Obama struggle was too dependent on the grassroots for the great leader syndrome to emerge.

There was another feature of this rally which was to become a feature of the mass mobilization. This was the importance of SMS or text messaging. Every person in the stadium was asked to leave a cell phone number so that they could get instant alerts and messages from the campaign. Jeremy Bird recalled the Oprah rally as the turning point in refining the use of text messages to get to supporters.[14]

Expanding the online reach of the campaign by collecting names, e-mail addresses, cell phone numbers, zip codes, and other information to build voter profiles took hold after December 2007. It was in South Carolina that the use of text messaging was refined in order to sift out different messages, so that the Obama headquarters "had the ability to text out to those team members' information about the campaign that we wouldn't text out to other folks."[15] After the rally, Scott Goodstein (the text-messaging specialist of the Obama campaign) sent texts to the numbers he had collected and asked supporters to make phone calls, volunteer in precincts, and vote on January 26, 2008 in South Carolina.

It was during the 2007–08 campaign that iPhones took off. Goodstein had created an iPhone application that could provide supporters with access to the campaign's news and videos. "The application also served as a mapping device to show the location of local campaign offices to new volunteers, which resulted in people showing up at the offices with iPhones in their hands."[16]

SMS communication had become part of political organizing in countries such as Spain and Kenya. Very early in the Obama campaign, a web page "Organizing for America" was set up. On entering that page readers were advised, "Sign up to the right to receive text messages on your phone or text GO to OBAMA (62262)."[17]

This appeal "To join Obama mobile" had come from one of the tools being developed throughout the campaign. With the tech-savvy team and advisers from Silicon Valley, the Obama campaign had the foresight to register a vanity common short code (CSC) that numerically represents the word "Obama" (62262). This code was used during the mobile message alert opt-in process. To get out younger voters, the Obama campaign used the page www. barackobama.com/mobile, which allowed potential supporters to download ringtones and wallpaper, sign up for Twitter updates, and receive text messages about policy and campaign events. Supporters of Obama became connected through various means through which they could receive updates on the campaign and on the policy positions of the Obama campaign.

Improvisation from South Carolina was to develop into a brand-new tool where the cell phone became the basis for information of all types to be transmitted to voters. From the massive rallies in Oregon to the acceptance speech at the Democratic National Convention, the proficiency of using "neighbor-to-neighbor" tools exposed how a tool developed at the micro level of one state or community could be carried forward at the national level.

Vastly expanded voter databases became one of the most

enduring legacies of the 2008 presidential election. (These are the scaling and cascading elements of fractals at work.) During 2007 and 2008, the Obama web operation collected hundreds of millions of new pieces of data on members of the electorate. The "triple O" strategy strengthened the capability for this collection of data.

Geodemographic databases had been developed as a "magic" political technology for over 30 years in the United States. This technology combined software applications in political campaigns with GIS (geographical information systems) technology.[18] Armed with the geodemographic databases beefed up with information from the US Census bureau, political campaigns had been able to develop a wealth of information on citizens. Statistics from these sources along with the nine-digit zip code provided a rich database for the neighbor-to-neighbor tools that were rolled out for the mapping of potential Obama supporters. New data-mining techniques developed by marketing research teams of the commercial world had been deployed by political consultants to map people's opinions, campaign activities, where they voted, responses to campaign messages, and other tidbits of information gleaned from e-mail traffic or phone conversations.

By the time of the election cycle of 2008, the old geodemographic technologies had been amplified by the tools of "reality mining." This is the name given by technology buffs to describe the collection and analysis of machine-sensed environmental data pertaining to human social behavior, with the goal of identifying predictable patterns of behavior. In 2008, the magazine *Technology Review* declared reality mining one of the "10 technologies most likely to change the way we live."[19] While there were plans for how this data on human behavior was being studied to adapt to the changes in the way we live, the Obama campaign was developing variants of this reality mining to develop the most sophisticated mapping of the voter and congressional districts. By 2008, the Obama campaign team did not allow their lack of funds to establish limits to their imagination for what could be done with information about people's cell phone number, e-mail address, and home address including zip code.

It was after that rally in December 2007 that neighbor-to-neighbor tools were refined. The same face-to-face and neighborly culture that had been deployed as a defense mechanism against the lynch mob was being harnessed for personalized campaigning by the Obama team. It was in light of the deployment of the tools refined after December 2007 that Goodstein remarked, "South

Carolina was a defining moment in what we were going to do with text messaging – not just with young voters but with all voters."[20]

From South Carolina there was the new plan, "meet the voters where they're at, and then get them engaged." Every volunteer was seen as a potential community organizer, and the task of the network of Team Obama was to get information to potential organizers so that they could go out and do the work, whether there were paid organizers from the Obama campaign or not. Tech-savvy volunteers were able to break the distinction between the professional and amateur political campaigner.

Jeremy Bird retold the South Carolina story and the massive effort in Maryland where, in Montgomery County, e-mails were able to mobilize 1,200 volunteers and organize an effective campaign with the Potomac primaries. The dynamics of innovation throughout the campaign ensured that national goals were rooted in the capabilities of grassroots efforts and not imposed from the headquarters in Chicago. This was indeed bottom-up politics, and it was clear in grassroots fundraising.

BUILDING A NATIONAL PRESENCE AND BOTTOM-UP FUNDRAISING

In the traditional Democratic Party model of presidential campaigns, the emphasis was on ensuring a massive win in the battleground states on Super Tuesday (February 5, 2008). This strategy of a decisive win on Super Tuesday had brought Bill Clinton his success in 1992. It meant that resources were concentrated in blue states, and states where the follow-on from the primary would win the general elections. When Howard Dean became the chairperson of the DNC in 2004, he decided to develop a multi-million-dollar 50-state strategy to rebuild the party from the ground up.

The 50-state strategy was a new way to be competitive in all parts of the country, so that the party was not only a presidential machine. Obama shared this vision of a 50-state strategy, which was consistent with a speech in 2004 where he said there were no blue or red states. Obama was particularly interested in setting up an organizational structure in the states that held caucuses. The Clinton machine did not pay attention to caucuses because these were intensely people-oriented, and required committed supporters who could turn up. Team Obama had studied the electoral map of the country and the rules for nominating a candidate. It calculated that winning caucuses would be part of the winning strategy, and required ground volunteers. Ground volunteers required money. It was this interface between volunteers and fundraising that distinguished the Obama effort.

For the Clintons, raising money from big donors and funding candidates had taken precedence over nurturing progressive and grassroots organizers. Dean had broken this model, and there was tension between Team Clinton and the shadow DNC after 2005.

Obama's entrance into the race for the presidency halted the feud between the Clinton team and the DNC because, after February 2007, the Clintons found that the Obama Team was a far more credible threat than earlier imagined.

OBAMA'S AMAZING MONEY MACHINE

Obama's message of hope created a dynamic that intervened to challenge the Clinton money machine. Three tools/instruments that governed US politics came together in a recursive manner for the Obama campaign: the message and the medium, the money, and the machinery-infrastructure. The medium of social networking was used to reach a very wide constituency with the message of hope. Hope motivated new forces to donate to the campaign, and the fundraising allowed for the infrastructure to mobilize the ground operations. Most of the major news outlets marveled at the fundraising capabilities of Obama, and thousands of articles were written on this aspect of the campaign. It could not be separated from the message of sharing and hope, along with the infrastructure of change.

By the end of the primary season, there were over 1.5 million people who had donated to the Obama campaign, and nearly half of them had made donations of US$200 or less. Most of these small donors were contacted and kept in touch through the social network mechanisms, especially web-based connections. Martin Kilson termed this phenomenon "the democratization of fundraising."[21]

This democratization was partly true, but the massive outpouring of grassroots support was going on at the same time as big donors were giving to the Obama campaign. Reports to the Federal Electoral Commission showed that more than half of the donors contributed more than US$200.

The figures in Table 5.1 show that in the primary phase, the Obama campaign raised nearly double the amounts raised by the

Table 5.1 Presidential candidates' fundraising activity, January 1, 2007 through August 31, 2008

	Total receipts	$200 or less	%	$201–999	%	$1,000–2,299	%	$2,300 & over	%
Obama	414,207,808	217,166,401	53	74,785,564	18	59,525,828	14	59,728,4431	15
Clinton	216,561,826	52,092,334	31	29,583,684	17	34,245,435	20	53,965,808	32

Source: figures from the Campaign Finance Institute http://www.cfinst.org/pr/prRelease.aspx?ReleaseID=205 9/25/200

Clinton machine. The Obama grassroots organization had become a money machine. Money attracted money, so that big donors gave generously to the Obama campaign. Information-age entrepreneurs were out in front in their support for the campaign. Not to be left behind, those in the financial services industry gave to everyone. Obama received large donations from bankers and hedge fund managers. Although the US$59 million from these sources represented only 15 percent of the amount raised in the primaries, this was more than the US$53 million raised by the Clinton campaign.

In an effort to present a safe face to these capitalists, Obama chose Penny Pritzker as National Finance Chair. Penny, a billionaire heiress of the Hyatt hotel chain, was from one of America's wealthiest business families. Obama wanted to move from the middle tier of the party to the top tier. To get to the top, he had to mobilize the bottom. Would he be trapped when he got to the top of the party? The answer had to await the outcome of the electoral struggle.

THE STRUGGLES IN THE PRIMARIES

Between January 3 and June 3, 2008, the Democratic Party set about the process of choosing its candidate for the 2008 Presidential Election. This choice came out of a grueling competition of election battles in over 59 primaries, caucuses, and conventions across the 50 states of the country (and beyond in Puerto Rico, Guam, Samoa, the US Virgin Islands, and among Democrats living abroad).

The most important outcome of the process of primaries and caucuses was that, at the end, Obama and his "amazing money machine" defeated the Clinton political machine. But for this study of politics for the twenty-first century, four factors distinguished this primary season:

- Most important was the collapse in March 2008 of Bear Stearns, the fifth largest investment bank in the United States. The US government had to intervene aggressively to prevent a collapse of the entire financial system.
- The surge in young voters and the increased participation of citizens.
- The attempt to make questions of racial identification the key question of the election.
- The internal collapse of the massive Clinton apparatus.

The fact that Obama won and went on to win the presidency is well known, and the disintegration of the Clinton political machine is well documented both by journalists and from the major election studies that have emerged since the elections. It is not necessary here to develop a state-by-state analysis of the results of the primaries because the drama of the gymnastics of the Clinton team was played out before the full view of the population. What are important from the point of this study are the four factors highlighted above, and how these factors can and will have a bearing on twenty-first-century politics.

THE CENTRALITY OF ECONOMICS AND POLITICS

Between March 10 and15, 2008 (in the middle of the campaign for the Democratic nomination), Bear Stearns collapsed. The media managed the news of this collapse in a way that would not panic the population, but the downfall exposed the fragility of the economic system, the limited future of the dollar as the reserve currency of world trade, and the thin basis of the superpower status of the United States. Throughout 2007, there had been news of the problems of the over-exposure of certain banks because of the securitaztion of mortgages. Bear Stearns and Lehman Brothers, two of the big names on Wall Street, were among the institutions mentioned in the financial press as being in danger.

One month before the collapse of Bear Stearns, economist Nouriel Roubini had alerted his clients to the depths of the crisis. He warned that the "housing market collapse would lead to huge losses for the financial system, particularly in the vehicles used to securitize loans," and that as trouble deepened, investment banks and hedge funds might collapse.[22]

In this "subprime crisis" the intricate relationship between mortgage-backed securities and the wider system of speculation was becoming public knowledge as Roubini's warnings went from the business pages to main street commentary. Citizens who did not own stocks and ordinary workers began to take an interest in how mortgages were repackaged and sold into new financial packages as they saw the impact of foreclosures. It was in this world of financial innovation that new instruments appeared in the name of collateral-ized debt obligations (CDOs), credit default swaps (CDS), and other concoctions in the trillion-dollar market of derivatives.

Finance, insurance, and real estate (FIRE) had become the central components of the economy of the United States as financialization and deregulation protected the bankers, allowing them to take more and more risks. These risk takers organized a new and elaborate system that some economists called the shadow banking system.[23]

This system operated in the world of "free markets" and deregulation that had been the political outgrowth of the neo-conservative and neo-liberal policies of the Reagan revolution and after. Political power became subsumed under economic and financial power in the United States.

Robert Rubin and Lawrence Summers represented the bridge between the shadow banking system and the real world of political and economic power.

Rupert Murdoch, one of the barons of the financial/communications world who had been an ardent supporter of the neo-conservative policies of the Bush period, threw his support behind Hillary Clinton. Murdoch, Bear Stearns, and Robert Rubin inhabited a world that transcended political affiliations, and it was in this sense that there was some truth to the charge that the United States had one political party. With a few exceptions, media houses were content to reproduce the belief that the financialization of the economy was in the best interest of American society, to maintain global economic dominance and for the centrality of the dollar as the global reserve currency of world trade.

As the full implications of the "credit crisis" became public beyond the codes, the real consequences of this shadow banking system were further concealed by the creation of mechanisms to hide "toxic assets."[24] Insiders of the financial and political system understood that their empire was in jeopardy and that many of the banks were insolvent. Between August 2007 and March 2008, there had been extreme tension within the financial services industry over the future of the complex financial instruments that Warren Buffet had likened to time bombs and "financial weapons of mass destruction" that could harm not only their buyers and sellers, but the whole economic system.

But in the midst of the primaries, media attention was on the Rev. Jeremiah Wright story, which only served to direct attention away from what would otherwise have been the number one question for everyone – the future of capitalism.

The collapse of Bear Stearns was a warning across the bows for the later fall of Lehman Brothers in September 2008, and revelations of the corruption and sleaze of the whole financial system, epitomized by the conviction of Bernard Madoff for a US$65 billion Ponzi scheme.

This episode is important insofar as the political system in the

United States was not organized to face reality of this sort. One day after the fall of Bear Stearns, Obama gave a major speech in Philadelphia. In a democratic society, it might have been expected that such a speech would have been about the biggest financial scandal of the country and the near collapse of the financial system. Instead, it focused on "race." The media was more concerned with the statements by the Rev. Jeremiah Wright than with the future of the capitalist system.

Obama had promised to change the political conversation and the political tone in the United States, and the fall of Bear Stearns provided an excellent opportunity to educate the population. However, because he believed in the liberal principles of free markets, he was unable to grasp the need for a new discussion. Those economists who were warning of the dangers of further explosions of the "financial weapons of mass destruction" were sidelined as Obama turned to the Chicago Boys and the followers of Milton Friedman.

In this, the media were complicit with the politicians in deciding what was newsworthy. For the politicians, Wall Street, and the media, the statements of Rev. Jeremiah Wright on the history of the genocidal past of the United States were far more important for the campaign. Obama was complicit in this diversion.

And yet, it could not be otherwise. The Philadelphia speech was billed as historic, and so it was. But the fact that American society was so preoccupied with questions of race rather than questions of the health of the financial and economic system was one indication of the philosophical-political world that the citizens of the United States inhabited. It was unthinkable that the media and the politicians would discuss issues such as the nationalization of banks, which would be so crucial for the future of society. Blogs became an outlet for alternative information, but their authors could not intervene effectively to change the news environment. It required the intervention of young people in the political spaces to begin to affect the political economy of the society.

THE INTERVENTION OF THE YOUTH VOTE AND THE GRASSROOTS

For decades, the role of big money in political campaigns had ensured that the political process in the United States was dominated by the financial–pollster consultant industrial complex. Images of men in smoke-filled rooms making decisions had become legend. Even the arrival of seemingly democratic instruments such as primaries and caucuses had not broken the dominance of big capitalists in elections. Efforts to clean up the role of big money in the political process had led to numerous legislative initiatives with respect to campaign finance reform.

Terry McAuliffe (the fundraiser for Hillary Clinton) saw his goal as that of surpassing the Karl Rove "genius" and building the machinery to get around the laws on spending limits. McAuliffe had to be careful, though, as the conviction of Jack Abramoff had exposed to the world that the United States deserved to be placed near the top of the list of corrupt countries in any global corruption barometer.

What saved the little democracy that existed in the United States was the emergence of new social networking tools that energized the grassroots and provided the basis for the rise of millions of small donors. The investments in grassroots campaigning by the Obama team had brought millions of grassroots people into the political system, and the interplay between message, money, and mobilization made the difference in the primaries. It was this expansion of participation, the initiatives of the volunteer teams, and the interplay between structure and spontaneity that gave the Obama campaign an advantage over other Democrats, especially Hillary Clinton.

The "small donor revolution" expanded participation and brought back new meaning to the concept of grassroots politics.[25] It was the youth, however, who made the decisive difference in the ground operations, especially the caucuses. Lawrence Lessig and those who were campaigning for the break-up of the conglomerates with a monopoly over software had challenged young people to be interested in more than simply downloading music, and they responded. Youth energy was one more link in the break away from the old.

Published records within the Clinton election team reveal the big debate over whether the young would be a factor. Journalists and political insiders who have been writing books on the 2008 campaign have reconstructed the dismissive position of Mark Penn and the Clinton planners on whether young people would have an impact on the elections. But the massive groundwork carried out by the Obama team denied the Clintons the knockout that they had planned. The Iowa caucus, in particular, demonstrated the importance of young people.

THE IOWA CAUCUS

Since 1972, the first caucus in the US Presidential elections has been held in the state of Iowa. The ritual of the caucus has been in the past a neighborly affair where politically active voters gather in schools, churches, and libraries to argue out their preferences. This was face-to-face politics where there could be no absentee voting. Caucuses were closer to people's assemblies than any other form of political forum in the United States. It was an electoral process where everything was done in the open. In the caucus, voters worked in groups to discuss their preferences and then held straw polls, the results of which would be broadcast. Later, the representatives would meet in a state convention to select delegates, but the caucuses were the first in the election cycle and therefore attracted national and international scrutiny.

Very early, the Obama team decided to work hard to expand the grassroots base and attract the youth vote. Chapters of high school students for Obama were created in 2007 with a view toward mobilizing those who would be 18 by the time of the caucus and the elections of November 2008. Every Obama campaign office in each caucus state developed competitive forms of attracting young people. This tradition was later carried over to the elections of 2008 with rewarding outcomes.

It is now history that young people provided the energy to propel the massive enthusiasm for the Obama victory in Iowa. The general message of hope, change, and being fired up gave an incentive to young people, as Obama quoted Gandhi who had called on his supporters to "be the change that you want to see in the world." Buttons bearing this slogan became one of the most prized souvenirs of the election period. From the experience of the Iowa caucus, this call to believe in something and work for change became the mantra of the campaign.

Obama's margin of victory came through on-the-ground, face-to-face, door-to-door, neighbor-to-neighbor organizing strategies that built a cohesive ground plan that could go from Iowa across the country. Despite all of the money and planning of the Clinton machine, Hillary Clinton came third in Iowa. From Iowa, the campaign gained momentum and went on to New Hampshire, where Hillary Clinton won marginally. On the night of the defeat in New Hampshire, Obama dug deep into the history of the struggles to prepare his team for a prolonged fight. He invoked the whispers of the enslaved while conveying the optimism of ultimate victory:

It was whispered by slaves and abolitionists as they blazed a trail toward freedom through the darkest of nights.
Yes we can.

It was the call of workers who organized; women who reached for the ballot; a President who chose the moon as our new frontier; and a King who took us to the mountaintop and pointed the way to the Promised Land.

Yes we can to justice and equality. Yes we can to opportunity and prosperity. Yes we can heal this nation. Yes we can repair this world.

These words were later put to music, and more than 12 million watched this song as it was performed. It connected past and present struggles, and spoke directly to the battles ahead in South Carolina, which marked a turning point in American politics.

THE CENTRALITY OF RACISM IN US POLITICS

If the youth and the potentialities of the assemblies of people (caucuses) offered one possibility for the building of democracy in the United States, the other window was opened by the concentrated power of the black vote in US politics. As if to throw off and slowly rid the state of the history of Benjamin Tillman, black voters in the state of South Carolina delivered a decisive victory in the January primary and sent the signal for the rest of the campaign.

When the voting was over on the evening of January 26, there was a new understanding that had been hidden from society since the period of radical reconstruction: that if blacks voted to defend their interests, they could hold the balance of political power.

Michelle Obama, who had understood the tradition of resistance in South Carolina epitomized by the militant collective spirit of the *Gullah* (African Americans who live in the low country area of Georgia and South Carolina), had campaigned extensively in the South so that even those pastors of black megachurches who endorsed Hillary Clinton found that they were supporting the Clintons while the rank and file supported Obama.

From the appearance of Michelle Obama at house meetings, the rank and file of the South had been quietly making a reverse brown paper bag test for her. The black middle class across the United States, from Andrew Young to Charles Rangel, Maxine Waters, and other officials of the Democratic Party machine, had underestimated the calculated mind of the children of those who had experienced Jim Crow. For these citizens, Obama was not a symbolic but a real candidate, and their intervention paved the way for his victory.

On the morning of the primary, Bill Clinton remarked, "Jesse

Jackson won South Carolina twice, in '84 and '88, and he ran a good campaign. And Senator Obama ran a good campaign here. He's run a good campaign everywhere." Media watchers immediately understood the coded message behind these words, as the *Atlantic* called it "advance spin.[26]

This rejection of racism by citizens was a rebuff to the old politics of division that had been practiced for over a century. Bill Clinton knew South Carolina well. He had carried out voter registration in the state when he was still a student. He won there handsomely in the 1992 primary. As an experienced triangulator (saying different things to different audiences), Bill Clinton had built a connection with rural Southerners. This connection was before the era of YouTube, where any statement made in a rural community could be on the Internet in seconds. Bill Clinton lacked this understanding because he was not part of the social networking generation.

Two years earlier, a Virginia politician, George Allen, had made a racist comment, referring to a voter as "*macaca.*" The words cost him the election. Similarly, the Jesse Jackson comment cost the Clintons the election, as younger voters who were averse to such racism were able to read between the lines and used their votes to register their disapproval of racism. However, the Clintons were not to understand that reality because, up to the end of the primary season, they had internalized the idea that a black man could not become the president of the United States. The simplicity of this racism ensured that the Clintons would make numerous racist comments, leaving many backs wondering how they could have designated Bill Clinton as the "first black president of the United States."

The Clinton comment was a tried and tested attempt to instigate a "white backlash" against the Obama candidacy. In 1984, after the victory of Jesse Jackson in South Carolina, the chair of the Democratic Party had said that in the face of the victory of Jesse Jackson, Walter Mondale had no choice but to go after the "blue-collar vote." This use of the term "blue collar," like the term "middle America," was a code for white Americans.

Scholars and pundits who were invested in the demobilization of the citizens had identified the white backlash against Jesse Jackson because "there was an association between white racism, fear and backlash and black demographic concentration in the immediate political environment."[27] Earlier in the month, Hillary Clinton had belittled Martin Luther King Jr. and the struggles of the civil rights movement, while Bill Clinton had likened Obama's run for the presidency to a "fairy tale." Hillary Clinton said, "Dr. King's dream began to be realized when President Johnson passed the Civil Rights Act, It took a president to get it done." The code: there needed to be someone white in the White House to get things done.

Anti-racist forces were taken aback by this overt display of racism by the Clintons, but with every victory by Obama, it became more and more blatant. By the end of January, Senator Edward Kennedy endorsed Obama. After a series of losses and the failure of the blow-out strategy of Super Tuesday, the Clinton camp went even further in an explicit appeal to white women, issuing an ad asking which of the two candidates would be ready for a crisis at 3 am in the morning. Far more powerful than the words were the images that were built into the message. The child on whom the camera first focuses is blond. Two other sleeping children, presumably in another bed, are not blond, but they are dimly lighted, leaving their appearance to the imagination of the viewer.

Despite this overt racist mobilization, after Super Tuesday, Obama continued to win in the Potomac primaries (Maryland, District of Columbia, and Virginia). Then, right in the middle of the meltdown of Bear Stearns, the media started to play short snippets from the speeches of the Rev. Jeremiah Wright.

Wright had been one of the civil rights leaders in Chicago, and pastor of Trinity United Church for 35 years. It was the church in which Obama became exposed to liberation theology. Obama titled his second book *The Audacity of Hope*, and praised the role of the church in its community work. The media overlooked this history of ministering to AIDS victims and others, and focused on one sermon where Wright had said, "The government wants us to sing 'God Bless America,' No no. Not God Bless America, God Damn America. God Damn America for treating our citizens as less than humans."

The media had a field day, and it was in the midst of this heightened discussion of the history of slavery and racism that Obama delivered his "A more perfect union" speech in Philadelphia. In an effort to use the episode of Wright as a moment to educate the population on the history of racism, Obama referred to his grandmother, and the need for tolerance and reconciliation to rid society of the cancer of racism.[28]

Obama used the occasion to reach those citizens who wanted to heal. For the Clinton campaign, the idea that a black man could be a leader, reconciler, and healer was foreign. Every effort to foreground racism was highlighted, and this was especially the case in the battles in Pennsylvania. The Clinton campaign refused to believe that Obama could be elected after victories in North Carolina and a spectacular rally of over 75,000 persons in Oregon. Whether it was Geraldine Ferraro who said that Obama was not qualified or Hillary Clinton herself who raised the prospect of the assassination of Obama, the investment in whiteness was not absent from the Clinton machine. In the end, citizens deserted the Clintons despite their effort to woo the superdelegates on the basis of whiteness.

INTERNAL COLLAPSE OF THE VAST CLINTON APPARATUS

The momentum for the Obama campaign after Iowa and South Carolina culminated in a clear victory in pledged delegates. According to the rules of the party, in order to secure the nomination at the convention, a candidate needed to receive at least 2,117 votes from delegates – a simple majority of the 4,233 delegate votes. Obama surpassed that total on June 3, 2008, becoming the apparent Democratic nominee.

From early May, it was clear that the Clinton campaign was heading for defeat. The collapse of the Clinton machine led to desperation. The shrillness of the machine was evident when Hillary Clinton declared that she was staying in the race because Obama might be assassinated like Robert Kennedy. Code words had not worked, and extreme anxiety had led to a desperate attempt to appeal to the superdelegates of the Party to deliver the nomination to her.

As far as the Clinton camp was concerned, Obama was a losing candidate. When the Clinton machinery were comfortable in the belief that Hillary Clinton would sweep the Democratic primary by February 5, the Clinton representative on the Rules and Bylaws Committee of the Party had agreed that only the four states of Iowa, New Hampshire, Nevada, and South Carolina would be permitted to hold primaries or caucuses before February 5, 2008.

After the failure of the Clinton strategy to win big on February 5, Hillary Clinton and her campaign started to argue that both Florida and Michigan should be seated at the convention. It was on the basis of the votes in both Michigan and Florida that the Clinton campaign argued that the nomination should be handed to Hillary Clinton because she had received more of the popular vote than Obama.

In the hour of defeat, the Clinton apparatus wanted to write new rules. But by then, the era of the Democratic Leadership Council was on the wane. The era of a more democratic and more anti-racist future had arrived. The Clinton machine disintegrated and fragmented. But there was one battle left: it was for the Democratic Convention. This is the subject of Chapter 6.

CONCLUSION

Thirty years after William Domhoff wrote his book *Fat Cats and Democrats*,[29] Kevin Philips wrote *Wealth and Democracy*.[30] The essential argument of both books was that the corrosive nature of big money had made a mockery of democracy in the United States. During the period of George W. Bush and the neo-conservatives, the machinery of Karl Rove had established a close-knit relationship between lobbyists, militarists, political careerists, and the new political philosophy of neo-liberalism for the Republicans to maintain a permanent majority.

It was the organized and patient work of the peace and justice movement that opposed the militarism, torture, and invasions that were organized under the "war on terror." Despite its small numbers, the peace and reparations movement had created a moral base for opposing the Republicans. Obama had been on the fringes of this peace movement and spoke out against the war in Iraq.

Before Obama, there had been previous attempts to "democratize the Democratic Party." One major attempt to clean up the graft and patronage in the party in the twentieth century had been undertaken by Eleanor Roosevelt in the 1950s after her son, Franklin Delano Roosevelt Jr., had been defeated in the race for attorney-general in New York by the old Tammany Hall machinery.[31]

Obama challenged the outmoded machinery, and succeeded where Eleanor Roosevelt and numerous reformers had foundered in the face of an entrenched machine that controlled fundraising and the dispensation of patronage. At the 1968 Democratic Party Convention, there were massive demonstrations by members of the peace and civil rights movements. Both of these constituencies had argued like Eleanor Roosevelt that the nominating system was closed to dissent and unrepresentative of popular opinion. There were other bold efforts to broaden the base of the party during the period of the run for the presidency by George McGovern and Jesse Jackson.

We started this examination of the Obama victory in the primaries with the efforts of the MFDP to ensure that blacks in the South were properly represented. Our analysis drew on the historic linkages between Marshall Ganz of Camp Obama and the teachings of Robert P. Moses and Ella Baker. The tradition of political organizers finding their own voice was carried forward from the civil rights movement, and enriched the organizing efforts of the Obama campaign.

Obama and his "machinery of hope" defeated the old Democratic Party machinery in June 2008, and built new networks as young people and the historically disenfranchised blacks made their claim to the democratic equation. The bottom-up self-organizing principles along with the break from the old forms of organizing brought out a central fractal principle of recursion.

Our recourse to the fractal conceptual framework was an attempt to go beyond the simple statement that it was the charisma of Obama that made him a transformative figure. Our reference to fractal optimism and the fractal conceptual frame was centered on the similar pattern of organization of each level of Obama's campaign, from the grassroots to the top, as opposed to the old "undemocratic" pattern of top-down, which was divisive and not all-inclusive. The old top-down pattern was the elitist money/power politics, which had formed a deep-rooted recursive loop, whose historical characteristics were manifested in systematic sidelining of blacks and Latinos, poor women, and young people.

Obama's campaign strategy was all-inclusive in terms of its message and medium, money (democratization of fundraising), and machinery/infrastructure (which was grassroots based). Obama's messages of hope and racial healing (reconciliation) and a sense of our shared humanity are central to fractal wisdom. They transcended the boundary of race, class, and gender. Indeed, there seems to be hope and optimism for a more democratic electoral politics in the twenty-first century if this new pattern (or mode of political organization) is consolidated, cascaded, and allowed to form a recursive loop and used as a reference point for politics.

Numerous writers have written on the fear of the concentrated black vote and the implications for the balance of power within the Democratic Party. The democratization of fundraising, the "triple O" strategy, and new forms of self-organization turned old politics on its head. It was when the professionals became amateurs in the era of social networking. Amateurs and volunteers became professional political operatives as millions were mobilized to believe in change. As one commentator noted, "On every metric, the campaign exceeded what has been done before."[32]

This was the essence of a quantum leap in the process of the democratization of US society. The quantitative change in numbers organized had a qualitative effect on the political system. Holistic concepts of healing and reconciliation in the "A more perfect union" speech touched millions by releasing new spiritual forces. It was this combination of spiritual energy, qualitative change, and sense of shared humanity that opened to door to quantum politics.

After Obama became president, the question of whether the door would be closed or open would depend on the extent to which democracy extended beyond voting, so that popular engagement and education could alert citizens to the dangers of reality mining. The same tech tools that were harnessed by the Obama campaign had been mobilized by the conservatives to establish the Total Information Awareness monitoring system.

Obama and his team embraced the information revolution and tapped into artistic and intellectual resources, so that classical music (structure) would meet jazz (spontaneity, improvisation, and self-organization). For this meeting to reach the ears of all, the media had to be democratized, the institutions of higher learning had to be open to all, and there had to be a concept of democracy that caught up with the realities of the twenty-first century. One section of the black liberation movement had identified three core elements of this twenty-first-century democracy:

- Cyberdemocracy –strengthening the general literacy of the society so that everyone would have access to computers and become active users of cyber technology.
- Collective intelligence – extending the halls and spaces of knowledge so that all intellectual production being collected, analyzed, and utilized will serve humans and not corporations.
- Information freedom – ensuring that intellectual production is freely available to everyone, as with clean air.

Yet, to move to the goals of cyberdemocracy and information freedom, American society had to move fast to undo the denial of the basic right to vote to black and Latino voters. Ronald Walters had been writing for 20 years on how the leadership of the Democratic Party was actually not keen for the Voting Rights Act to be implemented, and how the top leaders cooperated with the party activists in the South to suppress and dilute the black vote. Those who were connected to the financial oligarchy and the militarists understood clearly that the concentrated black vote in the United States, when mobilized along with the Latino vote, the votes of the working people, the peace movement, women, and young people, could transform the politics of the United States.

Working from inside and outside the mainstream political parties, the traditions of resistance and opposition to racism had fertilized the roots of another form of radicalism in the United States. Martin Luther King, Jr., Ella Baker, and the mass movements of the 1960s, along with the peace and justice movements, had generated another pole of politics and the struggle for democracy in the United States. Jesse Jackson tapped into this constituency in 1984 and 1988 to bring the peace and justice constituency into the Democratic Party.

However, far from welcoming the newly enfranchised activists, party leaders were filled with class and race fear. The party saw the Jesse Jackson candidacy as creating a white backlash, and developed codes to reproduce racist ideas by referring to "middle America" and the "middle class." The era of YouTube and blogs exposed the coded racism of Bill Clinton when he compared Obama to Jesse Jackson.

Obama had engaged the struggles for the nomination, and in the process, built from the traditions of Fannie Lou Hamer and Jesse Jackson. The Obama campaign was seeking to make up for the democratic deficit of the nineteenth and twentieth centuries. Throughout the twentieth century, getting the majority of citizens to vote was equated with the fulfillment of democratic rights. The numbers of new voters in 2008 showed that Obama had achieved this goal.

But by 2008, democratic demands included not only the right to vote but the right to breathe, to a decent standard of living, and to a healthy society. These democratic rights could not be supported by capitalism. Before people were able to go this next level of awareness, there had to be a struggle against the division of working people. In this enterprise, Obama made a great contribution.

Despite the diversionary focus on racism at the time of the fall of Bear Stearns, the call for reconciliation had been a necessary component of democratic struggles in the United States. When the Clinton machinery sought to invest in whiteness, voters who were concerned about their future supported the campaign of Obama. There had been an opening for the Obama campaign to "shift the discussion," but it became clear from the advisors around Obama that his vision did not include the question of the nationalization of the banks and financial houses.

Whether Obama was ready or not was not up to him. The insolvency of the banking system would bring attention back to the future of capitalism during September 2008, when Lehman Brothers was to follow the path of Bear Stearns.

Unlike the period of Frederick Douglass and Harriet Tubman, the anti-capitalist forces were not sufficiently organized to influence the direction of the debates on the economy. The financial rescue package for Bear Stearns required a new level of literacy about the working of the economy and global economic relations. As if in preparation for that moment, the mass of the working people rejected the investment in whiteness and refused to accept old divisions. In this, the young took the lead and used the caucuses across the country as a new school for politics. The caucuses had tremendous potential, as the assembly format could be enriched so that people used these assemblies not only to vote but also to govern. This would, for the first time in the history of the United States, make the establishment of democracy a real possibility.

Farsighted sections of the ruling class were not asleep to these possibilities. Hence the Obama campaign was monitored very closely. Obama himself was torn between the self-organization of the young and the commercial handlers of the campaign. Public relations firms such as GMMB and Blue State Digital were two enterprises that profited from the massive outpouring of democratic participation. At this moment, the professionalization of these corporate entities served the purposes of winning the Democratic primary. These forces were part of the netroots generation who believed that technical questions of social networking could be separated from political questions of the permanent empowerment of the young. Lawrence Lessig had symbolized one section of the Creative Commons network, which served as a bridge between the entrepreneurs and the political forces that wanted democratization.

When Hillary Clinton campaigned on the basis of "strength and experience," the younger creators of the new social networking technologies said, yes, we do not have experience but we want change. The call for changes in Silicon Valley and the call for change in politics merged in the Obama campaign. Which of the forces would win? This matter would be determined by the actual process of political struggle. This struggle further unfolded in the Democratic Party Convention and the presidential election in late 2008.

6

BETWEEN THE PAST AND THE FUTURE: THE DEMOCRATIC NATIONAL CONVENTION

BURDENS OF THE PAST

When the Democratic National Convention (DNC) met in Denver, Colorado, August 25–28, 2008, with over 50,000 accredited delegates, media, and assorted political followers, it was 100 years since the party had last convened in a state then called "the gateway to the west." Forty years before, at the 1968 Convention in Chicago, street demonstrations had overshadowed the proceedings on the convention floor. In every area of deliberation and presentation, the 2008 convention and the party were caught between the frontier past and the future of human cooperation, environmental justice, and peace.

The theme of the convention was "Changing the course of the nation," and there were numerous forces present that wanted change while others wished to hold on to the past. Obama had provided the leadership to bring the largest number of delegates to the nomination, but many of the seasoned elements of the state party machinery did not acknowledge his victory in the primaries and caucuses.

Denver, Colorado was a place in the United States where the history of the formation of the United States (the Louisiana Purchase and the Mexican American War) clashed with the future of the economic and political integration of the North American peoples and societies. Slowly, the geodemographers began to realize that the growth of the Latino/Hispanic population would have seismic implications for US political culture, especially at a moment of radicalization of Latin America and the Caribbean. Some of the more farsighted political strategists and intelligentsia understood the future and were hoping to muddy this reality by sowing divisions among the oppressed. Obama was to be the nominal head while the old thinking and Anglo-Saxon hegemony would not be disturbed.

Before the journey to the future could be embarked upon properly, the party and American society had to contend with the past. Would Obama and his campaign embark on a process of healing and repair that would set in motion real reparative justice for the society? Obama's ability to unleash trust, cooperation, and compromise was celebrated by those who were anxious for electoral victory, but the promise of redemption could not be fulfilled without an excavation of the truth of the past. Reparations and reparative justice were far from the minds and thinking of the planners of the Convention and the opinion makers.

In preparation for the 2008 convention, readers of a Denver newspaper were reminded that Native people were placed on display in 1908 for the Easterners to see real "Indians," complete with head-dress and the right dance, to entertain the Convention goers. Every-where in Denver, there were names associated with brutal history. One First Nation historian, Ward Churchill, who had sought to keep alive the question of the genocide of the First Nation peoples, was hounded out of the University of Colorado. Museums and libraries of the city contained celebratory memorabilia of civic and religious leaders, mayors, and governors who had been proud members of hunting parties that stole the land of the original peoples.

Other heroes had been outstanding leaders of the barbarous Ku Klux Klan in Colorado. The Denver Civic Center, where many of the meetings of the DNC were held, had been built by the long-time mayor, Benjamin Stapleton. Stapleton, like most members of the political establishment (Democratic and Republican), had been an active member of the Ku Klux Klan. Outside the South, Colorado had been one of the strongest bases of the Klan. Governors built their reputations on the extent to which they could keep out immigrants while sanctioning the super-exploitation of those who worked on farms, mines, and construction sites. Right up to the 1930s, the Klan had dominated all aspects of the politics of the state of Colorado, to the point where there is a respectable bibliography on the known Klan governor, Clarence Morley, along with the penetration of the Klan into political, religious, social, and commercial enterprises.[1]

The 2008 Convention was being held on the 88th anniversary of the ratification of the 19th Amendment of the US Constitution which granted women suffrage. Though women could not vote then, two had attended the 1908 convention in Denver. Native peoples, blacks, Hispanics, and Asians were excluded from the party.[2] Politics and the campaign for the office of president of the United States had been reserved for those whom the political leaders described as "100 percent Americans."

In 2008, there was some anxiety in Denver over possible drama from hardcore Clinton supporters. Although there was no on-camera drama, the usual consensus from the convention continued to elude Obama, as the diehards believed that he could not win the general election in November.

The nomination of Obama (a US citizen of biracial ancestry) as the presidential candidate in Denver pointed to one possible future for the United States, and represented an attempted break with the old party apparatus. In Chapter 5, we outlined the ways in which the Obama campaign had built a formidable alliance to defeat the machine politicians of the Democratic Party. In the process, the Obama team set in motion a new multinational and multiracial coalition to build grass-roots energies to expand the electorate in all 50 states of the United States. Obama's victory placed the party between the past frontier spirit of plunder and the future of a multinational and multiracial society.

Between the time of the victory over Hillary Clinton in June and the convention in August, the full reality of the nature of the economic meltdown had begun to sink into American minds. At the moment of the most serious economic dislocation in the history of the United States since the 1929 crash, corporate elements were very much in evidence in Denver as they sought to study and understand the Obama campaign. The Democratic faction of the corporate forces yearned for the victory of the party but was at the same time looking forward to the future demobilization of the forces that had been necessary for electoral victory.

This chapter begins with an analysis of why the Obama strategy for the West meshed with demographic trends in American society. From this analysis of the demographic future, we move on to an examination of the importance of the Latino/Hispanic constituency in the search for renewal and healing. The convention forms the backdrop as the experiences of the caucuses and speeches provide windows into the future forms of political organizing work within the United States.

NEW AND OLD FORCES AT THE CONVENTION

The briefing book for the delegates at the 2008 Denver Convention was full of the usual statements that Obama would "grow the economy, create jobs, restore fairness, and expand opportunity." Beyond these positions, there was the need for new thinking and political literacy, where people would be informed of the urgent need to break with the past celebration of ignorance.

There was unevenness between the specialists, consultants, public relations, and marketing personnel on one side, and the volunteers on the other, but for the campaign to be successful, the caucuses had to lift the general level of political education of the volunteers so that millions could be deployed for voter registration and get-out-the-vote drives. This division between marketing specialists and computer wizards on one side, and openness and multicultural literacy on the other, was played out in the convention.

While Obama had to build a ground organization to campaign for the presidency, the theme of "Changing the Course of the Nation" was caught between the old stage management of infomercials, marketing the ideas and personalities of the party to the public, and the spontaneous organizing and thinking that was required for the self-organized volunteer. Bloggers became the interface between the two.

The social networking tools of the Internet were enhanced by the democratization of information and the emergence of independent opinion makers who developed weblogs. The print and broadcast media would no longer have the monopoly of information on the course of the elections and the country.

Hundreds of bloggers and partisan citizens who were not part of the Democratic Party met daily in the Big Tent at Denver which was sponsored by Google, Netroots Nation, Blue State Digital, the Progressive Book Club, and about 20 other corporate and activist sponsors. Slowly, the death of the old media was releasing society from the stranglehold of the corporate news.

Throughout the United States, the domination of the sources of information by an elite crew of journalists has been challenged by the Internet, which has enabled thousands of individual commentators to communicate directly with others through new information platforms. As old-format newspapers died, media magnates experimented with new ways of charging for online news. What these moguls do not anticipate is the full democratization of information when conservative news outlets will be relegated to the fringe of society. This is an essential component of the revolutionary moment.

SHADOWS OF THE PAST AND THE DENVER SETTING

According to the US Census, "Latinos are the fastest growing population who are projected to comprise 30 percent of the US within thirty years."[3] The census adds, "Minorities, now roughly one-third of the U.S. population, are expected to become the majority in 2042."[4]

Neither of the mainstream parties had the political and intellectual infrastructure to fully grasp the historic possibilities of this demographic trend. Political scientists had been studying this phenomenon, and the 2006 Latino National Survey had yielded rich information on the political orientation of the fastest growing immigrant population. Progressive scholars from the Latino community were discussing, "Latino Political Engagement: Will Immigrants Revolutionize Politics?"[5]

Conservative forces in society had developed crude machinations to divide the Black and Latino communities. Probably the most nefarious was the planned and coordinated fights in the California prison industrial complex. Battles and fights between gangs in prisons spilled over into the wider community so that the violence and terror from these turf battles served to demobilize the poor and hindered their ability to organize against exploitation. Politicians inside and outside the United States were quite willing to fuel these divisions, as evidenced by the comment, "There is no doubt that Mexicans, filled with dignity, willingness and ability to work, are doing jobs that not even blacks want to do there in the United States." This statement by the president of Mexico, Vicente Fox in 2005 had been repeated by conservatives all across the United States. In all areas of interaction, jobs, health, education, housing, and environmental justice, the day-to-day solidarity between oppressed blacks and Latinos was overshadowed by a media that stoked the fires of division. It was in the prisons where the divisions were most brutal. Those who opposed the prison industrial complex noted that the US justice system had gone mad.

On the part of Karl Rove and George W. Bush, the strategy was to mobilize the Hispanic population on questions of family values (abortion, anti-communism, gay marriage, and other conservative questions) under the banner of morality. The Obama campaign and the Democratic Party had chosen the site of Denver as one way of mobilizing a different, more inclusive society to ensure that the Hispanic and Asian/Pacific Islanders along with their families were welcomed as citizens and as full Americans.

It was in the Latino/Hispanic caucus at the convention that the medium-term strategy was spelt out. Michelle Obama firmly stated the intention of the party and Obama to bring 12 million immigrants out of the shadows and on to the pathway to citizenship, with all the rights attendant to this status.

Coming from a black woman, this statement on citizenship carried a powerful repudiation of the hierarchical principles of citizenship that had been the reality of US society. The Western strategy of the Democratic Party under Barack Obama was different from the Western strategy of 1858, 1908, or 1968. Previously, states such as Montana and North Dakota had been considered "red states," that is, completely Republican dominated. Republicans had taken for granted that they would always win in the mountain states of Colorado, Arizona, New Mexico, Utah, Nevada, Wyoming, Montana, Utah, and Idaho. During the primaries, the Obama campaign had set up offices in all of these states. In some places such as Idaho, it was the first time these places witnessed a vibrant Democratic organization.

There was a short-term strategy for victory in the 2008 elections, a medium-term strategy to win Texas in the next round of elections, and a long-term future which was based on a multicultural alliance that would expand the electorate and draw into politics forces that had hitherto been excluded. This new political future was to be based on a vision of genuine multiculturalism and multinationalism. Denver was to be the gateway to the Southwest and West, and the Hispanic vote was central to this road to the new coalition.

Every aspect of the convention, especially the question of who received tickets to such events as Obama's speech on Thursday at the Invesco Stadium, had been determined by the short-term planning for the West. Spanish-language literature was to be seen in most centers, breaking the mindset of "English only," which is the mantra of certain conservatives in the United States.

THE PROMISE OF A GREEN CONVENTION

Convention cities are always linked to national and regional questions. In his book, *The Making of the Present, 1960,* Theodore H. White recorded for history the importance of the 1960 Los Angeles Convention in charting a future for a city that was to become one of the largest conurbations in the world.[6] Before the Second World War, Los Angeles was served by the largest electric/rail mass transit system in the country. But by the time of the Convention in 1960, powerful corporations had orchestrated the demise of the public transportation system. The deliberate destruction of the public transportation system paved the way for the "automobilization of transportation."[7] The other beneficiaries of this new system of transportation were the owners of construction companies with an interest in building freeways, real estate developers, and those who engaged in the expansion of suburbs. It was the extension of the Robert P. Moses model from the East coast to the West coast. The same forces of developers, construction operators, and real estate speculators were to congeal in the Democratic Party in the West.

Before the convention, the mayor of Denver had promised that the Democratic National Convention was to be "the greenest convention in history." The host committee had promised to focus on energy efficiency and minimal environmental impact. Here was a challenge to break with the wasteful practices of the past in order to inspire restraint in resource use, to reverse the destruction of the planet and people's lives. In the brochures marketing Denver, there were lofty statements about "the long history of environmental innovation." However, from arrival at the airport in Denver, there was a different statement on environmental innovation.

Denver Airport is located approximately 40 km (about 28 miles) from the city center. When it was built, the premise was that petroleum would forever be cheap and the urban sprawl from Denver would spread, with the motor car as the principal means of conveyance. Capitalists in the region envisaged Denver International Airport as a new aerotropolis. This is basically a city built around an airport and guided by the ideas of the unlimited spread of real estate values, increased production for international markets, and mega transportation points linking industries to foreign consumers. Under this vision of "development," certain industries are granted subsidies as an incentive to base their operations in or close to airports.

Efforts to develop a light rail system had been sidelined in the rush to support highway development for an aerotropolises. Developers, bankers, real estate speculators, and politicians plotted, as zoning regulations were organized to empower entrepreneurs, while there was a process of gentrification of the old neighborhoods close to the city.

Significantly, delegates to the convention who wanted to see real grassroots art about change had to travel beyond downtown Denver to the Manifest Hope Gallery. The fact that one of the most striking statements on the art, music, and culture of the political campaign was located in the Five Points neighborhood was one other indication of the struggle between the past and the future. Shepard Fairey's iconic poster of "Hope" on display in the Five Points district took the truly committed out of the glass and concrete of downtown Denver.

Reversing the gentrification and destruction of historic communities such as Five Points required new planning and a break from the priorities of real estate barons. From the planning of the convention, the Democratic Party and convention organizers paid attention to the ideas of a "green" future, without a clear reflection on the kind of democratic control that will be needed to break with the vision of the automobile and petroleum industries.

If people moved beyond the platform of the Democratic Party on renewable energy and the hype in Denver about a green future, it became clear from the Green Frontier Festival that far more than advertising and party statements would be required to make a break with economic activities that hastened global warming. Some of those who attended the convention benefited from the bike sharing and walkable distances between meetings, but these were symbolic initiatives. Environmental transformation required far more than words etched in the party platform. The cultural practices, economic relations, and politics of the past were not isolated from the environmental crisis of the present. To create a transformed environmental future required more than the free streetcar service that traversed the 16th Street mall in downtown Denver. This free transport using natural gas-powered buses and the efficient light rail system gave one glimpse of the future, but more than lip service will be needed for a true transformation of the energy policies of the United States.

T. BOONE PICKENS AND FORGIVENESS

Denver was like a universe unto itself, with new actors and actresses coming onto the political scene. It was also a space where old actors wanted to be seen in the new center of gravity. Van Jones, author of *The Green Collar Economy*,[8] had emerged at the convention as a link between the traditions of Ella Baker and the technological change necessary to break from the old destructive paths. His book sought to link questions of exploitation, the prison industrial complex, racism, and the environmental crisis. He maintained that a radical rethinking of the economy would lead to an end to subsidies for the banks and oil companies while creating an alternative basis for economic transformation.

Such a revolutionary vision of a green economy that would break from the past was different from the planning of those in power. The Denver 2008 Convention Round Table organized ten

discussions to "educate" delegates on health and wellness, education, philanthropy, transportation infrastructure, energy and climate
change, international relations, and so on.

What these discussions did was to bring conservative and
corporate elements to shape the discussion of the future of the
country. The transportation roundtable included top executives
from the financial services sector, while the international relations
roundtable was dominated by elements such as Madeleine Albright
and Richard Holbrooke (stalwarts of the Clinton campaign). At
least Albright and Holbrooke were from the Democratic Party, but
other discussions in the Big Tent included known conservatives such
as T. Boone Pickens.

The arrival of T. Boone Pickens at the convention cemented the
imagery of "fresh heroes and fools." T. Boone Pickens was one of
those billionaires on the Fortune 500 list who had made his fortune
out of the oil and gas industries.[9] He had managed to use his money
to sponsor one of the discussion groups in the Big Tent. His presence and that of other conservative planners pointed to the role of
conventions as a place for intelligence gathering.

In the recent past, Pickens had become famous for buying up
groundwater rights in Texas. A lifelong conservative associated
with the most backward wing of the Republican Party, Pickens had
supported the "Swift Boat" ads, which were used to rubbish John
Kerry's Vietnam war service, during Kerry's campaign as candidate
for the Democratic Party in 2004. Prior to the Denver Convention,
Pickens (one of the largest contributors to the Republican National
Committee) had become visible on national television, representing
himself as an oilman who is now a convert to wind energy. This was
in the month when the price of petroleum went over US$140 per
barrel. Pickens represented that "irrecapturable mood" of capitalists who had been complicit in crimes against nature but were now
seeking subsidies for "alternative" energy. One Denver newspaper
noted his presence at the Democratic Party Convention with the
headline, "T. Boone taps into forgiveness"[10]

Pickens wanted to influence the convention and foresaw a
future when people like him would be unable to influence voters in
primaries. Eight years earlier these same elements had supported the
energy policies of George W. Bush and Dick Cheney, and now they
wanted to be at the new center of gravity. Pickens had read the signs
of the new mood correctly, and wanted to be on board with the new
Obama administration after decades of supporting the conservatives
and the Republican forces in Texas and Oklahoma. He had been

embroiled in negative publicity relating to eminent domain powers and the removal of citizens from their homes in Texas and Oklahoma The truth about his relationship to communities had been concealed by the heavy press reportage about Pickens as a major donor of funds to the University of Oklahoma at Stillwater.

Universities, as recipients of the funds from corporate elements such as Pickens, covered up the plunder by focusing attention on so-called public–private partnerships. Other diehard conservatives donated large sums for the Denver Convention: for example, Thomas Golisano from upstate New York donated US$1 million. One year later, Golisano was up to mischief, engineering a coup against a Democratic Senate in the state of New York.

The search for forgiveness by Pickens was not without a price. He had seen the future, read the platform of the Democratic Party, the specialized studies on the billions that were to be invested in a new grid, and wanted to be on the side of the forthcoming federal subsidies for wind energy. Under the platform of the Democratic Party, the government of the United States would be committed to research and development and "deployment of renewable energy technologies – such as solar, wind, geothermal – as well as technology to store energy through advanced batteries and clean up our coal plants." Pickens wanted to see for himself whether this platform was just a ritual for the party activists to blow off steam in public, or real planning for the future.

Would there be teeth to the claim of the Obama team that after the elections, the new administration would "build a strong middle class through a green economy?" Would the Obama team be disciplined, be focused, and be decisive about a "green future? In terms of research on renewable energy technologies (especially solar), the United States was far behind societies such as China, Japan, Germany, and South Korea. Both the cost and scale of the investment in renewable technologies required new approaches to education, economics, and the needs of humanity.

In June 2007, Pickens announced the intention to build the world's largest wind farm in parts of four Texas Panhandle counties. Wind power politics is the term now being used in the energy sector to identify those forces who want the federal government to subsidize a new energy grid that can carry energy from different sources.[11] Because the investment needed for this new energy grid (compared with the investment in the Eisenhower interstate highway) required large outlays of federal funds, entrepreneurs from the energy sector were front and center of the lobbyists who converged on Denver. Those who had received subsidies in the oil and gas business for decades were now lining up in Denver to ensure that they were in the front row for government subsidies in the twenty-first century. A vision of subsidies and tax incentives for the future carrries on the same old thinking, where profits are front and center of planning.

Would the forms of regulation of the twenty-first century be similar to those of the nineteenth and twentieth centuries? This was the outstanding question in the discussions of green technology and a green future. Federal regulation and tougher environmental laws were needed to ensure that the form of regulation in the twenty-first century would be different from the past. Experience after experience, especially in the financial services sector, exposed the fact that, regulation or no regulation, capitalists were above the law. Regulations were supported only insofar as they strengthened the powerful.

Whether it was in railroads, banking, energy, commerce, telecommunications or automobile sectors of the economy, regulatory bodies were run for the powerful. Gabriel Kolko brought to the fore the reality that the forces that brought railroads under regulation at the end of the nineteenth century were the railroad barons themselves, who eventually sought regulation in order to divide up the market so that there was no real competition.[12]

Similarly, the Federal Trade Commission, established by Congress in 1914 presumably to regulate trusts, was found to be "carrying on its work with the purpose of securing the conditions of well intentioned business men, members of the great corporations as well as others."[13] Howard Zinn has chronicled this period of regulation serving big business in other areas such as city governments, where instead of presenting more democracy, they came under the domination of corporations.[14] Regulation, deregulation, controls, legislation, and oversight were all terms that held very little meaning in the absence of real democracy.

Lobbyists, political consultants, and representatives of more than 600 of the largest corporations in the United States made contributions to the Convention Host Committee so that their names could be prominently displayed at convention events. Meetings and networking among consultants, politicians, and capitalists had been one of the dominant features of 45 political conventions of the Democrats. Denver was no different. Because the Democratic Party is not really a national formation (but a conglomeration of 50 different state organizations), powerful state delegations at Denver such as California, Florida, Texas, New York, Illinois, Pennsylvania, and Ohio attracted a lot of traffic between consultants and corporate lobbyists.

One of biggest events was organized by the Boeing Corporation, a core part of the military industrial complex. It commemorated the 45th anniversary of the "I have a dream" speech by Martin Luther King, Jr. James A. Bell, president and CEO of the Boeing Corporation of Chicago, Illinois spent US$1 million on this breakfast for delegates to the convention. All of the black luminaries of the convention were invited. Nearly every speaker paid tribute to Martin Luther King, Jr., and the sacrifices that were made to pave the road for Obama.

The same sterile platitudes that are repeated every year on King's birthday were rolled out. Of the speakers, Joseph Lowery did not mince his words about the impact of the military industrial complex on the lives of poor people. His condemnation of the military and the wars in Iraq, Afghanistan, and US military bases overseas was clear and consistent.

However, for forces such as the Boeing Corporation, Lowery belonged to the past. Weeks before the convention, the top companies that were seeking bailouts from the Federal government made handsome donations to the Convention Committee. According to reports from the Center for Responsive Politics, AIG, Ford, Freddie Mac, and Citigroup were among biggest underwriters of the 2008 conventions (both Democrat and Republican).[15]

INSIDERS AND OUTSIDERS IN DENVER

The challenge of building a diverse progressive majority for the future was displayed in Denver without the benefit of a clear progressive constituency. At the 1968 Democratic Party Convention in Chicago, the peace movement and those supporting a new direction had been on the streets opposing the leadership of the Democratic Party. Forty years later, many of the peace activists and street demonstrators in Chicago had entered electoral politics and become political operatives.

Of the interest group caucuses, the faith-based caucus was a first. After eight years of George W. Bush and Karl Rove, the DNC had decided not to yield ground on issues of faith to the conservatives. The CEO of the convention was the Reverend Leah D. Daughtry, a member of a prominent Pentecostal family from Brooklyn, New

York. She was the daughter of another Reverend Daughtry, who over the previous 30 years had made history in Brooklyn, leading demonstrations and boycotts against police brutality and advocating the economic advancement of African Americans.

Obama's adviser for faith-based initiatives was Joshua Dubois, another young religious leader with roots in the traditions of the black church. Dubois was the classic outsider who was fast becoming an insider of big-time politics. He was later to become head of the White House Office of Faith-Based and Neighborhood Partnerships. It was given the mandate to work with faith-based communities across the country.

The biggest caucus was that of women. There was obvious overlap between the women, labor, and black caucuses, and many of the new insiders had been outsiders in previous years as Jesse Jackson's supporters of the Rainbow Coalition. Tom Hayden, retired state senator from California, was a representative of the new "insider/outsider" in the party. This category wanted to maintain its legitimacy with the historic peace and social justice movements while keeping linkages with the top political leadership.

Other insider/outsiders such as the writers of the *Huffington Post* maintained very close contact with the Obama campaign, and became a force in the new media competition.

There was intense competition to shape the story of the convention, and the top experts of "political spin" were on full display on the television channels. However, the convention as a political stage and political spectacle could not be contained by the mainstream media. The existence of bloggers, YouTube and other sources of information had empowered those who were not in the business of "political marketing" and staging the event in Denver. Slowly, the transformative potential of the information revolution was making its impact. During the convention, progressive forces worked diligently to challenge the monopoly on the party by big corporations.

Members of the party who were in the supposedly progressive Democratic organizations had continuous meetings on the party platform (health care, war, energy, education, jobs), but within the confines of historic name recognition. Organizations such as ADA (Americans for Democratic Action) as well as other formations called Progressive Democrats for America held their meetings at the Central Presbyterian Church, while the power lunches, dinners, and corporate receptions were being hosted in Denver Hotels and private clubs. What was unclear was how organizations such as the Sierra Club (the oldest and largest grassroots environmental organization in the United States) and the Daily Kos (a collaborative political blog publishing news and opinion from a liberal perspective) could share a platform with T. Boone Pickens. Was this an extension of Obama's bipartisanship?

Before the convention, the full effects of the sub-prime mortgage crisis were becoming clear, but the "discussions" at the meetings studiously avoided linking the economic crisis to the war against the people of Iraq.

Months before the convention, Joseph Stiglitz and Linda Bilmes had published a book outlining the ways in which the wars in Iraq and Afghanistan deepened the economic quagmire while leaving deep psychological and physical wounds for the society, especially for the veterans.[16] What was urgently needed at the convention was a rigorous debate on the ideological and political roots of militarism, so that society could make a break with the traditions that had decimated the First Americans and justified expansionism abroad. In Chapter 5, we outlined how the Democratic Leadership Council (DLC), child of the Coalition for a Democratic Majority, had been one of the parents of the neo-conservative movement. By the time of the convention in Denver, members of the DLC such as Rahm Emanuel and Harold Ford Jr. had maneuvered into becoming ardent spokespersons for the Obama campaign, seeking to blur the distinction between the former machine and the grassroots effort to elect Barack Obama. Emanuel would prove an adept survivor, and emerged as chief of staff of the White House when Obama won the presidency.

THE CLINTON BRIGADE IN DENVER

One sign of a successful convention is a minimum of confrontation on the main floor during prime-time broadcasting. Despite the fact that, the 2008 convention did not carry the kind of convention floor drama of 1960 or 1968, there was enough contention by the Clinton forces that Edward Kennedy had to be brought from his hospital bed to address the convention. Members of the Obama campaign had read the story of Lyndon Johnson in 1968, and how he unsuccessfully managed his operatives on the convention floor to thwart the nomination of Hubert Humphrey.[17]

Those members of the DLC and the Clinton primary team who believed that the United States was not ready to elect Obama refused to capitulate quietly, even though Hillary Clinton had pledged her support for Obama.

Older members of the party remembered when Adlai Stevenson was not running for the presidency but had been the beneficiary of massive floor demonstrations at the 1960 Convention, when delegates demonstrated and demanded "We want Stevenson." It was part of an attempt to stop John F. Kennedy from receiving the nomination in Los Angeles.

It was not possible to stop Obama from getting the nomination at this late hour, but disruptive demonstrations by opponents to the Obama presidency within the Democratic Party would signal great dissent and harm his general election prospects. The diehard supporters of Hillary Clinton found it difficult to move from making the comparison between Clinton and Obama, to the comparison between Obama and John McCain. Though few in numbers, they did everything to make themselves visible, and were as vociferous as the Obama supporters in Denver. In many ways, these Clinton supporters who opposed unity were important because of the old media. The *Los Angeles Times* correctly noted that "the amount of media attention on extremist Clinton-supporters seemed oddly disproportionate to the actual numbers on the ground."[18]

This writer saw a group of supporters with blue flags with the name of Hillary Clinton on them marshaled in the small park on 15th Street as shock troopers waiting to be deployed. The threat of the Hillary Clinton forces overshadowed the major discussion which was supposed to take place on Sunday August 24 on "From Fannie Lou Hamer to Barack Obama." Organized by *The Nation* magazine, Public Broadcasting Service, and the Denver Public Library, this panel was supposed to discuss how the civil rights movement changed American politics. John Conyers, a congressperson from Michigan (chair of the Judiciary Committee) was supposed to have a dialogue with John Nichols of *The Nation* to revisit the past militancy of the civil rights movement and the impact on the Democratic Party. Hundreds were gathered in the hall to listen to this dialogue, including three groups of high school students who had come to sing at this event. But anxiety over the drama of those who wanted respect for 18 million voters dominated the minds of attendees.

The high school students would have benefited by learning about the historic challenge of the Mississippi Freedom Democratic Party (MFDP) at the Democratic Party Convention in Chicago in 1964. Instead, John Conyers spent his time calling for unity, praising Hillary Clinton and the historic role of women in the Democratic Party.[19]

That Conyers spent more time on the 19th Amendment which gave American women the right to vote instead of linking the struggles of women to the civil rights movement, the struggles of the First Americans, and exploited immigrants was one indication of the panic that had overtaken delegates the day before the convention. John Nichols had sought to bring up the struggles of the civil rights movement and the historic run of Shirley Chisholm (a black woman) for president in 1972. Conyers, however, was focused elsewhere. The threat of those Hillary Clinton supporters marshalling around Denver was clearly on his mind, as he kept calling for future unity without dealing with the past disunity that had excluded African American, Hispanic, and First Nation voters from the party.

Next door to this session was a very loud and boisterous rally of trade unionists who had set aside their rivalries to support the Obama campaign. There were two distinct factions of the mainstream trade union movement. One, the AFL-CIO (American Federation of Labor and Congress of Industrial Organizations), had been the dominant force among the organized workers for 70 years. The other breakaway group, Change to Win Union Federation, had been critical of the AFL-CIO and embarked on a national campaign to strengthen the labor movement.

However, the long relationship between the trade unions and corporations in the United States had compromised the working-class organizations to the point where, in the midst of the biggest economic crisis since the Great Depression, the speeches and platforms of the unionists did not depart from standard call for change. Calls for "full employment," job security, and protection of workers from the neo-liberal paths of the policymakers were not vigorous enough to break out of the stranglehold of the consultants.

Twenty-first-century economic realities had dictated a new orientation about economic relations, but the history of Cold War ideology, a sense of entitlement from being the real labor aristocracy, and racial divisions had crippled militancy in the ranks of working people. Some of the leaders of the trade union movement referred to the fading of the "American Dream" without reference to what the dream had meant for the original people. One question that united both factions was the need for legislation to make it easier for workers to join trade unions. In this enterprise, the Obama campaign had promised to work vigorously for the Employment Free Choice Act.[20] Hilda Solis, a Democratic representative from the state of California, was an important speaker at the unionists' rally. The Clintons had worked hard to win support among the leadership of certain unions such as the American Federation of State, County, and Municipal Employees (AFSCME), but the overwhelming mood at the rally on Sunday August 24 was that the workers should plan for a new day with Obama. The trade unions were to contribute collectively more than US$450 million to the election campaign in 2008.

The other major progressive force at the convention was the California Nurses Association (CNA). It made itself felt with clarity on the need for single-payer health care in the United States. One of the strengths of this nurses association was its multinational and multiracial character. Similar to the Local 1199 of the Service Employees International Union, the CNA brought black, Latino and white workers together. Historically, Local 1199 was a militant trade union defending the rights of immigrants in the United States. It was not by accident that Patrick Gaspard emerged form this Local to be a leading organizer in the Obama team.

MICHELLE OBAMA AND THE CAUCUSES

One of the most visible persons at the convention was Michelle Obama. She spoke at the main convention on Monday night, at every one of the major caucuses, and at specialized events in Denver for veterans and military families. At the black and Latino caucuses she spoke firmly and clearly about her vision of the presidency. Thousands packed into the Wells Fargo room of the Convention Center to hear her address and vision to the black caucus. Departing from the scripted message that she delivered before prime-time television, she outlined the stakes for the oppressed in the United States. It was at this caucus where she said that sometimes she had to bite her tongue at some of Barack's statements. The black caucus was packed that morning of Wednesday August 27, as she exhorted the attendees to double their efforts. She said, "It is not easy, but because it is not easy does not mean that it is not possible."

Behind her words lay the burden of the increased security as she moved around Denver. The day before, up to four persons had been arrested over an alleged plot to kill Obama at the Democratic Convention Michelle Obama was testifying to the realities of the constant dangers that her husband faced. Yet the spirit that was displayed before the thousands in the Well Fargo room was one of strength and purpose. Speaking as a mother, she did not enter the discussions on health care reform from the point of view of legislation. She spoke of the realities of the families of service-persons and their sacrifices. Apart from this special section of the population, she noted that every family in the United States had faced a medical emergency.

It was in this caucus that the campaign rolled out the logistical plans to expand the electorate and increase turnout in the black community. Right before Michelle Obama spoke, Al Sharpton rallied the audience by saying, "They say that he is not black enough, not too white, but for us he is just right." Sharpton demonstrated that he grasped the historic moment when he said clearly to the black caucus that the fight was not black against white, but right against wrong. Sharpton was seeking to rehabilitate himself after he had been approached by anti-Obama forces in Iowa to divert attention from Obama's success. He left Jesse Jackson Sr. to whisper on Fox Channel about he would like to cut off Obama's testicles for allegedly talking down to black people. It was in the black caucus meeting more than any other place that the tale of the 2000 elections in Florida was repeated over and over again. The delegates and attendees were being called upon to be active, vigilant, and organized so that there would not be a repeat stolen election in 2008.

Graphs and figures were displayed to point out why every vote would count. The stress was on grassroots organizing in a digital age to increase voter registration by almost 20 million for the November elections. There was enough emphasis on how sheer human intervention could bridge the social divide and ensure that the black vote was sizeable in November. The job of Michelle Obama was to make the case for volunteering and motivating others to volunteer.

Her maturation in the election process came out of a long election campaign where she had had to study and understand the political process in the United States. The media had questioned her patriotism. Very early during the primaries, she had made a comment to the effect that "For the first time in my adult life, I am proud of my country." The peace movement understood the statement. Black people understood the statement. The media also understood the statement, but it fell to the conservative wing of the media to seek to destabilize the Obama campaign.

Michelle Obama was referring to the self-organization and the grassroots momentum that had been manifest in the primaries, but the mainstream media had a field day depicting her as an angry black woman. Cindy McCain, wife of John McCain, commented that she has always been proud of her country. The same depiction of militancy had been reproduced by the *New Yorker* magazine in July. Because of the stridency of the media campaign against Michelle Obama, especially by the outlets owned by Rupert Murdoch, Barack Obama had to personally confront Roger Ailes (Fox News) and Rupert Murdoch and tell them to back off from attacking his wife. Fox News had tagged Michelle Obama as anti-white, and she was referred to on the station as Obama's "baby mamma."

Michelle Obama was likened to angry "black women" because of her critique of the war in Iraq. She was compared unfavorably with Condoleezza Rice, former secretary of state to George W. Bush. Cynthia McKinney, the Green Party candidate for the presidency, was also depicted as "just another angry black woman." What the conservative media did not grasp was the fact that every attack on Michelle Obama endeared her to the rank and file, black and white, who were not in the conservative section of society.

As an independent person with ideas, Michelle Obama disrupted a stereotypical view of black women as maids, nannies, and cooks. It was the very same anti-Obama streak that had influenced his detractors to publish a photograph of Barack Obama in Somali traditional dress. This photograph had been taken when Obama had traveled to Kenya in the period of anti-Obama press. In the same period, the *New Yorker* magazine published a cartoon that depicted Barack Obama looking like Osama bin Laden next to his wife Michelle, who had a machine gun strapped to her back and looked very militant. Reproducing an image to suggest that the Obamas were unpatriotic, the cartoon showed the Obamas in the Oval Office looking like a pair of terrorists. Barack was depicted dressed in traditional Muslim clothing with a turban and sandals. Michelle Obama was shown with camouflaged military clothes, army boots, a bullet belt, an AK-47, and a giant afro hair style. Both are supposed to be fist bumping, while the American flag burns in the fireplace, below a portrait of Osama bin Laden hanging on the wall. This was the "humor" and satire of the supposedly liberal *New Yorker*.

It was the independent Michelle Obama who was presented to the country on the first night of the convention. As in the primary campaign in South Carolina, where the personal story was used as a motivational tool, now the traditions and legacies of Fannie Lou Hamer and civil rights testimonies were on display for a new politics. From the video that preceded her speech, it was clear that the objective of the public relations experts was to soften Michelle Obama's image. This was the verdict of the *New York Times* and other newspapers which carried commentaries of the speech that was watched by millions of households. The story dubbed her presentation and her story with Barack Obama as "embodiments of the American dream."[21]

What the media neglected to bring to readers was Michelle Obama's insistence on paying tribute to her father from the South Side of Chicago.

The speech linked Barack Obama to his early training as a community organizer in Chicago, and the optimism that came from that experience, where he had talked about "The world as it is" and "The world as it should be." Michelle Obama referred to the areas in Chicago that had been devastated by the closure of the steel plants in the 1980s, with the full understanding that all across the country there were similar shutdowns in the wake of the crash and home fore-closures. She described the common folks who invited Barack Obama back to their neighborhood after he had come back to Chicago.

Thus part of the speech was overlooked by the media. Instead, the concentration was on what she wore, what the children wore, and her hairstyle.[22] Michelle Obama had placed her patriotism not on the jingoism of the past but on the future "where the current of history meets this new tide of hope." It is this hope that was the key mantra of the campaign, and carried with zeal, as Michelle Obama emerged as one of the busiest people in the convention, shuttling between caucuses and engagements outside the convention with the veterans and wives of servicepersons.

THE LATINO/HISPANIC CAUCUS AT THE CONVENTION

The Hispanic caucus met in the Corbel room of the Colorado Convention Center. Tensions and struggles over the future of the Latino vote were on full display. In the first instance, the hetero-geneity of the Latino community eluded the consultants. Second, the divisions between the Obama and Clinton vision of the black/Latino alliance could not be concealed. Hillary Clinton had made a surprise appearance at the Latino caucus, where she pledged her full support for Obama and talked about the need for universal health care. After Governor Bill Richardson abandoned the Clinton campaign, the Latino caucus had been divided between the Clinton and Obama camps. On Wednesday morning, August 27, this caucus was addressed by Michelle Obama and Hilda Solis. Their appearance displayed the medium-term vision of the Obama campaign.

The response to both speakers reflected some of the ideological and regional divisions within the Latino community. Older members of the caucus sat on their hands while younger members stood and applauded Michelle Obama and Hilda Solis. Hilda Solis served in the US House of Representatives from 2001 to 2008, representing the 31st and 32nd congressional districts of California, which include East Los Angeles and the San Gabriel Valley. She was raised in La Puente, California by immigrant parents from Nicaragua and Mexico. Her roots in the labor movement, where her parents, who were migrant workers, had been labor organizers, placed her within an activist tradition. When Obama was elected president she was named the secretary for labor, becoming the first Latino woman to serve in the US cabinet. Her role as an organizer within two communities placed her in a position to transcend some of the divisions and regional differences within the Latino community.

WHO ARE THE LATINOS?

In the United States, the US Census Bureau determines Latinos to be Americans who identify themselves as being of Spanish-speaking background and trace their origin or descent from Mexico, Puerto Rico, Cuba, Central and South America, and other Spanish-speaking countries. This compounds the racial classifications in society, in so far as Latinos have many different racial and ethnic backgrounds. Of the 47 million Latinos in the United States 2008, 64 percent of Hispanic-origin people are of Mexican background. Another approximately 10 percent are of Puerto Rican background, with about 3 percent each of Cuban, Salvadoran, and Dominican origins. The remainder have other Central American, South American, or other origins. But far more important is the class background of these 47 million citizens.

The divisions between Latinos from different parts of the Americas had been exploited in the past. For decades after the Cuban Revolution, refugees in Miami had been one of the most vociferous sections of the Latino community, lending support to the Republican Party and conservative politics all over Latin America. However, Puerto Ricans and Salvadorans were not as conservative as the community of Cuban exiles. During the period of the civil rights movement, the Young Lords (a radical Puerto Rican group) made common cause with those blacks fighting against police brutality and the exploitation of the poor. Those Puerto Ricans who supported independence from the United States were branded as terrorists and forced to go underground. From time to time, vestiges of the struggles for self-determination reappeared in US politics, as in the struggles against the US naval presence on the island of Vieques.

Within the Latino community, the dominant media were in the hands of those who self-identified as whites. This was especially the case for the Spanish–language soap operas called *novelas*. Groomed by the anti-black establishment of the conservative forces in Latin America, these "whites" were to declare that a black person could not become the president of the United States. But among the youth, a different current flowed, "Hispanics voted for Democrats Barack Obama and Joe Biden over Republicans John McCain and Sarah Palin by a margin of more than two-to-one in the 2008 presidential election, 67% versus 31%."[23]

The other major finding of those researching the impact of the Latino vote was the effect of the radicalization of Latin America on immigrants. Though the pollsters wanted to make immigration the number one issue in their questions, the sentiments expressed at the Latino American Policy Forum during the convention was for the United States to develop better relations with Latin America.[24]

The spread of democratic ideas and relations in Latin America, symbolized by ALBA (the Bolivarian Alliance for Latin America and the Caribbean) radicalized the majority of indigenous and non-whites in the region who had been stirring to oppose the last vestiges of settler colonialism. Governments in Bolivia, Paraguay, Ecuador, Nicaragua, and St. Vincent had joined with the initiatives of Hugo Chavez of Venezuela.

The Obama campaign was being followed with keen interest all across Latin America. In Mexico the full effects of the North American Free Trade Agreement (NAFTA), the war on drugs, and the policies of neo-liberalism demanded new directions. Would the future realignment of international politics demand closer integration of the United States with other countries? These questions were sharpened by the economic depression, but before that discussion could start, Obama had to be elected and be open to starting a rethink on reparative justice and real conditions for healing.

ROLL CALL AND NOMINATION

By the time of the roll call to place Obama's name as the nominee for the party on Wednesday afternoon of the convention, the ritual had lost all the drama. The high point of the roll call was when a number of states yielded so that Senator Hillary Clinton from New York could formally nominate Obama as the candidate for the party.

Hillary Clinton, fresh from a large lunchtime rally of the women's caucus, "moved that the roll call be suspended and that Mr. Obama be declared the party's nominee by acclamation." History was being made, the future was being invoked, and millions watched as the convention roared when the motion was seconded.

Even as Hillary Clinton was nominating Obama, another drama was unfolding in the very picture of the leaders of the New York delegation. Before millions of viewers, the other New York senator, Charles Schumer, and the speaker of the New York Assembly, Sheldon Silver, were seen with the governor of New York, David Patterson, and senior representative Charles Rangel of Harlem lurking behind. The struggle over the New York machinery of the Democratic Party was being played out before the world. Obama would decide that in many states his campaign would be separated from the party machine for the general election.

ACCEPTANCE SPEECH AND MARKETING THE CANDIDATE

The setting and content of Obama's acceptance speech in Denver brought out the tensions and anxiety that surrounded the convention. As a marketing enterprise, the firm GMMB had come into prominence and worked closely with the Obama campaign. For the major speech, the PR forces had erected a giant stage. Jim Margolis of GMMB had studied the logistics of John F. Kennedy's acceptance speech in Los Angeles, and supervised the erection of a giant prop. There was division in the media whether the prop was similar to the columns of the Lincoln Memorial or a huge Greek temple.

The nature of the set built for television was dwarfed by the outpouring of enthusiasm by those who wanted to go in person to the Invesco Field, the stadium of the Denver Broncos football team. Press reports noted that Obama delivered his acceptance speech before a record-setting crowd of 84,000 people. It was estimated that another 38 million watched on ten different TV channels in the United States.

Of the estimated 84,000 who made it into the stadium, a large share of the tickets went to the estimated 30,000 delegates, party leaders, reporters, and so on. The rest were distributed to people who applied online, by phone, or at a campaign office. The Western strategy could be seen at work in the distribution of the tickets. As with the South Carolina organization strategy, this was another mechanism to get information for the campaign database. More than half the open tickets went to people from Colorado. Other tickets went to those from other nearby states.

Obama's speech was being delivered on an historic occasion. It was 45 years to the day since Martin Luther King, Jr. had delivered his "I have a dream" speech in Washington. It was also exactly 54 years since Emmet Till was killed in Mississippi. Obama was not unaware of the burden of history, and sought to reach the entire population in his speech. He did not try to cover up the challenges ahead, and called for hard work and sacrifice, paying attention to the centrality of labor in society. He said, in particular,

> Our government should work for us, not against us. It should ensure opportunity, not for just those with the most money and influence, but for every American who is willing to work. That's the promise of America, the idea that we are responsible for ourselves, but that we also rise and fall as one nation, the fundamental belief that I am my brother's keeper, I am my sister's keeper.

CONCLUSION

Obama embodied the promise of the future in August 2008, but the burden of the past and present weighed heavily over the Democratic Convention. On the Thursday evening after the speech, more than 100,000 people thronged the streets of downtown Denver, as the scene was like a carnival of the masses. From the stadium, tens of thousands mingled with the other tens of thousands who were out watching the speech in public venues. The masses briefly seized the streets, as peoples of all races, classes, genders, and sexual orientation mingled and claimed the freedom of the city. The fringe elements of the right-wing neo-conservatives who had been on the streets throughout the week, marching against abortion and gay rights, were smothered by the sheer numbers of those who were celebrating the historic moment.

At the time of the historic nomination of John F Kennedy in Los Angeles in 1960, Theodore H. White had declared, "A convention in American politics is frequently a place where the naked act of history and decision takes place in public."[25] The naked act of the nomination of the first candidate not from the dominant racial group was not lost on any commentator. Many remarked that Obama was the first African-American to be nominated for the White House by a major party.

For those who could not make it to Denver and witness history, the campaign rolled out a YouTube video, "Four days in Denver," about the Obama campaign.

Denver 2008 was very different from the Denver of 1908. This chapter began by pointing to the future of a multinational and multiracial United States. Projections from the census pointed to the make-up of a new electorate, and the convention worked hard to make solid pathways into that electorate.

On leaving the deliberations and planning of Denver, it was clear that the Obama team would win in November. It was already preparing for the challenge for Texas in 2010, which would be the bellwether of the future. We drew from the intervention of Michelle Obama and Hilda Solis in their efforts to build linkages between the caucuses, especially the women's caucus. Both Michelle Obama and Hilda Solis symbolized the future black/Latino coalition, but the old media insisted on stories of black/Latino rivalries. There was no shortage of pollsters who would pose questions about this rivalry, when the issues that united both oppressed groups called for more unity than disunity.

Barack Obama had worked tirelessly and diligently with the campaign team to ensure that the convention would not go down in history as a divided and contentious space. Senator Edward Kennedy was brought from his deathbed to address the convention. The speeches were memorable and historic.

James Carville (former Clinton campaign manager) and the "spin" specialists called the opening night a "wasted evening." Carville was working from the old playbook of the machine, and did not feel the weight of the social energy that made the PUMA (People United Means Action) group a footnote of history. The center of gravity of the Democratic Party had shifted from the Democratic Leadership Council – "the youth faced the old" and one generation had to give way to another. The media termed this generation the millennials, and the media congratulated Obama on being the best marketer of the year. In a year when General Motors went down and the banks were in crisis, politics became the number one source of revenue for advertisers. Obama was "*Advertising Age*'s marketer of the year for 2008."[26] For these Madison Avenue forces, the voters were like mindless consumers.

John Conyers, Barbara Lee, Bill Richardson, Ted Kennedy, and every major speaker pleaded for unity. The price of unity at the convention was the stifling of principled debate. Obama had come to Denver without a strong left wing of the party. In the stress for unity, real discussions were stifled at precisely the moment when society needed new thinking. It was in the caucuses away from the camera that the donkey work of planning and strategizing took place. An energized caucus of new forces had made their presence felt, to the point where the voice of the mainstream commented that "the Democratic Party today is different from the one that lost the last two presidential elections. It is bigger, younger and less visibly linked to traditional Democratic interest groups."[27]

Although the party was now bigger than traditional interest groups, these groups were not going away without a fight. Under the banner of the Rocky Mountain Round Table, some had gathered to promote neo-liberal solutions, when the collapse of the financial system demanded a break with the financial oligarchy. Conservatives and billionaires such as Tom Golisano and T. Boone Pickens did not want to be left out of this historic moment, so they used their millions to buy ringside seats at the Convention. For these forces, change was negotiable. It was on the question of environmental justice and repair that the reparations question stood out. Denver had mimicked Los Angeles, but the era of the automobilization of transport was coming to an end. Reparative and restorative justice required that full history be revealed so that the society could heal. Ghosts of frontiersmen and Ku Klux Klan leaders walked the convention center after which they were named.

At the start of the convention, *Time Magazine* had listed "Healer" as one of the five labels to describe Obama. Denver was a place where the healing could begin, because of the realities of how the previous convention was linked to the destruction of the First Nation peoples. The racism against Chinese workers who built the railroads and the contemporary racism against Latino workers cried out for exposure. Obama was not ready to discuss reparations because his attention was focused on winning an election, and he could not bring up the issue of reparative justice without alienating millions who refused to recognize the genocidal past. Joseph Lowery of the civil rights organization SCLC (Southern Christian Leadership Conference) was not shy in denouncing the war in Iraq and the crimes against peoples of the Earth. Boeing sponsored the breakfast where Lowery spoke, and was willing to tolerate his intervention, as long as the military industrial complex ploughed on.

This was then the strategy of big business. Obama could be president if there was to be business as usual. Under the banner of seeking bipartisanship, society would have to assess the direction of Obama. But before he could become president, he had to win the election. In Denver there was a formal rolling-out of the most breathtaking presidential campaign ever undertaken in the history of the United States. It is to the organization of this second ground operation for victory within one year that we now turn.

7

GROUND OPERATION FOR VICTORY: CHALLENGING THE RUTHLESSNESS OF THE WOUNDED CORPORATE BANKERS

Banking establishments are more dangerous to our liberties than standing armies.

Thomas Jefferson

These criminals have so much political power than they can shut down the normal legislative process of the highest law making body of this land.

Marcy Kaptur

The great wealth that the financial sector created and concentrated gave bankers enormous political weight – the American financial industry gained political power by amassing a kind of cultural capital – a belief system.

Simon Johnson

Economics dominates politics – and with that domination comes different forms of ruthlessness.

Sheldon Wolin

In his book *Democracy Incorporated: Managed Democracy and the Specter of Inverted Totalitarianism*, the noted political theorist Sheldon Wolin made the argument that if the United States does not radically alter course, it will become a totalitarian state. Because of the nature of US society, Wolin saw this as a rush towards what he called "inverted totalitarianism." What is significant about this analysis was the way in which Wolin placed the question of the repression of African Americans at the center of the rush towards totalitarianism.[1]

The question of instinctive racism deforming the politics of the United States has been at the heart of the analysis in this book.

During the eight years of the George W. Bush administration, the ruthlessness of corporate forces was on full display, and the challenge before the society was to put in motion a new kind of politics to halt the headlong rush to totalitarianism. Thus, the 2008 process was not only about the vote, but the larger question of whether the ruthlessness would move to a higher level. This was one of the challenges in the wake of the financial crisis. It is in the context of the massive powers in the hands of the corporate sector that the details of the ground operation for victory take on an added significance. This was especially the case in North Carolina, where bankers and conservatives wanted to entrench the instinctive racism that Wolin described.

Many of the sophisticated elements from the rebellious ranks understood what was at stake during the elections, so that in the election campaign of 2008, the massive voter registration drives by the Obama camp brought into play millions of new volunteers and tens of millions of new voters. From the period of the long primary season, the campaign embarked on the largest voter-registration drive in the history of US presidential campaigns. The organizational tasks that had been laid out in the caucuses in the Denver Convention took real form in the election campaign. Millions came forward, to the point where the distinctions between professionals and volunteers were blurred by the level of enthusiasm of the Obama supporters. In the words of *Wired Magazine*, the Obama campaign for the presidency in 2008 was "the most sophisticated organizing apparatus of any presidential campaign in history."[2]

Throughout the country, inventive forces emerged to engage the political system. This engagement with a phalanx of informed volunteers and voters proved to be the key to the challenge to the headlong rush to ruthlessness. The Obama team encouraged volunteers to take the campaign into their own hands.[3] Obama initiated the principle of getting volunteers to do things on their own, through inspiration, respect, and trust. Camp Obama and training sessions from the primary season through to the general elections of November honed these principles of respect and trust.

It was a campaign based on new strategies and tactics for mobilizing voters using the social networking tools of the twenty-first century. These tools, in isolation from real people, could not be the basis of what is now called the "inflection point" or the "decisive moment." The ground operation unleashed for the election was crucial for attempting to change the nature of political campaigns. More importantly, the ground operations employed scaling techniques, so that from the precinct level right up to the state organization, the command and control techniques for a particular state campaign could use the strategy most appropriate for that region.

The ground operation in this election campaign refers to the mobilization of grassroots and community forces to work on the ground in their communities, to register voters, get out the vote, and energize citizens in relation to the project of recovering real political democracy. The Obama campaign had placed an emphasis on expanding the electoral map as part of the task to counter the existing dynamics of power. The campaign was taking to heart the mantra of Barack Obama that there should not be red and blue states. Thus, though it was clear that states such as New York, Massachusetts, California, and New Jersey were traditionally Democratic states, volunteers in these states organized their own ground operations. In states such as Texas, Nebraska, Georgia, and much of the South which were supposed to be Republican territory, the Obama ground operation in targeted congressional districts took a long view of changing the electorate. To be on the ground in all parts of the country required a level of coordination and organization that had never been seen before in the United States (except by the military high command).

In the previous four decades, political consultants and advertisers were at the top of the campaign. Professional advertising firms used the latest techniques to hone a message, and the candidate usually flew into areas, gave a pep speech and encouraged volunteers. George W. Bush and Karl Rove had refined this technique of skilled advertising with a pep speech, where the mobilized ground volunteers were inspired by wedge issues such as abortion, same-sex marriage, or fundamentalist beliefs. One requirement of this technique was that the voter had to be as ignorant as possible.

The voluntary effort of Obama's field organization required a higher level of political and cultural literacy, and was not inspired by racism and wedge issues that encouraged divisiveness. Obama tapped into a popular mood and inspired a movement that pulled tens of millions of new voters to not only register but also vote. Voting in November 2008 was an act that was designed to inspire hope in a context where the financial system was imploding.

Obama's army of field operatives was part of a highly sophisticated voter education and outreach effort which operated with military precision in equipping voters with information to help them avoid problems at the polls.

The army of field volunteers needed to be people who could be trained and be educated on the political and economic realities of society. The map-reading skills of organizers had to be first rate. In door-to-door contacts, neighbor-to-neighbor, and professional networks all across the country, there was a new nested loop of energized citizens. For example, in a state such as Florida, there were over 19,000 neighborhood teams working with over 500 paid organizers. These organizers in Florida were just a fraction of the over 6,000 employed by the campaign. Remarkably, more than 95 percent of these full-time organizers were under the age of 30.[4]

The neighbor-to-neighbor networks supervised and managed by this youthful energy filtered through the overlap of networks and permeated the anti-war sentiments that were central to this election campaign. By having a presence in smaller towns and hamlets across the country, not only did field staff have the opportunity to contact new voters, they were also visible in the communities – eating with residents at restaurants, talking about issues in bars, and having an economic impact on these towns. In this way, there could be instant rebuttal of racist comments, such as Sarah Palin's cry that Obama was un-American, subtext for the fact that he was not white. Palin and the Republicans belittled Obama's experience as a community organizer, but the multiracial and democratic instincts that had been sharpened when Obama worked to register new voters in 1992 with Project Vote were now bearing fruit.[5]

The use of the term "ground operation" in this chapter is linked to the centrality of ordinary citizens, especially "fired-up youth," as volunteers in the election campaign. Earlier in the book, I highlighted the ways in which the embrace of Web 2.0 technologies made a difference in Obama's primary campaign. Then I compared the organization to the coming together of classical music and jazz. Classical music referred to the disciplined, regimented, and methodical command structure of the Obama operation. Jazz, in this context, referred to the improvisation, spontaneity, and enthusiasm of the volunteers and Obama supporters.

I want to highlight Ubuntu as a central aspect of the ground operation in so far as the Ubuntu of interpersonal networks was linked to a tech-savvy volunteer team. These were teams that zeroed in on voters using the kind of technology that had been used by the

Google search engine to target advertising to an individual's preferences. The campaign was able to develop a profile of voters based
on accumulated data on their employment status, credit card use,
car ownership, magazine subscriptions, and other intrusive information garnered through the mining of transaction footprints. From
this data, Obama campaign volunteers received detailed instructions
on whom to visit, including local maps of the area and walking
routes, and issues that each potential voter was likely to be most
concerned about. This ensured a high degree of sophistication in the
ordinary Obama supporter.

We will look deeply into the campaign in North Carolina to draw
out some of the key lessons for twenty-first-century politics. The
first lesson related to the importance of dealing with real people in
the study of politics. Political consultants and social scientists who
dealt with quantitative methods attempted to turn the question of
politics into statistical measurements about polls and voting behavior without dealing with the underlying issues of disenfranchisement
of large sections of the population.[6]

Second, the media had formed an alliance with the pundits to
frame the issues. Third was the high tolerance for racism and racist
politicians. In this election cycle, the Obama speech in Philadelphia
showed that there was a candidate who was not going to shy away
from dealing with the question of racism in society.

The Obama organization in the old Confederacy unleashed
unprecedented participation by citizens in many counties where
just a half century ago black people were systematically denied
the opportunity to even vote, much less run for president. North
Carolina, Virginia, Florida, and deep down in the South had begun
to turn from Benjamin Tillman and Jesse Helms. The civil rights
revolution was now moving to the next stage. The children of civil
rights were standing up. New networks were being strengthened,
and the election campaign benefited from these networks of women,
young people, and peace activists

The Obama campaign possessed three databases with unprecedented intelligence about the US electorate and society. An
intelligent electorate in a grassroots campaign for the presidency
fundamentally changed the political balance (if only temporarily).
It was in the face of this change in the electorate that the financial
oligarchy sought to extend its political muscle, and treasury secretary Henry Paulson became the "de facto leader of the country in
this time of crisis."[7] Other writers termed the turn of political events
a "coup."

This was the series of events in September which came after the fall of the Lehman Brothers investment bank. Simon Johnson, a former chief economist for the International Monetary Fund, called it a quiet coup.[8] Other congressional representatives called the bankers criminals, and demanded a diminution of their power. This open clash between democratic forces and the financial oligarchy became the dominant feature of US politics in 2008. The clash was a moment when "seemingly unrelated and disparate starting points converge to reinforce each other."[9]

September 15, 2008, will be recorded in the history, politics, and economics of the United States as an inflection point, or a moment of dramatic change. Inflection point is a mathematical term that has come into everyday usage to designate an event that changes the way we think and act. Our analysis of the revolutionary moment is seeking to grasp the evolution of the political and social struggles that emanated from this power grab by Wall Street oligarchs in the face of the implosion of the investment houses and the collapse of the international financial hegemony of the United States. Andrew Ross Sorkin, in his book *Too Big to Fail*, summed up the moment as a decisive one for the future of capitalism in the United States. But neither Sorkin nor film-maker Michael Moore made the important link between the levels of state intervention that had been orchestrated in September 2008 and the new possibilities for an educated population to intervene more forcefully to change the priorities of the society. The machinations to shore up this collapse of a failed economic model will go down in history as a real turning point for the United States.

This chapter seeks to link the intersection of the elections to the turning point of September 15, 2008, to the high-stakes struggle for power in the United States. Throughout this book, I have argued that capitalism cannot be separated from racism, sexism, and the destruction of the environment. While the Republicans took to the campaign trail with a less than subtle racist campaign that Obama was un-American, the financial aristocracy were cringing. The treasury secretary, Henry Paulson, organized a bailout of the banking system with trillions of dollars of public funds in the Troubled Assets Relief Program (TARP). By the end of the first year of the Obama administration over US$23 trillion had been pledged to save the bankers. At the moment of the financial coup in September, the amount that was being asked for was over US$700 billion. Revelations to the press one year later exposed the fact that the TARP document was actually written in April 2008, and that Paulson was waiting for the moment when the financial wizards could scare the population.[10] When Paulson and his aides were crafting the plan to support the financial oligarchs, one of Paulson's aides said plainly, "This is only going to work if you scared the shit out of them."[11]

It was an orchestrated scare that exposed the ruthlessness and panic that had taken over the financial sector. There was the biggest one-day drop in the Dow Jones Industrial Average in the history of the stock market. The old investment banking sector of the US economy disappeared. Merrill Lynch ceased to be an independent entity. At the start of 2008, there were five major investment banks. Two disappeared completely (Bears Stearns and Lehman). One was bought out by Bank of America and two others, Goldman Sachs and J. P Morgan Chase, became bank holding companies.

These changes demanded a robust discussion on the future of the twenty-first-century economy. Yet the demobilization of society had been so far advanced that the "bailout" did not become the number one issue in the election campaign. Though the word "coup" was employed by Simon Johnson, he did not identify the key players in the coup. Henry Paulson was a front for the bankers. Lloyd Blankfein, the CEO of Goldman Sachs, was a direct beneficiary of the interventions in September. He claimed that he was doing "God's work." Paulson, as a former CEO of Goldman Sachs, was operating in a world where the wishes of the bankers took precedence over the rest of the society.[12] After the election, the very same forces that had precipitated the crisis were promoted. This in itself is a statement on the power of Wall Street. That Lawrence Summers and Timothy Geithner were elevated inside the Obama cabinet told of the unseen power of the financial aristocracy. And yet the intensity of the struggle was simply heightened by the fact that in 2008, people were now watching and calculating. Though the debate was at the level of bonuses, press reports on the schemes called "derivatives" sparked new interest in the opaque world of bankers.

When Thomas Jefferson had written that banking establishments were more dangerous than standing armies, it was long before the US banking system had become enmeshed in the international financial system and international money laundering.

The financialization of the economy since Ronald Reagan laid the basis for a new framework for economic activities. Bubbles followed bubbles, and speculation trumped production, innovation, and work that elevated humans. The financial services industry became a dominant force in the world economy as the US stock market became the platform for new exotic products called "derivatives."

This was a fancy name for sophisticated gambling. The computer wizards who created these new "investment vehicles" were called "quants." Speculators dominated this circle of "investment" bankers. As long as US companies were able to expand overseas behind this military/financial strategy, US transnationals marched in line with this new drum beat. Risks begat risks and militarism inspired more adventures. Banks and standing armies had joined forces as the US financial empire was backed up by a far-flung system of military bases.

When the war against the people of Iraq was launched, capitalists in the technology sector remained silent. Capitalists who controlled giant corporations such as Microsoft and Google were complicit in this militarism as society celebrated the outrageous compensation paid to these "executives." It was not clear what anyone could do to earn a compensation of US$100 million per year. These forces expended more than US$3.2 billion in 2008 lobbying US government representatives. Bankers, real estate dealers, health insurance executives, pharmaceutical companies, manufacturers of armaments, and oil executives were the major forces in politics. Between September and December 2008, US citizens were being called upon to pay closer attention to this reality. They had no choice. Millions lost their jobs. Millions of others lost their homes. Increasingly, the question that was being discussed in the elections was the future of capitalism.

This chapter begins with the drama of the moment of September and the machinations of the gurus of Wall Street. Lehman Brothers had started in the era of slavery. The fall of Lehman was one effort to contain the recursive processes of US bank failures, but the laws of unintended consequences were slowly becoming clear to all those who wanted to see. This aspect of the banking crisis has been outside the mainstream media. From this analysis of the "quiet coup," we move to the ground operation in North Carolina.

THE MOMENT OF SEPTEMBER

After the Democratic and Republican conventions in August 2008, the election campaign was overshadowed by the financial crisis and the economic depression that threw millions out of work. Details of the financial collapse that seeped out to the public tore down the illusory world in which millions of Americans had lived. Less than eight weeks before the election date, panic overtook the country as the treasury secretary forced though a gigantic giveaway of trillions of dollars to the banks. One year later, continuous interventions had reached the point where over US$13.2 trillion had been committed to beating back the worst financial crisis since the Great Depression.

Months after the 2008 election campaign ended, Rep. Paul Kanjorski (D, Penn), chairman of the House Capital Markets Subcommittee, said on C-SPAN that the economic problems faced – by not just the United States, but indeed the entire world – were the result of an "electronic run on the bank" that resulted in the hemorrhaging of $550 billion in just "an hour or two." Kanjorsk said,

> The Treasury opened its window to help. They pumped a hundred and five billion dollars into the system and quickly realized that they could not stem the tide. We were having an electronic run on the banks. They decided to close the operation, close down the money accounts, and announce a guarantee of $250,000 per account so there wouldn't be further panic and there. And that's what actually happened. If they had not done that their estimation was that by two o'clock that afternoon, five-and-a-half trillion dollars would have been drawn out of the money market system of the United States, would have collapsed the entire economy of the United States, and within 24 hours the world economy would have collapsed.

This was his dire prediction: "the end of our political system and our economic systems as we know it." Why was this not a central issue in the election campaign? In the more than 20 books on the Obama campaign and victory, there is only passing reference to the activities of Paulson, Geithner, and the financial wizards. More than a year after emerging from the precipice, the very same bankers and financiers created new exotic and innovative products. Many economists inside and outside of government demanded rigorous control of the banks, even to the point of calling for nationalization.[13] Nationalization was one possible way to bring out of the shadows the interrelationships between the global financial system and the global drug trade. According to the UN Office on Drugs and Crime, these banks laundered over US$500 billion for international drug cartels.[14] During the 1990s, after the debacle of the Savings and Loans scandal, there had been efforts by some regulators to bring to the fore the role of the banks in the cocaine trade.

The secrecy of the banks in drugs followed the same path as the secrecy of the banks in the multitrillion-dollar derivatives market.[15] But then, and up to the present, the political power of the bankers had been so overwhelming that conscientious public servants were driven from their position by state officials who worked in the interests of the financial institutions.[16] One journalist noted that one of the banking institutions, Goldman Sachs, was the "best cash-making machine that global capitalism has ever produced, and, some say, a political force more powerful than governments."[17]

The drama of the moment of September brought to the fore the fact that bankers were more powerful than governments. Yet the scale and nature of the activities of the financial sector continues to be hidden from the public by a media that is complicit with the fraud. This was the conclusion of numerous writers who have written on how the political power of the financial sector was like an octopus choking the social system. Journalist Matt Taibbi called Goldman Sachs "a great vampire squid wrapped around the face of humanity, relentlessly jamming its blood funnel into anything that smells like money." One of the many challenges for twenty-first-century politics is how to break the stranglehold of the "vampire squid."[18]

In his article, "Inside the Great American Bubble Machine," Taibbi elaborated how the banks benefited from the Internet bubble, the housing bubble, and the commodities bubble. Authors who saw incompetence in relation to the Securities and Exchange Commission failed to grasp the full political implications for democratic participation and democratic action.[19]

Books and articles on the presidency of George W. Bush noted that he did not understand what was going on and repeated the mantra, "the fundamentals of the economy are strong."[20] The fundamentals referred to here lay in the political power of the financial oligarchy and the belief in the ideas of trickle-down economics. Behind this mantra was the realization that the economy was backed up by the US military and not by relations of production, exchange, and delivery of services such as education, decent health care, a clean environment, and housing. Politics was being dominated by organized interest groups, in short the financial capitalists.

RUTHLESSNESS AND RECKLESSNESS

While many writers have focused on the absence of regulation, it also emerged that this lack of regulatory oversight was not an accident but derived from the political and military interconnections between the financial sector, the military industrial sector, international drugs, and the top levels of the political system. "CIA Agents doing moonlighting work for the banks, consulting for Hedge Funds Consulting," private military contractors operating in the derivatives market and top generals on the boards of the Fortune 500 companies connected the link between the military and the banks. Eamon Javers wrote of these connections when he exposed the work of the CIA for banks.[21]

Arrogance, greed, recklessness, manipulation, and pettiness are now words associated with the politics of control fraud, and are attached to the titles of books on the hubris of the financial sector and the military industrial complex.[22]

Before its collapse in 2008, AIG (American International Group) had become a symbol of the misplaced power of Wall Street. Prior to the full exposure of its insurance, reinsurance, and derivatives business, AIG, as measured by asset value, was the largest insurer in the world. It was ranked ninth among the top Fortune 500 companies, with revenues of US$110 billion in 2007. In September 2008, after its AAA credit rating went down, AIG was without enough collateral for the credit default swaps it had sold to banks around the world, and was forced to accept a massive Federal bailout package in order to forestall a collapse.[23] The Federal bailout package was itself a testimony of the political power of the forces behind AIG.

In one of the historical accounts of the birth and evolution of AIG, Ron Shelp outlined the activities of the founder Cornelius Starr and the operations of the business during the Second World War.[24] There are now sources and documents that shed light on the connections between Starr and Bill Donovan of the Office of Strategic Services. These declassified documents revealed the ultra-secret Insurance Intelligence Unit, a component of the Office of Strategic Services, a forerunner of the CIA.

Before its collapse in 2008, AIG had grown from the operations set up by Starr to become the central operator in a nest of interlocking exposures in the market of credit default swaps. From its origins in Asia, AIG had matured from a small insurance business to a global business venture in financial services, asset management, life insurance and retirement services, and general insurance. As the global operations of AIG escalated with the spread of the US transnational corporations, this insurance giant acquired the International Lease Finance Corporation (ILFC). With this acquisition AIG became the largest aircraft lessor in the world, linking aircraft manufacturers to top executives and celebrities, the military, and bankers. Under chairman and CEO Maurice Greenberg, AIG operated in over 130 countries:

> as the company grew, it devolved a highly evolved structure of political exploitation. Step one, wherever possible, was to cultivate important relationships with political leaders. Step two was to fortify its influence abroad by cultivating even stronger relations with the US Foreign Policy establishment. One manifestation of that was Greenberg's leadership role with the Council on Foreign Relations in New York.[25]

From insurance, AIG had become enmeshed in the financial products business after its London unit decided to insure "collateralized debt obligations" (CDOs). It was in this opaque world of insuring derivatives that the world of economic ruthlessness converged with recklessness.[26]

In 2005 Greenberg was forced to step down after 20 years as CEO of AIG when an investigation initiated by New York's attorney general eventually resulted in a US$1.6 billion fine (US$1.15 billion after taxes) for AIG, and in criminal charges for some of its executives. In the financial crisis of 2008, AIG was not only too big to fail, its failure would expose the full history of AIG's close relations with the foreign policy establishment.

Newspapers such as the *Washington Post* and the *New York Times* became outspoken critics of the recklessness of AIG, but these same news organizations were enablers of the intellectual and ideological world of libertarianism, especially when AIG sponsored books and intellectual campaigns for the "liberalization of trade in services," and the papers showered praise on Alan Greenspan.

THE WORLD OF DERIVATIVES, POLITICS, AND RUTHLESSNESS

Entities such as the Carlyle Group, military industrialists who were now in the Wall Street business of "private equity," were ensconced within organizations with fancy names that disguised their links to the real players in the "iron triangle."[27] Very few citizens were aware of the links between asset management and financial services company Blackstone Group, investment management firm Black-Rock Inc., and the military industrial complex when the Obama administration awarded contracts to help the government "manage the complex rescues of Bear Stearns, the American International Group and Citigroup."[28]

Far from reflecting on the level of risk and the real consequences for ordinary citizens who placed their trust in the financial system, by the middle of 2009, the wizards of Wall Street had conjured new "products." Profits were not being made from lending to productive entrepreneurs but invented from trading in exotic products, essentially gambling. In the middle of 2009, less than a year after the near "collapse of the system," the financial oligarchy had regained their arrogance to the point where the "investment banks" in their new incarnations were repackaging old mortgage securities and offering to sell them as new products, a plan that was nearly identical to the complicated investment packages at the heart of the collapse of 2007–08. A predator state had arisen in a society where illusions of free market and competition had been used as a legitimizing myth to undermine the social weight and political influence of working people.[29]

In 1989 Michael Lewis, author of *Liar's Poker*, documented how the side bets made by the banks were created "out of a whole cloth, one hundred times over."[30] In our earlier chapter on the linkages between politics and economics during the primary season, we drew attention to the various names that had been affixed to the new practices relating to CDOs and other forms of derivative products.

With 20 years of experience in risk-taking backed up by the state, there were no assets to back up the bets being made. The risks from the 1990s were taken to an entirely new level. These derivatives were the instruments that Warren Buffet had labeled "financial weapons of mass destruction." Writers who commented on the interconnections between these banks in 2008 observed that:

> the unregulated $592 trillion market for over-the-counter derivatives, 41 times the size of the U.S. economy, contributed more than half of some banks' trading revenue and had never been tested by the bankruptcy of a major Wall Street firm.[31]

The derivatives market was a demonstration of the road to economics dominating politics, with the manifestations of the *Hidden Power* of the oligarchs of Wall Street.[32] It was a win–win situation because insurance firms such as AIG were integrated into this derivatives market. Credit default swaps were insurance-like contracts that insulated customers against the chances that the debt obligations they cover might not be paid. Buffet had warned in 2003 that "some derivatives contracts appear to have been devised by 'madmen.'" Madmen or not, the complicity of the Securities and Exchange Commission (SEC) and the US Treasury ensured that "financial innovators were able to create new products and markets without anyone thinking too much about their broader financial consequences."[33]

Financialization and securitization had enmeshed the financial services industry in highly complex financial instruments that harmed real people and destroyed the livelihood of millions of people in the United States and around the world. From Ireland to Latvia and from Iceland to Greece, the waste and carnage from neoliberalism inspired new political engagement. In Iceland nationalization was forced onto the country. New leaders emerged as society was forced to conduct criminal investigations, increase regulation, restore confidence in the economy, and clean out the parasitic bankers.

In the United States, the parasitism of the financial sector along with political power meant that the financial moguls had moved from being middle people in the economy to being central players in the political system.[34] It became clearer after scrutiny by investigative journalists and from diligent congressional representatives that this September 11, 2008 run on the bank, this near collapse, was all part of a larger political struggle in the United States to strengthen the bankers and the financial services industry.

With the knowledge that TARP was a scam to save the bankers, some progressive American politicians called for a bailout of the workers, instead of a bailout of the banks. But this call for the bailout of workers was at that particular minute of panic likened to a voice in the wilderness.

Six months before the "electronic run on the bank," the collapse of the investment bank Bears Stearns had been resolved by a "rescue" orchestrated by Henry Paulson. Using the power of his office, Paulson, one of the scores of alumni of Goldman Sachs in the top echelons of the bureaucracy, had arranged for the Federal Government to guarantee US$29 billion of Bear Stearns' toxic assets to facilitate the firm's sale to J. P. Morgan Chase. Some financial writers called this a gift. After the fall of Bear Stearns, it was known that Lehman Brothers was the next investment bank in trouble.

Together with bankers who had removed all of the regulations that had been implemented after the Great Depression, Lehman exulted in leveraging, as it became a household name among pensioners and those whose savings had been invested in its ventures from Hong Kong to London. Maturing from its cotton trade beginnings and profiting from slavery in the South, Lehman expanded in the era of monopoly capitalism and took off in the big league after the Second World War. Lehman was one of the banks that had been caught up in a long legal struggle over reparations for slavery.[35] The executives of Lehman had incurred the wrath of other bankers when it had apologized for its role in the enslavement of African Americans. This firm rode the waves of the expansion of US power after the dollar became the currency of international trade, and did business in investment banking, equity and fixed-income sales, research and trading, investment management, private equity, and private banking.

FINANCIALIZATION AS ECONOMIC TERRORISM

While short sellers were betting against the future of Lehman, the leaders of the bank took on more risk by borrowing more money. After August 2007, when the full exposure of the mortgage crisis came to light, the bank's leverage ratio skyrocketed as high as 44 to 1. In the period when the stocks were falling, the treasury secretary called numerous meetings to rescue Lehman and other exposed entities. By the end of August, these meetings had not produced results that could save the system. It will be up to history to divulge whether the electronic run on the bank was engineered. This is because there are now many writers who argue forcefully that the failure of Lehman was engineered to shock the system, another ruthless maneuver.[36]

During the month of August, the Obama campaign had hauled in a record US$66 million and John McCain's attack on Obama as a celebrity akin to Paris Hilton was running hollow as citizens focused on the economy. The Republicans had to search for scare tactics to frighten people, calling Obama a "terrorist lover." "In desperation, some in the White House speculated about a terrorist attack that would change the elections."[37] Kevin Phillips warned of this confusion over terrorism as early as 2002 when he wrote that:

The new US war against terrorism adds a further possibility that a US government concerned with protecting wealth may do so at the expense of democratic procedures and may try to blame terrorism rather than flawed economic hard times. There is also the possibility that the financialization processes of the 1980s and

1990s – securitizing so many income and debt streams, becoming electronically dependent, escalating the stock market as the center of commerce – have made possible a new manner of economic terrorism and warfare prior great powers never faced.[38]

Phillips was explicit when he likened financialization to a form of "economic terrorism" in the United States. This term had been used by the progressive left in the 1980s to characterize the war against the poor in Central America.[39] Earlier, Edward Herman had also used the term "economic terrorism" to characterize the neo-liberal policies of the government.[40] Now, within the upper levels of the US government, there was a revival of the concept of terrorism in the midst of the 2008 elections. What Matt Latimer had underestimated when he had heard talk in the White House about a "terrorist" attack was the very same scare tactics that he described in the machinations of Paulson. He had not understood the terrorism that was based on actual economic war against the poor.

After the details of the mortgage crisis had come out in the open in 2007, insiders in the big investment houses took on more risk even as there were calls for regulation. Lehman was one of the top innovators in the exotic instruments associated with the sub-prime mortgage crisis. This was one of the firms that had moved from outright engagement in slavery in the nineteenth century to be on the frontline of economic terrorism in the twenty-first century. In a world of terrorism and terrorists, there is a thin line separating victim from aggressor, so that Lehman in its turn became terrorized in 2008. Its stock began a steady fall from a peak of US$82 a share in 2007 to US$16.13 on September 2008, and then to US$3.65 ten days later. On Sunday afternoon, September 14, shares in Lehman Brothers were worth 3 cents. It was in this climate that Paulson called in the big moguls to alert them to save themselves from the contagion that had spread from Bear Stearns to Lehman and now exposed Goldman Sachs, J. P. Morgan, and Merrill Lynch. The top five investment firms in the United States were now about to become history.

Less than a decade after the revelations of the corruption and greed at Enron, the debacle of September 2008 was revealing to US citizens how the business aristocracy protected wealth and wielded power. Armed with the history of insider dealings since the era of Ronald Reagan and the unchecked powers of bankers, Richard Fuld, the CEO of Lehman, did not take into consideration the cut-throat legacies of the United States and the dangerous mix of "rational self-interest" and toxic competition. For Fuld, after the treasury secretary "rescued" Bear Stearns, it was logical that the government would also rescue the fourth largest investment bank.

The extent of the exposure of the entire banking system was becoming well known and could not be papered over. Henry Paulson, an unelected official as treasury secretary, and former CEO of Goldman Sachs, called together bankers to salvage the situation. Little by little, information is now coming out about the conflict of interest and the "waiver" that Paulson engineered in order to meet face-to-face with Goldman Sachs executives at the height of the crisis. Paulson made efforts to offload Lehman to Barclays (a UK bank), another bank that had its beginning in the enslavement of Africans.[41] When Paulson phoned the chancellor of the Exchequer, Alistair Darling, his counterpart in London, Darling told him he did not want to import the US cancer.[42] Managing this cancer occupied the treasury secretary up to January 2009, and history now reveals that the electronic run on the bank on September 11, 2008, was one more chink in the political armor of the bankers. Paulson had been searching far and wide, from the United Kingdom to South Korea, to ensnare other governments into the financial meltdown of the US financial oligarchy.

HENRY PAULSON AND THE DRAMA OF THE MOMENT OF SEPTEMBER

If Act 1, scene 1 of the political drama was the fall of Bear Stearns and the diversion of the Jeremiah Wright sideshow, Act 2, scene 1 was the panic induced by the electronic run on the bank, and the panic induced in September by the buzz that the United States was close to "the end of our political system and our economic systems as we know it."[43] Act 2, scene 2 of the dramatic week was the meeting of top bankers over the weekend of September 11–14. We now know that "two dozen of the world's most powerful bankers, brought together by Treasury Secretary Henry M. Paulson Jr. and Federal Reserve Bank of New York President Timothy F. Geithner the weekend of Sept. 13, 2008, to devise a rescue plan for Lehman, were too busy saving themselves to see the larger threat."[44] By Saturday morning, other investment banks sought cover as the treasury secretary along with the head of the New York Federal Reserve Bank connived to give shelter to Merrill Lynch, J. P. Morgan, and Goldman Sachs.

Paulson had been anxious to seal a deal before the opening of the Asian stock markets on Monday morning, September 15, which would be the evening of September 14 in New York. By Sunday night, the crisis management had been sealed. Deckchairs had been shuffled and Merrill Lynch was acquired by Bank of America. Months later, in February 2009, the CEO of Bank of America, Kenneth Lewis, testified before the attorney general of New York that Paulson and Fed chair Ben Bernanke "encouraged" (some might say, "conspired with") him to "keep silent about the deepening financial difficulties at Merrill Lynch."[45] When on the morning of September 15, 2008, Lehman Brothers filed for Chapter 11 bankruptcy protection, the filing marked the largest bankruptcy in US history. Revelations in the press now revealed that Bob Diamond of Barclays had "bought" the plum parts of the firm.[46]

After that day of September 15, 2008, it became clear that an old era had passed. The repercussions of the bankruptcy of Lehman and the acquisition of Merrill Lynch cascaded through the international financial system.

The fall of Lehman had unintended consequences as the commercial paper market froze. What the public had been told by the media was that Henry Paulson had sought to induce both Barclays and Bank of America to acquire Lehman Brothers. Books on the subject differ on the cause of the collapse.[47] Some writers claimed that Lehman had been sacrificed in order to shock the system, or that Lehman had to fail to save the US financial services sector. According to the public narratives reported in the media, the negotiations with possible buyers went on throughout that weekend. One year after the fall of Lehman, it became clear that the drama of the collapse of Lehman was part of a well-rehearsed strategy to strengthen the political power of the bankers.

ELEMENTS OF THE COUP

Johnson revealed that the victory of the financial services industry emerged from the fact that it had gained political power by amassing a kind of cultural-capital belief system. It was this cultural and political power that was to be displayed as Henry Paulson took the stage throughout the month of September to coax citizens to believe that what was good for Wall Street was good for America.

In his article in the *Atlantic*, Simon Johnson did not mention the connection between companies such as Blackstone and global private equity investment firm the Carlyle Group, or the fact that this connection along with the media persuaded US citizens that large financial institutions and free-flowing capital markets were crucial to America's position in the world.

SPEECHLESS AND POLITICS

The first candidacy to feel the impact of the financial collapse and the "quiet coup" was that of John McCain. During the campaign, McCain had been repeating all of the standard Republican lines that the government should adopt a hands-off attitude to the economy. McCain had exposed such a level of detachment from the realities of the everyday concerns of the US working people that he was insensitive enough to declare on the campaign trail that he did not know how many homes he possessed. Subsequent to the Republican Party Convention and the selection of Sarah Palin as the vice presidential running mate, the Republican Party seemed energized by the "grassroots and folksy" appeal of Palin. Democrats temporarily labeled her "Hurricane Sarah." However, two days after the collapse of Lehman and the fall in the stock market, John McCain used the Bush line that "the fundamentals of our economy are strong," despite what he described as "tremendous turmoil in our financial markets and Wall Street."

Following the fall of Lehman and the prolonged discussions to save the insolvent banks, Paulson had induced so much panic among representatives that he also warned that if the bailout bill was not passed, the situation would deteriorate to the point where it would be necessary to declare martial law.

While the threat of civil unrest was used to coerce members of Congress, it was clear that Paulson and his cronies were leading the country at that particular moment because the then president, George W. Bush, did not fully understand what was unfolding. In the book *Speech-less*, Latimer wrote,

> One of the president's staff members anxiously pulled a few of us aside. "The president is misunderstanding this proposal," he warned. "He has the wrong idea in his head. ... It wasn't that the president didn't understand what his administration wanted to do. It was that the treasury secretary didn't seem to know, changed his mind, had misled the president, or some combination of the three."[48]

Conservatives became outraged when Latimer wrote his book, but I quote at length to underscore the point that most politicians did not know what they were doing. There were a handful of representatives who opposed the railroaded legislation. Marcy Kaptur (D-Ohio) was one of the few members of the US House of Representatives who called the entire operation a criminal enterprise. She declared on the floor of the House,

> My message to the American people don't let Congress seal this deal. High financial crimes have been committed.
>
> The normal legislative process has been shelved. Only a few insiders are doing the dealing, sounds like insider trading to me. These criminals have so much political power that can shut down the normal legislative process of the highest law making body of this land.
>
> We are constitutionally sworn to protect and defend this Republic against all enemies, foreign and domestic. And my friends, there are enemies.

With hindsight, it is now clearer that Paulson himself, along with the bankers, did not know what the outcome would be. Paulson was simply exerting powers to support the financial oligarchy. They were manipulating the president, the public, and Congress.

Act 3 of the drama was the turbulence on Wall Street as the commercial paper market froze. Within a week, the US government stepped in to halt withdrawals from money market funds, leading to a US$1.6 trillion industry backstop, part of US$13.2 trillion it has committed to beating back the worst financial crisis since the Great Depression. These three acts of the financial coup and drama upended the election campaign. That dramatic week, as a pathway for the unfolding of the struggles in the United States, culminated in the first McCain–Obama debate. Prior to the moment of September, McCain had presented himself as the candidate of experience and proven leadership. Obama had acted calm and "presidential" during the crisis but he was also forced to defend the future of capitalism. In this period, the financial press was full of stories on the future of capitalism. Obama had to defend capitalism in the three debates in order to allay fears on the campaign trail that he was a socialist. When he made statements about the need to spread around the wealth of society, Palin declared that Obama was a socialist who had "palled around" with terrorists. One other Republican leader called the 2008 election "a referendum on socialism."[49]

OBAMA AND THE PRESIDENTIAL CAMPAIGN

While the Republican campaign crumbled in the face of the "inflection point," the Obama campaign for the presidency still had to demonstrate to the citizens that there were possibilities for a democratic opening, with citizens participating in a new form of campaign. The moment of September was defining in the sense that Obama was faced with talk of martial law and a potential terrorist attack. Later, we were to understand from former governor Tom Ridge that he had been pressured to raise the security alert on the eve of President George W. Bush's re-election in 2004.[50] The manipulation of security information for political purposes was not far from the minds of the Obama campaign, and the mantra of the campaign team was that Obama was to present himself as being steadfast and presidential. This steadfastness was also in response to the claim by the opposition that Obama was sympathetic to terrorism and had a past of "palling around with terrorists." Sarah Palin said at a campaign rally soon after the financial meltdown, "Our opponent ... is someone who sees America it seems as being so imperfect that he's palling around with terrorists who would target their own country." The Obama campaign responded immediately to point out that this attack on Obama was intended to distract attention from the financial crisis.[51]

Moreover, the 2008 elections were being held under the cloud of electoral fraud and the instruments in the hands of the private companies to manipulate election results.

The unleashing of the energy of a new constituency blunted the fraudulent operations of the Bush–Cheney infrastructure for election rigging.[52] In order to avert any possibility of the kind of fraud that had occurred in Florida in 2000, the Obama campaign threw such overwhelming force into the process that, in the end, the *machinery of hope* rendered the campaign so successful that it earned a place in history as a turning point for society. New organizers emerged to transform communities and revolutionize organizing itself in the United States.[53] The new organizers were young, energetic, anti-racist, and informed. Wired to the Internet and to the digital network, the young formed the backbone of the more than 13 million people who ended up on the Obama e-mail list.[54]

Andrew Rasiej confirmed this strategy of developing the media network for the Obama campaign in order to spell out the clear positions of Obama.[55]

The digital network had to have a base among real people, and it was the interface between young people building digital democracy and real communities that became the foundation of the ground operation. The ground operation was reinforced by the massive enthusiasm of ordinary citizens. These citizens had listened carefully to the talk of martial law and terrorist attacks, and were determined to intervene in the political process. One of the more enduring images of the 2008 election campaign was the final rally of over 85,000 people who had turned out and waited patiently in pouring rain to show their support for Barack Obama in Virginia. The grassroots were full of "hope," and it was at this rally that Obama announced the passing of his grandmother. He had used the history of his grandmother to remind the grassroots of how ordinary people had come together to survive during the Great Depression. Obama was calling for a new grassroots show of force in the 2008 election. In the words of David Plouffe, the campaign manager,

> We knew who we were, a grassroots campaign to the core. We started with our supporters on the ground and they led us to victory .... Obama felt in his gut that if properly motivated, a committed grassroots army could be a powerful force. Over time, the volunteers became the pillars that held the whole enterprise aloft.[56]

This powerful force was up against an even more powerful force that was contemplating ways to cancel, postpone, and hijack the elections.[57] Way back in April, Henry Paulson along with his assistant Neel Kashkari had nervously joked of the consequences of a possible Obama victory, comparing the possible emergence of Obama to Ronald Reagan bringing the hostages home in January 1981.[58]

Before the Democratic Party Convention in Denver, Obama had been on the road following a strategy that built on the organization that had been set in motion to win the primaries and caucuses. His general election plan, as laid out in the graphics and the strategy sessions of the campaign, had called for broadening the electoral map by challenging John McCain in "red" states, from North Carolina to Missouri to Montana. Obama sought to build on the voter turnout operations built in nearly 50 states in the long Democratic nomination battle. Planning for the election campaign had begun in the primary season, and included the organizational task to register new voters in all 50 states, to defend the Democratic majority in states that were won by John Kerry in 2004, and to compete in "battleground" states.[59]

The marriage of technology, sophisticated research, and messaging to the grassroots organization became a hallmark of the break from conventional forms of canvassing, phone banks and knocking on doors. The two aspects of the campaign – strategy and message – were interwoven in a way that provided consistency in the message for "Change that we can believe in" across all media channels. The strategy had been refined and perfected to contest the swing states, leverage the web – how and where to communicate the message. David Plouffe, the campaign manager, was at the core of a team[60] that harmonized message with strategy. One report noted that Plouffe knew every district in the country, where the Obama camp was, and where they could win.

With this knowledge of the electorate among members of the team, the campaign could make projections, slice and dice lists of volunteers by geographic micro region, and pair people with appropriate tasks. Centralized data collection and management gave this organization tremendous power in relation to basic information on citizens. Obama's key operatives laid out the campaign's strategic vision for the election in a PowerPoint presentation where Plouffe stressed that Georgia was home to 600,000 unregistered African American voters, all of whom the campaign was going to work hard to register and turn out. "Our volume is going to be enormous." In Florida, the Obama campaign had initiated an organization and planned to register 630,000 eligible Hispanics, 593,000 African Americans and 236,000 18- to 24-year-olds not yet on the rolls. By the end of September 2008, the Obama campaign had already spent close to US$39 million in Florida, and the more than 50 offices were staffed with 500 or more paid members, and hundreds of thousands of volunteers, organized in 19,000 neighborhood teams. These teams were part of the local communities where operatives were connected to the 770 offices opened across the country, more than twice the number used by McCain.

In these ground operations two fractal processes were clearly at work, scaling and recursion. From the neighborhood teams to the precinct level, the ideals of Ubuntu expanded the volunteer scheme in Florida, where the 2000 elections had been compromised. Paul Tewes, a veteran of ground operations for the Iowa caucuses, noted,

Volunteers pull in more volunteers who pull turn in more volunteers, and the campaign gives those volunteers wide latitude. ... Today the campaign counts 230,000 volunteers in Florida, including 19,000 "neighborhood team" members focused intensely on 1,400 neighborhoods across the state, usually covering four or five precincts. Those volunteers, many largely working free of a paid field organizer, become responsible to one another and motivate their cohorts to get out the vote in their own or an assigned neighborhood.[61]

I traveled to North Carolina to see the volunteer effort and to grasp how the ground operation unfolded in this state where there were officially 50 offices and 23,000 volunteers. In Plouffe's book, *Audacity to Win*, there is enough material in the chapter on "Rebuilding for the General Election" for readers to grasp the intense ground operation of the Obama campaign in other battleground states. Our task now is not to revisit the story of the ground operation in all of these states but to choose one of these states, North Carolina, to highlight how the organizational structures that were developed cascaded across the nation. Plouffe outlined how the campaign had targeted communities and states such as North Carolina that in the past had been written off by Democrats. Strategically, after the nomination in Denver, Obama made his first campaign stop in Southwestern Virginia where he could tap into supporters in both Virginia and North Carolina.

North Carolina is particularly important to our analysis because of the role that this state was playing in the unfolding financial crisis. If New York and Wall Street was the epicenter of the tremors from the fallout, North Carolina, especially Mecklenburg County, was the next major scene where the financial crisis and the election campaign had special relevance. The relevance was that the electoral victory was tied not only to the political campaign, but also to the desires of citizens to rise above control fraud and manipulation by the section of the "vampire squid" that had its base in North Carolina. Combating the twin challenges of the vampire squid and fraud required a level of cooperation across racial and ethnic lines in a state that had been at the forefront of the Jim Crow traditions symbolized by Senator Jesse Helms.

THE LEGACIES OF JESSE HELMS IN NORTH CAROLINA

During the period of the financial bubble, North Carolina had been touted as the new financial center of the United States. Charlotte became a banking hub second in importance to New York. Skyscrapers occupied by Bank of America and Wachovia dominated the skyline as the bubble of the banks boosted commercial real estate around Mecklenburg County, home of Charlotte and its bulging suburbs. At the moment when the bubble exploded, Bank of America, based in Charlotte, was one of the largest financial services companies, the largest bank by assets, the largest commercial bank by deposits, and the second largest by market capitalization in the United States. When the meltdown started to become public knowledge after September 15, 2008, both Bank of America and Wachovia were caught in the maelstrom of buying and selling that characterized the efforts of Henry Paulson and Timothy Geithner to save the bankers.

Bank of America was handed the chalice of Merrill Lynch the morning that Lehman fell, only to find out later its true level of toxicity. At the time of the takeover of Merrill Lynch, Kenneth Lewis, CEO of Bank of America, boasted to bank executives in New York that Charlotte was going to overtake Wall Street in political and economic influence.[62] When the real extent of the Merrill Lynch losses started to be revealed, Bank of America itself had to be rescued with over US$100 billion in handouts from the Federal government. Lewis himself was later forced to step down from Bank of America. In 2008, the Wachovia retail bank disappeared as an independent entity during the same week as the struggle over TARP, when Wells Fargo of San Francisco intervened to take it over. Commercial real estate values in the Mecklenburg County area had skyrocketed as Charlotte became politically and economically important. The bankers were comfortable in the surroundings that exulted in old Confederate culture. Senator Jesse Helms (R, North Carolina) had used his seniority in the Senate to support big capitalists and prop up the conservative Republican hold on this state during the last years of the twentieth century.

As a stronghold of politicians of the Ku Klux Klan variety, the white supremacist Democratic Party of the South dominated North Carolina until 1968, when the political establishment supported the Southern strategy of the Republican Party under Richard Nixon.

Jesse Helms, one of the senators for North Carolina from 1973 to 2003, had symbolized the white Southern backlash against racial integration and rights for all citizens. Helms was an open supporter of the apartheid regime in South Africa, and enjoyed the distinction of being one of the few lawmakers in the United States to boycott and protest when Nelson Mandela addressed the joint houses of Congress in 1990.

In this Dixiecrat territory of Southern conservatism, the Obama election campaign invested heavily to change the electorate. This decision on the part of the Obama team emanated from their study of the electorate and their knowledge that the political economy and demography of North Carolina had changed. Demographic change in the state from 1975 to 2008 had weakened the old conservative institutions, and there were millions of new immigrants. These immigrants were from four main categories:

- The skilled professionals who migrated to the banking hub of Charlotte and information technology firms around Raleigh-Durham.
- The new Hispanic migration elements. The Hispanic population multiplied from over 70,000 in 1970 to over 600,000 in 2004.[63]
- The large numbers of Asians migrating to North Carolina. According to Census data, the number of Asians doubled in the years from 1990 to 2002.
- The migration of African Americans from the North back to the South. North Carolina attracted the third largest number of blacks returning to the South.

Between 1990 and 2005, approximately 103,000 new African-Americans called the Charlotte area home. Hispanic migration during that same period totaled about 60,000. From 1995 to 2000, the Charlotte metropolitan area had the third-highest numbers of black migration in the nation, trailing only Atlanta and Dallas. The result was that the percentage of black Charlotte voters had increased from 26 percent in 1995 to 35 percent.[64]

Books by David Plouffe and other insiders on the campaign[65] reveal the strategy to win the South, where the largest section of the US population resided. Two states in this region, Florida and Texas, were among the four US states with the largest populations. It is clear from these books that the strategy for the South was not simply a short-term one relating to the 2008 election cycle, but was aimed at defeating the old racist divisions in the South and bringing millions of citizens into the political system to secure a "progressive majority."[66]

The Obama campaign had studied this demographic change, and talk about changing the face of the electorate at the national level had its local echo in the planning for the presidential elections in North Carolina. I traveled to the field offices in Forsyth County, Mecklenburg County, and Wake County to see the ground operation at first hand.

RESPECT, EMPOWER, INCLUDE – OBSERVING THE GROUND OPERATION AT FIRST HAND

My trip took place from October 2–5, 2008, in the heat of the registration process. The previous weekend of September 30, the state campaign had set itself a target of knocking on 100,000 doors for that weekend.[67]

In preparation for the trip, I had read the information on Obama sites and found the names of the offices and the field persons, but I had to go down to the offices to get a real sense of the work. The first office I visited was for Forsyth County, in the town of Winston Salem. There were six field organizers in this office. I requested permission to read the slogans on the wall, which instructed:

Vote 3 times –
1 President
2 State and local races
3 Judges (non-partisan).

The marching orders for volunteers were also scribbled on the wall:

1 Get people to register to vote.
2 Organize rides to the polls.
3 Whether people were going to vote.
4 Persuade people to vote for Obama.

While reading this I spoke to Rob, who was assisting a volunteer who had walked in. I saw for myself that the admonitions of "respect, empower, and include" were not simply slogans. The organizer had to be patient with volunteers so that the discussion and questioning would enable him to maximize their work. One clear issue that required a level of sensitivity was to handle the digital divide so that volunteers would be matched with jobs fitted to their skills.

Talking points for the phone bank people included (a) How to approach the call – based on information on file on the voter, and (b) How to answer questions – to dispel any form of intimidation.

YOUTH ACTIVISTS AND THE *WALL OF HOPE*

One of the most energetic areas of the office was the *Wall of Hope*. The *Wall of Hope* was a space where high school students made comments on the ongoing competition to determine which of the schools in Winston Salem could register the most voters. When I asked about the emphasis on the youth vote, especially high school students, it was explained that many of the high school students would reach voting age by November, and that a big push had been made to involve them during the primaries. The work with high school students was not only to generate foot soldiers for the 2008 elections, but also to prepare younger students for voting in 2012.

The Obama investment in youth went beyond high schools. The most enthusiastic volunteers for the Obama campaign all across the country were college students, and this was also the case in North Carolina.

TOLERANCE AND THE NETWORKS

I was told in Winston Salem that October morning that the goal of the campaign was to leave the county more organized than when it started. Nested into this goal were the tasks of changing the political situation in the country and strengthening the Democratic Party. In pursuit of these goals, the field operation invested time and resources in strengthening networks. Among the networks identified in the office were Women for Obama, Veterans for Obama, Independents for Obama, Active military/military spouses for Obama, People of faith for Obama (someone had to list their place of worship), Students for Obama, and Young Professionals for Obama Within these networks, volunteers deepened their own contacts beyond the neighborhood to reach out to their peers. Every one of these networks became a node of the new politics (see Figure 7.1).

I asked a local campaigner to give me two words to describe the campaign. He chose *excited* and *inspired*. I heard these words throughout the research trip. He spoke about the work and the efforts needed, that the field organization was at the core of the campaign.

Canvassing was the area of work that demanded the most people power. It is a labor-intensive aspect of the work that demands tact and tolerance. The Obama campaign had brought together the labor-intensive efforts of community organizing with high-tech information systems to process information from the millions of volunteers. The different teams were tasked to divide their work even further, dealing with faith groups, women, Hispanics, the armed forces, blacks, and so on.

Much of the literature on the campaign focused on its high-tech

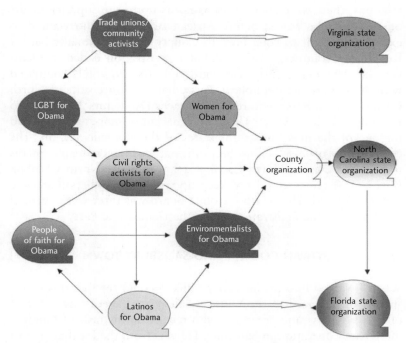

Within each of these spheres are three categories of people: 1) Mobilizers; 2) Connectors and 3) Core Organizers

Other forces not shown

Lawyrers for Obama held in reserve until the period of the Get out the Vote, registration and the election day

Website as the organizing tool for the groups

    Go to the website and log in to find the group in your area

Categories/groups that were created recently

    That Were Updated Recently

    With the Most Members

    With Recent Blog Posts

These search tools allowed for new levels of spontaneity and self organization

Figure 7.1 The Network of Networks

tools, but this focus conceals a class and racial bias that could only be seen in the field. One of the most striking aspects of interaction on the ground was the level of tolerance and respect showed to the walk-ins.

North Carolina was one of the states that had used schemes such as poll taxes, residency requirements, literacy tests, and grandfather clauses to disenfranchise non-white voters. Up to the 2008 elections, there were court cases as far as up to the Supreme Court on the obstacles placed before African Americans who wanted to exercise the right to vote. Forsyth County had traditionally been a Republican county. By the time voter registration ended in October, the Democratic Party had registered 103,996 voters compared with 74,879 for the Republican Party. For the entire state of North Carolina, the difference in registration was Democrats 2,871,589 to Republicans 2,005,386.[68] This was a margin of more than 866,000 for one of the most important states of the Confederacy, and the constituency of Jesse Helms. So proficient was the campaign operation of the Obama North Carolina team that the North Carolina Board of Elections could not keep up with the numbers that were being registered. The North Carolina Board was three weeks behind in computing the registrations from the Democratic Party.

ROWAN COUNTY AND SALISBURY TOWN

When I walked into the Salisbury office, I could see that this was a smaller operation than the Winston Salem one. There was one field officer, a very young organizer who reveled in his task of building the Obama operation in Salisbury. He was from the local area, and said that his task was to build a more informed electorate. It was he who made the crucial distinction between the Internet campaign and the human interaction on the ground. He noted, "Volunteers come in the door for the candidate; they come back for the field organizers."

The self-confidence of this young organizer came through as he related the efforts in Salisbury to clarify the issues for the voters. The sitting senator, Elizabeth Dole, had underestimated the strength of the Obama operation and had not invested resources in the campaign. After the massive voter registration and get-out-the-vote efforts, Dole became desperate and waged a campaign based on three core wedge issues: religion, abortion, and same-sex relations. She accused challenger Kay Hagan of being "godless." This type of divisive political advertising had been standard in North Carolina during the civil rights revolution. Prior to the 2008 elections, Dole had not resorted to a divisive campaign based on racial and religious issues, but with Barack Obama, a designated black person at the head of the rival ticket, she went back to the strategies and tactics of Jesse Helms. However, by the time she resorted to the old religious divide and rule, the electorate had moved past the Republican Party.

What was significant about this episode for the national campaign was the extent to which the old wedge issues were wearing thin in the face of the economic crisis. The Salisbury office volunteer related how numerous women had walked into the office to volunteer for the campaign after Sarah Palin has been nominated as the Republican VP candidate. Black and white voters were coming forward, including some who had never voted in an election before.

MECKLENBURG COUNTY AND CROSSING INTO SOUTH CAROLINA

Mecklenburg is the most populous county in the state of North Carolina. Class divisions there are deep, and income inequality is exaggerated by the high salaries of banking executives. Class and racial divisions are reflected in the differences in quality of housing, neighborhoods, and schools. Within the Obama campaign, these differences were papered over largely because the black middle class wanted to have equal access to state resources. Many of the black professionals who had moved into North Carolina were ideologically in tune with the financial elites. In the Charlotte office of the Obama campaign I could see the intense mapping and technical operation at work. The convergence between the field operation and the centralized web-mapping portals gave the organization a reach in all neighborhoods. However, the spatial and racial make-up of neighborhoods ensured that the self-organization and self-mobilization in the black and Latino communities carried the Obama campaign forward.

From the un-Obama-like feel of the Charlotte office and the Bank of America landscape, I proceeded to visit the campaign offices across the state line in South Carolina. In the county of Greenville, South Carolina, I met some of the unsung heroes and heroines of the campaign for change. South Carolina had fought hard to rid itself of the ghost of Benjamin Tillman and its racist heritage. It was in Greenwood that Obama had been fired up, and the slogan of the campaign, "Fired up: ready to go" echoed through the voice of Edith Childs, who represented that link between the civil rights generation and the new revolutionary moment.

While I was in the Greenville campaign office, reports came in of apartment buildings where voters were waiting to be registered. There were stories of hundreds who had never voted before in an election, but had now registered as a result of the office's blitz registration drive. One of the most moving stories was of a 90-year-old who had registered for the first time.

Witnessing the passion of the volunteers (young and old, black and white) was like a breath of fresh air in the midst of the Palin/McCain rhetoric about race and the fearmongering from Paulson. Blue Dog Democrats (a group of moderate-to-conservative Democrats committed to financial and national security) were now working side by side with former freedom riders of the civil rights movement. For the first time since the Reconstruction period of 1865–77, there was a new possibility of workers identifying with their own class interests before the interest of the capitalist classes. From Greenwood and Greenville I heard of the registration of white workers who were now turning their backs on the Republicans. Even though the Obama campaign was not as full-blown in South Carolina as it was in the top 14 battleground states, in its offices in Greenville and Rock Hill I saw levels of cooperation and collaboration between blacks and whites that, if translated beyond elections, could hold new meaning for political change.

THE NERVE CENTER IN RALEIGH-DURHAM

The main North Carolina office of the Obama campaign for president was in Raleigh, and here I saw full integration between the high-tech operation and the ground door-to-door operation. It integrated online activities with tasks that real people could perform in the multilingual, multicultural, and multiracial world of North Carolina. I visited before the registration campaign was in its final stage (registration closed on October 10). The Obama campaign had mobilized the resources of "reality mining" to put together data on voters that was way beyond any previous campaign organization.

It was able to put together a profile of every citizen it chose, and had done detailed studies of the voting patterns and demographic make-up of the South and the West. A block-by-block strategy mined the information base to identify new voters. The information was culled from a variety of sources, including magazine subscriptions, the types of cars people drove, where they shopped and how much they earned. Commuting patterns were also analyzed. Voting history in local races was factored in. For those who use the Internet, the Google effect of the Obama machinery meant that the tech geeks at Blue State Digital could know a great deal about the voters: what issues they cared about, what organizing and donating they did, who belonged to their social networks, whether they would volunteer and so on.

After the national data was studied and sorted at campaign headquarters in Chicago it was sent to every battleground state.

The names were bar-coded and ultimately showed up on the lists given to volunteers. The door-to-door operation was then armed with the information so that when a canvasser spoke to a voter, they had some information already. Information was verified, or disproved, through conversations at doorsteps or in telephone calls, where voting intentions were scaled from 1 (strongly for Obama) to 5 (strongly for McCain).

Although the campaign had promised that Obama would use technology to create "a new level of transparency, accountability, and participation," I did not see the mapping department that was the center for uploading the voter registration information into the databases of the Obama cyber world. This cyber world was a world unto itself, and the information from Forsyth County and Mecklenburg County was funneled to Raleigh, and then to Chicago and Blue State Digital in Boston.

When I visited the Raleigh office, the legal team was being set up to defend the vote. Lawyers for Obama all over the country had volunteered to ensure that there was no repetition of the 2000 electoral fraud in Florida. Updated Jim Crow practices had been refined by the Bush administration under the supervision of Karl Rove. Throughout the decade, the Bush White House had worked overtime to sharpen the tools to disenfranchise numerous citizens, especially African Americans. In 2002, the US House of Representatives had passed the Help America Voting Act (HAVA) to simplify electoral procedures, but the Justice Department under George W. Bush had worked to make voting harder. Many states had implemented new voter ID laws, restrictions on registration drives, and stricter rules for counting provisional ballots. These were new and legal ways to accomplish a longstanding GOP electoral tactic: thinning the ranks of likely Democratic voters. Under the George W. Bush White House, the attorney general Alberto Gonzalez had gone so far as to fire US attorneys who did not go along with the plans of deepening the disenfranchisement of the poor. Lawyers for Obama were on the frontline of the battle to defend the vote.

A DIVIDED MILITARY

One crucial constituency in the state of North Carolina was the military. There are currently eight active military installations in North Carolina, with a very large military presence at two major bases. Military opposition to the Republican wars had become so intense in the camps that even Republican Congressional representatives like Walter

Jones became outspoken critics of the wars in Afghanistan and Iraq. Jones's criticism was one more reflection of the *war within*, or the divisions inside the military itself. Veterans for Obama occupied a special place in the North Carolina offices. Michelle Obama had carved out a niche in the campaign working with military families. She had been a silent weapon in the campaign, galvanizing support in the Deep South while biting her tongue. At the Democratic National Convention, she made it known to one of the caucuses that she was surprised at some of the positions taken by Barack, especially on issues related to war and peace. However she did not make it clear whether she disagreed with her husband's bellicose stand on Afghanistan.

CONCLUSION

Barack Obama won the elections on November 4, 2008, by a landslide of 375 electoral votes to John McCain's 163. The turnout was the highest since the presidential elections of 1960 which brought John F. Kennedy to the White House. Three days after the elections, Michael Connell died in a plane crash. Connell had been implicated in the establishment of a computer architecture setup called "Man in the Middle," which had previously involved the shunting of the election returns from one state to the next. Connell had worked within the Bush–Cheney infrastructure for electoral fraud, and was being questioned by the Justice Department. His untimely death left unanswered questions about the extent of electoral fraud carried out by the Republican Party between 2000 and 2008. Later the company that was associated with voter fraud, Diebold, went out of business.

The Justice Department under the George W. Bush presidency had been politicized to the point where officials were more vigorous in disenfranchising the poor and blacks than in prosecuting theft and fraud from the financial barons. Although Obama won by a landslide in November 2008, one researcher estimated that in fact,

> Obama probably won by twice as many votes as we think. Probably a good seven million votes for Obama were undone through vote suppression and fraud, because the stuff was extensive and pervasive, in places where you wouldn't expect it.[69]

Mark Crispin Miller, author of *Loser Take All: Election Fraud and the Subversion of Democracy, 2000–2008*,[70] was among the few scholars and commentators who had perceived the ways in which US democracy had been subverted under the Bush administration. This subversion has been assisted by the social science disciplines that tried to befuddle citizens with statistical methods and mathematically based models of politics. What was being raised by Miller was simple: can society move in a new direction where voter suppression, fraud, and disenfranchisement will not be covered up and papered over?

My analysis in this chapter was intended to bring to the fore the reality that even the little democratic expression that existed was threatened by the political and economic power of the barons of Wall Street. From my research, I agree with those who claim that Paulson's actions were intended to scare the population, with an aggressiveness and ruthlessness that indicated the full extent to which the financial oligarchy dominated the politics of the United States. What Simon Johnson had called a "quiet coup" had failed to connect the fraudulent election of Florida in 2000 to the voter disenfranchisement and empowering of the super-rich in the United States. The crisis is so deep that sections will contemplate moving from a quiet coup to more overt forms of intervention. Numerous books are now coming out on the moment of September 2008. Few have raised the fundamental question of the future of capitalism in general, and the future of capitalism in the United States in particular. Yet the discussion cannot be postponed.

The campaign to elect Obama as president of the United States threw up new organizational forms. I agree with Zack Exley's observation that the way organizing is understood has itself been revolutionized by the campaign. It is the ideological and intellectual underdevelopment of the society that holds back the full explosion of forces in combat. Yet the contradictions are so deep that the resolution will not await neat and clear theories of social change. The mobilization of voters has temporarily stalled a harder form of a more explicitly repressive state that could move from "inverted totalitarianism" to full-blown fascism.

During the electoral contest, there was already talk of a declaration of martial law. Increasingly armed, the conservative forces have sought to draw on the racist and sexist past to mobilize against social justice. Unfortunately for these conservative forces, for the first time since Reconstruction in 1865, the Federal Government is not totally in the hands of conservative forces. A divided military confronts a divided society where citizens are calling for books not bombs, and schools not jails. These calls strike at the heart of the military industrial organization that held society together.

Working people understand that, in times of crisis, the capitalist classes will drop the "front" of democratic participation and unleash brute force. Obama's election was a holding action to postpone this clenched fist of capitalism.

Timothy Tyson, the author of *Blood Done Sign My Name*,[71] speaking about the prospect of an Obama victory in North Carolina, went on to say, "It would show that we are on the edge of yet another new South, a forward-looking South that will rise again but with school books, not bayonets, with health care, not a Confederacy of Dunces."[72]

The expectation of a society rising with schoolbooks and health care and not bayonets was not unique to North Carolina. American society is on the edge of a new era. The postponement of the task to dismantle militarism can only be temporary insofar as the United States is involved in wars in all parts of the world, and the crisis of capitalism is simultaneously a crisis of imperialism. The confluence of wars, financial crisis, environmental degradation, and unemployment brought society to a new turning point.

Would the turn be towards repression or the deepening of democratic participation and expression? Our discussion and reflection on the moment now turns to the networks that can break with the traditions of racism and militarism.

8

BEYOND MESSIAHS: NETWORKS FOR PEACE AND TRANSFORMATION IN THE TWENTY-FIRST CENTURY

He is not operating on the same plane as ordinary politicians ... the agent of transformation in an age of revolution, as a figure uniquely qualified to open the door to the 21st century. Barack Obama is our collective representation of our purest hopes, our highest visions and our deepest knowings. ... He's our product out of the all-knowing quantum field of intelligence.

Gary Hart

INTRODUCTION

There was happiness worldwide on Wednesday morning, November 5, 2008, after Barack Hussein Obama's victory in the campaign to become the president of the United States. With the memory of the stand-off in Florida over the elections of November 2000, the Obama campaign had mobilized more than 250,000 people to attend the victory rally at Grant Park in Chicago. After the rumors of martial law and threats of a potential "terrorist attack," the victorious candidate wanted to show that there was popular support to thwart possible mischief. A similar mass mobilization was undertaken for the inauguration on January 20, 2009 when Barack Obama was sworn in as the 44th president of the United States. More than 2 million people assembled on the National Mall in Washington to witness the inauguration, where Obama proclaimed that there was "A new birth of freedom." Which freedom was this, the freedom of the liberal democratic creed or the freedom of those who followed the North Star of the underground railroad?

There were many occasions when Obama used the story of the North Star to refer to the escape from slavery through the underground railroad. But Obama used metaphors about the North Star instead of speaking plainly about the tasks of transcending the traditions of institutional racism, sexism, exploitation, and the destruction of the environment. This begged the question: was he trapped by liberalism? Whether Obama was trapped or captured had to await the experience of the actual occupation of office as 44th president.

When Obama was entering the White House in January 2009, he was certainly trapped by a totalitarian presidential tradition bequeathed by George W. Bush and Richard Cheney. Whether he could escape the inheritance of the previous political directions of an imperial state was dependent on his ability to understand the imperial nature of the society, and on the networks for peace that had to grow to manifest an alternative source of people power. The inheritance of throwing trillions to the financial oligarchy necessitated a critical appraisal of the ideation system that had suggested only the salvaging of the big banks could save the system. Obama wanted to occupy the "middle ground" in US politics, but in revolutionary moments, leaders are forced to take sides. Revolutionary forces, whether in the areas of climate change, the economic hothouse, or the impatience of the young, had undermined the middle road. Leaders had to lead, take sides, or be cast aside.

Many progressives understood that something was fundamentally wrong with US society, but pinned their hopes on the election of Obama. These elements had no coherent movement. The old Left had virtually disintegrated, with disagreement over whether to support electoral politics or not. In the midst of the indecisiveness of the progressives, the mainstream media took the missionism and messianic traditions of society to the point of comparing Barack Obama to a black Jesus. Society was trapped by its religiosity, just as history weighed as an albatross around its neck. Obama was entrapped within these traditions of messianism, the presidency, inherited wars, neo-liberalism, and the incompetence of a class that promoted religious intolerance and hatred in order to destabilize people.

Throughout history, religiosity and the sense of Americans as a chosen people had been popularized in society. "Manifest Destiny" and the view that the United States was "the last best hope for humanity" had been trumpeted for decades in the nineteenth century. Throughout the twentieth century, the United States was presented as the savior of the planet, rescuing humanity from communism. This doctrine of salvation was so deep that there was a slogan, "better dead than red." Every politician, whether Republican or Democrat, parroted the slogan that the United States was like a "shining city upon a hill whose beacon light guides freedom-loving people everywhere." George W. Bush had taken this Christian mission even further after September 2001, when he framed the war against terror as a moral mission blessed by God. This morality was embodied in the proposition that the United States was fighting against an "axis of evil."[1]

Our challenge is to grasp the limits of messianisn, liberalism, and charismatic leadership in American society. In a profound way, the ideas of technological determinism, of unlimited capabilities of technocrats, reinforced messianism and the concept of US society as comprising "a chosen" people. Thus, liberalism carried within its logic the privileging of the profit motive over human relations. This same logic of capital accumulation comes into conflict with the future of the planet, but the blind belief in individual accumulation carries with it visions of technological determinism. This determinism influenced scientists and policymakers in the United States to predict that "technology could save the economy."[2]

In this chapter, we argue that it was the very belief in technological progress that has brought humanity to the point where the planet is in peril. Technological determinism and liberalism were two aspects of an ideological outlook that captured the presidency of Barack Obama. This trap of the liberal ideology was compounded by the messianism of the inherited wars against terrorism.

At precisely the moment when the peace and justice forces were being called upon to awaken to the sharp struggles locally and internationally, sections of the peace movement silenced themselves by looking to answers from Obama.

Conservatives and racists had no such hesitation. Their networks of intolerance, hate and ugliness, racism, sexism and homophobia sought to take over the debate about the future of American society. These networks of conservatism and whiteness occupied public spaces with weapons, and were given much publicity in a conservative media. Right-wing militias and white supremacists came out of the woodwork, spreading their venomous ideas to sections of the military.

The songs and sounds of the election period had tapped into the large reservoir of the cultural wealth of society that was repressed by Eurocentrism. Messages of change, hope, and peace during the election campaign had resonated with a population that wanted an end to a monolithic culture, especially the armaments culture. Millions had turned out to join networks during the campaign, and were now in a holding pattern. These forces projected their existence into a new self that wanted to escape the militaristic culture, but those who sought a second life had to go through the rituals of reparations and repair.

Those seeking to repair the environment and retreat from the repression of society were slowly beginning to understand that twenty-first-century politics had to transcend electoral forms. Reparative justice for people and repairing the headlong rush to the destruction of the planet would spark new engagements.

Before his "crucifixion," Van Jones had put forward some bold ideas on confronting climate change through his ideas about a *Green Collar Economy*. However, Van Jones's vision was based on a nineteenth and twentieth-century conception of employment and work. Was he holding back on the Ella Baker part of the vision because he was in the White House as energy czar? Obama and his advisers repeated the wish to return to "full employment." This was the same vision as that of a fractured trade union movement which wanted to return to the Works Progress Administration (WPA) of the New Deal. But the changes in the nature of the economy required new thinking for new circumstances, where construction of public buildings and roads, and environmental clean-up would not be based on the segregated enclaves of oppression and super-exploitation.

Confronting the environmental clean-up and mobilizing the creative energies of people require a different kind of thinking from the economists of the twentieth century. How would a country headed toward full unemployment rethink its ideas on society and economics? How could it grasp the reality that we were on the threshold of a workless society? What values were necessary to replace the old dogma that humans received affirmation of their humanity from being gainfully employed? The era of the "end of work" and full unemployment required new thinking about the real purpose of society. This era was not only an indictment of the old Left in the United States, but another critique of the liberal credo of the male breadwinner in the family. This trap of the old Left was being reinforced by the supposed view that progress entailed "development of the productive forces." This attention to productive forces, devoid of a focus on the quality of people's lives, devalues human worth.

Because of the global dehumanization that flowed from the mode of economic organization, the question of the day-to-day policies of the US government was watched by billions. The polarization and pauperization at the global level were slowly becoming manifest in all areas of social life inside the United States, to the point where sections of society were slowly being released from messianic leadership and the belief that capitalist organization could solve the problems of humanity. The most articulate sectors of this anti-capitalist struggle were those involved in the networks of the environmental justice movement. Climate scientists who clarified that global warming was more severe than predicted were among those who were not waiting for a messiah.

THE TRAP OF MESSIANISM AND MILITARISM

In Chapter 5, in the analysis of the South Carolina electoral contest, I drew attention to the rally in the stadium and the claim by Oprah Winfrey that Obama was "the one." This reference to Obama as the "one" met the emotive needs of a number of audiences, and particularly the secular tech-savvy and networked youths who followed the movie trilogy, *The Matrix*, where the hero, Neo, was referred to as The One or the Liberator. The second and wider audience was the Christian followers who believed in the Messiah and messianic leadership. For these forces, the United States was God's country. Capitalism and the pursuit of profit were doing God's work. This was the audience which believed in the Second Coming, and that a new Savior would come to redeem US society. The third audience was that sector of US society that was looking for a reincarnation of the hope and optimism that had been alive during the period of John F. Kennedy. During the election campaign there was the delicate dip into the well of the prophetic traditions in the call, "Yes we can" and the slogan, "We are the ones that we've been waiting for." Thus, in the midst of the Obama victory were those who believed that he combined the qualities of liberator, redeemer, and savior.

After the euphoria of the election victory and the celebrations associated with the inauguration, reality intervened. It was the reality of the polarization between the 1 percent at the top and the increased immiserization of the majority of citizens. It was also the reality that the working people were being squeezed by the banks, the militarists, and the insecurity generated by the depression. By the end of December of the first year of the Obama administration,

Table 8.1 Compendium of instruments and commitment to support the financial oligarchy

Facility	Estimated total as of Dec 2009
Troubled Asset Relief Program	$700 billion
Federal Reserve rescue efforts	$6.4 trillion
Federal stimulus programs	$1.2 trillion
American International Group	$182 billion
FDIC bank takeovers	$45.4 billion
Other financial initiatives	$1.7 trillion
Other housing initiatives	$745 billion
Total	$11 trillion

the US Government had committed over US$11 trillion to save the financial system.

While Congress and the media were focused on the US$700 billion of the TARP, the Federal Reserve was quietly developing new opaque instruments to transfer funds to the bankers.[3] There was no shortage of economists who were presenting information to the government and to society that the cumulative results of the interventions by the government were preparing the ground for another financial meltdown. In July 2009, Neil Barofsky, the special inspector general of TARP, testified before a Congressional Committee that "the total potential Federal Government support could reach up to $23.7 trillion."[4]

When the outcry against the banks intensified, the CEO of Goldman Sachs retorted that he was only doing "God's will." The head of Goldman Sachs was tapping into the fundamentalist mindset of the divine mission that had been nurtured for generations. This same mindset was manifest in the defense industry, where one company was stamping bible verses on rifles to be used by the military in Afghanistan.[5] Fighting terrorism was also a divine mission.

The mindset and belief system had been drilled into US society that America was the land of opportunity, where everyone who works hard can make it to the top. Thus, those elements at the top had the right to make unlimited profits, regardless of the societal costs. The right of the bankers to make profits and to get rich was part of the liberal dream of freedom. James Carroll had noted that religiously inspired violence and "missionizing in the name of freedom" were basic American impulses.[6] The idea of the special mission evolved as a kind of American ideology associated with "fundamental liberalism."[7]

Obama was trained within the liberal tradition, and he believed in this vision of the United States as "the city on the hill." It was this fundamentalism that led to expectations after the election of Obama that he was the "chosen one" with special gifts for leadership. This messianic label had been fostered by political pundits who lavished praise on Obama, seeking to make a distinction between him and the social organization and social networks that elected him.

Belief in the ability of a chosen leader was not confined to US society. This belief that a leader would emerge as the liberator was also strong among liberation movements in Africa and in the *caudillo* traditions of Latin America.

Within the United States, leaderism, liberalism, and messianism had been promoted by a system that wanted to overturn the grass-roots mobilization of the peace movement and replace this force with a movement that supported war in the name of fighting terrorism. During the civil rights movement, the spontaneous and organized efforts of grassroots forces had sustained the anti-war movement. The media had elevated Martin Luther King, Jr. above the movement that created him, placing emphasis on the symbolism of his speech at the National Mall in Washington, instead of the content of his message. King had been trained in the fundamental liberalism of US society, but in the process of the struggles against racism and for peace, King transcended its liberalism and fundamentalism. The movement for social justice had released him from the conservative brand of Christianity and brought him closer to the traditions of liberation theology.

The social justice part of his "arc of a moral universe" was deleted from young minds, and what was usually invoked were King's charisma and leadership skills. The conservative media and many of his supporters preferred to see Obama as a fully formed messiah, instead of moving to interrogate what it would take to strengthen the moral arc of justice so that society escapes spiritual death.

Obama himself understood the limitations of his generation and his own class background. On numerous occasions, he likened King and his compatriots to the Moses generation that made the sacrifices for civil rights, just as Moses led the children of Israel out of bondage in Egypt. Those who reaped the fruits of the Moses generation were up-and-coming entrepreneurs and other sections of the rising black bourgeoisie who had not been involved in struggle. The *New Yorker* described this group of entrepreneurs around Obama as "the Joshua generation – the successful, talented, networking, and, in many cases, idealistic daughters and sons who benefited from struggles that they could not have known firsthand."[8]

Unlike King, there was no mass movement that was organized to hold Obama accountable within the "Joshua generation." The structures of the government and the Democratic Party contained the pollution and corruption of values that King had fought against. There was a grassroots coalition that had come together from different networks to elect Obama, but from the corridors of the Denver Convention, corporate elements strategized how to win the elections and then demobilize the enthusiasm of youth. After the elections, pictures of Obama dominated the news. This media blitz created false expectations of overnight changes, and perpetuated the imagery of a liberator for society.

After the election, it slowly became clear that Obama had neither an organization nor a vision that was independent of the political consultancy business, where political campaigns were part of a multi-billion-dollar business. His campaign managers and advertising guru entrepreneurs of the political consulting industry exulted in their new business organization that tapped into social networking technologies. Conservative media commentators buttressed the ammunition of political consultants in the determination of the choices of the team for the transition. This was most evident in the campaign against Linda Darling-Hammond, who had led the transition team for the Education Department.[9]

What is now clearer to people was that Obama was engaging in self-deception when he spent quality time with conservatives such as David Brooks and George Will in the name of bipartisanship. These conservative commentators had a base in the corporate media, while progressive social activists such as Linda Darling-Hammond and Van Jones had bases in the education and environmental justice networks. Caught in the social and intellectual world of his classmates from Harvard Law School and the Chicago economists, Barack Obama took for granted the allegiance of the peace and justice forces in society.

Consistent with the belief that the liberal ideas of trickle-down economics would save the system, Obama selected the same team of economic advisers who had been overseers of the asset bubbles. From the figures in Table 8.1 of the over $11 trillion committed to the financial industry, it becomes clearer why Geithner had to be at the Treasury to ensure continuity for the bankers. Instead of working with the mobilized grassroots to turn the campaign slogan "Change we can believe in" into a clear policy for reconstruction, Obama deferred to the bankers, to assure them of continuity they could trust. Hence the retention of Geithner and Summers. Overseeing the life-support systems for the bankers went from Henry Paulson, Timothy Geithner, and Ben Bernanke to Lawrence Summers, Geithner, and Bernanke.

To inspire confidence in the very forces that precipitated this crisis, Obama named insiders such as Lawrence Summers and Timothy Geithner to top positions in the Treasury and the National Economic Council. To the wider society, Paul Volcker, the head of the Federal Reserve under George W. Bush, was presented as the balancing force to Geithner and Summers in the financial team around Obama. Older citizens of the United States and the rest of the world remembered Volcker's draconian policies during the Reagan administration, when the poor and the countries of the Third World were squeezed so tight by US interest rate policies that scholars dubbed his policies the Volker Shock.[10]

By naming Lawrence Summers to be his chief economic adviser, Obama was making his peace with the hedge fund and derivatives forces who believed that they were doing God's will. Summers had been treasury secretary under the Bill Clinton administration, and was probably the most arrogant and sexist force that was brought into this administration of "Change." As chief economist of the World Bank before he became Clinton's treasury secretary Summers had written an internal memo highlighting the benefits of dumping toxic waste in poor countries: "The economic logic behind dumping a load of toxic waste in the lowest wage country is impeccable and we should face up to that .... I've always thought that under-populated countries in Africa are vastly under polluted."

This same Summers graduated from his position as treasury secretary under the Clinton administration to become the president of Harvard University. From Harvard, Summers again exposed his white supremacist ideas by waging war against the intellectual and philosophical contributions of Cornel West. Where there is racism there is also sexism, and Summers as president of Harvard University laid bare his contempt for women when he opined that "innate differences between men and women might be one reason fewer women succeed in science and math careers."

Tim Geithner had interned at the IMF, worked at the Federal Reserve on Wall Street, and was moving in a natural escalator ladder to the Treasury.

As a new president of the United States committed to real change, Obama could not have been unaware of the controversial nature of the chokehold of the Wall Street–Treasury–IMF complex. Instead of bringing in a new team to reflect change and steering clear of those forces that had organized the control fraud., he succumbed to his liberal advisers, who believed that the safety and survival of the banks was in the interests of humanity. The economic team of Geithner and Summers (a disciple of the banker and political insider Robert Rubin) represented one wing of entrapment for Obama. The barons of the armaments industry backed up the bankers, so that when Obama entered the White House, the financial wing of the entrapment reinforced the security wing held by Rahm Emmanuel, General Jones, and Robert Gates. Obama understood that he was trapped between the financial oligarchs and the military industrial complex. However, after his balancing between the sharks and the people in the politics of Illinois, Obama was of the view that a similar balancing could be undertaken in Washington. The stakes were much bigger and the rules of the game had been tightened. After September 15, the president of the United States had to show unquestionable support for the bankers at home and for the military projects abroad.

LIBERALISM, MISSIONISM, AND THE LONG WAR

As Obama descended into the abyss of being a messenger for Wall Street, there was no alternative political force in the society strong and mature enough to challenge that direction. The progressive forces were marginalized. Blogging by some had become a substitute for collective mass action. Without a social movement strong enough to turn the "Audacity of hope" into a bold break with liberalism and pragmatism, Obama could not escape the moral cowardice of talking tough one day, while Geithner called the banks and reassured them the following day. Neither could Obama grasp the interpenetrating linkages between the bankers and the forward planning of the military industrial complex for permanent war. This forward planning has been exposed as part of the long-range war planning intended to ensure the United States remains hegemonic for the next 50 years.[11]

The consumer-led economy, the speculation and risk taking by banks, and the militarism of the leadership were all interconnected. Militarism abroad, fear and repression at home, fulfilled the needs of a small class that consolidated power. This consolidation strengthened the corporate welfare recipients of the military industrial complex, reinforced and reproduced global exploitation, strengthened the class and racial divisions in society, while hiding behind words about globalization and free markets. It was none other than Tom Friedman who had noted that:

> America cannot be afraid to act like the almighty superpower that it is. ... The hidden hand of the market will never work without the hidden fist – McDonald's cannot flourish without McDonnell-Douglas, the designer of the F-15. And the hidden fist that keeps the world safe for Silicon Valley technologies is called the United States Army, Air Force, Navy and Marine Corps.[12]

Friedman was not as crude and brutal as the more obvious neo-conservatives of the "Project for a New American Century" (PNAC), who had developed the long-term military strategy based on the view that the global system could not be held together without US militarism. The militarists were sophisticated enough to infiltrate both political parties, so that while the PNAC became the activist arm of the crude neo-conservatives, the Center for a New American Security (CNAS) had been formed as the militarist arm of the Democratic Party.

The submission of the people of the Middle East and the pretense for the war against the people of Iraq confirmed this thesis of liberalism and permanent war. The wars in Iraq and Afghanistan should not be seen as errors of foreign policy, but understood in the context of the crisis of US hegemony, where only a strong military can sustain the dollar as the currency of world trade. Herein lay the linkages between the financial system and the militarism of the United States.[13]

Obama had campaigned on ending the war in Iraq, but the Pentagon forces organized a well-thought-out plan to build a network of military bases and to maintain military personnel in Iraq in the same magnitude of occupation that had been witnessed in Germany and Japan. Similarly, just when the citizens of the United States had overwhelmingly registered their opposition to military operations in Afghanistan, in December 2009 Obama ordered an escalation of that war. This sent tremors throughout the region, with Pakistan brought into the forefront of the war planning, and contingency operations for its full-scale occupation. Military contingency and planning for decisive action in Pakistan were deemed even more urgent for the securocrats because Pakistan possessed nuclear weapons.

Ambushed in the White House, Obama could only escape if he was able to demonstrate leadership and boldness beyond liberal platitudes about freedom. In October 2009, when Obama was reviewing his options for the escalation of the war in Afghanistan, *Rolling Stone* magazine said, "As Obama rethinks America's failed strategy in Afghanistan, he faces two insurgencies: the Taliban and the Pentagon."[14]

John F. Kennedy had faced an insurgency in the security apparatus and did not survive it. Kennedy had chosen leadership and long-term strategy but was overtaken by forces beyond any leader in the United States, because the military industrial complex remained at the center of the political economy. Obama needed the strength of the peace and justice forces to release him from the trap of the empire. Until the re-emergence of the peace and justice networks, Obama was destined to repeat the missionary statements of war as peace. And so he did in his justification for the escalation of the war in Afghanistan. Obama's leadership within the liberal tradition had reached its limits. Twenty-first-century politics required a leap out of the nineteenth-century missionary practices.

WAR AS PEACE

The story of spin, scandal, and selling the Iraq war did not go to the depths of the emasculation of one section of the peace movement, and the attempts to diminish, if not derail, the peace networks in the United States. The Bush administration and their intellectual allies studied the tactics of the peace movement, followed their arguments, sought to demonize peace activists, and developed campaigns to show that the United States must mobilize for war in order to preserve peace. George W. Bush communicated the philosophies of "just cause" and "just war," and rekindled the classic missionary role of the United States in international politics. For the ruling class, Obama was a godsend in so far as he could present a more gentle face of US imperialism. Thus, while the network of young people had campaigned for Obama to bring real change, the militarists and the Wall Street–Treasury complex embraced Obama and surrounded him with Moynihan democrats, the other arm of the PNAC. Obama himself was trapped by his own rhetoric during the campaign, when he had argued that the war in Afghanistan was a war of "necessity," but that the war in Iraq was one of choice.

The language and posture of Obama while receiving the Nobel

Peace Prize came weeks after he had announced a build-up of US forces to fight against the people of Afghanistan. It is important to link these militaristic and offensive positions, and shift the discussion from the actual acts of militarism to the ideas and state of mind of societies that carry out genocide. The important point that is being made is that this state of mind did not arise spontaneously, but out of a popular culture and popular history that taught citizens ideas of inferiority and superiority, and celebrated an instrumental rationality which reinforced the bifurcation of people. It was the mission of superior beings to bring peace and democracy to inferior beings. Many are now cognizant of the adage of Albert Einstein that we cannot solve problems with the mindset that created the problems in the first place. Obama was trapped by the military establishment and the supporters of the military industrial complex, by his own liberal training, and by the Saul Alinsky view that it is necessary to work within the system. His administration could only escape with the support of a vibrant peace and justice movement. This peace movement was being forced to come to the forefront so that the lessons of Toussaint L'Ouverture in Haiti would not be repeated. What were these lessons?

WOULD OBAMA END UP LIKE TOUSSAINT?

The most important lesson was that through its twists and turns, a revolution devours its children. In the specific case of the Haitian Revolution, there was a grassroots revolution and a number of grassroots leaders who brought great inspiration to the rebellion against enslavement. Three of these leaders of the revolution were Jean Francois, Biassau, and Jeannot. Toussaint was a brilliant strategist who had joined the revolution and placed himself as the military strategist for a people fighting for freedom. After winning many victories with the commitment of the masses, Toussaint had reached the point where he stood in the path of the revolution and the independence of Haiti. His internalization of the French ideas of liberty and equality had blinded him to the realization that France wanted to return the people to servitude. In the name of modernizing the economy, Toussaint wanted the former enslaved people to return to the plantations. There were two lessons from the rise and fall of Toussaint. The first was that a revolutionary leader who is trapped by the ideas of the forces of oppression will stagnate. Second, and more profoundly, was that as the revolution and contradictions deepen, the violence and bloodletting can hold back a society for decades.

Like Toussaint, Obama was dithering and seeking negotiations with the oppressive forces. While Obama dithered, the grassroots movement that had been mobilized for the elections stood still, while the conservative forces whipped up the anger of outraged citizens who were genuinely afraid for their future. The cogent lesson for this revolutionary moment was that the full mobilization of the peace and justice forces was necessary to ensure that the Obama entrapment and polarization in a period of financial depression did not degenerate into struggles around the state where violence engulfs the entire society. The militarization of society requires a kind of mobilization where militant non-violent civil disobedience and mass struggle can break the powers of the oligarchy. One year after the election of Obama, the Supreme Court handed down the decision that the government may not ban political spending by corporations in candidate elections.[15] The ruling effectively meant that corporations could flood the political space with money and dominate the electoral process. Already during the struggle to enact a health care measure that could extend coverage to millions, the drug and pharmaceutical industries had expended billions to block legislation that would benefit ordinary citizens.

Direct corporate contributions in elections would strengthen the conservative and militaristic wing of the polity. Despite the fact that Obama was already in a trap, the forces of inverted totalitarianism would not want to take the chance of seeing another upsurge in popular participation in elections. The bankers understood that the economic depression would require far more government intervention on the side of the financial oligarchy. Obama would be forced to make even harder choices than the ones he made in his first year in office. Comparing the choices before Obama to the challenges faced by Franklin Delano Roosevelt in 1933, Bill Fletcher, the peace activist, summed up the challenges for the peace forces in this way:

> So, the question is whether Obama will feel the Roosevelt-tug, or whether he will continue to dive into the middle – or worse – in response to voter anger. I would suggest that the answer depends less on Obama and more on us. Will we be in the streets around war, or will we be sending emails reflecting our despair? Will the unemployed be organized through groups like ACORN, National People's Action, and labor unions, or will they simply be a statistic that is referenced in speeches? Will workers move

to organize despite every obstacle that corporate America puts before them, or will they cringe awaiting the next pink slip? These are the sorts of questions that progressives need to be asking and, more importantly, acting upon.[16]

Fletcher was calling for a new mode of organization and new levels of consciousness to confront the economic and political crisis. Correctly arguing that the answer did not lie with Obama but with the progressive forces, he was calling on progressives to pose new questions in order to come up with new answers. Imamu Baraka made the same argument by drawing an analogy with the period before the rise of Hitler, when the forces of social democracy and radicalism bickered among themselves while the fascists manipulated working people as the capitalist depression deepened. Liberalism could not survive in a depression, so new energies and forces had to break the missionism and messianism of the "shining city on the hill."

NETWORKING AND SOLIDARITY

Cindy Sheehan represented a deep sentiment for peace that was blossoming in slow and imperceptible forms across society. She was one of the founding members of Gold Star Families for Peace which was formed in January 2005. The idea behind Gold Star came from mothers whose children were killed and maimed in war. Each mother became a Gold Star individual, and the idea was expanded to include all family members. Here was a fractal form of self-similarity iterating at different scales all across the country. It was a fast-developing brand of local self-organizational networks that defied party loyalties. Mothers used family connections to educate each other about how to cope with the alarming cases of mental illnesses and post-traumatic stress disorder among veterans.[17] The activities of the peace networks among these families brought to the national level a bottom-up movement that exposed the strength and power of self-organization, self-mobilization, and non-violence.

Sheehan had exposed the possibilities of self-organization and self-mobilization when she took the decision to engage other mothers whose children had been wasted in the senseless and illegal war in Iraq. Self-organization typically refers to a process by which systems organize themselves without external direction, manipulation, or control. So although there were many established peace organizations such as United for Peace and Justice, Black Voices for Peace, the American Friends Service Committee, and numerous local peace councils, the autonomous actions of millions of citizens delegitimized the war in Iraq. These self-directed actions from citizens who were open, willing to share, and had a global perspective represented a crack in the mindset of savior mentality that was being promoted as the basis for wars in Afghanistan and Iraq (messianism and imperialism).

During the election campaign of 2007–08, the networking model of Obama supporters grew out of robust opposition to war and the general anxiety associated with the social, economic, and environmental crisis. The war on terror had inspired its opposite, a global peace movement that linked citizens in over 130 countries.

This international mobilization created a new awareness of the need to reconceptualize peace in a way which will provide the spiritual and intellectual powers to make a break with the ideas that made the twentieth century the most violent in human history. One scholar who sought to develop the theme of the second superpower also invoked the importance of self-organization and self-mobilization in the process of cementing this power: "the second superpower, emerging in the 21st century, depends upon educated informed members. In the community of the second superpower each of us is responsible for our own sense-making."[18]

These educated and informed members had become active in the 2008 election. They were the same educated and informed members who formed the basis of the social networking teams that brought Obama to power. The sense of self-organization, multiple sources of energy, and the various forms of organizing social life drew from the understanding that the peace movement was not monolithic and or vanguardist. This movement had deep roots in all communities across the country, and was motivated by a framework that is very different from the ideas of American exceptionalism and superpowers. One of the many challenges of the massive mobilization against the Iraq war was to transform ideas about peace from a negative concept of peace (absence of war) to a positive engagement with issues of justice in order to initiate real changes in the society. Many who followed the campaign of change had high expectations that peace forces would have a greater say in the new Obama period. At the minimum, there was the expectation that government-financed think-tanks such as the United States Institute for Peace (USIP) would be taken out of the hands of the neo-conservatives, who used this "Institute of Peace" as a platform for refining war-making.[19]

There were very few in the peace movement who grasped that the massive build-up of US forces was first and foremost to intimidate and subjugate US citizens. Hence, even though the peace and self-determination movements won victories in rolling back the enormous Congressional support for the war in Iraq, they did not sufficiently affect the dissemination of knowledge and the concept of the mode of economic organization. The classes that profited from the armaments culture regrouped and re-emerged with more determined efforts, as manifested in the ambush of Barack Obama and the December 2009 announcement of a surge in Afghanistan. Networks of peace organization had to go back to their toolboxes to make a decision about how to oppose the Pentagon and the war-making machinery in a way that strengthens democracy at home and peace abroad.

The Tea Party movement that labeled Barack Obama a "socialist" was a manifestation of the confusion of white supremacy and militarism mixed together. Sarah Palin was being promoted as a front for counter-revolution and militarism, as the Tea Party movement became the voice of Cheney calling for more robust military action. Palin echoed the call to arms by declaring, "America is ready for another revolution." The conservative forces in the United States were calling for a return to the period of racist oppression, violent repression, segregation, and imperialist aggression. Revolution and counter-revolution were in contention, and the peace movement was being challenged to become the force for social transformation and change from racism and militarism. In essence, conservative forces believed that the masses of working people were so ignorant that the deep racism of the Tea Party movement would lead to more repression against the poor, diverting attention from the economic depression with millions unemployed. Liberalism and militarism in the United States were at a crossroads, and the peace forces had to sharpen their understanding of revolutionary non-violence in order to confront the rising racist and counter-revolutionary forces.

Throughout the maturation of the peace movement in the United States, concepts of peace and non-violence that were offered by Gandhi and Martin Luther King, Jr. were analyzed in relation to an exotic view of multiculturalism. It was not a rigorous critique of the structural and physical violence of the social system and the ideation system that justified the hierarchies of human beings. W. E. B. Dubois as early as the period of the First World War had called on peace activists in the United States to move beyond the statistics of military spending in order to be able to grasp the mindset that generated war.[20]

Extending the democratic ideal required far more than elections. The election of Obama to be the president of the United States opened one window beyond the "economy of influence" and the mindset of war. Repair and renewal were required to make a break with the iterations of warfare and destruction, but in order to move to reparative justice there had to be a national understanding that genocide was a crime.

THE PEACE, ANTI-RACIST, AND REPARATIONS NODES OF THE REVOLUTIONARY PROCESS

In essence, the reparations movement became a cornerstone of the revolutionary moment in the United States. Reparations and the truth about past harms constituted one slow form of healing society from the kind of counter-revolution that the Tea Party was threatening. First Nation peoples and African descendants had been the anchor of the reparations movement, which was feared because its revolutionary momentum threatened all of the holy scripts about the "the shining city on the hill." Reparative ideas confronted the ideas of racism, sexism, anti-Semitism, homophobia, and militarism. In the fight back against the Bush–Cheney administration, there was the embryo of a new multinational, multicultural, and broad-based movement which had the potential to become a dominant political force (or in the words of the *New York Times,* a "superpower"). Gandhi's idea that an eye for an eye made everyone blind percolated and brewed in the peace movement, but it was drowned out by the Bush call that "you are either with us or against us." The attack on the World Trade Center had demanded truth and reparations. Instead, the media whipped up hysteria for war and invasions.

Sections of the US political leadership understood the changed world situation, and on Thursday, June 18, 2009, the US Senate approved a resolution formally acknowledging the "fundamental injustice, cruelty, brutality, and inhumanity of slavery and Jim Crow laws" that enshrined racial segregation at the state and local level in the United States well into the 1960s. Congress apologized "to African Americans on behalf of the people of the United States, for the wrongs committed against them and their ancestors who suffered under slavery and Jim Crow laws." The mainstream peace movement in the United States was silent on this apology, but it was noted by the Congressional Black Caucus and by the international forces of reparations.

The next major task was to ensure that textbooks in the United States are rewritten to reflect this apology by the US Senate. One claim that will be followed by cultural and intellectual forces is that social studies textbooks in the United States now properly reflect this resolution, so that there is a process to reverse the ideas and practices that supported enslavement.

This conception of reparative justice beyond material manifestations confused many, especially liberal forces in the United States. In the face of the fear of liberals, the right wing unleashed a vicious campaign spearheaded by conservative pundits such as Glen Beck and David Horowitz. Beck went so far as to claim that Obama (who as a liberal did not identify with the reparations movement) wanted to bring in reparations through health care reform.[21]

This assault by the Right was a deliberate effort to confuse poor whites who wanted health care and a clean environment. Beck and Rush Limbaugh were given massive publicity through radio, television, and print media to argue that Obama was a racist and that, in the words of Limbaugh, "Obama's entire economic program was based on reparations." Reparations was an issue that whites (even progressives) were cautious about. Steven Colbert on *Comedy Central* used humor to mock the racists, but Keith Olbermann and Rachel Maddow were unwilling to take on the implications of reparations and reparative justice.

The urgency for clarity on this issue was heightened by the multi-million-dollar Save Darfur coalition, which presented itself as a peace movement calling for military intervention in the Sudan. I agree with Mahmood Mamdani's conclusion that the Save Darfur coalition was a sophisticated effort to undermine the peace movement and divert attention from the over 1 million lives lost in Iraq since 2003. Ultimately, in spite of the multi-million-dollar advertising and media campaign to support US military intervention in Darfur, this campaign faded as the reality of the capitalist depression became clear to the young people who were being manipulated. Despite the economic recession, the biggest expenditure of the United States was on war making. Millions were opposed to the escalation of the war in Afghanistan, but the media presented the war as the effort of brave US soldiers to save the citizens of Afghanistan from the evil Taliban.

Obama had jumped on the bandwagon of opposing the war in Iraq after the massive demonstrations and the activities of groups such as United for Peace and Justice, Black Voices for Peace, Code Pink, Gold Star Families for Peace, and numerous groups agitating for peace. Those that grasped the interconnections between war and plunder were moving to embrace the international reparative spirit that was needed for the twenty-first century. Groups such as Black Voices for Peace understood that environmental justice and reparations were interwoven with the need for health care and a retreat from crimes against nature.

Before the untimely passing of their founder Damu Smith, the National Black Environmental Justice Network and Black Voices for Peace educated the broader peace movement on the fact that crimes against the environment committed in Louisiana's "cancer alley" could not be separated form the history of slavery and Jim Crow. There was a wide variety of criminal acts against the environment by the capitalist classes, which required a robust reparations movement in the United States. These crimes against the environment – including toxic waste dumps, logging, wildlife smuggling, bio-piracy, gas flaring, and mountain top removal by coal companies – ensured that there were environmental activists and networks sharing information in all parts of the world.[22]

Vandana Shiva summed up the challenges of moving in a new direction:

> Globalization is threatening survival itself – by robbing millions of their right to life and by creating a political climate in which negative identities thrive. Human rights must focus on the right of the human species to survive, in peace with each other and the rest of the earth family. Economic globalization does not create global markets. The madness must be stopped. With our collective will and our courageous interventions we must cure not the symptoms of insecurity but the root causes.[23]

Curing the root causes was not going to be easy, but the reparative break was simmering as society tottered between reaction and reparations, between Palin's revolution and the revolution of values that Martin Luther King, Jr. championed. Reparation continues to be one element of going to the root causes of global insecurity.

PEACE AND THE MEANING OF WORK

This peace movement had many nodes, but the primary goal was to move society progressively away from the messianism and missionism that had induced the "savior" mentality. Slowly, workers and other citizens in the United States were beginning to see their jobs disappear while the bankers and barons of finance paid themselves huge bonuses. The labor movement was in a strategic position to support peace and to mobilize organized and unorganized workers to oppose militarism. However, this task was a major challenge for the trade union movement, as well as for the old Left. As the realities of the war sank into communities across the country, numerous city councils passed resolutions against the wars in Afghanistan and Iraq. A National Priorities Project continuously outlined the costs to individual communities and the costs to the society as a whole.

Widespread opposition to the war in Afghanistan by the first year of the Obama administration was a turning point for US workers away from the old "patriotism" that had been generated after the Second World War. Labor activists had to overcome the leadership of the AFL-CIO, which had developed close relations to the Central Intelligence Agency (CIA) and supported the Cold War since the 1950s. The end of the Cold War and the deindustrialization of America have led to a new mood in the workers movement. The tragedy was that the Left had not awakened to the full implications of deindustrialization. Sheldon Wolin, in his broadside against "inverted totalitarianism," had critiqued the academic Left in the United States, arguing that,

> The American left has crumbled. It sold out to a bankrupt Democratic Party, abandoned the working class and has no ability to organize. Unions are a spent force. The universities are mills for corporate employees. The press churns out info-entertainment or fatuous pundits. The left no longer has the capacity to be a counterweight to the corporate state.[24]

Wolin was pessimistic in relation to the ability of the Left to resist the extreme Right. What he did not do was to explore the inability of large sections of the Left to transcend the Eurocentric ideas about work, the old conceptions of full employment, and the labor theory of value. Valorization in the era of robots and clones held a different meaning from the nineteenth-century factory. More importantly, US society could not recover as long as the educational system was premised on destroying the poor and peoples of color. Trade unionists in the United States still harbored conceptions of full employment when changes in the organic composition of capital had created a workless society.

In his January 2010 State of the Union address, Obama repeated statements about seeking to achieve full employment. Here was one more manifestation of the trap of liberalism. Unemployment and underemployment were forcing society to develop a new idea of work and humanity. The women's movement for peace called for investing in caring instead of killing. This advanced section called for wages for housework. This was a call for a different idea of work, rather than one where capitalists only considered work in relation to the production of goods and services that yielded a profit for the capitalist class. Millions of citizens could be mobilized to create and envision a new society, but this vision was linked to demilitarization and the conversion of the military industrial complex. It was a new concept of work that was linked to human creativity, innovative spirit, and happiness.

People are now at the point where they understand Che Guevara's view of work and happiness. Guevara had envisioned a society where humans worked to be happy and where labor power was not coerced. It was a form of society where people were totally emancipated from the despotism of the factory. At the dawn of the twenty-first century, US society was faced with the need to reconstruct cities, clean up the toxic dumps and the criminal polluting systems of 200 years of industrialization, and rebuild society to serve the needs of healthy people instead of a small capitalist class.

After one year and the expenditure of close to US$1 trillion in the American Recovery and Reinvestment Act of 2009 (the stimulus package), there were millions of citizens who were unemployed because the Obama administration had internalized the views that tax credits and tax relief for small business could provide jobs. Economists such as Paul Krugman and Joseph Stiglitz criticized the Obama administration, saying that the stimulus package was too small, but their critique did not go to the heart of the matter, which was that the reorganization of the economy could only begin with a new mindset about governments and the financial and real estate conglomerates that dominated urban centers. Obama had read the book on life of Robert Moses, *The Power Broker,*[25] but there was nothing his administration could do to reverse the spatial organization of a society that ensured that Federal dollars strengthened racism in cities. Movements that were dedicated to living change in urban areas in cities such as Detroit, which faced over 50 percent unemployment, declared,

> The old industrial economy is gone. We face nothing short of the responsibility and challenge to create a new kind of economy. The capacity to do this, based on principles that value meaningful work

and caring relationships with one another and with the Earth, will never come from Washington. New ways of living will have to be created by us.[26]

This warning by Grace Lee Boggs in 2010 echoed the call made by James Boggs more than 40 years earlier. Boggs had warned that the United States was moving towards a workless society, and that new ideas of revolution were necessary. Explaining why the concept of full employment was reactionary, Boggs argued that:

> To talk about full employment and getting the unemployed back to work at this point when we are on the threshold of the workless society, is as reactionary as it was for the "rugged individualists" to say in the 30's that the only reason why a man wasn't working was that he didn't have the initiative to go out and get himself a job.[27]

The "end of work," the exhaustion of the ideas of the male breadwinner, and the delegitimization of the ideas of US exceptionalism were all forcing new ideas on society. New ways of living were being created as old stereotypes and Calvinistic notions of self-worth confronted twenty-first-century realities. Old divisions between black and Latino workers, and between US citizens and immigrant communities, were being exposed as divisions that held back the organizing capabilities of all citizens. After the Great Depression the struggle of working people and socialist movements aspired to a condition of full employment. Full employment was envisaged as the economic condition when everyone who wished to work at the going wage rate for their type of labor was employed. After the Second World War most Western governments adopted measures to maintain high levels of employment, with a social welfare cushion for workers. By the time of Reagan and Thatcher a more exploitative model of economic relations was adopted, called neo-liberalism. In this model, unemployment was welcomed because it drove down the bargaining possibilities of employed workers. Under this neo-liberal regime, privatization and liberalization transferred state resources into the private sector.

Faced with growing unemployment after the crash of 2008, the Obama administration embarked on Keynesian policies to invest in infrastructure in order to stimulate demand. These infrastructure projects went to established construction firms and other organizations that were already securely vested in the old economic relations.

Economists who wrestled with nineteenth-century ideas of inflation and the Phillips curve could not begin to rethink the requirements of community transformation in the twenty-first century.

Massive deaths from cancer epidemics, absence of health care, the prison-like conditions of many communities, along with the actual extension of the private and public prison system, demanded political change that transcended electoral politics. Slowly, the depth of the economic crisis cracked open the cultural space to challenge the "dumbing down" of working people. An educational system rooted in eugenics and built on the celebration of genocide was not geared to produce critical citizens. The United States spent more resources on the incarceration of the youth of color than on education, spending an average of US$ 22,000 per inmate. The United States has the highest total documented prison and jail population in the developed world, with 2,304,115 incarcerated in 2008. Private contracting of prisoners for work fostered incentives to lock people up, as the prison system represented a new kind of slavery.

In 2004, news broke worldwide that there had been "systematic and illegal abuse of detainees," including torture and degrading treatment, by US interrogators and guards at Abu Ghraib prison, outside Baghdad. These features were external manifestations of the abusive treatment of prisoners within the United States.

The New Abolitionist movement against the prison industrial complex became a dominant peace force opposing both the military industrial complex abroad and the prison industrial complex at home. Like the military industrial complex, the prison industrial complex represented an interweaving of private business and government interests. Its twofold purpose remains the maximization of profit and repression of people of color in urban areas. The public rationale was and remains the fight against crime. However, the exposure of control fraud by the bankers led more and more citizens to grasp who were the real criminals.

It is in opening up the spaces for repair of the human spirit where the current struggles against counter-revolution will make a fundamental break with the wrongheadedness of the enlightenment of the dominion of humans over nature. This struggle against the wrongheadedness will also call for a fundamental rethinking of human relationships. It is here where the struggles against militarism, masculinity, and patriarchy meet the goal of supporting healthy spaces on Earth.

James Boggs had penetrated this need in his call for revolution. He had noted,

This means that the new generation, the outsiders, the workless people, now have to turn their thoughts away from trying to outwit the machines and instead toward the organization and reorganization of society and of human relations inside society. The revolution which is within these people will have to be a revolution of their minds and hearts, directed not toward increasing production but toward the management and distribution of things and toward the control of relations among people, tasks which up to now have been left to chance or in the hands of an elite.[28]

Boggs was articulating the sentiments of emancipation that were echoed by Bob Marley in 1980 in "Redemption Song," "Emancipate yourselves from mental slavery; none but ourselves can free our minds. Have no fear for atomic energy cause none of them can stop the time."

REVOLUTION AND THE TIPPING POINT

The cascading effect of revolutionary ideas was nowhere more apparent than on the question of the challenges of environmental justice. The window of a decade to solve climate change had been given by scientists who warned humanity that global warming was already beyond the tipping point.[29]

These scientists presented two alternatives, either business as usual without reducing carbon emissions or cutting CO_2 emissions by changing our way of life. The network of environmentalists who were at the forefront of the fight to save the planet slowly emerged as the connectors and information specialists who were cementing the linkages between environmental justice activists all around the world. Environmental justice networks were intergenerational, and had connections in communities of different races and social groups. Their activists warned that if the planet was to survive, industrialized countries had to seek a 90 percent reduction in carbon emissions. This would involve cutting all emissions from coal and a drastic change in consumption patterns.

Al Gore had become an activist in this movement for climate change, but was hindered by his belief that environmental justice was compatible with the existence of capitalism. Gore, like some of the peace activists who are afraid to embrace the reparations movement, has been calling for political will to cut emissions without seeking structural economic changes.

The US Congress and Senate acted to support "special interests," and from time to time participated in discussions about "green jobs" and a "green economy," but this transition was supposed to take place without fundamental changes in consumption and production. For some who actually agreed that there was global warming, there was the belief that scientific and technological changes would solve the problems of climate change. This version of technological determinism guided the inaction of the United States at international climate change meetings. Obama himself was trapped by intellectual and political impoverishment when he continuously used a contradictory formulation, "clean coal."

Liberalism and expediency in the United States have only been exacerbated by the belief that technological breakthroughs will solve the problems of climate change without a fundamental restructuring of the mode of economic organization. This complacency ensures that the most oppressed sections of the society are the ones suffering from the impact of hazardous waste landfills, cancer alleys, and abuses of uranium mining, pesticides, pollution, and environmental degradation. Blacks, Latinos, poor whites, Native Americans, and workers in the above-named sectors of the economy are the citizens most affected by the destruction of the Earth. By the time of the failure of the Copenhagen summit in December 2009, many environmental justice activists were moving beyond the "inconvenient truth" to struggle for system change.

There was a recognition that only revolutionary changes in the mode of economic organization could bring about a genuine response to climate change. It took another international conference to fully expose the deep conservatism of the political system in the United States.

As the full contradictions of capitalism and environmental degradation exploded, the environmental justice front of the networks had the potential of bridging old divisions between communities, different peoples, and classes. Environmental justice connected peace activists, health activists, reparations activists, anti-racist activists, women's groups, and immigrant workers as these groups became a force for bringing society to understand the meaning of a common and shared humanity. However, in order to move to transform society, activists needed to transform themselves and shed ideas of possessive individualism that corrupted the mind. Here there was an urgent need to fully comprehend the politics of Ubuntu. George Monbiot, an activist in the international environmental justice movement, summed up the task,

I came back from the Copenhagen climate talks depressed for several reasons, but above all because, listening to the discussions at the citizens' summit, it struck me that we no longer have movements; we have thousands of people each clamoring to have their own visions adopted. We might come together for occasional rallies and marches, but as soon as we start discussing alternatives, solidarity is shattered by possessive individualism. Consumerism has changed all of us. Our challenge is now to fight a system we have internalized.[30]

PEACE AND THE INHERITANCE OF BLACK LIBERATION

While the organizational forms of the twenty-first century revolution eschew all forms of vanguardism and hierarchy, the history of the struggle for black liberation gave this movement a special place in the memories of liberation. Whether these memories came in the form of the Harriet Tubman principles of self-organization, the Ella Baker guidelines for participatory democracy from the grassroots, Martin Luther King Jr.'s dream of equality, or Tupac Shakur's call for changes, the cultural and political voices from this section of the American progressive camp acted as a force against outright fascism. Inverted totalitarianism could not find a base because of the organized and spontaneous activities of black revolutionary forces. Whether in the Jericho Movement, National Welfare Rights Organization (NWRO), black women's movement, underground and revolutionary hip hop artists for peace, the liberation theology forces or *Black Youth Rising*,[31] the *Radical Black Imagination*[32] ran deep inside the African American community. Angela Davis, Mumia Abu Jamal, Assata Shakur, Bob Moses, Stevie Wonder, bell hooks, Mohammad Ali, Frances Beal, Imamu Amiri Baraka, and hundreds of thousands of other freedom fighters formed the link and living testimony of the traditions of peace and liberation. Books such as Stokeley Carmichael's *Ready for Revolution*,[33] the history of the Black Panther Party, and of revolutionaries such as Malcolm X and Martin Luther King, Jr., ensured that revolutionary ideas in society had a firm base.

In this sense, I would differ with those journalists who had declared the death of revolutionary traditions in the United States. I have drawn heavily from the theoretical and political insights of Grace Boggs and James Boggs, revolutionaries who were involved in the struggles of Detroit from the period of the CIO (Congress of

Industrial Organizations) to the current era of deindustrialization. Grace Boggs combined the histories of involvement in numerous formations, from the women's movement to the environmental justice movement to the present struggle for new ways of organizing life. She had been part of the Old Left in Detroit, and had gradually grasped the limitations of a liberation tradition that focused on liberation from exploitation at the point of production.

I have made reference to the Marxist traditions of revolution, where the concept of liberation involved the freedom from exploitation and an end of the alienation of the working people. This is the alienation of the labor power of the workers. This is the process of surplus extraction from workers that is central to capital accumulation. When finance capital took new forms such as new financial products, and the forms of oppression became diversified, the struggles had to also take multiple forms. We must add to the alienation of workers the racial alienation that was and remained embedded in ideas of scientific racism, oppression based on the forms of the family, heterosexism that oppresses persons of the same sexual orientation, environmental destruction, ageism, and sexism. From the experiences of fighting the prison/industrial complex and racial profiling, the black liberation movement served as a bridge for building alliances with members of the Arabic, South Asian, Latino and Islamic communities in opposing the present racial profiling and labeling of ordinary citizens as terrorists.

The hip hop cultural revolution united all of the forces fighting against injustice. As in most movements for change, hip hop combined the dialectic of the negative and the positive in society. Hip hoppers for peace presented their manifesto for peace to the United Nations, seeking to distinguish the conscious forces within hip hop from the violence and misogyny that was promoted by the media and the cultural apparatuses of oppression. African American citizens suffer from both the physical and structural violence of the social system, and remain the most resolute revolutionary forces, at the forefront of exposing the complex, multidimensional crisis whose facets touch every aspect of our lives – health and livelihood, the quality of our environment and our social relationships, our economy, our technology, and politics.

Military oppression under the Bush administration and the passing of the Homeland Security legislation brought linkages between wars at home and abroad. Because of the high percentage of black and Latino youths in the army, the state could not guarantee that the long-term plans for military operations in urban areas will be smooth in the event of "civil unrest." Hence, the US government resorted to private contractors as mercenary forces who were being trained to occupy and oppress the black community. With memories of the resistance of black soldiers during the Vietnam War, the military planners of the United States poured billions of dollars into a semi-mercenary force of very conservative militarists. Peace and transformation required an end to the conditions that bred terrorism, racism, sexism, class exploitation, homophobia, and insecurity. This understanding of peace and revolution had inspired the kind of calculations within the black community to use the right to vote to remove Bush and Cheney and the forces of counter-revolution. Networks from the old civil rights period understood that elections did not bring about change. The change had to come from organized actions of citizens.

PROGRESSIVE WOMEN AND THE PEACE MOVEMENT

If the progressive networks among African Americans served as one hub or node at the grassroots, it was progressive women who served as the ultimate bridge between the different forces struggling for peace and justice in the United States. African American and Latino women built new sites of struggle to mobilize women to move beyond single issues and link up with a broad-based movement of women fighting for freedom. These women could be distinguished from liberal feminists who wanted equality within the capitalist system. Networks of progressive women were to be found in every area of struggle in US society, including the areas of health provision, education, child care, environment, safety of communities and the general levels of violence and repression in the society. Progressive women had to reject the militaristic macho role-model for youths. Young men also need to reject this militaristic macho role model to prevent more and more Americans from going out on shooting sprees or joining the armed forces as if it were the only means of national service. Domestic violence served as the initiation into war, which later spilled out onto the international arena on the pretext of "total war" on terrorism.

Earlier, I drew attention to the self-organization techniques of women such as Cindy Sheehan, who defied the big organizations to make her mark for peace. Her example represented the kind of decentralization and autonomy which was an antidote to the old forms of vanguardism and top-down organization for change. Women in all spheres of activities such as those fighting for health care, breast cancer survivors, women against violence, and hundreds of thousands of other organizations exposed the depth of social organizing in the United States. The more the depth of the movement for change, the more intense was the propaganda war against women as vehicles for the reproduction of capitalist ideas. The advertising industry in the United States remains at the front line of this war against women. Yet the more the war against women waged, the sharper the struggle became. Space does not allow for an elaboration of the depth of the struggles, but suffice it to say that the traditions of Harriet Tubman and Ella Baker reawakened a new generation of activists in this revolutionary moment. As the peace movement liberated itself from the messiah complex, new formations appeared to rise above single issue considerations in the radical feminist movement. One such formation, Ella's Daughters, grew as a national network of diverse activists, scholars, artists, and workers advancing justice in Ella Baker's democratic tradition, and facilitating connections between different social justice movements.

BUILDING A NEW DEMOCRACY

The struggles for the minds of the young, especially women, intensified after the Obama campaign showed the potential for organizing young people who were written out of politics. Grace Boggs had this to say of the Obama victory:

> my support for Obama was never based on his policies or promises which, with few exceptions, are not that different from those of other Democrats. From the outset my eyes were on the people at his rallies, especially the youth who, inspired by his persona and his eloquence, shed the fears instilled by the Nixons, Reagans and Bushes since the 60s and, imbued with a new hope, began organizing on his behalf. For me, not just Obama's victory but that transformation of "we the people" from Fear to Hope, from passivity to activity, from looking on as spectators to participating as citizens was what was so historic about this period.[34]

Young people from all races and classes had mobilized themselves in the election campaign. They had harnessed social networking technologies and took the campaign of Obama to be the site to demonstrate new possibilities for political engagement. In the elections, another notable level of "domestic" transformation took place with millions who had acquired technology almost merely for fun and leisure, who then turned the same tools into part-time tools of change in the total society. The future will tell the extent to which these tools and cyberspace itself can deepen the emergence of what is in fact a partly virtual democratic transformation.

The speed with which corporate forces asserted their power within the apparatuses of the US state served as an education for the evolving revolutionary confrontations in society. Within one year, it became crystal clear that that while representative demo-cratic participation (as manifest in the electoral struggle to elect Obama) was an important component of change, the central aspect of change was not in the contest for positions. Democratic transfor-mation involved more than voting every four years. In the face of electoral reversals for the Democratic Party, Obama started to make small gestures towards regrouping with the grassroots, with an eye towards the 2010 midterm elections. However, the more far sighted understood the adage of C. L. R. James, who had observed at the time of the French Revolution that "phases of revolution are not decided in parliaments, they are only registered there."

Voting under the current system could always be undermined by corporate power in the repressive and productive apparatuses. This is part of the neo-liberal or "low intensity democracy." That is the democracy where there is no accountability once a person is elected. C. L. R. James had written extensively about a new democracy, a democracy where "every cook can govern."

This is the new revolutionary place that we are in at this moment, in this new century, when popular forms of expressions are break-ing out as peoples develop new techniques at self-organization. This revolutionary moment is slowly producing new revolutionary ideas and forms of organization, to draw a line of steel between the kind of revolution that was being called for by the Tea Party and the kind of liberation that would end destruction of people and the environment. At the same time, the slow awareness of the strengths of self-organization breaks down the vanguardism and leaderism of the old Left.

It is also now possible to enrich the observations of C. L. R. James by looking not only at Greek democracy (which was limited) but also at the social collectivism of the African village community, the cooperative institutions of the indigenous peoples in Latin Amer-ica, as well as the Iroquois concept of democracy. It is now possible to draw on the memory of these forms of democratic participation to inform this revolutionary moment.

The strength of new social movements emanated from their

autonomy and self-organization. In one year, the Obama administration expended more than US$13 trillion to save the banking system. Yet the system was on the brink because the forms of accumulation that had been organized required total control by the bankers. As analyzed earlier, it was not *if* there was going to be another collapse of the financial services, the question was *when*. As the capitalist crisis deepened, the new networks will be able to draw on their accumulated experiences to fight back against militarism. Informed networks are slowly liberating society from the savior mentality, and this liberation is supported by the creative abilities of cultural workers. Now, in the context of the revolutionary moment, networks for reparations, peace, and justice are struggling for the freedom of peoples and individuals to continue building a new society to practice a better way of living.

The insights of C. L. R. James of envisioning a society where every cook can govern brought back to the fore the idea of politics without intermediaries or great leaders (messiahs). Women from all races and classes organized in numerous formations were tenacious in promoting the "lela principles" of caring, which advocates using the nurturing love and care between a mother and her child as a reference point for societal relations between the government and the citizens. The Wages for Housework movement developed a global slogan, "Invest in caring, not killing." This moment called on citizens to organize with their neighbors to establish assemblies at places of social engagement (church, mosque, work, school, community and so on). Every cook with the capability to govern or the deepening of the politics of self-organization required everyone to participate directly in the transformation of society, starting from their own immediate living environment and to connect, in debates and actions, the concrete immediate problems with the structural causes which produce them.

This new basis for democracy is informing the Zapatistas of Mexico, who have joined the Cuban people as the forerunners of the new revolution of the Americas. This self-organization for revolution is very different from self-organization for representative politics. The former is a type of politics where people take themselves from one level of consciousness to the next. At the same time, one of the most profound aspects of the Zapatistas has been the way in which they have deepened the mobilization of positive cultural values from their history. It is not by accident that informed observers have identified the homegrown concepts associated with the revolutionary project in Mexico. Another important aspect of this revolutionary approach is the need to build community power so that people shift away from the old state machinery of violence and domination. In every community in the United States, local struggles for social justice were nurturing new forms of politics. Slowly, the accumulated experiences of struggles were distinguishing the new radical forces from those that had been compromised by the "non-profit" form of mobilization that depended on handouts from private corporations.

CONCLUSION

Within one year, the limitations of achieving change through the electoral process became clear to American society. Those who were looking to Obama as a messiah were disappointed. The contradictions between the requirements of capitalist accumulation and the reproduction of human life precipitated a clash that could not be postponed. The missionary spirit of society and the history of genocide came face to face with the future of humanity and the planet. Both climate scientists (James Hansen) and economic analysts (Nouriel Roubini) gave society a ten-year window of reflection to step back from the tipping point. The tipping point of global warming had the most profound impact on young people, and this was manifest in the networks of environmental activists. Roubini's warning was about the end of the dollar hegemony. Presently, the US military acts as the primary basis for the power of the United States. It is a matter of time before countries such as China cease propping up the dollar, which allows the United States to project military force.

There are sections of the United States that drew up long-term plans for militarization well into the next three decades. The future of this militarization is challenged by a peace and reparations movement in the United States. The election of Obama to be the president of the United States was a manifestation of the hunger for change among the population. This election, however, served as a lesson that far more profound forms of political organizing and political interventions were necessary to intervene to prevent outright fascist politics. The call of the right-wing forces for "revolution" challenged the liberals to grasp the depth of the social and economic crisis. At the same time, there were many lessons that could be learnt from Germany in the midst of the Great Depression. Before the Reichstag fire and the rise of Hitler, the Left and the communists bickered among themselves, while the Right organized and brought in Hitler.

Obama's victory in November 2008 temporarily removed the most conservative forces from the top levers of power, but these forces regrouped very quickly. The Right removed the middle ground and bipartisanship that Obama craved. He was trapped by liberalism and his view that capitalist recovery could transform society. From this entrapment, Obama could not but utter the confused words of seeking peace in Afghanistan through war and seeking to bring about a green economy with clean coal.

With every passing day and night, the polarization deepened between wealth and poverty, war and peace, racism and anti-racism, environmental destruction and repair, and between schools and jails. The ruling of the Supreme Court to give more power to corporations solidified the power of the same corporations that have given themselves the right to determine that life is an invention.

Obama will either be released from the traps or he will be pushed aside by the forces that will be impatient for outright repression. I have drawn lessons from the dithering of Toussaint L'Ouverture in the Haitian Revolution. Toussaint wanted to maintain the same economic system as that of the former French colonists even after the revolution. Our experiences from the period of Martin Luther King, Jr. ensured that a Jean-Jacques Dessalines will not be the one to emerge after Obama is being freed from the traps. How young people will move "from passivity to activity" in this era will be dependent on the strengthening of the alliances of the forces that have the most to gain from reparations, peace, and justice. Progressives must be prepared for the battle ahead. They can succeed by building on the long tradition of struggle that preceded this moment. In this book I have emphasized the moment of opportunity more than the moment of danger in order to re-energize the forces that were organized for the 2008 break with Bush and Cheney.

Obama used "Wake up" as his theme song for the elections. Was it possible that he was reminding the youths of the words of Martin Luther King, Jr.. that "There is nothing more tragic than to sleep through a revolution"?[34]

9

UBUNTU AND TWENTY-FIRST-CENTURY REVOLUTION

THE SETTING AND THE CHALLENGES

This book has been inspired by the history of freedom fighters and the premise of the optimism of the will and the healing of the human spirit. Cheikh Anta Diop has written on the existence of a vibrant African optimism and the ideas of peace and justice along with the emancipation of women in domestic life.[1] The emancipation of women and the humanization of the male are tasks bound up with building another world. Throughout this book, we have also gained inspiration from the cultural workers who have sought to keep alive the spirit of Ubuntu that said, "We are the world, let us come together as one."

The word Ubuntu comes from the Bantu languages spoken in southern Africa, and is related to a Zulu concept – "*umuntu ngumuntu ngabantu*" – which means that a person is only a person through their relationship to others. This concept is termed "*unhu*" in Shona and "*utu*" in Kiswahili. It is a concept that is to be found in all parts of Africa. Archbishop Desmond Tutu, who sought to be a healer in South Africa, has written extensively on the question of Ubuntu. In his book, *No Future Without Forgiveness*, Desmond Tutu noted that: "Ubuntu is very difficult to render into a Western language .... It is to say, 'My humanity is caught up, is inextricably bound up, in what is yours.'"[2] Ubuntu is an ethic or humanist philosophy focusing on people's allegiances and relations with each other. It is important to *restate* that this ethic focuses on people's allegiances to and relations with each other. In short, we share a common humanity.

At the British Labour party conference in 2006, the former president of the United States, Bill Clinton, told the assembled delegates that all that was needed to solve the problems of the world was Ubuntu. Clinton declared that "Society is important because of Ubuntu."[3] Characteristically, he did not carry this message in the United States. At the US State Department under Hillary Clinton, some staffers have introduced the concept of "Ubuntu diplomacy," but this appropriation of the word Ubuntu by imperial officers is similar to the way George W. Bush attempted to present war as peace.

It is among the most creative people in American society that Ubuntu is catching on. Even without using the word Ubuntu, progressive scholars in the Latino community have introduced a concept of "linked fate" to underline the reality that the future of all the peoples of the Americas is linked together.

Ubuntu is also the name that has been adopted for a computer operating system based on Debian GNU/Linux, which is distributed as free and open source software with additional proprietary software available. Lawrence Lessig has been at the forefront of the open source movement as one more node in the struggles for information freedom and a new form of "literacy."[4] This literacy is an integral component of revolutionary citizenship.

David Harvey, as a scholar of the present nature of imperial plunder and "accumulation by dispossession," called on us to draw from the spirit of love and peace. He noted that "we have something of great importance to accomplish by expressing optimism of the intellect in order to open ways of thinking that have for too long remained closed."[5] How do we open up this expression of optimism of the intellect?

Is grasping the revolutionary possibilities of this historical moment one way of making the break with the past crimes against humanity and crimes against the environment? It is the thesis of the book that young people in the United States reject white supremacist doctrines and looks to a new future for the twenty-first century in the United States. This was a major theme in my approach to an analysis of the political conjuncture. I have argued throughout the book that the depth of the contradictions is so immense that the old liberal form of democracy cannot hold. Society needs a new popular democracy, "where every cook can govern."

From the outset of the book, I have sought to grasp this historical moment as one of opportunity rather than danger. Even in the face of the new right-wing populism characterized by deep conservatism and institutional racism, I have sought to bring to the fore the traditions of peace and love rather than fear and hate. I drew from the cultural forces of the anti-racist and anti-capitalist networks to understand the conditions for a change in the politics of reconstruction.

The majority of the population in the United States understood that there could be no economic recovery on the basis of the old forms of exploitation. White racism no longer offered material incentives for poor and working-class whites. Recovery could only come with new leadership, new ideas about society, and new social structures to place people before profit. I have stressed the interconnections between politics and economics, finance and the military, and the institutionalized racism that held back the educational system and the full potential of the whole of American society.

Throughout the book, I have eschewed predictions about the exact nature of the twenty-first-century revolution, except to highlight the central ethic of Ubuntu in the search for a common humanity where every one could live in peace. This book builds on the radical imagination and spiritual energies of those activists who labored for peace and transformation. John Lennon was one of those who called on humans to imagine all peoples living in peace and as one. Grace Boggs imagined a new city where the right to the city was linked to the needs of the people. Cindy Sheehan imagined a world where children are not dying for corporations.

These were dreams for us to transcend the hierarchy of humans, to imagine a new brotherhood and sisterhood of humans, and for humans to consider sharing as a basic organizing principle Both John Lennon and Martin Luther King, Jr. were peace activists of the twentieth century who recognized the possibilities for a break with the old mechanistic, atomistic and deterministic paradigms about rational actors who are encouraged by competition, greed, and a careful, self-interested calculus. This break is a central component of recursion.

Ron Eglash, who wrote on the implications of recursion in fractal geometry,[6] also spelt out the ways in which Aristotelean conceptions of politics and math found discomfort with the concept of infinity. Greek philosophers were uncomfortable with the concept of infinity because of the implications relating to chaos and uncertainty. African peoples were humble enough to grasp the infinite beauty of the universe and the relationship between the living, their ancestors and the unborn.

How did the election of Obama make a break with the old patterns of bifurcated humans of the Aristotelean model?

How will a twenty-first century theory of democracy rise beyond the old concept of democracy, where economic management is separated from political management, and where equality was for whites only?

There are important implications for the revolutionary moment from one of the core elements of recursion, memory. From these memories, I have drawn from the ideas, organization, and leadership of revolutionaries in the United States as well as revolutionaries from all other parts of the world, to draw out the best lessons for struggles in the twenty-first century.

New progressive grassroots political leadership, ideas, and forms of organization are germinating to make a break with top-down politics and the multi-million-dollar political consulting business. Here, the insights of James Boggs are most prescient,

> Very few revolutions start with a conscious attempt to take power. No revolution has ever started with everyone in the country agreeing with the goal of the revolutionary movement. It is clashes, both ideological and physical, among segments of the population and usually the whip of the counter-revolution which give the revolution its momentum. Sometimes the revolution is violent, sometimes it is non-violent, but always it is the revolution. Sometimes those in the revolution are conscious of the consequences of their actions, sometimes they are not, but always there is action.[7]

It is through the lens of chaos theory that we are able to grasp the simultaneity of the contradictory presence of revolution in counter-revolution and counter-revolution seeking to derail revolutionary breakthroughs. Boggs correctly noted that "Who will and who will not start a full-scale revolution cannot be foretold. The basis for a revolution is created when the organic structure and conditions within a given country have aroused mass concern."

Here, Boggs was warning against predictions, but at the same time alerting us to grasp the moment when there are fundamental changes in the organic structure of society. These are the changes that bring about contradictions so pronounced that the old institutions cannot contain them any more. These fundamental changes are called an "inflection point" in ruling circles. This inflection point has rattled the old ideas so much so that the energy and motivation that lay behind the new white supremacist calls for revolution and civil war remain attached to the memory of the genocidal history of the United States.

But in this book, I argue that the extreme right will have to be careful about what they are calling for. The United States is not the Germany of 1932, and the followers of the John Birch Society and other militarist forces are unable to understand the full depth of the economic depression in the United States.

Dick Cheney emerged as a spokesperson for a branch of the military industrial complex, but the more sophisticated members of the Carlyle Group and "private equity" understood that US corporations benefited from the more friendly face of Barack Obama in the international marketplace. Rupert Murdoch and his media empire News Corp. had such a deep ideological affinity to militarism and masculinity that editors, writers, and commentators from this stable were enthusiastic supporters of war. But the owners of News Corp. were opportunistic capitalists, and as the economic crisis deepened, the future of the vitriol was challenged as Murdoch and his children were wrestling over overt support for fundamentalism and homophobia.

While that struggle in the media simmered, forces such as the Tea Party Nation were given media coverage far beyond their real political support in American society. It was not by chance that on that same platform of the Tea Party Convention in Nashville, Tennessee, Tom Tancredo (who had made his reputation as a politician who mobilized on the basis of anti-immigrant sentiments) said that Barack Obama won because "we do not have a civics, literacy test before people can vote." Preaching hate and xenophobia were never far from the structural violence and institutional racism of American society, but the moment called for a grasp of revolutionary non-violence.

When one writes of revolution, it is expected that the focus will be on violence, bloodshed, and disaster, but for this period, armed revolutionary actions had to be an option of the last resort when all other forms of struggle had been exhausted. Self-defense of the most oppressed can be guaranteed by pushing the legal, political, and ideological struggles to dismantle the military and coercive apparatuses so that the power of the people will be reflected in the state. Martin Luther King, Jr., Mahatma Gandhi, and the Student Non-Violence Coordinating Committee (SNCC) have exposed the potential of revolutionary non-violence. Ella Baker enriched this understanding with her insights, participatory grassroots leadership, and democratic engagement. This is a different kind of leadership from that which focuses on the great leader, messiah or emancipator.

At the start of this book, I sought to lay out the challenges of the elaboration of our humanity in an era when multiple forces have sought to diminish us. We have noted that the concepts of Ubuntu and healing offered one revolutionary opening for the twenty-first century away from the ideology of might as right and rational individual actors and actresses in the marketplace. There may be many revolutionary openings, but I have found that Ubuntu (the ideas of forgiveness, willingness to share, reconciliation, peace, justice, and love) offers tremendous possibilities for new human relations in the twenty-first century. Che Guevara stated simply that revolutionaries are guided by strong feelings of love.

Throughout every chapter of this book, I have sought to deepen the revolutionary ideas of Ubuntu with an approach to contemporary politics that rises above eugenic ideas about people, linear conceptions of progress, and technological determinism. It was my analysis that the repair of people away from concepts of dominion and progress sheds more light on the recursive processes necessary to break from "the most terrible century in history."[8]

In the nuclear age, our challenge is to dig deep for a philosophy of life that can repair the human spirit and unleash new energies for transformation. This is where reparative justice draws from Ubuntu and a fractal outlook. This is the outlook that links the reparations issue to the entire knowledge system that justified colonialism as progress and genocide as an unfortunate byproduct of "modernity." A veritable revolution in education is a clear requirement if society is to break out of the eugenic ideal that has blocked creativity and innovation.

Many Europeans on the Right and Left are uncomfortable with reparative break and rupture, because such a break undermines the dominant basis of state ideological legitimation since 1776. Some Americans who believe that the United States is the "shining city on the hill" cannot face the truth of the past. It is in the rewriting of the entire history of humanity, where the politics of memory becomes central in the formulation of long-term concepts of the new politics. This rewriting of the history of people has the potential to break the preoccupation with monetary compensation, and highlight the revolutionary possibilities that are open when there is a change in the entire social order.

The experience of the current moment reinforces the concept that revolutions cannot be understood as an event (such as the formation of parties and elections, or the fall of a government), but as a process where people take themselves from one level of political consciousness to the next. This is the essence of self-emancipation. It is in this sense that the four sequences of revolutionary politics in the United States built on each other, not in a linear sense of "prog-ress" as in the Newtonian model, but in the spiritual and healing sense of clarifying the forms of consciousness needed for building a new planetary civilization for the twenty-first century.

UBUNTU, QUANTUM POLITICS, AND THE REVOLUTIONARY MOMENT

In the history of the United States, emancipatory politics did not always thrive: when it did, it existed under conditions. Revolution-ary moments are therefore precarious and sequential. As we learnt from the second revolution (Civil War) and its aftermath with the rise of the Ku Klux Klan, from the civil rights revolution and the aftermath of the Reagan counter-revolution, revolutions do not proceed in a straight line. There are many zigs and zags, twists and turns. Quantum politics assists us in understanding the unpredict-able, contradictory nature of people and social phenomena. It alerts us to political and economic philosophies that are more appropriate to the realities of the twenty-first century, where separation and compartmentalization have no meaning.[9]

Quantum politics holds many possibilities in a fast-changing society with the innovative capabilities of the young. The bottom-up or insur-gent motion of intergenerational links between the SNCC training sessions and the Camp Obama sessions no longer accepted authority without question, so that the old mechanistic paradigms cannot deal with the multiple challenges of the twenty-first century. A new reality of the sense of community that inspires the insurgent forces is at the heart of "fractal optimism." This is the thinking about complexity and interconnectivity that reinforces the holistic concept of Ubuntu. The main point is that we must have a sense of the people of society, the conditions of their existence, their cosmos, and the quest for a new mode of politics that serves as the basis for emancipation.

In the aftermath of the attacks on the World Trade Center in September 2001, the political leaders of the United States used that event to heighten the militaristic traditions of society, and to spread fear and insecurity in all parts of the globe. Despite the books, inves-tigations, and reports on the intrigue-ridden story of the fraudulent build-up for war, the militarists are so addicted to armed engage-ments that the truth is smothered to ensure prolonged and perpetual war.[10] Until the elections of 2008, it seemed as if the politics of revenge and blindness inspired by fear had taken over US society.

However, as people were losing their homes, they were more afraid of the insecurity generated by capitalism than by "Islamic terrorists," even though the media kept up the hysteria about terrorism.

During the Cold War, fear of communism had been the rallying cry for strategic planners. After September 11, 2001, US citizens were called upon to embrace both fear and imperial arrogance. At the same time, citizens were coerced into fearing "Islamic terrorists" while supporting US oil companies and the military occupation of Arab lands. Coerced and living in fear, "patriotic" citizens were called upon to be proud to be called imperialists.[11]

Scholars such as Laurie Mylroie[12] were brought from the fringes of the conservative think-tanks to spew conspiracy theories that had no basis in reality. As a student of Harvard, Laurie Mylroie was simply reproducing what she had learnt from the realist theoreticians of international relations. Mainstream political scientists stressed the importance of "power," influence and authority.

Samuel Huntington, who provided some of the intellectual fodder for the "war on terror" with his book *The Clash of Civilizations*,[13] reproduced some of the eugenic concepts of democracy by claiming that the concept of democracy emerged from Anglo-Saxon protestant culture and that American democracy was the triumph of White Anglo-Saxon protestant values. In his book *Who Are We? The Challenges to America's Identity*, Huntington employed the trope of social Darwinism to define US politics and culture, and called for a return to protestant culture as the source of US identity so that the country could return to the moral leadership of the world.[14] In his broadside against immigrants, especially Latinos, Huntington did not exclude the possibilities of a multiracial politics, but only insofar as African Americans accepted the values and ideas of individualism, competition, and American exceptionalism. Huntington's book was written to counter a true multinational, multilingual, and multicultural unity that valued all the contributions of those who live in the United States.

Unlike the apologists for imperialism who trumpeted US corporate culture as another savior in the twenty-first century, David Harvey, Angela Davis, Chalmers Johnson, Vandana Shiva, and Samir Amin, among others, have exposed the militaristic basis of US corporations and the conditions for permanent war. Chalmers Johnson, in his book *Sorrows of Empire,* exposed how the United States has built an empire of bases, creating in the process a government that is obsessed with maintaining absolute military dominance over the world.[15]

Barack Obama inherited this military infrastructure for permanent war, and it was naiveté on the part of some in the peace movement that made them believe he could, as president, change the militaristic direction without the power of a mobilized grassroots movement. In this sense, I would agree that: "A revolution would be required to bring the Pentagon back under democratic control."[16] This movement needs to use as its reference the call of Martin Luther King, Jr. for a "revolution of values." It is a revolution that will hark back to that period, albeit briefly, during the Civil War when the US army became an army of liberation.[17]

The fear of this break in the armed forces continues to inspire the drivers of the "war on terror." During the Bush years, the "war on terror" was routinely leveraged for the purposes of social control, military mobilization, and electoral advantage. In the midst of this period of insecurity, characterized by millions who are unemployed, without health care, and losing their homes, the peace movement was being called on to renounce the preoccupation with terrorism and to challenge the Obama administration, which like Lincoln's, dithers in the face of threats to civil peace.

The wholesale reorganization of American society for war abroad and repression at home has been noted by the liberal think-tank the National Priorities Project, pointing to the fact that the government was spending over US$2 billion per day on the military when there were clear social needs to be met. It is this militarization and repression that reflects the principal characteristics of a militarist state.

Peace activists were conscious of this deep militarism, and understood that the forces of hope must be at the forefront in creating spaces for non-violence and peaceful change. Under the Obama administration, this tradition of subordinating all other interests to those of the military has been carried forward with a massive military budget and additional outlays for the militaristic agency called Homeland Security. This militarism ensured that, in the midst of a deep economic crisis when all other sectors of the federal budget were coming under deep cuts, the military budget was the only area of expansion.

This militarism set the pattern for the expansion of government surveillance internationally and domestically through wiretapping, rendition, torture, and secrecy. Those from the conservative Right and the angry populists who railed against big government were also taking their poisonous ideas of race hatred and homophobia to the armed forces.

The politicization of the military sharpened the divisions in its ranks. The forward planners for permanent war were not unaware of the fissures in the ranks. So the more conservative sectors of the political establishment pushed for the engagement of the mercenary sector, organized into what were called "private military contractors."[18] Whether society can continue this pace of militarism and warfare in all corners of the globe will be dependent on how the networks for peace and justice will be able to intervene forcefully to reverse US militarism at home and abroad.

At the start of this book, I restated the position of James Boggs that the American Revolution was bound up with the revolution in the Americas. I agree with the view that the Cuban Revolution had been a forerunner for the revolutionary current that will sweep through the Americas in the twenty-first century. This reminder became explicit when an earthquake struck Haiti in January 2010. Twelve thousand nurses petitioned to be deployed to Haiti; instead, Washington mobilized the "private corporations" that are integrated into the military humanitarianism of the US empire.

With the clear inability of the Obama administration to provide leadership against the forces of finance capital and militarism, the peace movement in the United States will need to slowly develop new tactics and strategies to intensify the struggles for demilitarization and the dismantling of the military industrial complex. In this way, sections of the movement will be ahead of the official discourses that seek to impose democracy and represent military occupation as liberation.

It is pertinent here to go back to the UNESCO view of peace:

> There can be no genuine peace when the most elementary human rights are violated or while situations of injustice continue to exist; conversely, human rights for all cannot take root and achieve full growth while latent or open conflicts are rife .... Peace is incompatible with malnutrition, extreme poverty and the refusal of the rights of self-determination. Disregard for the rights of individuals, the persistence of inequitable international economic structures, interference in the internal affairs of other states .... The only lasting peace calls for the establishment of an equitable international order which will preserve future generations from the scourge of war.[19]

In Chapter 8, I argued that the messiah and savior mentality predisposed some US citizens to see themselves as superior to other people.[20] This is because many in the peace movement accept the ideas of individual liberty of John Locke and the libertarian ideas of Ayn Rand and Alan Greenspan. These ideas have been reinvented by the neo-liberal state to promote militarism.[21]

After years of bashing governments, there are many young people who now understand that the non-profit sector acted as a prop for the system of capitalism. It is in this section of the peace movement where human rights and humanitarianism are debased by marketized philanthropy. Similarly, there are many scholars who have brought a deep critique of imperialism without a corresponding critique of the enlightenment project and the devaluation of the lives of non-Europeans. Ubuntu and reparative justice challenge all of the myths about linearity and progress.

James Hansen called for a dramatic change in the direction of society so that there is a drastic cut of CO_2 emissions to the point where they level off, slowly decline for a few decades, and by mid-century decrease rapidly, aided by new technologies. However, at the Climate Change Summit in December 2009, it became clear that the present political establishment in the advanced capitalist countries is paying lip service to reversing global warming. In the main, these societies and their leaders did not want to acknowledge the crimes against nature that have been committed over the past 250 years of industrialization.

War, as an extension of androcentric "conquest of nature," underlies the imperial brotherhood's notions of "manliness" and "toughness." Peace is the antidote to subduing nature, because it implies living in complete harmony with fellow living beings and the environment. If you cannot love all human beings and accuse some of being "evil," then you will have the intent to destroy not only those falsely accused but also their habitats, their forests, and their lands. When intent is combined with the might of the military industrial complex, then we can foresee a war on nature and natural habitats as a component of the "war on terrorism."

ENVIRONMENTAL JUSTICE, A FRACTAL OUTLOOK, AND QUANTUM LEAPS

My analysis of environmental challenges brought to the forefront the awareness that changing our mode of economic organization requires nothing less than system change. Health and peace are linked just as environmental repair and peace are inseparable. The Obama administration has tepidly introduced "reforms" of the health care system but this was a stillborn effort because the question of health could not be separated from the powers of insurance companies, health maintenance organizations, and the multi-billion-dollar drug industry. The marriage between the priorities of the private educational corporations and pharmaceutical companies in the area of genetic research, and the interest of the Pentagon in chemical/biological warfare, has created a new force to fundamentally inform the nature of the diseased mind and diseased soul of an unhealthy society.

The history of racism and eugenics in the United States graphically surfaced in the form of the Tuskegee experiments from 1932 to 1972. When the Nazis were being tried at Nuremberg for the sterilization of inmates in the death camps, the US government was carrying out similar practices. There are no safeguards in society to ensure that similar tests are not now underway in the life sciences industry. Peace activists and scientists, and all of those who want to retreat from the spread of the ideas of the "master race," are being challenged by the ways in which policymaking bodies and research institutions are implicated in supporting research for the breeding and preservation of the master race.

Racial profiling in the United States is being taken to a completely new stage in the scientific community as the possibility of genetic discrimination increases. Obama was elected as the era of technological singularity approaches. This is the era when scientists want to create super human beings. The digital divide, the health divide, and the environmental divisions are all interrelated, and American society is learning that health care cannot be separated from environmental justice or the control of the big corporate entities.

During the Copenhagen Summit, the cry went out: "system change, not climate change." Activists and scholars who have critiqued the rationalist thinking behind the ideas of human domination over nature have been able to warn about the moment of ecological collapse in which we live and the urgent necessity for Earth democracy.[22]

John Bellamy Foster argued that the system of capitalism was "a failed system."[23]

The challenges to the future of human existence are so profound that they require a radical break with the ideas and structures of the capitalist mode of production. A fractal approach to society and life has opened new possibilities for grasping the interconnectedness among humans, nature, and the wider universe. Fractal thinking sharpens our understanding of why it is necessary to grasp the interconnections with nature and the biosphere.

Slowly, networks of environmental justice forces are presenting a new framework for human relations, which calls on us to retreat from business as usual, which threatens the planet Earth. Fractal thinking and fractal geometry open the space for us to understand how different parts of the universe fit together: in short, understanding that "everything is connected to everything else."[24] As temporary inhabitants of the physical space on Earth, we begin to appreciate the reality that the biosphere is the global ecological system integrating all living beings and their relationships, including their interaction with the elements of the cooperating systems (atmosphere, geosphere, and hydrosphere).

Birds and animals are offering new warnings on the changes in the biosphere. In the twenty-first century, the butterfly effect is allowing us to understand the fact that complex and unpredictable results can and will occur in systems that are sensitive to their initial conditions. In other words, it is possible that a very small occurrence can produce unpredictable and sometimes drastic results by triggering a series of increasingly significant events.

Chaos theory makes a break with the certainty and simplicity of mechanical ideas that have brought humans to the brink of disaster. Determinism, whether technological or historical, has been one of the byproducts of the mechanical world view that influenced Western social sciences in the nineteenth and twentieth centuries. Chaos theory and the new insights into the biosphere opened a new revolutionary way of understanding the universe, and it is not by accident that in this book, I have pointed to the inflection point of climate change as one of the key markers of the revolutionary moment.

Writing on the contributions of Ed Lorenz to the revolutionary understandings of chaos theory and climate change, his colleagues said some scientists have since asserted that the twentieth century will be remembered for three scientific revolutions – relativity, quantum mechanics, and chaos.[25]

The move to break from the Cartesian universe in the field of the physical sciences has occurred steadily in the last century. These three revolutions have opened great possibilities for new scientific breakthroughs with the innovations associated with television, computers, cat scans, lasers, and cellphone technology all connected to the application of quantum insights. Yet, at the same moment when we are experiencing and living through these scientific revolutions, some social scientists want to confine our human potential and political capabilities to the ideas and practices associated with the same Cartesian world that reproduced assumptions about the hierarchy of human beings.

Isaac Newton, Francis Bacon, Rene Descartes, and other intellectual luminaries of the Enlightenment "drew nearly every influential social, political, and economic thinker of the seventeenth, eighteenth, and nineteenth centuries" into a "distorted perception" of nature as an other, "only to be conquered and used."[26]

Feminist geopolitics seeks to forge a more inclusive mode of politics, one grounded in the local context and therefore honoring multiplicity of meaning in scholarly discourse.[27] This kind of feminism is distinguishable from the liberal feminism that promotes the concept of equality without a fundamental challenge to the ideas of patriarchy, masculinity militarism, and imperial domination.[28] It is also this radical feminist analysis that opens up the discussion on the relationship between the state and the family form.

The nervousness of the state and the conservatives is nowhere more apparent than on the question of the survival of the "nuclear" family. This nuclear, heterosexual family has been at the center of state ideological legitimization, and the "fear" of terrorists in society has only been surpassed by the fear of gays and lesbians and people of the same sexual orientation. More than a decade ago, Stephanie Coontz helped to shatter the myths about traditional family values in her book, *The Way We Never Were: American Families and the Nostalgia Trap*.[29] There are many family forms in the United States, and the debates on the right to create new family forms represent one aspect of the revolutionary struggles. Debates on same-sex marriages are only one facet of a deeper challenge to the unrealistic idealization of the past, and old conceptions of inheritance and family relations. These debates also reflect the binary concepts of humans.

The explosion of the myth of WASP middle-class suburban lifestyle and nuclear family form will be a slow process. Anti-sexism and new forms of tolerance have been developing since the civil rights period, and many young people do not accept the oppression of gays and lesbians in society. This anti-racism and anti-homophobia movement gained strength from the leadership of Obama on the question of the rights of gays and lesbians to serve in the armed forces. While peace activists call for the dismantling of the military, the reversal of the "don't ask, don't tell policy" will be one more issue that will deepen the fissures and divisions in the armed forces between the democratic forces and the more fundamentalist and white supremacist elements.

During the 2008 elections in the United States, it was this democratic force that temporarily engaged the electoral process, and in its relations sought to shatter the hierarchies associated with mechanical thinking and the hierarchy of humans. An intergenerational movement that connected the spirit of the 1960s to the current moment brought new techniques of networking and engagement which greatly expanded the democratic space in the United States. Barack Obama was a beneficiary of this engagement of the intergenerational movement and the expansion of the democratic space.

The delicate dance between revolution and counter-revolution that characterizes the moment requires human intentions and actions to create democratic societies. Young people brought the full creativity of their vision of a new society along with a new sense of purpose to transcend the fictive biological categories between humans. Some of these young people have deepened the oppositional culture and since gone on to build a new virtual world called "Second Life." However, their ability to interact with this future world will be dependent on how this planet survives. The key aspect of the search of all progressives for a better life inspires revolutionaries, whether they are in the first life or second life movement. Once we start down this road of self-awareness, we begin to be liberated from the rational conceptions of domination over nature. We have also sought to understand how tapping into the ideas and spiritual energies that are motivated by fractal optimism and Ubuntu, along with bottom-up, self-organizing principles, can generate qualitative political changes.

UBUNTU, SELF-ORGANIZATION, AND SELF-MOBILIZATION

If Ubuntu became one signpost for the fractal optimistic future, the other sign led down the road to self-realization and self-confidence of the people. My quest was to unearth those ideas and practices in society that could accelerate and strengthen self-emancipation and the transformation of society. I drew heavily from the mobilized networks for the electoral process of 2007–08 to focus attention on the revolutionary potentialities of American society and the growing networks of men and women who are becoming engaged in international, local, religious, and educational formations for change. Quantitatively, the more the networks continue to be formed in this period of social and economic stress, and the more they develop, the more there will be possibilities for a leap in the nature of political organizing.

In Chapter 5 on fractal optimism, I drew from the skills and knowledge that had been brought to the elections process by the netroots generation. Numerous writers have written on the energy of youth and the social networking technologies that had been brought to bear on the Obama effort. In that analysis, I concluded with the observation that the professionals became amateurs in the era of social networking. The Ubuntu of common humanity met with the Ubuntu of the open source movement. Amateurs and volunteers became professional political operatives as millions were mobilized to believe in change. As one commentator noted, "On every metric, the campaign exceeded what has been done before."[30] This was the essence of a quantum leap in the process of the democratization of US society. This book was written with the same philosophy as the author of *Quantum Politics*,[31] who argued that "true democracies are self-organizing systems."

The quantitative change in numbers organized had a qualitative effect on the political system. Holistic concepts of "hope and change" touched millions by releasing new spiritual forces. The combination of spiritual energy, qualitative change, and a sense of shared humanity cemented the foundations of quantum politics. After Obama became president, the question of how these foundations would be cemented depended on the organizational capabilities of the peace and justice forces who were not constrained by party politics.

The delegitimization of the neo-liberal experts has already opened room for creative and humorous broadsides against the bankers and their protectors. The new media have offered a platform for new cultural products, films, songs, and other ways to expose the bankers. It is the anti-racist sentiments of young people that prevents the real anger that is directed in the populist realm from breaking out to a mass neo-fascist force. Humor and new images can galvanize American society to a point where these bankers no longer have a chokehold over it.

However, beyond humor, there is need for new organizations. The embryo of the new forms of organizing is already there in the networks organizing for life, decent education, the right to the city, environmental justice, and peace. In practical terms the networks of networks form the kernel of the new move towards a new revolutionary form of organizing. These networks create spaces for creativity, and transcend the racialized spaces of the society. Quantitatively, the more there are of these networks, the more there is the possibility of a leap. This leap reproduces a new recursive process as the arc of the moral universe turns towards justice.

The central argument of this book has been that Obama embraced a revolutionary moment in the history of the world and of the United States. His campaign for the US presidency had tapped into new forms of self-organization and self-mobilization. He learnt from listening, and moved politics to a new level by collectively applying this approach. In this new relationship, the campaign inspired nested loops of new social networks that old-school politics and the pundits did not understand, but that are second nature to young people. Thus far we have identified the idea of Ubuntu on which this period is grounded. The second major question is the revolutionary form of organization.

ABRAHAM LINCOLN AND THE SECOND REVOLUTION IN THE UNITED STATES

Self-reference is at the heart of recursion and recursion is the motor of fractals. US citizens constantly referred to their revolutionary past, but it was a past tainted by the ideals of inequality. Obama sought to refer to this revolutionary past in a way that drew from the positive assumptions about liberty and freedom. There have been many commentaries on the parallels between Barack Obama and Abraham Lincoln. Obama himself acknowledged his own debt to Lincoln when in February 2009, Lincoln's birthday was celebrated. Obama said, "It's a humbling task, marking the bicentennial of our 16th president's birth – humbling for me in particular because it's fair to say that the presidency of this singular figure who we celebrate in so many ways made my own story possible." When he announced his candidacy in Lincoln's former home of Springfield, Illinois, in February 2007, Obama repeatedly invoked Lincoln's legacy:

> Abraham Lincoln ... had his doubts. He had his defeats. He had his setbacks. But through his will and his words, he moved a nation and helped free a people. It is because of the millions who rallied to his cause that we are no longer divided, North and South, slave and free.

This recollection of Lincoln is pertinent because many writers such as C. L. R. James and W. E. B. Dubois called the presidency of Lincoln the second revolutionary sequence in the United States. In that revolutionary moment, Lincoln dithered on the question of full emancipation of the enslaved. Lincoln and the federal behemoth would be persuaded on the question of full emancipation not by "moral urgency, but by contradictions."[32]

Lincoln believed that Africans were from an inferior mould to white people, and he said and wrote this often. The Southern racists and slave masters had started the war, and Lincoln had no choice. Lincoln was pressed from the start of the war to declare slavery abolished. He refused. Lincoln was doubtful of the capacity of the enslaved to fight for freedom, but after three years of battle with major reversals for the Union army, many formerly enslaved people distinguished themselves in battle and in the cause to end slavery. Their organized and spontaneous actions pushed the US army into an army of liberation. In the words of Cedric Robinson, "It was the slaves and the exigencies of war that changed Lincoln's mind and provided the abolitionists in Congress, the military, and various loyal state governments with the leverage required to secure emancipation."[33]

Lincoln and the majority of the Northern industrialists in the Republican Party had sought to limit the objectives of the war to ending the rebellion of the Confederate states while preserving property in the form of blacks. Black people had another objective. They wanted freedom and nothing but freedom, and Lincoln was pushed towards the emancipation proclamation. By the time of his second inaugural address, he had grown, and he denounced slavery.

Lincoln made a revolutionary declaration after coming to power by traditional, not revolutionary, means. But he had grown, and his growth was pushed by the contradictions of the society and his recognition that there could be no union that was based simply on democracy for whites.

It is pertinent to study the organizational forms of the militant abolitionists, and their autonomous relationship with President Lincoln. Frederick Douglass, Harriet Tubman, and the team of militant abolitionists understood that within the boundaries of the two dominant parties, Abraham Lincoln was best able to carry forward the program of the abolitionist movement. Douglass and the militant abolitionists carried out their work using all methods available.

After the rebellion of John Brown at Harpers Ferry in West Virginia, there was a vigorous division within the US military between those who supported slavery and those who opposed it. The militant abolitionists carried out prolonged propaganda and educational work among the troops. It was their opposition to enslavement that precipitated a break in the ranks of the military. One section of the military wanted to fight to preserve slavery, and one group did not. Abolitionist generals and officers worked with the enslaved, who had the most to gain from emancipation. Abraham Lincoln, as president of the United States, at first wanted to preserve the union (even at the price of deporting blacks back to Africa), but because Douglass and Tubman were organized, the shift in politics was decisive at that historic moment. Blacks proved decisive in the Civil War because they did not liquidate their independent organizations.

What were the organizational lessons that can be learnt from the references to Harriet Tubman and the underground railroad? The elaboration of the arguments about slavery and the Civil War would take us deeper into the period of the Civil War, which is outside the scope of this conclusion. The more pertinent issues are the thinking and organization that inspired the militant abolitionists, and the detailed planning that was carried out by independent teams. The historical tasks of these independent and autonomous teams elicited the following points, which I have termed the Harriet Tubman Principles of Revolutionary Organization:

- self-organization – belief in the necessity for political organization and mobilization at all levels: personal, community, and national
- belief in freedom from oppression – freedom from mental and physical slavery
- thirst for knowledge in the pursuit of freedom – the abolitionists studied geography, history, law, and astronomy in order to carry out missions
- developed networks and spaces of peace and freedom
- deeply spiritual human beings
- passionate belief in the rights of women
- lack of fear of big military forces, slave masters or other oppressors
- readiness to defend self and supporters
- belief in victory and inspiring others to fight for freedom
- building networks and alliances all through society to advance the cause of freedom.

I have outlined these principles to elaborate the key differences between self-organization and vanguardism. One other major principle that Tubman lived by was the need for proper care for older and retired people.

The revolutionaries in this moment must build their organization to ensure that young people are not carried away by nostalgia about a genocidal past. Are we carrying out a similar campaign to educate the generals to engender a broader debate between those who want to end the imperial wars in Iraq and Afghanistan, and those who want to carry the war to Iran? Is there room within the progressive ranks to see the possibility of "growth" in Obama?

We hear the same criticisms of Obama that were made of Abraham Lincoln. Wendell Phillips, who had campaigned for Lincoln, called him "stumbling, halting, prevaricating, irresolute, weak and besotted." After two years, as the conditions of war and the losses intensified, Lincoln was transformed from being an ordinary leader into a revolutionary leader. Frederick Douglass and Harriet Tubman supported Lincoln, but they did not liquidate their own organization. It is one observation that part of the attraction of Obama from so many quarters is people's sense of a crisis that calls for a break-out, without necessarily understanding the real nature of that crisis.

Obama and his team are at present incapable of delivering without the pressures of a movement that Lincoln faced. More importantly, the contradictions of the moment will intensify. As a liberal, Obama will want to save the present system, and the issue will be, at what price?

The numerous forms of independent political organizing in the United States can be enriched in this period. It is also important to spell out the fact that new organizations must develop independent and autonomous leadership at the grassroots in order to survive. This was another lesson from the period of the SNCC. Ella Baker encouraged young people to build organizations independent of their elders, and she also influenced the empowerment of women.

Revolutionary organizations strengthen the momentum for change in those historical moments that are characterized by unstoppable drives for change. These moments are sometimes captured in one major event, but the moment captures the spirit and creativity of those social forces in society with the most to gain from change in politics. Revolution is itself a process, and though sometimes identified with one event, the event encapsulates processes that emerged long before that moment, and processes that engender transformations in a new direction long after the revolutionary event.

UBUNTU, SELF-ORGANIZATION, AND NEW LEADERSHIP

During the Obama election campaign, the slogan of self-empowerment, "Yes we can," echoed from young people, workers, environmentalists, pensioners, peace activists, students, cultural artists, women, civil rights workers, and gay and lesbian mobilizers. Peer-to-peer networks that started as house parties blossomed in the United States. Young people and women brought out hidden aspects of Ubuntu, as networks of networks grew on new platforms such as Facebook, My Space, and Twitter.

This was where the new leadership emerged. In 2004, when the netroots forces first emerged in the campaign of Howard Dean, they had introduced new leadership styles. By 2007, these netroots forces had grown into a formidable force, to the point where it was recognized that they had revolutionized organizing itself. With the fast pace of political, economic, cultural, and technological change, the revolutionary organizational forms of 2008 were being enriched as young people searched for ways of understanding the financial crisis, and were seeking to liberate themselves from mental slavery. Many of the technical breakthroughs developed by Blue State Digital in 2008 have already been superseded by new technological breakthroughs in wireless communication.

In conventional US political science, it was never calculated that ordinary people could enter the political process in large numbers, because the idea that the US government was oppressive was foreign to the mainstream theoreticians of liberal democratic theory. It is for this reason that, up to the present, the conventional teachers of political science in the United States cannot grasp the enormous contradictions of the moment. For many, the economic crisis is simply another of the cyclical crises of the "free enterprise system."

The challenge for women and men is to ask how the open source campaign and the tools that were mobilized and harnessed can shape a new understanding of politics and political engagement. How can the movement develop, independently of the political formations that were business enterprises? Obama in the White House abandoned the mobilized networks and became trapped in the presidency. The revolutionary forces will have to develop their own program, one that is independent of electoral politics and the lobbies for big oil, big coal, and the military industrial complex.

NEW LEADERSHIP AND OPTIMISM IN SOCIETY

This analysis of the moment of Obama's electoral victory has sought to introduce a unified emancipatory approach: liberating humanity from the mechanical, competitive, and individualistic constraints of Enlightenment philosophy, and reunifying humans with each other, the Earth, and spirituality. In tandem with much of the current discussion of fractal optimism, this intervention calls for a revolutionary paradigmatic transformation, but one that is intrinsic to human knowledge and its capacity to intervene to stop the destruction of the planet.

Within one year of taking office, it became clear that Obama and his political team cannot bring about the change needed for peace and justice. Neo-liberalism has run its course, and the chaos and ruin that ensued have forced citizens in all parts of the world to articulate the real meaning of change. The slogan after the election is "Making change real." We can see the clarity of Albert Einstein in his comment that we cannot solve a problem with the mindset that created the problem in the first place. In Chapter 8, pointing out that Obama was not a messiah, I drew attention to the fact that he was trapped by the ideas of liberalism. I wanted to give Obama agency, and grasp the dynamics behind his inability to see beyond the parliamentary game. However, the contradictions within the contradictions are too interwoven to await Obama's reeducation.

The interconnections between momentum, fractal theory, and Einstein's insights have created an unprecedented opportunity for transformation of political processes in the United States. Here, it must be underlined that we must distinguish between the Newtonian principle of momentum and the ideas of momentum that are linked to transformations: that is, transformation of consciousness, ideas, gender relations, and family structures, and grassroots leadership. I have invoked Ubuntu as a new discourse of transformation. I have linked this discourse to a particular historical moment which some have called an inflection point, and third, I sought to grasp the moment not from a linear perspective of the old replacing the new, but as a complex process of transformation, where freedom from fear and oppression is informed by bold insights about building a better future and saving Planet Earth.

Can self-organization and mobilization be resuscitated in the face of the economic crisis? Tim Geithner and Obama's economic team have argued that their policies have staved off an economic crisis and saved the financial system. However, writers such as Simon Johnson and Neil Barofsky have warned that another crash is coming. Roubini predicts a ten-year period of decline. I would argue that replacing Geithner and Lawrence Summers is an urgent requirement, but that this removal will be insufficient until society begins to understand the call by representative Mary Kaptur, who declared from the floor of the U.S. Congress that:

These criminals have so much political power that [they] can shut down the normal legislative process of the highest law making body of this land. We are constitutionally sworn to protect and defend this Republic against all enemies, foreign and domestic. And my friends, there are enemies. The people pushing this deal are the very ones who are responsible for the implosion on Wall Street. They were fraudulent then and they are fraudulent now.[34]

Beside Marcy Kaptur, economists were calling for the return to the days when banks served communities. William Black and Elizabeth Warren are two economists who have championed democratic control over the bankers.

Obama remains true to the liberal ideology that he was trained in. He is not a revolutionary, but has been caught up in a revolutionary moment in world history. It is now much clearer after one year that there are limitations to the electoral project, insofar as the task of restructuring US society is a gigantic one that cannot be done overnight. Obama may not be the solution, but his election is a small step in the direction of making the break with the old binary conceptions that dominated Enlightenment thinking. It is the laws of unintended consequences that will emanate from this break, and can lead to a new direction where all can live in peace.

When Obama accepted the Nobel Peace Prize in Oslo, he referenced the idea of the North Star. This was the guiding star for Harriet Tubman. This was an indication that Obama understood the unfinished tasks. As president of the United States, he had to speak in codes. Our task is to push society to the point where leaders can speak about peace without fear of retribution from the intelligence services and the heirs of James Jesus Angleton.[35]

The expectations from the 2008 victory triggered new possibilities, as young people began to be released from the fears, insecurities, and phobias that had been rained on them by the media and the image makers of the military/industrial/cultural complex. Here was one crack in the edifice of mind control. Would this crack unleash a new cultural apparatus in the United States? This break was not only possible, it is slowly developing, as we can see from powerful work in film and music. James Cameron's film *Avatar* showed what Hollywood will be able to do in the future, when there is a full-blown critique of the history of racial genocide.

This book seeks to build on the call for happiness in order to inspire an understanding of Ubuntu as the core theory of the politics of inclusion for the twenty-first century

I will join the call, "Don't stop the movement. Being fired up must be maintained to develop a path for peace, justice, and health for all. A new morality awaits the citizens who want to retreat from the imperial past."

OPTIMISM AS A POLITICAL ACT

In this concluding chapter, I cited the vibrant African optimism of Cheikh Anta Diop. I added the words of David Harvey to urge the revolutionaries of the twenty-first century to create spaces of hope. It was my argument that the new recursive processes in these new spaces will gradually challenge and eventually make a break with the old, and engender repair. This was not a prediction but an observation borne out of the conjuncture. It was a conjuncture where there were new energies being reproduced in the new media and in new networks. One of these networks argued correctly that optimism can be revolutionary:

> Optimism, by contrast, especially optimism which is neither foolish nor silent, can be revolutionary. Where no one believes in a better future, despair is a logical choice, and people in despair almost never change anything. Where no one believes a better solution is possible, those benefiting from the continuation of a problem are safe. Where no one believes in the possibility of action, apathy becomes an insurmountable obstacle to reform. But introduce intelligent reasons for believing that action is possible, that better solutions are available, and that a better future can be built, and you unleash the power of people to act out of their highest principles. Shared belief in a better future is the strongest glue there is: it creates the opportunity for us to love one another, and love is an explosive force in politics.[36]

I am drawing from the Gandhian and Guevara principles of love, and the basic principle of a shared belief in a better future. This book agrees that the election of Obama opened the floodgates of optimism from many networks in society. I have drawn extensively from writers and artists who have sought to extend this optimism, and called for revolution and happiness.

Alice Walker, the radical feminist, made this call. She had sent a message to Obama before he became president:

> I would advise you to remember that you did not create the disaster that the world is experiencing, and you alone are not responsible for bringing the world back to balance. A primary responsibility that you do have, however, is to cultivate happiness in your own life.[37]

This book also endorses the call by Alice Walker for a society freed from fear. John Lewis, a veteran freedom fighter who bore the scars of the civil rights revolution in the United States, called Obama's election victory "a peaceful revolution." Speaking on television the morning after the win, Lewis (who had spoken on the platform with Martin Luther King, Jr. at the massive civil rights march in 1963) went on to the ideas of King, to note that,

> a revolution of values, a revolution of ideas. I've been saying over and over again – that the vote is the most nonviolent instrument that we have in a democratic society. And the American people used that vote ... to make Barack Obama the next president of the United States of America.

I agree with the non-violent instrument, but would also caution about the focus on elections in a society where there is really only one party with two branches. John Lewis was not the only commentator adding the prefix "revolutionary" to the description of the victory. One writer in a mainstream political blog called the election "the Obama Revolution." This writer commented, "Beyond the symbolism of Barack Obama's victory, the reality of power in Washington changed more profoundly than meets the eye. Nov. 4, 2008, was the day when American politics shifted on its axis."[37]

Not to be outdone in this labeling of the elections, H. Orlando Patterson from Harvard termed the Obama victory a component of the eternal revolution. Falling back on his exposure to C. L. R. James, Patterson invoked the traditions of American democracy, and called the victory the triumph of the intervention of blacks, women, and the young. After lauding the vision of the framers of the US constitution, Patterson observed that:

> Three groups, in particular, were excluded from the process: blacks, women and the young. The history of American democracy can

be read in good part as the struggle of all three to become fully included in the process. The 2008 campaign was remarkable in the way all three groups worked together to realize, finally and fully, the ambivalent vision of the founders.[38]

Patterson was more than charitable when he called the vision of the founding fathers of the United States "ambivalent." This term was meant to neutralize the reality of enslavement, the genocidal wars against the First Nation peoples, the military invasion and theft of the land of the Mexican people, along with the brutal exclusion of the working poor from the political process. Patterson was straddling the historical divide between revolution and reaction in his rendition of the meaning of Obama's victory.

No such straddling was evident in the commentary of death row prisoner Mumia Abu Jamal. Mumia properly summed up the historic meaning of the victory. Calling on progressives to continue organizing to put pressure on Obama, Mumia differed from those scholars who called Obama's victory symbolic. Mumia noted, "But beyond symbol is substance, and substantively, some scholars have defined Obama as little different from his predecessors." After noting the substantive implications of Obama's Presidency, Mumia continued, "Yet, symbols are powerful things. Sometimes, they have a life all their own. They may come to mean something more than first intended. History has been made. We shall see exactly what kind of history it will be."[39]

Unlike those who simply noted the revolutionary moment, Mumia was pointing to the historical possibilities unleashed by the laws of unforeseen circumstances. I am of the view that the quantum leap in the politics that will emerge from the new political life in the period of economic decline will fundamentally shake the society from its genocidal past. History will emerge from the processes of self-emancipation and self-organization that first appeared in peace activities, in the environmental justice forces, and are now maturing in the midst of the crisis. I will reassert the statement that "It is not up to Obama, it is up to us."

The pacific goals of the revolutionary moment represent a major step away from the doublespeak of the present capitalists, who seek to manipulate the concepts of peace to reinforce repression. The major question before the citizens of the United States, and indeed before all people, is the form of human organization necessary to fulfill the need for the dignity of human beings. These questions are integrally related to what form of human organization can best use the resources of the planet for the reproduction of the human species while cleaning up the destruction of the past forms of production and consumption. This would break with the past idealism that peace can be achieved within the context of a racist, sexist, and capitalist society. However, before that point is reached, all of the horrors of the present investment in militarism will have to be revealed in order awaken the whole population to the fact that another world is possible.

NOTES

Preface

1 Saul Relative, "Large Hadron Collider, breaks records in search of 'God' particle", associatedcontent.com <http://www.associatedcontent.com/article/2841650/large_hadron_supercollider_breaks_records.html> (accessed May 19, 2010).

1 Revolutionary Moments and Ruptures

1 Simon Johnson (2009) "The Quiet Coup," *Atlantic*, May, <http://www.theatlantic.com/doc/200905/imf-advice> (accessed November 15, 2009).

2 Andrew Ross Sorkin (2009) *Too Big to Fail: The Inside Story of how Wall Street and Washington Fought to Save the Financial System – and Themselves*, Viking Books, New York.

3 Charles Gasparino (2009) *The Sellout: How Three Decades of Wall Street Greed and Government Mismanagement Destroyed the Global Financial System,* Harper Collins, New York.

4 Harriet Washington (2006) *Medical Apartheid: The Dark History of Medical Experimentation on Black Americans from Colonial times to the Present,* Anchor Books, New York.

5 James Boggs (1963) *The American Revolution: Pages from a Negro Worker's Notebook*, Monthly Review Press, New York.

6 The analysis of the Civil War as a revolutionary moment in the United States was made by W. E. B. Dubois (1998) in *Black Reconstruction in America 1860–1880*, Free Press, New York and C. L. R. James (1943) "Negroes in the Civil War Their Role in the Second American Revolution," *New International*, December.

7 Mmatshilo Motsei (2007) *The Kanga and the Kangaroo Court: Reflections on the Rape Trial of Jacob Zuma*, Jacana Media, Johannesburg.

8 Michael Battle (2007) *Reconciliation: The Ubuntu Theology of Desmond Tutu*, Pilgrim Press, Cleveland, Ohio.

9 David Stannard (1992) *American Holocaust: The Conquest of the New World*, Oxford University Press, New York.

10 Quoted in Kevin Phillips (2002) *Wealth and Democracy: A Political History of the American Rich,* Broadway Books, New York.

11 Samir Amin (2009) "Emerging from the crisis of capitalism," *Pambazuka News*, September 20. For an elaboration of the argument

see also Samir Amin (2004) *The Liberal Virus: Permanent War and the Americanization of the World*, Monthly Review Press, New York.

12 Matt Latimer (2009) *Speech-less: Tales of a White House Survivor*, Crown Books, New York.

13 Nouriel Roubini (2009) "The Almighty Renminbi?" *New York Times*, May 13.

14 R. Paul Stimers (2004) "President signs major nanotechnology bill," January 1 <http://www.metrocorpcounsel.com/current.php?artType=vi ew&artMonth=September&artYear=2009&EntryNo=1003> (accessed May 13, 2009).

15 Quoted in Natasha Lomas (2008) "Nanotech to solve global warming by 2028" Silicon.com, November 20 <http://www.silicon.com/management/ cio-insights/2008/11/20/nanotech-to-solve-global-warming-by-2028-39345604/> (accessed April 20, 2010).

16 Fritz Althoff, Patrick Lin, James Moor, and John Weckert (2007) *Nanoethics: The Ethical and Social Implications of Nanotechnology*, John Wiley, New York.

17 Vandana Shiva (2005) *Earth Democracy: Justice, Sustainability and Peace*, South End Press, Boston, Mass.

18 Vladimir. I. Lenin (1929) *What is to be Done?*, International Publishers, New York.

19 Eugene Debs cited by Todd Chretien (2007) "Lenin's Theory of the Party," *International Socialist Review*, Issue 56 (November/December).

20 Martin Luther King (1967 "Beyond Vietnam – A Time to Break Silence." Speech at the Riverside Church in New York, available in audio and text online at <http://www.americanrhetoric.com/speeches/ mlkatimetobreaksilence.htm> (accessed on January 18, 2009).

21 Walter Rodney (1980) *Sign of the Times*, Last speech, June 6.

22 Barbara Ransby (2003) *Ella Baker and the Black Freedom Movement: A Radical Democratic Vision*, University of North Carolina Press, Chapel Hill, North Carolina.

23 Boggs (1963).

24 Gene Koo (2008) "A network analysis of the Obama 08 campaign" <http://blogs.law.harvard.edu/anderkoo/2008/10/14/a-network-analysis-of-t...> (accessed January 24, 2009).

25 David Plouffe (2009) *The Audacity to Win: The Inside Story and Lessons of Barack Obama's Historic Victory*, Viking Books, New York.

26 Zack Exley (2010) "The New Organizers, What's really behind Obama's ground game," Huffington Post, March 10 <http://www. huffingtonpost.com/zack-exley/the-new-organizers-part-1_b_132782. html> (accessed November 12, 2009).

27 Boggs (1963).

28 Exley (2010).

29 Cornell West (2004) *Democracy Matters: Winning the Fight Against Imperialism*, Penguin Books, New York.

30 C. L. R. James (1963) *The Black Jacobins: A Study of Toussaint L'Ouverture and the San Domingo Revolution,* Vintage Books, New York.

2 The Political Training of Barack Obama

1 Shiva (2005), p. 112.
2 *Los Angeles Times* (2001) "The Politics of Cloning," June 2 <http://www.newamerica.net/publications/articles/2001/the_politics_of_cloning> (accessed March 3, 2009).
3 Janny Scott (2008) "A Free-Spirited Wanderer Who Set Obama's Path," *New York Times,* March 14 <http://www.nytimes.com/2008/03/14/us/politics/14obama.html?pagewanted=all> (accessed March 16, 2008).
4 Samir Amin (1977) *Imperialism and Unequal Development,* Harvester Press, Sussex.
5 Jonathan Kozol (1992) *Savage Inequalities: Children in America's Schools,* Harper, New York.
6 Michael Parenti (1991) *Make Believe Media: The Politics of Entertainment,* Wadsworth, Belmont, Calif. See also Noam Chomsky and Edward Herman (2002) *Manufacturing Consent: The Political Economy of the Mass Media,* Pantheon, New York.
7 The direct link between Obama and the organizing legend of Chicago, Saul Alinsky, was manifest in his relationship to Jeremy Kellman and Marshall Ganz. For an overview of Alinsky's life, see "Empowering People, not Elites," <http://www.progress.org/2003/alinsky2.htm> (accessed February 3, 2010).
8 Inferiorization is the conscious, deliberate and systematic process utilized specifically by a racist social system to brainwash "functional inferiors." See Barry D. Adam (1979) "The Survival of Domination: Inferiorization and Everyday Life," *Contemporary Sociology,* 8(3), (May), p. 465 and William Oliver (1989) "Black Males and Social Problems: Prevention through Afrocentric Socialization," *Journal of Black Studies,* 20(1), (Sept), pp. 5–39.
9 Barack Obama (2004) *Dreams from my Father: A Story of Race and Inheritance.* New York, Three Rivers Press, p. 24.
10 David Stannard (1993) *The American Holocaust: The Conquest of the New World,* Oxford University Press, New York.
11 Claudia Card (2003) "Genocide and Social Death," *Hypathia,* 18(1) (Winter), pp. 63–79.
12 Obama (2004), p. 23.
13 Ron Takaki (1983) *Pau Hana: Plantation Life and Labor in Hawaii, 1835–1920,* University of Hawaii Press, Honolulu, Hawaii.
14 Obama (2004), p. 12.
15 Obama (2004), p. 70.
16 Malcolm Caldwell (1975) (ed.) *Ten Years' Military Terror in Indonesia,* Spokesman, Nottingham, England; and Peter Dale Scott (1985) "The

United States and the Overthrow of Sukarno, 1965–1967," *Pacific Affairs*, 58, (Summer), pp. 239–64.

17 Obama (2004), p. 48.
18 Tim Jones (2007) "Barack Obama: Mother, not just a girl from Kansas, Stanley Ann Dunham Shaped a future Senator," *Chicago Tribune*, March 27, <http://www.chicagotribune.com/news/politics/obama/chi-0703270151mar27-archive,0,5853572,full.story> (accessed April 24, 2009).
19 Scott (2008).
20 Ron Eglash (1999) *African Fractals: Modern Computing and Indigenous Design*, Rutgers University Press; New Jersey. For an elaboration of the implications for theories of peace see Bertha Amisi (2008) "Indigenous Ideas of the Social and Conceptualising Peace," *African Peace and Conflict Journal*, 1(1), (December).
21 "A more perfect union," speech delivered by Barack Obama in Philadelphia, March 18, 2008 <http://www.youtube.com/watch?v=zrp-v2tHaDo> (accessed March 22, 2008).
22 Obama (2004), p. 20.
23 Obama (2004), pp. 85–7.
24 Obama (2004), p. 89. The Frank referred to in the text is Frank Marshall Davis.
25 Obama (2004), p. 97.
26 Obama (2004), p. 115.
27 Obama (2004), p. 133.
28 Kenneth Walsh (2007) "On the Streets of Chicago, a Candidate Comes of Age," *US News and World Report*, August, 26 <http://www.usnews.com/usnews/news/articles/070826/3obama.htm> (accessed May 12, 2009).
29 See Andrew Sabl (2002) "Community Organizing as Tocquevillean Politics: The Art, Practices, and Ethos of Association," *American Journal of Political Science*, 46(1), (January), pp. 1–19.
30 Robert Pruger and Harry Specht (1969) "Assessing Theoretical Models of Community Organization Practice: Alinsky as a Case in Point," *Social Service Review*, 43(2), (June), pp. 123–35.
31 Alexis de Tocqueville (1945) *Democracy in America*, Vintage Books, New York, pp. 412–13.
32 By this, I mean the crack cocaine epidemic and the allegations of Gary Webb (1999) in *Dark Alliance*, Seven Stories Press, New York.
33 May Day is a commemoration of the Haymarket Massacre in Chicago in 1886, when Chicago police fired on workers during a general strike, killing a dozen demonstrators. See Louis Rucharnes (1964) "John Brown, Jr. and the Haymarket Martyrs," *Massachusetts Review*, 5(40) (Summer), pp. 765–8.
34 Reginald Horsman (1981) *Race and Manifest Destiny: The Origins of American Racial Anglo-Saxonism*, Harvard University Press, Cambridge, Mass..

35 David Roediger (2007) *The Wages of Whiteness: Race and the Making of the American Working Class*, Verso Books, New York. See also Matthew Frye Jacobson (1998) *Whiteness of a Different Color: European Immigrants and the Alchemy of Race*, Harvard University Press, Cambridge, Mass.
36 *Playboy* interview with Saul Alinsky in 1972. Se Part four of the interview as reproduced on http://www.progress.org/2003/alinsky5.htm (accessed May 21, 2010).
37 Cf. Sanford D. Horwitt (1989) *Let Them Call Me Rebel: Saul Alinsky, His Life and Legacy*, Knopf, New York.
38 Obama (2004), p. 165.
39 David Moberg (2007) "Obama's Community Roots," *Nation* April 16 <http://www.thenation.com/doc/20070416/moberg> (accessed February 22, 2009).
40 Bob Secter and John McCormick (2007) "Obama: Portrait of a Pragmatist," *Chicago Tribune*, March 30.
41 Obama (2004), p. 202.
42 For an analysis of how neoliberals used NGOs to create a "social cushion," see James Petras (1997) "Alternatives to Neo-Liberalism in Latin America," *Latin American Perspectives*, 24(1).
43 Nelson Blackstock (1976) *The FBI's War on Political Freedom*, Vintage, New York, and James Kirkpatrick Davis (1997) *Assault on the Left: The FBI and the Sixties Anti-War Movement*, Praeger, Westport, Conn.
44 Jean Stefaniac and Richard Delgado (1996) *No Mercy: How Conservative Think Tanks and Foundations Changed America's Social Agenda*, Temple University Press, Philadelphia, Pa.
45 Matthew Bishop and Michael Green (2008) *Philanthro-Capitalism: How the Rich Can Save the World*, Bloomsbury, New York.
46 Davis (1997).
47 In the United States, this is the 501(c)3 sector.
48 Malidoma Patrice Some (1999) *The Healing Wisdom of Africa: Finding Life Purpose through Nature, Ritual and Community*, Putman, New York, p. 22.
49 Tom Shachtman (2009) *Airlift to America: How Barack Obama.Sr, John F. Kennedy, Tom Mboya and 800 East African Students Changed their World and Ours*, St. Martins Press, New York.
50 Barack H. Obama (1965) "Problems Facing our Socialism," *East African Journal*, July.
51 Obama (2004), pp. 214–15.
52 Obama (2004), pp. 429–30.
53 Jodi Kantor (2007) "Obama Found Political Voice in Law School," *New York Times*, January 28.
54 Lawrence Graham (1999) *Our Kind of People: Inside America's Black Upper Class*, Harper Collins, New York.
55 After the election in November 2008, the media identified Valerie

Jarrett, Martin Nesbitt and Dr. Eric Whitaker as close advisers of Barack Obama. Bob Johnson, the billionaire owner of BET, represented one wing of the black establishment that opposed Obama.

56 For the history of corruption and kickbacks in the state, see Thomas J. Gradel. Dick Simpson, and Andris Zimelis (2009), "Curing Corruption in Illinois," *Anti-Corruption Report, No.1*, Department of Political Science, University of Illinois at Chicago, February.

57 Ron Takaki (2006) "A Different Mirror: Studying the Past for the Sake of the Future," Commencement Address for Whitman College, Sunday, May 21.

58 "Statement on Race, American Anthropological Society," in Evelynn M. Hammonds and Rebecca M Herzig (eds.), *The Nature of Difference: Sciences of Race in the United States from Jefferson to Genomics*, MIT Press, Cambridge, Mass., p. 324,

3 Confronting Racism and Sexism in US Politics

1 Abraham Lincoln, "Gettysburg Address," Gettysburg, Pa., November, 19, 1863.

2 Frantz Fanon (1956) "Racism and Culture," speech delivered before the First Congress of Negro Writers and Artists in Paris in September 1956 and published in the Special Issue of *Presence Africaine*, (June–November).

3 Daniel Kevles (1985) *In the Name of Eugenics,* Harvard University Press, Cambridge, Mass. See Edwin Black (2003), *War Against the Weak: Eugenics and America's Campaign to Create a Master Race,* Four Walls Eight Windows, New York.

4 Jeremy Rifkin (1998) *The Biotech Century, Harnessing the Gene and Remaking the World*, Putman, New York (see in particular Chapter 4, "A Eugenic Civilization").

5 Ward Churchill (1992) *Indians Are Us? Culture and Genocide in Native North America*, Monroe, ME: Common Courage.

6 Gary Oldfield (1993) "The Growth of Segregation in American Schools: Changing the Patterns of Segregation and Poverty since 1968," *Harvard Project on School Desegregation*, (December).

7 Jonathan Kozol (2005) *The Shame of the Nation: The Return of Apartheid Schooling in America*, Random House, New York.

8 Ronald Walters (2003) *White Nationalism, Black Interests: Conservative Public Policy and the Black Community*, Wayne State University Press, Detroit, Mich.

9 The Obama Birther movement claims that Barack Obama was born in Kenya, and is not a US citizen. See Ben Cohen (2009) "Why the Birthers matter," Huffington Post, July 23 <http://www.huffingtonpost.com/ben-cohen/why-the-birthers-matter_b_243647.html> (accessed July 28, 2009).

10 "Finding of the Human Genome Project," <http://www.ornl.gov/sci/

techresources/Human_Genome/elsi/minorities.shtml> (accessed July 30, 2009).

11 Fanon (1956).

12 Speech by Barack Obama in Selma, Alabama March 4, 2007 also speech to the 100th anniversary of the NAACP in New York City, July 16, 2009.

13 David R. Roediger (2007) *The Wages of Whiteness: Race and the Meaning of the American Working Class,* Verso, New York.

14 Sheldon Wolin (2008) *Democracy Incorporated: Managed Democracy and Inverted Totalitarianism,* Princeton University Press, Princeton, N.J., p. 58.

15 *New York Times* (2008) Editorial, "Abolish Electoral College," November 20.

16 Greg Palast (2003) *The Best Democracy Money Can Buy: The Truth About Corporate Cons, Globalization and High-Finance Fraudsters,* Plume, New York; and Bev. Harris (2004) *Black Box Voting: Ballot Tampering in the 21st Century,* Talion, Renton, Wa.

17 Scott McClellan (2008) *What Happened: Inside the Bush White House and Washington's Culture of Deception,* Public Affairs, New York.

18 The conservatism of the mainstream political science in the United States came out in the ways in which it did not condemn the stolen elections. See Stephen P. Nicholson and Robert M. Howard (2003) "Framing Support for the Supreme Court in the Aftermath of "Bush v. Gore," *Journal of Politics,* 65(3) (August); James L. Gibson, Gregory A. Caldeira, and Lester Kenyatta Spence (2003) "The Supreme Court and the US Presidential Election of 2000: Wounds, Self-Inflicted or Otherwise? *British Journal of Political Science,* 33(4), (October).

19 Ronald Walters (2005) *Freedom is Not Enough: Black Voters, Black Candidates and American Presidential Elections,* Rowman & Littlefield, Lanham, Md. (see especially Chapter 4, "Diluting Black voting power: the Supreme Court in the 1990s and the 2000 presidential elections in Florida").

20 "People for the American Way, The Long Shadow of Jim Crow: Voter Suppression in America (2004)" <http://site.pfaw.org/site/PageServer?pagename=report_the_long_shadow_of_jim_crow> (accessed June 13, 2009).

21 Akhil Amar and Vikram Amar, "The Electoral College Votes Against Equality" Yale Law School <http://articles.latimes.com/2004/sep/08/opinion/oe-amar8> (accessed January 12, 2009).

22 It was written into Article 1, Section two of the American Constitution.

23 Cheryl Harris, "Whiteness as Property," *Harvard Law Review,* 106(8), p. 1707.

24 Roediger (2007) *The Wages of Whiteness: Race and the Making of the American Working Class,* Verso, New York.

25 For a critique of the Hobbesian concept of enlightened self interest see Mary Midgley (2009) "Hobbes *Leviathian,* Part 1: Strange Selves,

Guardian, UK, April 6 <http://www.guardian.co.uk/commentisfree/ belief/2009/apr/03/religion-philosophy-hobbes-midgley> (accessed May 10, 2009).

26 Dorothy Roberts (1997) *Killing the Black Body: Race, Reproduction and the Meaning of Liberty*, Pantheon, New York, p. 9.

27 Amin (2004).

28 Dubois (1998).

29 See one of Lincoln's famous letters at <http://showcase.netins.net/web/ creative/lincoln/speeches/greeley.htm> (accessed February 12, 2010).

30 Cedric Robinson (1977) *Black Movements in America*, Routledge, New York.

31 Nell Irvin Painter (2006) *Creating Black Americans*, Oxford University Press, Oxford, p. 117.

32 Darlene Clark Hine (1989) "Rape and the Inner Lives of Black Women in the Middle West: Preliminary Thoughts on the Culture of Dissemblance," *Signs,* 14 (Summer). See also Lisa Cardyn (2002) "Sexualized Racism/Gendered Violence: Outraging the Body Politic in the Reconstruction South," *Michigan Law Review*, 100(4) (February).

33 The testimony of Harriet Jacobs fully revealed the day to day outrages against black women: see Nellie Y. McKay (1991) "The Girls Who Became the Women: Childhood Memories in the Autobiographies of Harriet Jacobs, Mary Church Terrell, and Anne Moody," in Florence Howe. (ed.), *Tradition and the Talents of Women*, University of Illinois Press, Urbana, Ill., pp. 105–24.

34 Thomas Jefferson was one of the founding fathers of the US Republic. He fathered five children with Sally Hemings, who was an enslaved woman. This history is even more controversial insofar as Hemings was supposed to have borne the first child when she was still a minor.
    See Annette Gordon-Reed (1997) *Thomas Jefferson and Sally Hemings: An American Controversy*, University of Virginia Press, Charlottesville, Va. Since the development of DNA technology it has been proven conclusively that Jefferson was the father of her children.

35 Dubois (1998) p. 670.

36 Noel Ignatiev (2008) *How the Irish Became White*, Routledge, New York.

37 Arica Coleman (2008) "Hillary Clinton and the Possessive Investment in Whiteness," *History News Network*, May 19 <http://hnn.us/ articles/50540.html> (accessed May 20, 2008).

38 Cardyn (2002); Laura Edwards (1991) "Sexual Violence, Gender, Reconstruction, and the Extension of Patriarchy in Granville County, North Carolina," *North Carolina Historical Review*, 68; Stephen Kantrowitz (2000) *Ben Tillman and The Reconstruction of White Supremacy*, University of North Carolina Press, Chapel Hill, N.C.; and Diane Miller Sommerville (1995) "The Rape Myth in the Old South Reconsidered," *Journal of Southern History*, 61(3) (August) .

39 Quoted in Cardyn (2002) p. 726.

40 Roberts (1997).

41 Cardyn (2002) p. 678.
42 Kathleen M. Blee (1991) *Women of the Klan: Racism and Gender in the 1920s,* University of California Press, Berkeley, Calif., p. 16.
43 Kantrowitz (2000) p. 255.
44 Kantrowitz (2000) pp. 255–6.
45 Kantrowitz (2000) p. 259.
46 Kantrowitz (2000) pp. 284–6.
47 David Blight (2001) *Race and Reunion: The Civil War in American Memory,* Belknap Press, Cambridge, Mass.
48 David Brion Davis (2001) "The Enduring Legacy of the South's Civil War Victory," *New York Times,* August 26.
49 Ethel Tobach and , Betty Rosoff (eds.) (1994) *Challenging Racism and Sexism: Alternatives to Genetic Determinism,* Feminist Press at CUNY, New York (see especially the chapter by George Allen, "The Genetic Fix: The Social Origins of Genetic Determinism").
50 Edwin Black, "American corporate complicity created undeniable Nazi nexus" <http://jta.org/news/article/2009/03/12/1003678/op-ed-american-corporate-complicity-created-undeniable-nazi-nexus> (accessed March 14, 2009).
51 See Edwin Black (2009) *The Nazi Nexus: America's Corporate Connections to Hitler's Holocaust,* Dialog Press, New York. In his analysis of the role of US corporations, Black argued that Hitler had indispensable help that virtually shaped the size and scope of the Holocaust itself.
52 Arthur R. Jensen (1968) "How Much Can We Boost IQ and Scholastic Achievement?" *Harvard Educational Review,* 39, pp. 1–123.
53 Rifkin (1998) p. 117. Foundations financed by Carnegie, Rockefeller and Ford were associated with not only the financing of race science in the United States but also establishing the idea that society would be better off to weed out undesirable humans.
54 Rifkin (1998).
55 Michael J. Sandel (2007) *The Case against Perfection: Ethics in the Age of Genetic Engineering,* Harvard University Press, Cambridge, Mass.
56 Roberts (1997).
57 Bob Herbert (2009) "The Howls of a Fading Species," *New York Times,* June 1.
58 Michelle Alexander (2010) *The New Jim Crow: Mass Incarceration in the Age of Colorblindness,* New Press, New York.
59 Chris Hedges (2007) *American Fascists: The Christian Right and the War on America,* Free Press, New York.
60 Raymond Kurzweil (2005) *The Singularity is Near,* Viking, New York; see also Raymond Kurzweil (1987) *The Age of Intelligent Machines,* MIT Press, Cambridge, Mass.
61 "Ray Kurzneil on How Technology Will Transform Us." Ted Talks <http://www.ted.com/talks/ray_kurzweil_on_how_technology_will_transform_us.html> (accessed January 22, 2009).

62 Sidney Wilhelm (1971) *Who Needs the Negro?* Schenkman, Cambridge, Mass.

63 Bill Joy (2000) "Why the Future Doesn't Need Us," *Wired Magazine.*

64 Martin Luther King Jr, "Beyond Vietnam: A Time to Break the Silence," speech delivered at the Riverside Church, April 4, 1967.

65 Mary Midgley (1985) "Persons and Non-Persons," in Peter Singer (ed.), *In Defense of Animals,* Blackwell, New York:

66 Midgley (1985).

67 Karl Marx (1967) *Capital,* Vol. 1, International Publishers, New York, p. 345.

68 C. L. R. James (1963) *The Black Jacobins: A Study of Toussaint L'Ouverture and the San Domingo Revolution,* Dial Press, New York, p. 283.

69 Cathy Cohen (1999) *The Boundaries of Blackness: AIDS and the Breakdown of Black Politics,* University of Chicago Press, Chicago, Ill.

70 Harriet Washington (2006) *Medical Apartheid: The Dark History of Medical Experimentation on Black Americans from Colonial times to the Present,* Anchor, New York.

71 Plouffe (2009).

72 Roediger (2007), p. 6.

73 Martin Luther King, Jr. (2001) *The Measure of Man,* Fortress, Augsburg, p. 43.

4 Grassroots Organizing Confronts the Machine

1 Boggs (1963).

2 Kevin Philips (2002) *Wealth and Democracy: A Political History of the American Rich,* Random House, New York, p. xiii.

3 Charles M. Payne (1995) *I've Got the Light of Freedom: The Organizing Tradition and the Mississippi Freedom Struggle,* University of California Press, Berkeley, Calif.

4 William Pepper (2008) *An Act of State: The Execution of Martin Luther King,* Verso, New York; see also Ward Churchill and Jim Van Der Wall (2001) *The COINTELPRO Papers: Documents from the FBI's Secret Wars Against Dissent in the United States,* South End Press Boston, Mass.; see also Paul Wolf's detailed website on the COINTELPRO activities, <http://www.icdc.com/~paulwolf/cointelpro/cointel.htm> (accessed October 2, 2009).

5 Peniel E. Joseph (2007) *Waiting 'till the Midnight Hour: A Narrative History of Black Power in the United States,* New York: Owl Books.

6 F. Capra (1982) *The Turning Point: Science, Society and the Rising Culture,* Bantam, New York, p. 41.

7 Marshall Ganz (2000) *Five Smooth Stones: Strategic Capacity in the Unionization of California Agriculture,* unpublished Harvard PhD thesis.

8 Boggs (1963).
9 James W. Douglass (2008) *JFK and the Unspeakable: Why he Died and Why it Matters,* Orbis, New York.
10 Stokely Carmichael (2005) *Ready for Revolution: The Life and Struggles of Stokely Carmichael (Kwame Ture),* Scribner, New York.
11 William G. Martin and Michael West (2009) *From Toussaint to Tupac: The Black International in the Age of Revolution,* University of North Carolina Press, Chapel Hill, N.C.
12 Ransby (2003).
13 Lecture by Marshall Ganz on "Distributed Leadership and the Obama Campaign," on You Tube <http://mitworld.mit.edu/video/662> (accessed November 12, 2009).
14 Robert Moses (2001) *Radical Equations: Civil Rights from Mississippi to the Algebra Project,* Beacon Press, Boston, Mass., p. 81; see also Charles Payne (1997) *I've Got the Light of Freedom: The Organizing Tradition and the Mississippi Freedom Struggle,* University of California Press, Berkeley, Calif.
15 Jeffrey H. Birnbaum (2000) *The Money Men: The Real Story of Political Power in the USA,* Crown Books, New York.
16 Phillips (2000). For a comprehensive account of political corruption in the United States see Mark Grossman (2003) *Political Corruption in America: An Encyclopedia of Scandals, Power, and Greed,* ABC-Clio, Santa Barbara, Calif.
17 G. William Domhoff (1972) *Fatcats and Democrats: The Role of the Big Rich in the Party of the Common Man,* Prentice-Hall, Englewood Cliffs, N.J.
18 Vladimir I. Lenin (1972) *What is to be Done?* Progress, Moscow.
19 Domhoff (1972).
20 Donald T. Critchlow (2005) *Phyllis Schlafly and Grassroots Conservatism,* Princeton University Press, Princeton, N.J.; Robert Brent Toplin (2006) *Radical Conservatism: The Right's Political Religion,* University Press of Kansas, Lawrence, Ks; Joseph Crespino (2007) *In Search of Another Country: Mississippi and the Conservative Counterrevolution,* Princeton University Press, Princeton, N.J.; and Philip Jenkins (2006) *Decade of Nightmares: The End of the Sixties and the Making of the Eighties America,* Oxford University Press, New York.
21 Eric Shragge (2003) *Activism and Social Change: Lessons for Social and Community Organizing,* University of Toronto Press, Toronto; and (2009) *Incite, Women of Color against Violence. The Revolution Will not be Funded: Beyond the Non-Profit Industrial Complex,* South End Press Boston, Mass.
22 Philips (2000), p. xvi.
23 Lucius J. Barker and Ronald W. Walters (1989) "Jesse Jackson's 1984 Presidential Campaign," in *Challenge and Change in American Politics,* University of Illinois Press, Champaign, Ill.

24 Judith A. Center (1974) "1972 Democratic Convention Report and Party Democracy," *Political Science Quarterly*, 89(2).

25 Paul Rockwell (2008) "Never Mind the Voters, Here's the Super Delegates," <http://www.inmotionmagazine.com/opin/pr_super.html> (accessed August 12, 2008).

26 "Money Wins Presidency and 9 of 10 Congressional Races in Priciest U.S. Election Ever" < https://opensecrets.org/news/2008/11/money-wins-white-house-and.html> (accessed November 10, 2008).

27 Richard Wolff (2007) "Twenty Years of Growing Inequality," *Monthly Review*, November 1.

28 Paul Krugman (2006) "The Great Wealth Transfer," *Rolling Stone*, November 30 <http://www.rollingstone.com/politics/story/12699486/paul_krugman_on_the_great_wealth_transfer/print> (accessed November 12, 2009).

29 Emmanuel Saez, "Striking it Richer: The Evolution of Income Inequalities in the United States," accessed through <http://elsa.berkeley.edu/~saez/> accessed February 16, 2020).

30 James Boggs (1976) "Towards A New Concept of Citizenship," <www.boggscenter.org/new_concept_citizenship_jboggs_1976.html> (accessed March 28, 2010).

31 Jo Freeman (1986) "The Political Culture of the Democratic and Republican Parties," *Political Science Quarterly*, 101(3), p. 320.

32 Harold Gosnell (1933) "The Political Party versus the Political Machine," *Annals of the American Academy of Political and Social Science*, Vol. 169, *The Crisis of Democracy* (September), pp. 21–8.

33 Warren Moscow (1971) *The Last of the Big-Time Bosses, The Life and Times of Carmine De Sapio and the Rise and Fall of Tammany Hall*, Stein and Day, New York.

34 Ronald Walters (2007) *Freedom is Not Enough: Black Voters, Black Candidates, and American Presidential Politics*, Rowman & Littlefield, Lanham, Md.

35 Speech of Senator Trent Lott as reported in the *Washington Post*; Thomas Edsall (2002) "Lott Decried for Part of Salute to Thurmond," December 7.

36 Crespino (2007).

37 Walters (2007).

38 Raymond E. Wolfinger (1972) "Why Political Machines Have Not Withered Away and Other Revisionist Thoughts," *Journal of Politics*, 34(2) (May).

39 Jerome Krase and Charles LaCerra (1992) *Ethnicity and Machine Politics,* University Press of America, Lanham, Md.

40 Nathan Glazer and Daniel Patrick Moynihan (1970) *Beyond the Melting Pot: The Negroes, Puerto Ricans, Jews, Italians and Irish of New York*, MIT Press, Boston, Mass.; see also Noel Ignatiev (2004) *How the Irish Became White*, Routledge, New York.

41 David R. Colburn and George E. Pozzetta (1976) "Bosses and

Machines: Changing Interpretations in American History," *The History Teacher*, 9(3), (May), p. 458.

42 Mike Royko (1971) *Boss: Richard J. Daley of Chicago*, Dutton, New York.

43 Jonathan Kandell (2004) "Carmine De Sapio: Political Kingmaker and last Tammany Hall Boss," *New York Times*, July 29.

44 For a mainstream analysis of the system of bribery and corruption in the party under the banner of patronage see, James Q. Wilson (1961) "The Economy of Patronage," *Journal of Political Economy*.

45 Robert A. Caro (1975) *The Power Broker: Robert Moses and the Fall of New York*, Vintage, New York, p. 18.

46 David Harvey (2008) "The Right to the City," *New Left Review*, 53 (September–October).

47 Dennis W. Johnson (2007) *No Place for Amateurs: How Political Consultants are Reshaping American Democracy*, Routledge, New York.

48 The breakdown was as follows: US$5 billion spent by the financial institutions, US$1.6 billion by pharmaceuticals, US$850 million private insurance companies and drug companies, US$447 million defense contractors, US$830 million big oil etc. See Bernie Sanders (2009) "Who Owns Congress?" September 25 <http://www.huffingtonpost.com/rep-bernie-sanders/who-owns-congress_b_300104.html> (accessed January 10, 2010).

49 Jeff Taylor (2006) *Where did the Party Go? William Jennings Bryan, Hubert Humphrey and the Jeffersonian Legacy*, University of Wisconsin Press, Madison, Wisc.

50 John Feffer (ed.) (2002) *Power Trip: US Unilateralism and Global Strategy after 9/11*, Seven Stories Press, New York.

51 Jacob Heilbrunn (2008) *They Knew They Were Right: The Rise of the Neocons*, Doubleday, New York.

52 Joshua Green (2008) "The Frontrunners Fall," *Atlantic Monthly* (September).

53 Terry McAuliffe (2007) *What a Party: My Life Among Democrats: Presidents, Candidates, Donors, Activists, Alligators and other Wild Animals*, New York: St. Martin's Press.

54 Michael Barnett (2003) *Eyewitness to Genocide: The United Nations and Rwanda*, Cornell University Press, Ithaca, N.Y.

55 Hillary Clinton (2004) *Living History*, Simon & Schuster, New York.

56 Robin D. G. Kelly (2002) *Freedom Dreams: The Radical Black Imagination*, Beacon Press, Boston, Mass.

5 Fractal Wisdom and Optimism in the Primary Campaign of 2008

1 Barack Obama (2006) *The Audacity of Hope: Thoughts on Reclaiming the American Dream*, Crown, New York.

2 The importance of leverage politics was discussed extensively in Ronald

W. Walters (1998) *Black Presidential Politics: A Strategic Approach*, State University of New York Press, Albany, N.Y.; see also the discussion of leverage in Walters (2005). This issue of leverage politics is also discussed by Clarence Lusane (1994) *African Americans at the Crossroads: The Restructuring of Black Leadership and the 1992 Elections*, South End Press, Boston, Mass.

3   Zillah Eisenstein (2007) *Sexual Decoys: Gender, Race and War in Imperial Democracy*, Zed, London.

4   Clarence Lusane (1994) *African Americans at the Crossroads: The Restructuring of Black Leadership and the 1992 Elections*, South End Press, Boston, Mass. The Bradley effect describes the inaccuracy of pre-election polls in which white respondents refused to give their true feelings about a black candidate. This name came after the election of Tom Bradley who campaigned to be the governor of California in 1982. He lost the elections although the polls had shown that he was ahead. The pollsters claimed that whites did not communicate their true feelings about black candidates to pollsters. It was this idea that suggested that whites would not vote for Barack Obama, despite his impressive poll numbers.

5   Joshua Green (2008) "The Hillary Clinton Memos," *Atlantic Monthly*, August 11 <http://www.theatlantic.com/doc/200808u/clinton-memos> (accessed October 3, 2008).

6   Phillips (2002), p. xvi.

7   Bruce H. Lipton (2005) *The Biology of Belief: Unleashing the Power of Consciousness, Matter and Miracles*, Hay House, Carlsbad, Calif.

8   Tim Dickinson (2008) "Obama's Brain Trust," *Rolling Stone*, July 10 <http://www.rollingstone.com/politics/story/21470304/obamas_brain_trust/print> (accessed August 3, 2008).

9   Joshua Green (2008b) "The Front-Runner's Fall," *Atlantic Monthly*, September, <http://www.theatlantic.com/doc/200809/hillary-clinton-campaign> (accessed December 15, 2009).

10 Lawrence Lessig (2005) "The People Own Ideas," *Technology Review*, June.

11 Jerome Armstrong (2006) *Markos Moulitsas, Crashing the Gate: Netroots, Grassroots, and the Rise of People-Powered Politics*, White River Junction, Vt.: Chelsea Books,

12 Marshall Ganz, "Distributed Leadership in the Obama Campaign," lecture at MIT leadership Center, April 2009 <http://mitworld.mit.edu/video/662> (accessed November 12, 2009).

13 *Time* (2008) Special Issue, August 21, "A Leader of Obama's Grassroots Army."

14 "A Conversation with Jeremy Bird," YouTube, December 13, 2008, <http://www.youtube.com/watch?v=1-3h77Xyb18> (accessed December 15, 2008).

15 Conversation with Jeremy Bird (2008).

16 For two differing accounts of the work of Goodstein as part of the

triple O team, see Jose Antonio Vargas (2008) "Obama's Wide Web: From YouTube to Text Messaging, Candidate's Team Connects to Voters," *Washington Post*, August 20; "How Obama Used Social Networking Tools to Win," *Insead Knowledge*, <http://knowledge.insead.edu/contents/HowObamausedsocialnetworkingtowin090709.cfm> (accessed July 25, 2009).

17 <http://www.barackobama.com/mobile/>.

18 See Jon Goss (1995) "We Know Who You Are and We Know Where You Live: The Instrumental Rationality of Geodemographic Systems," *Economic Geography*, 7(2), (April). For another critique of the potential misuse of this technology see Patrick Novotny (1997) "Geographical Information Systems and the New Landscape of Political Technologies," *Social Science Computer Review*, 15(3).

19 Kate Green (2008) "Reality Mining," *Technology Review* (March–April). For another analysis of the collection of personal information for the campaign see David Talbott (2009) "Personalized Campaigning," *Technology Review*, March/April.

20 Vargas (2008).

21 Martin Kilson (2008) "Dynamic of the Obama Campaign's Historic Achievement," *Black Commentator*, May, <http://blackcommentator.com/279/279_obama_campaign_dynamics_kilson_ed_bd.html> (accessed January 22, 2009).

22 Nouriel Roubini (2008) "The rising risk of a systemic financial meltdown: the twelve steps to financial disaster," February 5, <http://www.rgemonitor.com/blog/roubini/242290> (accessed January 22, 2009).

23 Paul Krugman (2008) *The Return of Depression Economics and the Crisis of 2008*, W. W. Norton, New York; and Nouriel Roubini (2008) "The Demise of the Shadow Banking System and of the Broker Dealers," RGE Monitor, September 15 <http://www.rgemonitor.com/roubini-monitor/253598/the_demise_of_the_shadow_banking_system_and_of_the_broker_dealers_some_media_appearances> (accessed November 12, 2008).

24 Cf. Robin Blackburn (2008) "The Sub-Prime Crisis," *New Left Review* (March–April).

25 Interestingly, it was Lawrence Lessig – the champion of the Creative Commons – who was also at the forefront in claiming the need to clean up the political system, See Lawrence Lessig (2008) *Remix: Making Art and Commerce Thrive in the Hybrid Economy*, Penguin, Harmondsworth, UK.

26 Blog by Andrew Sullivan (2008) on the web page of the *Atlantic Monthly*, "Clinton's Advance Spin," January 26, <http://andrewsullivan.theatlantic.com/the_daily_dish/2008/week4/index.html> (accessed February 22, 2009).

27 Analysis of the American National Election Study, quoted in Lucius J. Barker and Ronald W. Walters (1989) *Jesse Jackson's Presidential*

Campaign: Challenge and Change in American Politics, University of Illinois Press, Champaign, Ill., p. 210.

28 Barack Obama, "A more perfect union," Speech delivered in Philadelphia, March 18, 2008.

29 G. William Domhoff (1972) *Fatcats and Democrats: The Role of the Big Rich in the Party of the Common Man*, Prentice-Hall, Englewood Cliffs, NJ.

30 Phillips (2002).

31 Joseph Lash (1972) *Eleanor: The Years Alone*, W.W. Norton, New York, pp. 274–6.

32 David Talbott (2008) "How Obama Really Did It," *Technology Review* (September/October).

6   Between the Past and the Future: The Democratic National Convention

1 The Governor Clarence Morley Collection in the Colorado State Archives contains a respectable file with a list of information on the Ku Klux Klan and its activities in Colorado. See also Robert Alan Goldberg (1981) *Hooded Empire: The Ku Klux Klan in Colorado*, University of Illinois Press, Urbana, Ill.; and Shawn Lay (ed.) (1992) *The Invisible Empire in the West: Toward a New Appraisal of the Ku Klux Klan of the 1920s*, University of Illinois Press, Urbana, Ill.

2 Democratic Party Platform of 1908 <http://www.presidency.ucsb.edu/ws/index.php?pid=29589> (accessed February 12, 2010).

3 See US Census Bureau news, August 2008 <http://www.census.gov/Press-Release/www/releases/archives/population/012496.html> (accessed January 13, 2009).

4 US Census Bureau News (2008) press release, August 14.

5 See the paper by the same title presented by Elaine Rodriquez at the conference on Latinos at Brown University, October 2009. See her book (2008) *The National Voter Registration Act: Impact and Implications for Latino and Non-Latino Communities*, University Press of America, Md.

6 Theodore H. White (1961) *The Making of the President, 1960*, Atheneum, New York.

7 Bradford C. Snell, "American Ground Transportation: A Proposal for Restructuring the Automobile, Truck, Bus & Rail Industries," Senate Judiciary Committee Subcommittee on Antitrust and Monopoly, February 1974. See also Jonathan Kwitny (1981) "The Great Transportation Conspiracy," *Harper's* (February), and Jane Holtz Kay (1988) *Asphalt Nation: How the Automobile Took Over America and How We Can Take it Back*, University of California Press, Berkeley, Calif.

8 Van Jones (2010) *The Green Collar Economy: How One Solution Can Fix Our Two Biggest Problems*, HarperCollins, New York.

9 T. Boone Pickens (2008) *The First Billion is the Hardest: Reflections on a Life of Comebacks and America's Energy Future*, Crown, New York.

10 "T. Boone Pickens taps into forgiveness" <http://www.denverpost.com/dnc/ci_10340061> (accessed November 6, 2008).

11 Mark Svenvold (2008) "Wind Power Politics," *New York Times Magazine*, September 12.

12 Gabriel Kolko (1976) *Railroads and Regulations 1877–1916*, Greenwood Press, Westport, Conn.

13 Howard Zinn (1980) *A Peoples History of the United States*, Harper & Row, New York, p. 345.

14 Zinn (1980), p. 345.

15 Center for Responsive Politics (2008) "Struggling Companies and Industries Still Found Funds to Sponsor Political Conventions," December 10, <http://www.opensecrets.org/news/2008/12/struggling-companies-industrie.html> (accessed October 3, 2009).

16 Joseph Stiglitz and Linda Bilmes (2008) *The Three Trillion Dollar War: The True Cost of the Iraq Conflict.*, W. W. Norton, New York.

17 Justin A. Nelson (2000) "Drafting Lyndon Johnson: The President's Secret Role in the 1968 Democratic Convention," *Presidential Studies Quarterly*, Center for the Study of the Presidency and Congress.

18 Meghan Daum (2008) "A Few PUMAs on the Loose," *Los Angeles Times,* August 30.

19 On August 26, 1920 this Amendment was incorporated into the Constitution. The Amendment proclaimed, "The right of citizens of the United States to vote shall not be denied or abridged by the United States or by any State on account of sex." It ended more than 70 years of struggle by the suffragist movement.

20 *New York Times* (2009) "Pace of Change Under Obama Frustrates Unions," September 6.

21 Adam Nagourney (2008) "Appeals Evoking American Dream Rally Democrats," *New York Times*, August 26.

22 Avis Thomas-Lester (2009) "He Dresses Michelle's Tresses," *Washington Post*, March 26.

23 Mark Hugo Lopez (2008) "The Hispanic Vote in the 2008 Elections," *Pew Hispanic Center*, November 7. See also <http://pewhispanic.org/reports/report.php?ReportID=108> (accessed May 2, 2009).

24 "DNC: Courting the Latino Vote," *New America Media*, August 29, <http://news.newamericamedia.org/news/view_article.html?article_id=d7cde9b4c0c6e930bef9a0472dab248b> (accessed October 20, 2009).

25 White (1961), p. 166.

26 *Advertising Age*, "Marketer of the Year," <http://adage.com/moy2008/article?article_id=131810> (accessed January 10, 2010).

27 *New York Times* (2008) Editorial, August 29.

7 Ground Operation for Victory: Challenging the Ruthlessness of the Wounded Corporate Bankers

1 Sheldon Wolin (2008) *Democracy Incorporated: Managed Democracy*

and Inverted Totalitarianism, Princeton University Press, Princeton, N.J., p. 58.

2 Quoted on Net Routes: On the Media, National Public Radio, November 7 2008, <http://www.onthemedia.org/transcripts/2008/11/07/04> (accessed November 8, 2008).

3 Plouffe (2009), p. 92.

4 Plouffe (2009), p. 320.

5 Christopher Hayes (2008) "Obama's Voter Registration Operation," *The Nation*, August 13.

6 Patricia Cohen (2009) "Field Study: How Relevant is Political Science?" *New York Times,* October 19.

7 Sorkin (2009), p. 470.

8 Simon Johnson (2009) "The Quiet Coup," *Atlantic* (May). Sorkin (2009) noted that the original name of the plan was "Break the Glass" and it was written in April 2008.

9 Sheldon Wolin (2008) *Democracy Incorporated: Managed Democracy and the Specter of Inverted Totalitarianism,* Princeton University Press, Princeton, N.J., p. 46.

10 For details see Sorkin (2009), p. 83.

11 Sorkin (2009), p. 441.

12 Henry Paulson (2010) *On the Brink: Inside the Race to Stop the Collapse of the Global Financial System,* Business Plus, New York.

13 Paul Krugman (2009) "Wall Street Voodoo," *New York Times,* January 18.

14 Francisco E. Thoumi, (2005) "The Numbers Game: Let's All Guess the Size of the Illegal Drug Industry!" *Journal of Drug Issues,* 35(1), (Winter).

15 A derivative is a tradable product whose value is based on or "derived" from, an underlying security. The classic example of a derivative is the option to buy a stock in the future. For an elaboration on the world of derivatives see Gillian Tett (2009) *Fool's Gold: How Unrestrained Greed Corrupted a Dream, Shattered Global Markets and Unleashed a Catastrophe,* Little, Brown, London.

16 This was the case of Brooksley Born of the Commodities Futures Trading Commission, who was driven from her position by Alan Greenspan, Robert Rubin, and Lawrence Summers. These were the forces at that time of the Clinton administration which was then the political front for the financial oligarchy.

17 John Arlidge (2009) "I'm doing God's Work. Meet Mr. Goldman Sachs," *Sunday Times,* London, November 8.

18 Matt Taibbi, "Inside the Great American Bubble Machine," *Rolling Stone,* issue 1082–83.

19 Dean Baker (2009) *Plunder and Blunder: The Rise and Fall of the Bubble Economy,* Polipoint Press, New York. For an analysis that takes into consideration the class and political implications of the bubbles see John Bellamy Foster and Fred Magdoff (2008) *The Great Financial Crisis: Causes and Consequences,* Monthly Review, New York.

20 Latimer (2009).
21 Eamon Javers (2010) *Broker, Trader, Lawyer, Spy: The Secret World of Corporate Espionage,* Harper Collins, New York.
22 William D. Cohan (2009) *House of Cards: A Tale of Hubris and Wretched Excess on Wall Street,* Tantor Media, New York; and Michael Scheur (2004) *Imperial Hubris: Why the West is Losing the War on Terror,* Brasseys, Dulles, Va. See also Roger Burbach and Jim Tarbell (2007) *Imperial Overstretch: George W. Bush and the Hubris of Empire,* Censa, Berkeley, Calif.
23 Michael Lewis (2009) "The Man Who Crashed the World," *Vanity Fair* (August).
24 Ron Shelp (2009) *Fallen Giant: The Amazing Story of Hank Greenberg and the History of AIG,* Wiley, New York.
25 Shelp (2009), ppp. 9–10.
26 Joe Nocera (2009) "Propping up a House of Cards," *New York Times,* February 22. See also Report of Neil Barofsky Special Inspector General of TARP to the House Committee on Oversight and Government Reform, October 14, 2009, House Committee on Oversight and Government Reform.
27 For an elaboration of the interconnections see Dan Briody (2004) *The Iron Triangle: Inside the Secret World of the Carlyle Group,* Wiley, New York.
28 *New York Times* (2009) "Wall St. Firm Draws Scrutiny as U.S. Adviser," May 18.
29 James Galbraith (2008) *The Predator State: How Conservatives Abandoned the Free Market and Why Liberals Should Too,* Free Press, New York.
30 Michael Lewis (1989) *Liar's Poker,* W.W. Norton, New York.
31 Bob Ivry, Christine Harper and Mark Pittman (2009) "Missing Lehman Lesson of Shakeout Means Too Big Banks May Fail," Bloomberg.ccm, September 8 <http://www.bloomberg.com/apps/news?pid=20601170&sid=aX8D5utKFuGA> (accessed January 10, 2010). See also Sorkin (2009).
32 BBC (2003) "Buffet Warns of Investment Time Bomb," March 4. For an analysis of the hidden power of the financial oligarchy see Charles Derber (2005) *Hidden Power: What You Need to Know to Save Our Democracy,* Berrett-Koehler, New York.
33 Michael Lewis and David Enhorn (2009) "How to Repair a Broken Financial World," *New York Times,* January 3.
34 William K. Black (2009) "How the Servant Became a Predator: Finance's Five Fatal Flaws," Huffington Post, October <http://www.huffingtonpost.com/william-k-black/how-the-servant-became-a_b_318010.html> (accessed October 13, 2009).
35 "Reparations Suit Leaves Opening," *In These Times,* February 2, 2004. http://www.inthesetimes.com/article/506 (accessed July 5, 2009).
36 Sorkin (2009); Lawrence G. McDonald (2009) *A Colossal Failure of*

Common Sense: The Inside Story of the Collapse of Lehman Brothers, Crown Business, New York.

37 Latimer (2009), p. 275.

38 Phillips (2002), p. xvii.

39 Jack Nelson-Pallmeyer (1990) *War against the Poor: Low-Intensity Conflict and Christian Faith*, Orbis Books, Maryknoll, N.Y.

40 Edward S. Herman (1998), "The Global Rogue State, *Z Magazine*, February. See also his book with Gerry O'Sullivan (1990) *The Terrorism Industry: The Experts and Institutions That Shape Our View of Terror*, Random House, New York.

41 Eric Williams (1994) *Capitalism and Slavery*, University of North Carolina Press, Chapel Hill, N.C., p. 101. For another elaboration of the role of the banks and the enslavement of Africans see Sam E. Anderson (1996) *Black Holocaust for Beginners*, Readers and Writers, New York.

42 Bob Ivry, Christine Harper and Mark Pittman (2009) "Missing Lehman Lesson of Shakeout Means Too Big Banks May Fail," Bloomberg News, September 8 <http://www.bloomberg.com/apps/news?pid=20601170&s id=aX8D5utKFuGA> (accessed January 10, 2010).

43 The drama itself was played out in the PBS Frontline Production "Breaking the Bank" <http://www.pbs.org/wgbh/pages/frontline/ breakingthebank/etc/script.html> (accessed June 17, 2009).

44 Bloomberg News, September 8, 2009.

45 The threats to Kenneth Lewis were confirmed in the letter from Andrew Cuomo, attorney general of New York, to Hon. Christopher Dodd, chairperson of the Senate Banking Committee, April 23, 2009. Months later when the House Government Oversight Committee held hearings on the bailout of the Federal Government for Bank of America, Paulson admitted that he strongly urged Lewis not to go forward with his threat to follow "the material adverse change" MAC clause to back out of the deal.
   See also press reporting by Liz Rappaport (2009) "Bank of America Chief Says Bernanke, Paulson Barred Disclosure of Merrill Woes Because of Fears for Financial System," *Wall Street Journal*, April 23.

46 John Waples (2009) "How Bob Diamond took Barclays into the Top League of Investment Banks," *Sunday Times,* June 14.

47 Lawrence MacDonald (2009) *A Colossal Failure of Common Sense: The Inside Story of the Collapse of Lehman Brothers*, Crown Books, 2009; David Wessel (2009) *In Fed We Trust: Ben Bernanke's War on the Great Panic*, Crown Books, New York.

48 Latimer (2009).

49 Hendrik Hertzberg (2008) "Barack Obama is a Socialist?" *New Yorker,* October 27.

50 Tom Ridge (2009) *Test of Our Times: America Under Siege and How We Can be Safe Again*, Thomas Dunne Books, New York, pp. 238–9.

51 See *Christian Science Monitor,* October 5, 2008

52 Mark Crispin Miller (2008) *Loser Take All: Election Fraud and the Subversion of Democracy, 2000–2008*, Ig publishing, New York.

53 Exley (2010).
54 Plouffe (2009), p. 364.
55 Quoted in David Talbott (2008) "How Obama Really Did It: Social Technology Helped to Bring Him to the Brink of the Presidency," *Technology Review* (September/October).
56 Plouffe (2009), pp. 364.
57 Michael Connell was the chief IT consultant to Karl Rove and created websites for the Bush and McCain electoral campaigns. He also set up the official Ohio state election website reporting the 2004 presidential election returns. He was to testify about electoral fraud but died in a plane crash three days after Obama's electoral victory. For details see "Republican IT Specialist Dies in Plane Crash," December 24, 2008 <http://rogerhollander.wordpress.com/2008/12/24/republican-it-specialist-dies-in-plane-crash/> (accessed December 24, 2008).
58 Sorkin (2009), p. 93.
59 In the book *How Barack Obama Won: A State by State Guide to the Historic 2008 Presidential Election* (Vintage, New York, 2009), Chuck Todd and Sheldon Gawiser identified eight battleground states for the general elections as follows: Colorado, Florida, Indiana, Iowa, Missouri, North Carolina, Ohio, and Virginia. These same authors identified twelve states as receding battleground states. These were Michigan, Minnesota, Nevada, New Hampshire, New Mexico, Pennsylvania, Wisconsin, Arizona, Georgia, Montana, Nebraska, and Texas.
60 For a thorough list of the massive organization of the Obama campaign see "Key People- Senator Barack Obama" <http://www.gwu.edu/~action/2008/obama/obamaorggen.html> (accessed November 2, 2009).
61 Adam C Smith, Alex Leary and David Adams (2008) "Obama Assembles a Volunteer Army," *St. Petersburg Times*, October 2.
62 Sorkin (2009).
63 <http://www.ncatlasrevisited.org/Population/ethncpop.html> (accessed February 15, 2010).
64 William Frey (2004) *The New Great Migration: Black Americans' Return to the South, 1965–2000,* Brookings Institute, Washington D.C., May.
65 David Plouffe (2009) *The Audacity to Win: The Inside Story and Lessons of Barack Obama's Historic Victory,* Viking Books, New York.
66 Quoted in Christopher Hayes (2008) "Obama's Voter-Registration Drive," *The Nation,* August 13.
67 <htttp://my.barackobama.com/page/community/group/North CarolinaNativeAmericansforOBAMA> (accessed October 2, 2009).
68 North Carolina State Board of Elections, Voter Registration Statistics <http://www.sboe.state.nc.us/content.aspx?id=41> (accessed April 20, 2010).
69 Commentary by Mark Crispin Miller, on Democracy Now, <http://

www.democracynow.org/2008/12/22/republican_it_specialist_dies_in_
plane> December 24, 2008

70 Miller (2008).

71 Timothy Tyson (2004) *Blood Done Sign My Name*, Crown, New
York.

72 Quoted in Yuna Shin (2008) "North Carolina Provides Insight into
Changing Southern Politics," Huffington Post, October 30.

8 . Beyond Messiahs: Networks for Peace and Transformation in the Twenty-First Century

1   James Carroll (2004) *Crusade: Chronicles of an Unjust War*,
Metropolitan Books, New York.

2   *Technology Review* (2009) "Can Technology Save the Economy?"
(May/June).

3   See the papers of the Center for Economic Policy Research (CEPR).
For the figures of the amounts that were going, see CNNMoney.com
bailout tracker <http://money.cnn.com/news/storysupplement/economy/
bailouttracker/index.html> (accessed February 20, 2010).

4   "Following the Money: Report of the Special Inspector General for
the Troubled Asset Relief Program (SIGTARP)." Neil M Barofsky, the
special inspector general for TARP (SIGTARP) in report to the House
Committee on Oversight and Government Reform, July 21, 2009.

5   It was reported in the media that a Michigan defense contractor,
Trijicon, stamped references to bible verses on combat rifle sights made
for the U.S. military.

6   Tomdispatch Interview: James Carroll, American Fundamentalisms,
September 17, 2007.

7   Amin (2004), p. 68.

8   David Remick (2008) "The Joshua Generation," *New Yorker*, November
17.

9   David Brooks (2008) "Who Will He Choose? *New York Times*,
December 5.

10 See Patrick Bond (2008) "The Volcker Shock – Can Africa Survive Obama
and His Advisers," <http://countusout.wordpress.com/2008/11/28/
the-volcker-shock-can-africa-survive-obama-and-his-advisers> (accessed
November 21, 2008).

11 Andrew Bacevich (2007) *The Long War: A New History of U.S.
National Security Policy Since World War II*, New York, Columbia
University Press. See also Tom Hayden (2009) "Understanding the Long
War," *The Nation*, May 7.

12 Thomas Friedman (1999) "A Manifesto to the Fast World," *New York
Times*, March 28; extracts from the book (by the same author) *The
Lexus and the Olive Tree: Understanding Globalization*, Farrar, Straus
& Giroux, New York, 1999.

13 One indication of the close relationship between the military and

intelligence agencies and Wall Street was revealed in Eamon Javers (2010) *Broker, Trader, Lawyer, Spy: The Secret World of Corporate Espionage*, Harper, New York.

14 Robert Dreyfuss (2009) "The Generals' Revolt." *Rolling Stone*, October 28, <http://www.rollingstone.com/politics/story/30493567/the_generals_revolt> (accessed January 12, 2010).

15 In a landmark case, *Citizens United v. Federal Election Commission*, 558 U.S. (2010), United States Supreme Court ruled that corporate funding of independent political broadcasts in candidate elections cannot be limited, because doing so would be in noncompliance with the First Amendment. This ensured that corporate entities could spend unlimited amounts on elections.

16 Bill Fletcher Jr. (2010) *Black Commentator*, January 21.

17 Shoshana Johnson (2010) *I'm Still Standing: From Captive U.S. Soldier to Free Citizen – My Journey Home*, Simon & Schuster, New York.

18 James F. Moore, "The Second Superpower Raises its Beautiful Head," <http://cyber.law.harvard.edu/people/jmoore/secondsuperpower.html> (accessed January 25, 2010).

19 Sreeram Chaulia (2009) "One Step Forward, Two Steps Backwards: The United States Institute of Peace," *International Journal of Peace Studies*, 14(1) (Spring /Summer).

20 W. E. B. Dubois (1978) *The African Roots of World War 1*, Black Liberation Press, New York. For an elaboration of the development of this race thinking at the turn of the twentieth century see Jan Nederveen Pieterse (1995) *White on Black: Images of Africa and Blacks in Western Popular Culture*, Yale University Press, New Haven, Conn.

21 Glen Beck (2009) "Is Massive Health Care Plan Reparations?" July 23 <http://www.glennbeck.com/content/articles/article/198/28317/> (accessed July 24, 2009).

22 Robert F Kennedy Jr (2005) *Crimes against Nature: How George W. Bush and His Corporate Pals Are Plundering the Country and Hijacking Our Democracy*, Harper Collins, New York. See also Karl Jacoby (2001) *Crimes against Nature: Squatters, Poachers, Thieves, and the Hidden History of American Conservation*, University of California Press, Berkeley, Calif.

23 Shiva (2005), p. 106.

24 Sheldon Wolin (2008) *Democracy Incorporated: Managed Democracy and the Specter of Inverted Totalitarianism*, Princeton University Press, Princeton, N. J.

25 Robert A. Caro (1974) *The Power Broker: Robert Moses and the Fall of New York*, Knopf, New York.

26 Shea Howell (2010) "Beyond Budget and speeches," The Boggs Blog, February 7 <http://boggsblog.org/> (accessed February 15, 2010).

27 James Boggs (1963) *The American Revolution: Pages from a Negro Worker's Notebook*, Monthly Review Press, New York.

28 Boggs (1963).

29 Michael D. Lemonick (2008) "Global Warming: Beyond the Tipping Point," *Scientific American,* October.
30 George Monbiot (2010) "Consumer Hell," *Guardian,* January 5.
31 Shawn A. Ginwright (2009) *Black Youth Rising: Activism and Radical healing in Urban America,* Teachers College Press, New York.
32 Robin D. G. Kelly (2002) *Freedom Dreams: The Radical Black Imagination,* Beacon Press, Boston, Mass.
33 Stokeley Carmichael (2005) *Ready for Revolution: The Life and Struggles of Stokely Carmichael (Kwame Ture),* Scribner, New York.
33 Grace Lee Boggs (2008) "Our Time is Not the 1930s," *Michigan Citizen,* November 30.
34 Commencement address of Martin Luther King Jr. at Oberlin College, 1965.

9 Ubuntu and twenty-first-century revolution

1 Cheikh Anta Diop, *The Cultural Unity of Black Africa: The Domains of Matriarchy and Patriarchy in Classical Antiquity,* Karkak House, London, 1989, p. xiv.
2 Desmond Tutu (1999) *No Future Without Forgiveness,* Doubleday, New York.
3 Reported in *BBC News Magazine,* September 28, 2006: "Society is important because of Ubuntu."
4 Lawrence Lessig, *Remix: Making Art and Commerce Thrive in the Hybrid Economy,* Penguin, New York.
5 David Harvey (2000) Spaces of Hope, University of California Press, Berkeley, Calif., p. 17.
6 Eglash (1999).
7 Boggs (1963).
8 See Eric Hobsbawm (1994) *The Age of Extremes: A History of the World 1914–1991,* Penguin, London.
9 Theodore L. Becker (1991) *Quantum Politics: Applying Quantum Theory to Political Phenomena,* Praeger Books, New York.
10 Michael Isikoff and David Corn (2007) *Hubris: The Inside Story of Spin, Scandal and the Selling of the Iraq War,* Crown Publishers, New York.
11 Quoted in Michael Parenti (2010) "What Do Empires Do?" *Common Dreams,* February 13.
12 Laurie Mylroie (2003) *Bush vs. The Beltway: How the CIA and the State Department Tried to Stop the War on Terror,* Regan, New York.
13 Samuel P. Huntingdon (1996) *The Clash of Civilizations and the Remaking of World Order,* Simon & Schuster, New York.
14 Samuel P. Huntington (2004) *Who Are We? The Challenges to America's Identity,* Simon & Schuster, New York.
15 Chalmers Johnson (2004) *The Sorrows of Empire, Militarism, Secrecy, and the End of the Republic,* Metropolitan Books, New York.

16 Johnson (2004).

17 Robinson (1977).

18 Peter Singer (2004) *Corporate Warriors: The Rise of the Privatized Military Industry*, Cornell University Press, New York.

19 Birgit Brock Utne (1987) *Educating For Peace: A Feminist Perspective*, Pergamon Press, New York, p. 3.

20 James Petras (1997) "Imperialism and NGO's in Latin America," *Monthly Review*, 49(7).

21 David Harvey, "Neo Liberalism and the Restoration of Class Power," See also David Harvey (2005) *A Brief History of Neo-liberalism*, Oxford University Press, New York.

22 Vandana Shiva (2005) Earth Democracy: Justice, Sustainability, and Peace, South End Press, Boston, Mass.

23 John Bellamy Foster (2009) "A Failed System: The World Crisis of Capitalist Globalization and its Impact on China," *Monthly Review*, March.

24 Albert-László Barabási (2003) *Linked: How Everything Is Connected to Everything Else and What It Means,* Plume Books, New York.

25 See the obituary on the MIT web site, <http://web.mit.edu/newsoffice/2008/obit-lorenz-0416.html> (accessed January 12, 2010).

26 I. Marshall and D. Zohar 1994) *The Quantum Society,* HarperCollins, New York, ch. 1.

27 For more on feminist geopolitics please see Gillian Rose (1993) *Feminism and Geography: The Limits of Geographical Knowledge*, University of Minnesota Press, Minneapolis, Minn.

28 Spike Peterson (ed.) (1992) *Gendered States: Feminist (Revisions of International Relations Theory*, Lynne Rienner, Boulder, Colo.

29 Stephanie Coontz (2000) *The Way We Never Were: American Families and the Nostalgia Trap*, Basic Books, New York.

30 David Talbott (2008) "How Obama Really Did It," *Technology Review* (September /October).

31 Becker (1991).

32 Robinson (1977) p. 71.

33 Robinson (1977) p. 72.

34 Mary Kaptur speaking in Congress, September 2008. See the report in Guardian UK, <http://www.guardian.co.uk/world/uselectionroadtrip/2008/nov/03/uselections2008-marcy-kaptur> (accessed January 22, 2010).

35 James Jesus Angleton was the head of counter-intelligence in the Central Intelligence Agency (CIA) His career was shrouded with the deepest drama of assassinations and deceptions at home and abroad. See James Douglass (2008) *JFK and the Unspeakable: Why He Died and Why it Matters,* Orbis, New York.

36 Climate Change needs inspiration and optimism, <http://climatechange.thinkaboutit.eu/think2/post/climate_change_needs_inspiration_and_optimism> (accessed January 22, 2010).

37 *The Obama Revolution*, Politico.Com, November 5, 2008, <http://find.politico.com/index.cfm?key=obama&currentPage=13> (accessed January 22, 2010).

38 Orlando Paterson (2008) "An Eternal Revolution," *New York Times*, November 7.

39 Mumia Abu Jamal, " The Meaning of Victory," , November 9, 2008, http://another-green-world.blogspot.com/2008/11/mumia-abu-jamal-welcomes-obama.html (accessed January 12, 2009).

FURTHER READING

Althoff, Fritz, Patrick Lin, James Moor and John Weckert (2007). *Nanoethics: The Ethical and Social Implications of Nanotechnology*. New York: John Wiley.

Amin, Samir (2004). *The Liberal Virus: Permanent War and the Americanization of the World*. New York: Monthly Review Press.

Armstrong, Jerome and Markos Moulitsas (2006). *Crashing the Gate: Netroots, Grassroots, and the Rise of People-Powered Politics*. White River Junction, Vt.: Chelsea.

Bacevich, Andrew (2007). *The Long War: A New History of U.S. National Security Policy Since World War II*. New York: Columbia University Press.

Baker, Dean (2009). *Plunder and Blunder: The Rise and Fall of the Bubble Economy*. New York: Polipoint Press.

Balz, Dan and Haynes Johnson (2009). *The Battle for America 2008: The Story of an Extraordinary Election*. New York: Viking.

Barabási, Albert-László (2003). *Linked: How Everything Is Connected to Everything Else and What It Means*. New York: Plume.

Barker, Lucius J. and Ronald W. Walters (1989). *Jesse Jackson's Presidential Campaign: Challenge and Change in American Politics*. Urbana, Ill.: University of Illinois Press.

Battle, Michael (2007). *Reconciliation: The Ubuntu Theology of Desmond Tutu*. New York: Pilgrim Press.

Becker, Theodore L. (1991). *Quantum Politics: Applying Quantum Theory to Political Phenomena*. New York: Praeger.

Birnbaum, Jeffrey H. (2006). *The Money Men: The Real Story of Political Power in the USA*. New York: Crown.

Black, Edwin (2009). *The Nazi Nexus: America's Corporate Connections to Hitler's Holocaust*. New York: Dialog Press.

Black, William K. (2005). *The Best Way to Rob a Bank is to Own One: How Corporate Executives and Politicians Looted the S&L Industry*. Austin, Tex.: University of Texas Press.

Blackstock, Nelson (1976). *The FBI's War on Political Freedom*. New York: Vintage.

Boggs, James (1963). *The American Revolution: Pages From an American Worker's Notebook*. New York: Monthly Review Press.

Briody, Dan (2004). *The Iron Triangle: Inside the Secret World of the Carlyle Group*. New York: John Wiley.

Carmichael, Stokely (2003). *Ready for Revolution*. New York: Scribner.

Caro, Robert A. (1975). *The Power Broker: Robert Moses and the Fall of New York*. New York: Vintage.

Carroll, James (2004). *Crusade: Chronicles of an Unjust War*. New York: Metropolitan Books.

Chaulia, Sreeram (2009). "One Step Forward, Two Steps Backwards: The United States Institute of Peace," *International Journal of Peace Studies*, Vol. 14, No 1, Spring/Summer.

Chomsky, Noam and Edward Herman (2002). *Manufacturing Consent: The Political Economy of the Mass Media*. New York: Pantheon.

Churchill, Ward and Jim Vander Wall (2001) The COINTELPRO Papers: Documents from the FBI's Secret Wars Against Dissent in the United States. Cambridge, Mass.: South End Press.

Cohan, William D. (2009). *House of Cards: A Tale of Hubris and Wretched Excess on Wall Street*, New York: Doubleday.

Crespino, Joseph (2007). *In Search of Another Country: Mississippi and the Conservative Counterrevolution*. Princeton, N.J.: Princeton University Press.

Critchlow, Donald T. (2005). *Phyllis Schlafly and Grassroots Conservatism*. Princeton, N.J.: Princeton University Press.

Davidson, James West (2007). *They Say: Ida B. Wells and the Reconstruction of Race*. New York: Oxford University Press.

Davis, Kirkpatrick James (1997). *Assault on the Left: The FBI and the Sixties Anti-War Movement*. Westport, Conn.: Praeger.

Derber, Charles (2005). *Hidden Power: What You Need to Know to Save Our Democracy*. New York: Berrett-Koehler.

Domhoff, William G. (1972). *Fat Cats and Democrats: The Role of the Big Rich in the Party of the Common Man*. Englewood Cliffs, N.J.: Prentice-Hall.

Douglass, James W. (2008). *JFK and the Unspeakable: Why he Died and Why it matters*. New York: Orbis.

Dubois, W. E. B. (1998). *Black Reconstruction in America 1860–1880*. New York: Free Press.

Dubois, W. E. B. (1978). *The African Roots of World War 1*. New York: Black Liberation Press.

Edwards, George C. (2004). *Why the Electoral College is Bad for America*. New Haven, Conn.: Yale University Press.

Eglash, Ron (1999). *African Fractals: Modern Computing and Indigenous Design*. Piscataway, N.J.: Rutgers University Press.

Eisenstein, Zillah (2007). *Sexual Decoys: Gender, Race and War in Imperial Democracy*. London: Zed.

Feffer, John (ed.) (2003). *Power Trip: US Unilateralism and Global Strategy after 9/11*. New York: Seven Stories Press.

Foster, John Bellamy and Fred Magdoff (2008). *The Great Financial Crisis: Causes and Consequences*. New York: Monthly Review Press.

Galbraith, James (2008). *The Predator State: How Conservatives Abandoned the Free Market and Why Liberals Should Too*. New York: Free Press.

Ganz, Marshall (2000). *Five Smooth Stones: Strategic Capacity in the Unionization of California Agriculture*, Harvard Ph.D. dissertation.

Gasparino, Charles (2009). *The Sellout: How Three Decades of Wall Street Greed and Government Mismanagement Destroyed the Global Financial System*. New York: Harper Collins.

Ginwright, Shawn A. (2009). *Black Youth Rising: Activism and Radical Healing in Urban America*, New York: Teachers College Press.

Goldberg, Robert Alan (1981). *Hooded Empire: The Ku Klux Klan in Colorado*. Urbana, Ill: University of Illinois Press.

Goodman, Laurie (2009). *Subprime Mortgage Credit Derivatives*. London: Wiley.

Graham, Graham (1999). *Our Kind of People: Inside America's Black Upper Class*. New York: Harper Collins.

Grossman, Mark. *Political Corruption in America: An Encyclopedia of Scandals, Power, and Greed*. New York: ABC Clio.

Hammonds, Evelyn M. and Rebecca M Herzig (eds.) (2008). *The Nature of Difference: Sciences of Race in the United States from Jefferson to Genomics*. Boston, Mass.: MIT Press.

Hansen, James (2009). *Storms of My Grandchildren: The Truth about the Global Climate Catastrophe and Our Last Chance to Save Humanity*. New York: Bloomsbury.

Harris, Bev. (2004). *Black Box Voting: Ballot Tampering in the 21st Century*. Renton, Wa.: Talion.

Harvey, David (2007). *A Brief History of Neoliberalism*. New York: Oxford University Press.

Harvey, David (2003). *The New Imperialism*. New York: Oxford University Press 2003.

Harvey, David (2000). *Spaces of Hope*. Berkeley, Calif.: University of California Press.

Hedges, Chris (2007) *American Fascists: The Christian Right and the War on America*. New York: Free Press.

Heilemann, John and Mark Halperin (2010). *Game Change: Obama and the Clintons, McCain and Palin, and the Race of a Lifetime*. New York: Harper.

Herman, Edward S. and Gerry O'Sullivan (1990). *The Terrorism Industry: The Experts and Institutions that Shape Our View of Terror*. New York: Random House.

Huntington, Samuel P. (2004). *Who Are We? The Challenges to America's Identity*. New York: Simon & Schuster.

Ignatiev, Noel (2008). *How the Irish Became White*. New York: Routledge.

Isikoff, Michael and David Corn (2007). *Hubris: The Inside Story of Spin, Scandal and the Selling of the Iraq War*. New York: Crown.

Jacoby, Karl (2001). *Crimes against Nature: Squatters, Poachers, Thieves, and the Hidden History of American Conservation*. Berkeley, Calif.: University of California Press.

James, C. L. R. (1992). "Abraham Lincoln: The 150th Anniversary of His

Birth." In *The C.L. R. James Reader*, ed. Anne Grimshaw. Oxford: Blackwell.

James, C. L. R. (1963). *The Black Jacobins: A Study of Toussaint L'Ouverture and the San Domingo Revolution*. New York: Vintage.

Javers, Elmon (2010). *Broker, Trader, Lawyer, Spy: The Secret World of Corporate Espionage*. New York: Harper.

Johnson, Chalmers (2004). *The Sorrows of Empire, Militarism, Secrecy, and the End of the Republic*. New York: Metropolitan Books.

Johnson, Dennis W. (2007). *No Place for Amateurs: How Political Consultants are Reshaping American Democracy*. New York: Routledge.

Johnson, Simon (2009). "The Quiet Coup." *Atlantic*, May. <http://www.theatlantic.com/doc/200905/imf-advice> (accessed April 20, 2010).

Johnson, Simon and James Kwak (2010). *13 Bankers: The Wall Street Takeover and the Next Financial Meltdown*. New York: Random House.

Jones, Van (2008). *The Green Collar Economy: How One Solution Can Fix Our Biggest Problem*. New York: Harper One.

Jordan, Winthrop H. (1974). *The White Man's Burden: Historical Origins of Racism in the United States*. New York: Oxford University Press.

Kantrowitz, Stephen (2000). *Ben Tillman and The Reconstruction of White Supremacy*. Chapel Hill, N.C.: University of North Carolina Press.

Kelly, Robin D. G. (2002). *Freedom Dreams: The Radical Black Imagination*. Boston Mass.: Beacon Press.

Kennedy Robert F. Jr. (2005). *Crimes against Nature: How George W. Bush and His Corporate Pals Are Plundering the Country and Hijacking Our Democracy*. New York: Harper Collins.

Kevles, Daniels (1985). *In the name of Eugenics*. Boston, Mass.: Harvard University Press.

King Martin Luther Jr. (1967). *Beyond Vietnam: A Time to Break the Silence,* speech delivered at the Riverside Church, April 4.

Klein, Joe (2006). *Politics Lost: How American Democracy was Trivialised by People who Think You're Stupid*. New York: Doubleday.

Kovel, Joel (1971). *White Racism: A Psychohistory*. New York: Vintage.

Kozol, Jonathan (1992). *Savage Inequalities: Children in America's Schools*. New York: Harper.

Kozol, Jonathan (2006). *The Shame of the Nation: The Restoration of Apartheid Schooling in America*. Boston, Mass.: Three Rivers.

Krugman, Paul (2008). *The Return of Depression Economics and the Crisis of 2008*. New York: W. W. Norton.

Latimer, Matt (2009). *Speech-less: Tales of a Whitehouse Survivor*. New York: Crown.

Lipton, Bruce H. (2005). *The Biology of Belief: Unleashing the Power of Consciousness, Matter and Miracles*. Carlsbad, Calif.: Hay House.

Lusane, Clarence (1994). *African Americans at the Crossroads: The Restructuring of Black Leadership and the 1992 elections*. Boston, Mass.: South End Press.

MacDonald, Lawrence (2009). *A Colossal Failure of Common Sense: The Inside Story of the Collapse of Lehman Brothers*. New York: Crown.

Makik, Kenan (1999). *The Meaning of Race: Race, History and Culture in Western Society*. New York: New York University Press.

Martin, William G. and Michael West (2009). *From Toussaint to Tupac: The Black International in the Age of Revolution*. Chapel Hill, N.C.: University of North Carolina Press.

McClellan, Scott (2008). *What Happened: Inside the Bush White House and Washington's Culture of Deception*. New York: Public Affairs.

Miller, Mark Crispin (2008). *Loser Take All: Election Fraud and the Subversion of Democracy, 2000–2008*. New York: Ig.

Moses, Robert (2001). *Radical Equations: Civil Rights from Mississippi to the Algebra Project*. New York: Beacon Press.

Nichols, John and Robert W. McChesney (2006). *How the American Media Sell Wars, Spin Elections, and Destroy Democracy*. New York: New Press.

Obama, Barack (2004). *Dreams from My Father: A Story of Race and Inheritance*. New York: Three Rivers Press.

Obama, Barack (2006). *The Audacity of Hope: Thoughts on Reclaiming the American Dream*. New York: Crown.

Obama, Barack H. (1965). "Problems Facing Our Socialism." *East African Journal*, July.

Palast, Greg (2003). *The Best Democracy Money Can Buy: The Truth About Corporate Cons, Globalization and High-Finance Fraudsters*. New York: Plume.

Patterson, Scott (2010). *The Quants: How a New Breed of Math Whizzes Conquered Wall Street and Nearly Destroyed It*. New York: Crown.

Payne, Charles (1997). *I've Got the Light of Freedom: The Organizing Tradition and the Mississippi Freedom Struggle*. Berkeley, Calif.: University of California Press.

Pepper, William (2008). *An Act of State: The Execution of Martin Luther King*. New York: Verso.

Phillips, Kevin (2002). *Wealth and Democracy: A Political History of the American Rich*. New York: Broadway.

Pieterse, Nederveen (1995). *White on Black: Images of Africa and Blacks in Western Popular Culture*. New Haven, Conn.: Yale University Press.

Plouffe, David (2009). *The Audacity to Win: The Inside Story and Lessons of Barack Obama's Historic Victory*. New York: Viking.

Ransby, Barbara (2003). *Ella Baker and the Black Freedom Movement: A Radical Democratic Vision*. Chapel Hill, N.C.: University of North Carolina.

Roberts, Dorothy (1997). *Killing the Black Body: Race, Reproduction and the Meaning of Liberty*. New York: Pantheon .

Robinson, Cedric (1997). *Black Movements in America*. New York: Routledge.

Roediger, David R. (1991). *The Wages of Whiteness: Race and the Making of the American Working Class*, New York: Verso.

Roediger, David R. (2007). *The Meaning of Whiteness: Race and the Meaning of the American Working Class.* New York: Verso.

Sandel, Michael J. (2007) *The Case against Perfection: Ethics in the Age of Genetic Engineering.* Boston, Mass.: Harvard University Press.

Sanger, David (2009). *The Inheritance: The World Obama Confronts and the Challenges to American Power.* New York: Harmony.

Savage, Sean J. (1991). *Franklin D. Roosevelt, the Party Leader, 1932–1945.* Lexington, Ky.: University Press of Kentucky.

Shawcross, William (1997). *Murdoch: The Making of a Media Empire.* New York: Simon & Schuster.

Shawn, Lay (ed.) (1992). *The Invisible Empire in the West: Toward a New Appraisal of the Ku Klux Klan of the 1920's.* Urbana, Ill.: University of Illinois Press.

Shelp, Ron (2009). *Fallen Giant: The Amazing Story of Hank Greenberg and the History of AIG.* New York: Wiley.

Singer, Peter (2004). *Corporate Warriors: The Rise of the Privatized Military Industry.* Ithaca, N.Y.: Cornell University Press.

Some, Malidome (1999). *The Healing Wisdom of Africa: Finding Life Purpose Through Nature, Ritual and Community.* New York: Penguin Putman.

Sorkin, Andrew Ross (2009). *Too Big to Fail: The Inside Story of How Wall Street and Washington Fought to Save the Financial System – and Themselves,* New York: Viking.

Soyinka, Wole (2000). "Memory, Truth and Healing." In *The Politics of Memory, Truth, Healing and Social Justice,* ed. Ifi Amadiume and Abdullah An-Na'im. London: Zed.

Stanage, Nail (2009). *Redemption Song: An Irish Reporter Inside the Obama Campaign,* Chester Spring, Pa.: Liberties Press.

Stannard, David (1989). *Before the Horror: The Population of Hawaii on the Eve of Western Contact.* Honolulu: University of Hawaii Press.

Stannard, David (1992). *American Holocaust: The Conquest of the New World.* New York: Oxford University Press.

Stefaniac, Jean and Richard Delgado (1996). *No Mercy: How Conservative Think Tanks and Foundations Changed America's Social Agenda.* Philadelphia, Pa.: Temple University Press.

Stiglitz, Joseph and Linda Bilmes (2008). *The Three Trillion Dollar War: The True Cost of the Iraq Conflict.* New York: W. W. Norton.

Takaki, Ron (1983). *Pau Hana: Plantation Life and Labor in Hawaii, 1835–1920.* Honolulu, Hawaii: University of Hawaii Press.

Talbott, David (2008). "How Obama Really Did It: Social Technology Helped to Bring Him to the Brink of the Presidency." *Technology Review,* September/October.

Taylor, Jeff (2006). *Where did the Party Go? William Jennings Bryan, Hubert Humphrey and the Jeffersonian Legacy.* Columbia, Miss.: University of Missouri Press.

Tett, Gilian (2009). *Fool's Gold: How Unrestrained Greed Corrupted a*

Dream, Shattered Global Markets and Unleashed a Catastrophe. New York: Free Press.

Thompson, Michael J. (ed.) (2007). *Confronting the New Conservatism: The Rise of the Right in America*. New York: New York University Press.

Todd, Chuck and Sheldon Gawiser (2009). *How Barack Obama Won*. New York: Vintage.

Toplin, Robert Brent (2006). *Radical Conservatism: The Right's Political Religion*. Lawrence, Kans.: University Press of Kansas.

Tucille, Jerome (2003). *Rupert Murdoch: Creator of a Worldwide Media Empire*. New York: Beard.

Walters, Ronald W. (1988). *Black Presidential Politics: A Strategic Approach*. New York: State University of New York Press.

Walters, Ronald W. (2005). *Freedom is Not Enough: Black Politics, Black Candidates and American Presidential Politics*. New York: Rowman & Littlefield.

Walters, Ronald W. (2007). *Freedom is Not Enough: Black Voters, Black Candidates, and American Presidential Politics*. Lanham, Md.: Rowman & Littlefield.

Walters, Ronald W. (2003). *White Nationalism, Black Interests: Conservative Public Policy and the Black Community*. Detroit, Mich.: Wayne State University Press.

Washington, Harriet (2007). *Medical Apartheid: The Dark History of Medical Experimentation on Black Americans from Colonial Times to the Present*. New York: Doubleday.

Wells, Ida B. (2009). *A Red Record: Tabulated Statistics and Alleged Causes of Lynchings in the United States*. California: Dodo Press.

Wessel, David (2009). *In Fed We Trust: Ben Bernanke's War on the Great Panic*. New York: Crown.

West, Cornell (2004). *Democracy Matters: Winning the Fight Against Imperialism*. New York: Penguin.

White, Theodore H. (1961) *The Making of the President 1960*. New York: Atheneum.

Wolfe, Richard (2009). *Renegade: The Making of a President*. New York: Crown.

Wolin, Sheldon (2008). *Democracy Incorporated: Managed Democracy and the Specter of Inverted Totalitarianism*. Princeton, N. J.: Princeton University Press.

INDEX